WHICH LIE DID I TELL?

More Adventures in the Screen Trade

WILLIAM GOLDMAN

BLOOMSBURY

For Ingmar and Ernie and Bob
For Bobby and Peter and Scott
For Joel and Ethan and Nora
For Callie and Tony and John. And Sue

For screenwriters suffering everywhere (It's what we do)

First published in Great Britain 2000
This paperback edition published 2001

Grateful acknowledgement is made to the following for permission to reprint previously published and unpublished material: **Applause Theatre & Cinema Books:** Material adapted from the introductions to *The Ghost and the Darkness: The Screenplay* and *Absolute Power: The Book of the Film* by William Goldman; and material adapted from the introductions to *The Princess Bride, Misery,* and *Maverick* by William Goldman from *William Goldman: Four Screenplays with Essays* and *William Goldman: Five Screenplays with Essays.* Adapted and reprinted by permission of Applause Theatre & Cinema Books. • **Faber and Faber Limited:** Excerpts from *Fargo* by Ethan Coen and Joel Coen. Copyright © 1996 by Ethan Coen and Joel Coen. Reprinted by permission of Faber and Faber Limited. • **Henry Holt and Company, LLC:** "Stopping by Woods on a Snowy Evening" from *The Poetry of Robert Frost,* edited by Edward Connery Lathem. Copyright ©1923, 1969 by Henry Holt and Company, LLC. Copyright renewed 1951 by Robert Frost. Reprinted by permission of Henry Holt and Company, LLC. • **Alfred A. Knopf, International Creative Management, Inc., and Nora Ephron:** Excerpt from the screenplay *When Harry Met Sally* by Nora Ephron. Copyright © 1990 by Castle Rock Entertainment. Reprinted by permission of Alfred A. Knopf, a division of Random House, Inc., and Nora Ephron. • **Ernest Lehman and Turner Entertainment:** Excerpt from the screenplay *North by Northwest* by Ernest Lehman. Directed and shot by Alfred Hitchcock. Reprinted by permission of Ernest Lehman and Turner Entertainment.

Permissions acknowledgements continue on page 486

Bloomsbury Publishing Plc, 38 Soho Square, London W1D 3HB
A CIP catalogue record of this book is available from the British Library

ISBN 0 7475 5317 3
10 9 8 7 6 5 4 3 2 1

Printed and bound in England by Clays Limited, St Ives plc

CONTENTS

INTRODUCTION

This book began a decade ago because of one single moment that happened at Oberlin College.

One of the salvations of my life is that I went to Oberlin—a great school if you don't mind the weather and if you've realized that it's okay to be just a little bit strange.

Anyway, there I was back in Ohio and one afternoon I met with a bunch of student writers to answer their questions about Hollywood. I remember the moment so clearly. This girl stood up. Slender, wearing red, so obviously bright and intense, and before she spoke I realized whatever she was about to ask *mattered*. She was leaning in toward me and she was almost trembling, and when she spoke it was with such clarity and power. These were her words: **"Mr. Goldman, Mr. Goldman, do you always begin your second theme by page seventeen?—"**

I was so stunned. The question would not stop echoing inside me: **"Mr. Goldman, Mr. Goldman, do you always begin your second theme by page seventeen?—"**

Because, you see, I didn't know what a second theme *was*. I literally did not know what language she was speaking. But she had this nugget, this bit of data, and she was going to build her church on it—and it would not stand. Her church would crumble the moment weight was applied. (There are, scattered throughout this book, sidebars that deal with specific questions. I wish I'd had a sidebar for that girl in red.)

But she made me realize, truly she did, that I would have to write another book about screenwriting. Because movies are not about second themes or about dialogue or pretty stars. Because if screenplays are structure, and they are, then movies are story.

And this is a book about storytelling on film . . .

It's also about the screenwriter's life. Has to be. You meet people in this business, and one thing you must know is that just about everyone you come in contact with seems shockingly normal. Executives, producers, directors, stars. *Do not be fooled.* Since movies succeed by word of mouth, something you cannot manufacture, everyone in the business is constantly in fear of losing their spot by the fire. Since they have no idea what got them there in the first place, this all makes for a certain lunacy and insecurity. (Everyone assumes, correctly, that being writers, we are already loony and insecure.)

I was in Las Vegas once with a producer who was promoting his various projects on the phone. We were in his hotel suite and he clearly wanted me to listen, since he chose not to go into the bedroom. On and on he went, phone call after phone call, spouting inaccurate grosses, potential star castings, stuff like that.

Perversely, since he wanted me to know what a big deal he was, and since I already did know he was an asshole, I decided to hear nothing. I picked up a copy of *Sports Illustrated,* read for quite a while—

Until suddenly I heard my name, whispered sharply, "—Bill—*Bill*"— I glanced over and there he was, his hand over the mouthpiece. Then came these words: **"Which lie did I tell?"**

Understand, he had no look of shame on his face. This was all said in the interest of accuracy.

Storytellers tell lies too. We must. Story ideas surround us, but they need shading, shaping, climaxes, beginnings; that's our job. What we must try and learn is which are the best lies, best in the sense of helpful. When we try and tell our stories, we all need help. I hope there's some here. For you.

I.
More Adventures

The Leper
[1980—85]

I don't think I was aware of it, but when I started work on *Adventures in the Screen Trade,* in 1980, I had become a leper in Hollywood.

Let me explain what that means: the phone stopped ringing.

For five years, from 1980 till 1985, no one called with anything resembling a job offer. Sure, I had conversations with acquaintances. Yes, the people whom I knew and liked still talked to me. Nothing personal was altered in any way.

But in the eight years prior to 1978, seven movies I'd written were released. In the eight years following, none.

I talked about it recently with a bunch of young Los Angeles screenwriters, and what I told them was this: If I had been living Out There, I don't think I could have survived. The idea of going into restaurants and knowing that heads were turning away, of knowing people were saying "See him?—no, don't look yet, okay, now turn, that guy, he used to be hot, can't get arrested anymore," would have devastated me. In L.A., truly, there is but one occupation, the movie business. In New York, the infinite city, we're all invisible.

Example: my favorite French bistro is Quatorze Bis, on East Seventy-ninth. Best fries in town, great chicken, all that good stuff. Well, I was there one night last year when another guy came in, and we had each won two Oscars for screenwriting, and we lived within a few blocks of each other—

—and we had never met. (It was Robert Benton.)

Impossible in Los Angeles. But that kind of thing was my blessing during those five years.

My memory was that the leprosy didn't really bother me. I asked my wonderful ex-wife, Ilene, about it and she said: "I don't think it did bother you, not being out of Hollywood, anyway. But one night I remember you were in the library and you were depressed and I realized it was the being alone that was getting to you. You always enjoyed the meetings, the socialness of moviemaking. You were always so grateful when you could get out of your pit."

I wrote five books in those five years (couldn't do it now, way too hard) and then the phone started ringing again.

This is why it stopped in the first place.

———

There is a famous and *amazingly* racist World War I cartoon that showed two soldiers fighting in a trench. One was German, the other an American Negro who had just swiped at the German's throat with his straight razor. (When I say racist, I mean racist.) The caption went like this:

German Soldier: You missed.
American Soldier: Wait'll yo' turn yo' head.

The point being, in terms of my screenwriting career, I never turned my head. Looking back, there was no real reason to. I was on my hot streak then. I was a Good Housekeeping Seal of Approval in those years. Between '73 and '78 this is what I wrote:

Three novels:
The Princess Bride	(1973)
Marathon Man	(1974)
Magic	(1976)

And six movies:
The Great Waldo Pepper	(1975)
The Stepford Wives	(1975)
All the President's Men	(1976)
Marathon Man	(1976)
A Bridge Too Far	(1977)
Magic	(1978)

If you had told me, that 1978 November day when *Magic* opened, that it would be *nine years* before my next picture appeared, I doubt I would have known what language you were speaking.

It wasn't as if I'd stopped writing screenplays after *Magic*. But the lesson I was about to learn was this: studios do not particularly lose faith in a writer if a movie is terrible. Producers do not forget your name if a movie loses lots of money. Because *most* studio movies lose lots of money (they survive on their hits). If, say, they chose directors who had only hits, they would be choosing from a practically nonexistent list. All anybody wants, when they hire you, is this: **that the movie happen.**

The change came after *A Bridge Too Far.*

Joseph E. Levine, the producer of that film, thought of me as a kind of good luck talisman. His career was not exactly rocketing the years before *Bridge,* and when that movie brought him back close to the fire, he attributed a lot of it to me. And he wanted to go into business with me. He bought my novel *Magic,* made that movie, and then proposed a three-picture deal: I would write three original screenplays for him, pretty much of my own choosing. I had never signed a multiple deal before, never thought I would. But I jumped at it. The work experiences with him had been so decent, unlike a lot of the standard Hollywood shit we all put up with.

One thing that made Mr. Levine unique was that *he was the bank*. He made his movies with *his own money,* took no studio deals until late in the game, when he had something to show. He was gambling that he would find movie studios who would want to buy, and he had gotten rich that way. *Bridge* had cost him $22 million. An insane gamble in today's world, nuttier back then. But the day it opened it was $4 million in profit. Mr. Levine sold the movie everywhere, Europe, Asia, country by country, territory by territory; he had collected $26 million by opening day.

Typical of his bravery was one day when he was in a hospital in New York after surgery. I was visiting him, and the director, Richard Attenborough, called from Holland. They were shooting the crucial parachute drop, and the weather had been dreadful. The parachutists were willing to work the next day, a Saturday.

Attenborough requested that extra day. It would cost Levine seventy-five thousand of his own dollars. Levine *screamed* at Attenborough for even suggesting such a thing. Attenborough repeated his request. Levine asked if he had sufficient footage for the sequence as it was. Attenborough said he had more than enough but it was all drab-looking. Levine screamed at him again. It was a ridiculous request. Attenborough held tough, saying the extra day might make all the difference. Levine then asked what was the weather report for Saturday. Attenborough admitted it was for more of the same: dreary.

Now Levine really let fly. You limey bastard, on and on, and he finally hung up on Attenborough. But not before he agreed to the extra day. The weather turned glorious and almost the entire wonderful drop sequence comes from that extra day.

Try getting a studio to do that.

So the fact that Mr. Levine did not need studio backing, that he cared not at all for studio money or thinking, was a huge factor in my agreeing to the three-picture deal.

It turned out to be a huge contributor to my downfall.

————

The Sea Kings was the first of the three-picture deal. A pirate flick. Came from a *great* snippet of material. In the early 1700s, the most famous, and most lethal, pirate was Blackbeard. At the same time, living on the island of Barbados, was a fabulously wealthy planter, Stede Bonnet.

Bonnet had been a soldier but had never seen action. He had a monstrous wife. Had almost died the previous winter. And, in a feat of great lunacy unmatched just about anywhere on earth, Bonnet decided to become a pirate. He commissioned a ship—the only such one in history, by the way. Pirate ships were always stolen.

So off he sailed.

And met, for a blink, Blackbeard.

They did not sail together for very long, but the idea of these two strange and remarkable men knocked me out. So I wrote *The Sea Kings* about them. (Butch and Sundance on the high seas, if you will.)

The decision that I made was this: Bonnet, rich beyond counting and miserably unhappy, a student of piracy, wanted one thing more than any other: an adventure-filled life (and if that included death, so be it). Blackbeard was sick up to here with his adventure-filled life. Piracy was getting tougher and tougher, and he was broke, as all pirates (save Bonnet) were. What he wanted was a long, comfortable life and a sweet death in bed.

So I wrote a movie about two men who were each other's dream.

It was filled with action and blood and double crosses and I hoped a decent amount of laughter. When I was done, I gave it to Mr. Levine.

Who just loved it.

The Year of the Comet was my second original, a romantic thriller, about a chase for the world's greatest bottle of wine, and you can read all about it in the chapter with its name on it. I will add only this here—

—Mr. Levine loved it too.

I wrote the part of Blackbeard for Sean Connery, and Mr. Levine got the idea of casting the two James Bonds, having Roger Moore play the more elegant Bonnet. Another casting notion was the two Moores: Dudley (*10* had happened) as Bonnet, Roger shifting over to Blackbeard.

In the wine movie, he wanted Robert Redford in the Cary Grant part.

Obviously, you did not see these movies.

What happened?

When Mr. Levine had come to me for *A Bridge Too Far,* he was pushing seventy, and he hated being out of the loop, was willing to take almost any gamble. Now that *Bridge* and *Magic* had helped restore him, his needs were lessened.

He was also older now.

But most critical: the price of movies had begun to skyrocket. So the fact that he was his own bank, so wonderful earlier, was now a huge problem—he was rich, but not *that* rich. Some research was done on the cost of constructing that everyday little item, the pirate ship.

You don't want to know.

Stars' salaries.

You don't want to know.

He had chances to lay the scripts off to studios but he couldn't do that, y'see, because then he'd be just like everybody else, taking shit from the executives. When he was the bank, he *gave* shit. I heard him blow studio heads out of the water. I saw him sit at his desk, smiling at me, while he hurled the most amazing insults at these Hollywood powers—

—and they had to take it—

—because he had movies they wanted.

That was the fucking staff of life for the old man. His ego would not allow him to be just like everybody else. *He didn't need it.*

So both scripts just lay there. (They very well may have been unusable scripts—always a very real possibility when I go to work—but that was not the governing principle here.) I never wrote the third original—Mr. Levine and I parted company.

I was O for two.

The Ski Bum began as an article in *Esquire* by Jean Vallely. Briefly, it concerned a ski instructor in Aspen who led a very glamorous life. Wealthy and famous clients, the kind of romantic existence most of us only moon about.

That's by day.

By night he was aging, broke, scraping along in a trailer with a wife and little kid.

I thought it would make a terrific movie.

The producer had bought the underlying rights. I signed on, went to Aspen, noodled around, did my research, went to work on the screenplay. Got it to the producer and the studio, Universal.

The producer loved it.

Alas, Universal's studio head *hated* it. When the producer left for another studio, he asked to buy it back, take it with him. Universal said, *no conceivable way. We hate this piece of shit and we are going to keep it forever, thank you very much.*

I always thought that was strange. If you hate something so much and you're offered a fair price to unload it, why keep it around? I did know, of course, the most usual reason—fear of humiliation. What if a studio gives up a piece of material that turns into *Home Alone* (happened) or *E.T.* (happened)?

But this was all company stuff, taking place far far above my head.

Dissolve, as they say (they really do), Out There.

It's a couple of years later and another executive has come to power at Universal. The guy who hated it so much is still above him, but this secondary power likes the screenplay and wants to see the movie made. We met and his first words to me were these: *"You don't have the least idea what happened, do you?"*

I didn't then.

I do now.

The producer had been, at the time, relatively new in the picture business. But he was a gigantic figure in the music business: Name a superstar singer, he handled him.

Well, Universal owned an amphitheater and needed talent to fill it. So the very great Lew Wasserman made a deal personally with the producer to handle the amphitheater and also have a movie-producing deal. *Anything* he wanted to make was an automatic "go."

With one teensy proviso: it had to cost less than an agreed-upon amount. Anything that cost more, Ned Tanen, the head of Universal Pictures, would have to agree to.

The Ski Bum, which needed stars and snow and all kinds of other expensive stuff, obviously needed Tanen's okay.

This presented kind of a problem for the picture because, decades ago, Tanen and my guy had been together in the mailroom at William Morris, where so many great careers were launched.

And they had hated each other with a growing passion since then.

Not only that, Tanen was pissed that the producer had gotten a movie deal at his company by going over his head to Wasserman.

So there it was.

Tanen, of course, rejected it. And, of course, rejected any attempt to buy the screenplay back.

The new executive and I tried an end run. Tanen never budged.

O for three.

———

The Right Stuff came next. A ghastly and depressing saga (recounted in magnificent detail in *Adventures in the Screen Trade,* so I won't repeat it here). I left the project angry and frustrated. These were bad times in America—the hostages had just been taken in Iran—so I had wanted to write a movie that might have a patriotic feel. The director wanted something else.

O for four.

———

On Wings of Eagles was not called that when I got involved. The famous Ken Follett book and the miniseries were still in the future.

But Ross Perot, who controlled the material, was interested in making a movie about the wonderful time when he masterminded breaking his employees out of an Iranian prison. I still had my patriotic need. I signed on.

The problem with this material was always very simple: it was an expensive action film but the star, the main guy, Perot's hero, "Bull" Simons, was not a young man. And Perot would never have betrayed the basic reality by allowing a younger man to do it.

There was only Eastwood. Had to be Eastwood. No one else but Eastwood. Dead in the water without Eastwood.

He took another military adventure movie, *Firefox.*

I was the one dead in the water now.

Until late in 1986, when the telephone rang . . .

Memoirs of
an Invisible Man
[1986]

On the other end of the phone, a quiet voice said, "Bill? My name is Michael Ovitz. I'm in town, and if you have a minute I'd like to come talk to you."

One of the problems with trying to bring old material to some kind of life is this: nobody cares about the past. Because of the explosion of media, everything has become *now*. But it's important when you read about Hollywood to know *who* people were *when*.

There are three people involved in this little story, and none of them now are remotely what they were a dozen years past. Alphabetically, Chevy Chase, Michael Ovitz (along with his agency, CAA), and Ivan Reitman.

The Michael Ovitz that came so promptly to see me a few hours after that phone call is nothing like the man today. Today he is rich, very famous, and, I suspect, more than a little haunted. Or maybe he always was.

In this mid-'80s time, he was *underground* famous. There were few newspaper quotes, fewer articles anywhere, almost no interviews. He was, and had been for several years, one of the founders of Creative Artists Agency, an organization that was as hated then as now, but back then was so low-key as to be almost mysterious. More than that, this—**the industry was terrified of them.**

Ovitz was the reason for the fear.

I remember two things about his call as being strange: (1) that he made it himself, and (2) that *he* was willing to come to *me*. In Hollywood, *you* travel to the power.

He was certainly not frightening in person. Trim, soft-spoken, conservatively dressed, a gentleman, he arrived impeccably on time and we went into the library. He spoke. Briefly. He said there was no point in not dealing with the facts, and the facts were essentially that my career was in the toilet and that was a shame. He said the feeling Out There was that I was no longer interested in dealing with the major studios. He said he thought CAA might be able to help me. He explained they work in groups, so that I would always have someone looking after me. (Not true, by the way; or maybe it is for stars.) He said the decision was mine. He hoped I would think about it.

And then he was gone.

There was really no doubt in my mind that I would go to CAA. This was only complicated by the fact that I resist change—I have had more agents leave me over the decades than the reverse.

Feeling guilty and failed (my longtime law firm), I still managed to switch to CAA within a month, and a month after that I was offered *Memoirs of an Invisible Man,* a novel by H. F. Saint, to adapt. It was a special-effects comedy-thriller, the kind of thing I had never done, might never *have* done if my hot streak had continued. But that winch was dead.

Besides, I thought I could make the novel work. More than that, there was talent connected with the project. Chevy Chase was set to star, Ivan Reitman to direct.

Chevy Chase is in his mid-fifties now, and his career as a major movie star is over. But when we met, he had the *National Lampoon* series going for him, he had the *Fletch* series going for him, he was the number 5 box-office star in the whole wide world. These were the four above him:

4. Michael J. Fox
3. Clint Eastwood
2. Eddie Murphy
1. Sylvester Stallone

(See what I mean about *when?*)

Chase, a lovely fellow, was also this: *tall.*

Now is as good a time as any to admit my fetish: I am hopelessly smitten with finding out the truth about how tall performers are. Especially male performers. Most especially male action performers.

I think part of it must be my fascination with the phoniness of Hollywood. I saw Gwyneth Paltrow being interviewed—she was a few weeks away from winning her first Oscar for *Shakespeare in Love*—and she said essentially that her chief thought of the coming ceremony was to be sure to remember to wear comfortable shoes, that she had given no thought to winning and of course didn't care. Well, there aren't enough lightning bolts in heaven to cover all the falsehoods in that little discourse, but the interviewer just hung on every humble word out of little Gwyn's head.

Most movie stars are short. (I'm six-one, and the only major stars who are taller that I have met are Eastwood and Connery.)

Stars' stumpiness is the beginning of my obsession. But when you throw action stars into the blend, guys who slay legions, well, it's just too yummy for me to resist.

Okay. True story. I am at the Hotel du Cap with friends during a recent Cannes Festival. And one of the friends, who knows my fetish, out of the blue says to me: "I guess we know where you're going, Bill." I didn't understand, glanced around, and lo, my prayers were answered—

—Sylvester Stallone had entered the swimming pool.

Panting like a schoolgirl, I left my friends, wandered casually to the pool, went in, stood maybe six feet away from Stallone—never once looking at him, understand. That would be insufferable and rude. I knew where he was and I also knew this: we were leaving together.

If he stayed an hour? Not a problem. Two? Tricky for me—this was late morning and we had a lunch reservation at the great hotel restaurant, the Eden Roc. But I was determined to get the truth.

I had a hot lead that Sly was sixty-seven inches. My source was a woman who had been a publicist on a movie he had been in and one early morning she was out jogging and they ran into each other and went back to the hotel, stride for stride, and she is five foot seven.

Now I would at last know.

You see, stars have lifts in their boots—why else, pray tell, do you think they wear them all the time? They have lifts in their shoes, their loafers, their slippers. I know one who has lifts in his socks.

But no one has figured out a way to put lifts in his feet. (Yet.)

Do not doubt my excitement.

Since this is not a book about my neuroses—well, maybe it is—but anyway, I will cut to the chase. After maybe ten minutes, he got out, grabbed a towel. I got out, grabbed a towel. He stood. I stood.

Sixty-seven inches, dripping wet. (There. Now you know everything.)

I am going to try and save face by connecting that anecdote to a book about screenwriting. Here it is: stars are not *not* **not** what you think.

They are not remotely what the world believes them to be, either. Most of them are smaller than you think, and all of them are more frightened than you think—and don't you *ever* forget that if you are lucky enough to work with them.

The director of *Memoirs of an Invisible Man* was Ivan Reitman. Reitman was never famous, which was very much his own choice. But he sure could have been. Here is what one film encyclopedia says: "Although he received less personal publicity than his box office powerhouse contemporaries, George Lucas and Steven Spielberg, Reitman had a comparable impact on filmmaking trends of the late '70s and '80s. When the demographic of moviegoers shifted to favor teens, these visionary showmen went beyond merely understanding their target audience, they molded them with their own distinctive tastes and obsessions. What Lucas and Spielberg did for fantasy/adventure, Reitman did for comedy."

In the late '70s, Reitman developed and produced *Animal House,* a shocking success that, as much as any movie of the last twenty years, changed comedy. He then directed and produced *Stripes* and *Meatballs* and, for an encore, in 1984, did the same for *Ghostbusters,* the most successful comedy in film history up to that point. (Since surpassed by *Home Alone.*)

So now you know the cast of characters. But I was *not* involved with the Chevy Chase and Ivan Reitman you picture as you read this now. Think of these two names—Jim Carrey and James Cameron—for those are the equivalents today.

And between them, trying to come back from the dead and make everybody smile, little Billy Goldman, that well-known pleaser from Highland Park, Illinois . . .

———

In my experience, you work with the director. Stars come later, and though they can be helpful, usually they are concerned not with the story but rather their part in it, and how can they be made even more adorable. Often, my main chore on a first draft is to nail a director.

Here, Reitman was involved from the initial go-round, so I met him. Reitman had talked with Chase; together they had decided what the movie should be.

(Pssst . . . remember that last sentence.)

I liked Ivan Reitman from the very beginning. A couple of interesting things about him: for a comedy figure, he was never remotely funny. For a superstar director, there was a total absence of bullshit. (Later, when he brought me in to doctor *Twins,* there was no secrecy. He had the other writers there when I was there. In the same room.)

When we started, we were both well aware that *Memoirs of an Invisible Man* was not *The Battleship Potemkin.* But Reitman was on the project for one very good reason: he felt absolutely confident that he was on the track of another *Ghostbusters:* a special-effects-filled comedy-action flick. (The plot of the novel—all you ever need to know—is that it's about a guy who accidentally gets caught in a lab explosion and is rendered invisible. And has ensuing adventures.)

We talked for a couple of days, then I went off and did the first draft, sent it to Reitman and Chase.

It was an okay first draft, meaning that lots of work needed to be done but at least a version of the story was there. Reitman felt it was a good start, called me out from New York to talk about draft two. Before that happened, I spent a few minutes with Chevy Chase.

I liked him, too. He wasn't just tall, he was nice and bright and funny.

He, too, was supportive enough about the first draft, knowing it was just that, the beginning of something. He clearly saw the potential in the project. And as I was leaving he casually mentioned that he hoped this time through we would be a little more forthcoming on what most interested him in the material, and which he had talked to Ivan about—namely, an investigation of **the loneliness of invisibility.**

Nice phrase, that. Interesting rhythm, unpretentious, but all kinds of swell echoes. Want to know how those words sounded to my ears? Like this:

AAARRRGHHHH

Why? Because my director wanted to do a funny farce with special effects and my star wanted to do a serious sad drama.

I went running to my new agents, CAA. "Listen to me," I told them, "there's going to be a train wreck and I'm in the middle."

Here's what they said: "Bill, you've been away a while, things are a little bit different now. Ivan is represented *by us.* Chevy is represented *by us.* It is what we at CAA specialize in. It is called '*a package.*' And there will be no train wreck. Just write the script. It will all sort itself out."

I met with Ivan. "Chevy is kind of interested in investigating the loneliness of invisibility," I told him.

His reply? Total unruffled calm. "Let me handle Chevy."

Off we go into the wild blue yonder. Ivan had some ideas for how to make the second draft better than the first. Terrific for me to work with. "Let's try this, let's see if that works, it's going to be a very funny movie."

Back to Manhattan, and I tried this, saw if that worked, wrote for weeks and more, because I knew certain absolute truths: Ivan was one of the three hottest directors on Planet Earth, he wanted this to be his next picture, Chevy was a huge star and a bright fellow, so fret not, this would indeed all sort itself out. Good. Because the most important thing, for me anyway, was this: after my years in the desert, *this picture had to happen.*

The second draft is sent off. Ivan likes it better, feels we have made strides, still need to make more.

I hear from Chevy, too—he had thought by this draft the loneliness of invisibility would be a little more clearly set out.

Back to CAA I go. "Listen to me," I inform them again. "*There's going to be a train wreck and I'm in the middle.*" (In point of fact, there was a little reality here in addition to my paranoia: Ivan had met with Bruce Bodner, Chevy's manager, partner, and protector, and pretty soon it was not a love nest.)

Here is what CAA told me. "Bill, do you know how many packages we have made? Do you realize we have changed the industry with our packaging skill? Just go write the third draft and we promise you this: *it will all sort itself out.*"

Round thr—ooops, draft three. Talk with Ivan, hopefully make things better, chat with Chevy about the loneliness of invisibility, back to New York and write and write, and in truth, whenever there was a chance to toss a little loneliness into the flick, I did so.

And do you want to know why? Because Chevy had a valid point. How could you deal with this material without discussing the awful reality of what it would be like if no one could see you? If you were, I guess, the ultimate freak on Earth?

But this had to be considered too—Olivier was not playing the lead. Young Brando was not playing the lead. Or Cagney. *My* truth was this: I had no problem investigating the loneliness of invisibility, *I just didn't want to investigate it with Chevy Chase.* Bright as Chase was, he had not gotten famous playing drunks or scientists or death-row convicts, he had become so playing a goof who had trouble with stairs.

Draft three made its way to both powers. Ivan wanted to go into production. Chevy stood his ground.

I made my standard run at CAA. "Have I ever mentioned a fucking train wreck to you guys?" I inquired. "Well, run for cover."

They smiled and chortled and reassured but I could see in their eyes I was not the loony of a few months before.

Ivan went to the Brothers Warner. Your pick, he told them, knowing they had to pick him. Me or Chevy?

They picked Chevy.

I think I quit first but I really don't remember; it was probably a dead heat. Half a dozen years later, Chevy came out in the flick. My name is mentioned among the writers. I have no idea if it should have been, since I never saw the movie. I have blocked out so much of that period, but a couple of things I do remember.

One is that I was cheated for the first time in decades of movie work.

Understand this: all the sleaze you've heard about Hollywood? All the illiterate scumbags who scuttle down the corridors of power? They are there, all right, and worse than you can imagine.

But Hollywood is one of the last of the handshake businesses. I don't think I have ever signed a contract before my work was finished. You just know you are going to be reimbursed whatever you were told you would be. Studios may have their creative accounting, sure, but they don't rob you up front.

Mark Canton was head of production then and he flipped when Ivan and I quit, but Ivan was much too powerful for him to do anything about. I wasn't, and he refused to pay me for work handed in. His message was essentially this: Sue us, we've got lots of lawyers, how many do you have?

I remember being shocked when this happened. Pissed, too. Finally a settlement was made, not even remotely a fair one. When you hire me, you are hiring my work and my time. Never happened since.

The second memory is something I think I said. (I read in a magazine that I did, although I have no real recollection of it.)

Chevy and Bodner tried to bring me back after the fiasco. For one final whack at the material. To write into the script what was so important to them. (Class, repeat after me: the loneliness of, *riiiight*, invisibility.)

They were both gentlemen and I listened. Then I got up, said this: **"I'm sorry, but I'm too old and too rich to put up with this shit."** And left.

Wouldn't that be neat if it was me . . . ?

Bill the Virgin

This is the opening of the first movie I was ever hired to do, thirty-five-plus years ago. (The movie became Cliff Robertson's Oscar winner, *Charley*.) In other words, I am letting you read my very first words as a screenwriter. This is clearly one of the brave acts of my young life.

It's pretty clunky stuff.

The only sign of talent I can find is this: the scene appears nowhere in Daniel Keyes' glorious short story, "Flowers For Algernon," on which the whole enterprise is based. We knew it must have taken place, but we don't see it or talk about it.

When I was fired immediately after turning in the screenplay, I remember feeling so failed, wanted desperately to have another chance. Looking back now, I couldn't have asked for a better introduction to the screen trade.

<u>GOOD OLD CHARLEY GORDON</u>

First Draft   Screenplay by:

April, 1964   William Goldman

                       Based on the short story

                       <u>Flowers For Algernon</u>

                       By Daniel Keyes

FADE IN ON:

A MACHINE.

This particular machine is the most modern
and up-to-date model yet manufactured for
the use of anesthetists. It has gauges and
tubes and a black, bladder-like bag with
which an anesthetist can control a patient's
breathing, and it has tanks of gas labeled
Nitrous Oxide and Oxygen and Cyclopropane.
This machine, in other words, is an anesthetist's dream of heaven and it would only
be used in operations of major import.

CUT TO:

A surgeon's face. (It is DOCTOR STRAUSS.)
Now it is clear that we are in an operating
room and that an operation is very much in
progress. And now the camera begins to move.

A SLOW CIRCULAR SHOT begins, taking in all
the people around the operating table. They
are deadly serious and terribly concerned.
Among the people we pass are:

ANOTHER DOCTOR (this is DOCTOR NEMUR), TWO
SCRUB NURSES, then a CIRCULATING NURSE, another CIRCULATING NURSE, then one ANES-
THETIST, then another ANESTHETIST and then
finally, we are back on the face of the SUR-
GEON. He pauses, closes his eyes while a
gloved hand dabs the perspiration from his
forehead. Turning, the glances at the operating room door, or more specifically, at the
round window in the center of the door.

CUT TO:

The window. Behind it, staring through the
glass, is MISS KINNIAN. As it registers on
her face that DR. STRAUSS is watching her,
she nervously tries for a smile, doesn't
quite make it, then holds up two fingers and
crosses them slowly, as a child might.

CUT TO:

DR. STRAUSS. He nods, turns back to operation, very, very serious. And so is everyone
in the room, very, very serious. Everything
suggests an operation of major import.

CUT TO:

Long shot that takes in all the people, the
nurses, the anesthetists, the doctors.
Everyone is seen but the patient.

A drum begins.

Slowly, with an awesome steadiness, the camera starts to move in closer to the operating
table.

The drum beats louder.

A nurse scurries around the table.

Louder on the drum; louder, but no faster.

DR. STRAUSS is perspiring heavily and again a
gloved hand dabs at his skin.

Relentlessly, the camera moves on, wedging
in between the shoulders of two nurses.

We still do not see the patient.

Slowly the camera tilts up, up toward the
great circular light high above the operating table. For a moment, the light is almost
blinding.

The drum stops.

The camera swoops down to the table, revealing that the patient is ALGERNON.

ALGERNON is a white mouse.

<u>A VERY FAST FADE-OUT</u>.

C

R

E

D

I

T

S

The Princess Bride
[1987]

Here is how the novel *The Princess Bride* happened.

I loved telling stories to my daughters. When they were small, I would go into their room and stories would just be there. Anyone who knows me knows that I don't think much of what I do is very terrific, but, my God, I was wonderful those early evenings. Stuff just *came*. I knew that because the girls would sneak out and tell their mother and she would say to me, "Write it down, write it down," and I told her I didn't need to, I was on such a hot streak I knew I'd remember.

All gone, of course, and of all the stuff I've done over almost forty-five years of storytelling, more than anything I wish I had those moments back. Doesn't matter, really. Woulda shoulda coulda . . . At any rate, I was on my way to Magic Town around 1970, and I said to them both, to Jenny, then seven, and Susanna, then four, "I'll write you a story, what do you most want it to be about?" And one of them said "princesses" and the other one said "brides."

"Then that will be the title," I told them. And so it has remained.

The first snippets are gone. A couple of pages maybe, maybe a little more, sent from the Beverly Hills Hotel to home. Since it was to be a kid's saga, the early names were silly names: Buttercup, Humperdinck. I'm sure those pages weren't much. I have never been able to write in Southern California. (My fault, of course. I find it just too, well, *wun*-derful. There was a time, before the recent madness, when people actually thought of L.A. as being that, *wun*derful.

Wandering now, I suppose nothing surprises me more than Los Angeles's becoming a place people *leave*. For the first half-century of my life, it was, he says in as cornball a way as he can muster, the American dream. Walls closing in? Just drive to the western ocean, you'll be fine. For me, abrasiveness helps, so I have always written in New York.

Anyway, the early pages disappeared. As did the notion of writing something for my ladies. At least consciously. (I don't understand the creative process. Actually, I make more than a concerted effort *not* to understand it. I don't know what it is or how it works but I am *terrified* that one green morning it will decide to not work anymore, so I have always given it as wide a bypass as possible.)

There is a story of Olivier after a particularly remarkable performance of *Othello*. Maggie Smith, his Desdemona, knocked on his dressing room door as she was on her way out of the theater and saw him staring at the wall, holding a tumbler of whiskey. She told him his work that night was magic. And he said, in, I suspect, tears and despair, "I know it was . . . and I don't know how I did it."

This relates to me in but one way: *The Princess Bride* is the only novel of mine I really like. And I don't know how I did it.

I remember doing the first chapter about how Buttercup became the most beautiful woman in the world. And the second chapter, which is a rather unflattering intro of Prince Humperdinck, the animal killer in his Zoo of Death.

But then I went dry.

The nightmare of all of us who put words on paper. I stormed around the city, wild with ineptitude, because, you see, all these moments had already happened in my head—the sword fight on the Cliffs of Insanity, for example; Inigo and his quest for the six-fingered man, for example; Fezzik and his rhymes—but I didn't know how to *get* to them, had no way to string them together. And I could feel the window of creativity starting to close. We move on, we move on, it's okay, we'll find other stories left to tell . . .

But I didn't *want* to tell other stories, I wanted to tell *this* one. And I couldn't find a way. I suppose the most desperate I have ever been was when I was twenty-four and done with grad school and done with the army and about to become an accursed copywriter in some ad agency in Chicago when I wrote my first novel, *The Temple of Gold*, in three weeks. It was a couple of hundred pages long and I had never written anything more than thirty and I remember thinking, when I was on page 75 or 100 or 150, "I don't know where I am, all I know is I've never been here before." But the book got published and suddenly I was what I always dreamt of but never thought I'd be, a writer.

Then I got the idea of the "good parts," that the whole *Princess Bride* story would be an abridgment of another, longer, book.

That made the novel possible. *My* book would be an abridgment of an earlier book, written by S. Morgenstern. Morgenstern's book would be one my father had had read to him by his father when he was sick (in the movie it's the grandfather reading it to me) and from which my father read me only the good parts because he didn't want to bore me.

Which meant I could jump wherever I wanted. I was free. So I did the opening chapter which explains how I got sick and my father started reading to me—

—and then I started to fly.

For the only time, I was happy with what I was doing. You can't know what that means if, most of your life, you haven't been stuck in your pit, locked forever with your own limitations, unable to tap the wonderful stuff that lurks there in your head but flattens out whenever it comes near paper.

The most startling creative moment of my life happened here. I remember going to my office and Westley was in the Zoo of Death (the Pit of Despair in the movie—budgetary reasons), and he was being tormented by the evil Count Rugen, who got his Ph.D. in pain (or would have, but doctorates didn't exist then, this was after education but before educators realized the real money was in diplomas). Westley is strapped in The Machine and Prince Humperdinck roars down and turns it all the way up and Inigo and Fezzik are on the way to the rescue when the Deathscream begins and they track it and as I was going to work that morning I kind of wondered how I was going to get Westley out of it. I sat at my desk and had coffee and read the papers and fiddled a while. Then I realized, I *wasn't* going to get him out of it. And I wrote these words: Westley lay dead by The Machine.

I think I must have looked at them for a long time. *Westley lay dead by The Machine.* He was perfect and beautiful but it hadn't made him conceited. He understood suffering and was no stranger to love or pain, yet the words were still there.

Westley lay dead by The Machine . . .

You killed him, I thought. You killed Westley. How could you do such a thing? I stared at the words, and I stared at the words some more, and then I lost it, began to cry. I was alone, you see, no one could help me get out of where I was and I was helpless. Even now, more than twenty years after, I can still truly feel the shocking heat of my tears. I pushed away from my desk, made it to the bathroom and ran water on my face. I looked up and there in the mirror this red-faced and wracked person was staring back at me, wondering who in the world were we and how were we going to survive?

I tell you this because I guess I want you to know that although I don't think it is a good life, writing, not insofar as having relationships with other people, having loves, all that emotional stuff we all long for, or say we long for, still, there are worthwhile times. And if you were to ask me the high point of my creative life, I would say it was that day when Westley and I were joined.

The rest of the book went the way it's supposed to but never does. Hiram Haydn, my editor, loved it, but more than that, I loved it. After it was done I got very sick, was hospitalized, thought I was going to die.

———

Here is how the movie *The Princess Bride* happened.

The Greenlight Guy at Fox liked the book. (Note: those Premiere 100 types Out There have all these different titles. Vice President in charge of this, Executive in charge of that, on and on. All salad. In movies, there is but one power, that of being able to greenlight a picture. Each studio has a grand total of one greenlighter. Understand, most of us alive in the Continental United States can greenlight a picture. Of course, a movie can cost five thousand dollars. That is an affordable sum for a lot of us to be, at least for a little while, a mogul. Now, what kind of picture will you get? You will not have car crashes. You will not enjoy the services of Mr. Schwarzenegger. It may not be what sets hearts aflutter on Saturday night in Westwood. But, if you can purchase enough film stock, it will be a movie. That's *our* movie. At each major studio there is a guy who can greenlight *any movie,* and today, "any movie" can mean up to $100 million. Those other executives at that studio, regardless of their titles, they are only oil slicks.

As I was saying, the Greenlight Guy at Fox liked the book.

I was in.

Problem: he was not remotely sure if it was a movie. So an odd deal was struck. They would buy the book and I would write a screenplay but they would not buy *that* unless they decided to make the movie. In other words, we each had half of the pie.

I wrote the screenplay. The GG at Fox liked it but wasn't 100 percent convinced yet that it was a movie. So he sent me to London to meet with Richard Lester, who was just coming off a considerable success with *The Three Musketeers*. Lester, most famous for the Beatles pictures, is a brilliant man, a Philadelphian who lives in England.

We met, he had some suggestions, I did them, he liked what I did, but better than that, the only man of true import in the whole matter, the GG at Fox, liked what I did.

Home and dry.

Except: the GG at Fox was fired.

Here is what happens when that happens. The old GG is stripped of his epaulets and his ability to get into Morton's on Monday nights, and off he goes, rich—he had a deal in place for when this happened—but humiliated.

The new GG takes command with but one rule writ boldly in stone: *nothing* his predecessor had in motion must ever get made. Why? Say it gets made. Say it's a hit. Who gets the credit? The *old* GG. So when the new GG, who can now get into Morton's on Mondays, has to run the gauntlet there, he knows all his peers are sniggering, "That asshole, it wasn't his picture."

Death.

So *The Princess Bride* was buried, conceivably forever.

Of course, I was upset by this, but I was too frantic to give it the weight it deserved. Because there had been a reaction to my sickness, and it was that I realized I was forty-two years old, had zero money in the bank, and a wife and two kids I had to provide for. So I provided. Movies and books and rewrites of books and endless rewrites of movies, and it was all honorable work, I wasn't throwing a bag over my head and doing it for Old Glory. I *cared*. (There are no rules to writing, but if there were, caring would be up there. Or, as we intellectuals are fond of saying, you had better give a shit.)

But none of it meant to me what *The Princess Bride* did. And I finally realized that I had let control of it go. Fox had the book. So what if I had the screenplay, they could commission another. They could change anything they wanted. So I did something of which I am genuinely proud. I bought the book back from the studio, *with my own money*. I think they were suspicious that I had a deal or some plan. I didn't. I just didn't want some idiot destroying what I had come to realize was the best thing I would ever write.

After a good bit of negotiating, it was again mine. I was the only idiot who could destroy it now.

I read recently about the fine Jack Finney novel *Time and Again*, which has taken close to twenty years and still hasn't made it to the screen. *The Princess Bride* didn't take that long, but not a lot less either. I didn't keep notes, so this is from memory. Understand, in order for someone to make a movie, they need two things: passion and money. A lot of people, it turned out, loved *The Princess Bride*. I know of at least two different GGs who loved it. Who shook hands with me on the deal. Who wanted to make it more than any other movie.

Who each got fired the *weekend* before they were going to set things in motion. Believe this: one *studio* (a small one) closed the weekend before they were going to set things in motion. The screenplay began to get a certain reputation—one article listed it among the best that had never been shot.

The truth is that, after a decade and more, I was always waiting for the other shoe to come clunking down, and it always did. But events that had been put in motion a decade before eventually would be my salvation.

When *Butch Cassidy and the Sundance Kid* was done, I took myself out of the movie business for a while. (We are back in the late '60s now.) I wanted to try something I had never done: nonfiction. I got a very silly idea from listening to some very disturbed acquaintances talking of the pluses and minuses of their respective mental institutions. "The Hatches" was what I decided to write—a magazine-length piece based on the premise that mental institutions might send out brochures as if they were colleges and universities. "Our Manic-Depressive Department is known worldwide." I decided to visit them and talk about the entrance requirements, class size, size of student body, quality of food, like that. I realized before I had gone much further that the piece was dead if Meninger's didn't cooperate. I dropped the idea. I have never liked being at anyone's mercy.

I fiddled for a while, wondering what I could investigate where I knew someone would always talk. I decided on Broadway. I had been a failed playwright already, had three plays on by the time I was thirty, hated it—it was just too brutal. Unlike a movie or a novel, where there is often a year between when you finish and when the public is allowed in, on Broadway it's immediate—you are often still rewriting as Opening Night comes thundering down. Your scar tissue never gets a chance to heal. Agony.

So I knew a lot about the theater, had a lot of friends and acquaintances who worked that side of the street, had done my graduate work in theater. Plus, the theatrical world is so filled with envy, hatred, and bile, I knew someone would always tell me what was going on. If the producer or writer wouldn't talk to me, well, I could get to stage managers.

So I wrote a book about Broadway called *The Season*. In the course of a year I went hundreds of times, both in New York and out of town, saw everything at least once. But the show I saw most was a terrific comedy called *Something Different*.

By Carl Reiner.

He was terribly helpful to me and I liked him a lot. When the book was done I sent him a copy. And a few years later, when *The Princess Bride* was done, I sent him the novel. And one day he gave it to his eldest son. "Here's something," he said to his boy Robert one day. "I think you'll like this."

Fortunately for all concerned, Carl was right. Rob was years away from being a director at that point. He was starring in the number-one TV show of the decade, *All in the Family*, created and produced by Norman Lear. Ten years later Rob was a director and had formed a little company with his friend and producer Andy Scheinman. Rob had directed *This Is Spinal Tap*, had just finished a rough cut of his second movie, *The Sure Thing*. They were sitting around one day wondering what to do next, when Rob remembered the book, talked about it, reread it, got excited.

Eventually we met and the movie happened. But in between there was a lot of frustration because the movie that established him as a commercial director, *Stand By Me*, had yet to happen. But he can be magnificently stubborn, and eventually Norman Lear got us the money. I was grateful then, still am, always will be.

We had our first script reading in a hotel in London. Rob and Andy were there. Cary Elwes and Robin Wright were there, Westley and Buttercup. Chris Sarandon and Chris Guest, the villains Humperdinck and Count Rugen. Wally Shawn, the evil genius Vizzini. Mandy Patinkin, who played Inigo, was very much there. And sitting by himself, quietly—he always tried to sit quietly—was Andre the Giant, who *was* Fezzik.

Not your ordinary Hadassah group.

Sitting suavely in a corner was *moi*. Two of the major figures of my time in the entertainment business—Elia Kazan and George Roy Hill—have both said the same thing to me in interviews: that by the time of the first cast reading, the crucial work was done. If you had gotten the script to work and cast it properly, then you had a chance for something of quality. If you had not, it didn't matter how skillful the rest of the process was, you were dead in the water.

This probably sounds like madness to the uninitiated, and it should, but it is very much true. The reason it sounds like madness is this: *Premiere* magazine isn't around when the script is being prepared. *E.T.* isn't around for the casting. They are only around during the shooting of the flick, which is the *least* important part of the making of any movie. Shooting is just the factory putting together the car. (Postproduction—editing and scoring—is waaaay more important.)

But shooting is all most people know—from those awful articles in magazines or stories on the tube that purport to be on the inside but are only bullshit. The movie company knows who is watching and they behave accordingly. Stars do not misbehave when the enemy is about. Directors do not admit their terrors when the enemy is about. Writers, to give us our due, are not even *there* when the enemy is about. (And when I am forced to be there, and the enemy is about, I lie. "Oh, this is an amazing shoot, it's just been a dream." "I don't know where Dusty [or Barbra or Sly or Eddie or fill in your own blank] gets this bad rap about being hard to work with, he's [she's] been a dream here." So it goes.)

I was there in London, at the script reading. And I was terrified. Not only is that my natural state when I am around actors, this was almost a decade and a half from when I helped scale the Cliffs of Insanity. Most of the people in the room I knew of. The others I had heard read. But there were two who were essentially new to me.

Robin Wright, our Buttercup, was new to everybody, except the faithful watchers of the soap *Santa Barbara*. A California kid of maybe twenty, she was neither experienced nor trained. She was being asked to be first a farmgirl, unspoiled and in love, then a princess, regal and emotionally dead, all this, by the way, with an English accent. (Turns out she has a brilliant ear.)

It also was important that she be the most beautiful woman in the world, and of course that is all a matter of personal taste, there is no single most beautiful woman. Except looking at Robin that London morning, watching her as she sat there with no makeup, she sure made one hell of a case. We started the reading then, and this is what I thought when we were done—

—I thought she was going to be the biggest lady star in the world.

Hasn't happened. I don't know her, have seen her once in five years, we have no friends in common. Still, I think I know why. *She doesn't want it.*

To be a star, yes, you have to have talent, and my God, do you ever have to be lucky, but riding alongside is this: desire. One so consuming that you are willing to piss away everything else in life. Stars have no friends, they have business acquaintances and serfs. They can only fake love on screen.

But they get the good table at Spago.

And if that is your heart's desire, and it is a lot of people's heart's desire, get rid of everything personal that might hinder you, and good luck. I promise to stare as you go by.

Wright has been in a few movies, and her work is always fine. But I think what she wants is to spend some time on the occasional job, and to spend a lot of time with her family. She had not been in a big commercial success until *Forrest Gump*. She was almost in one earlier; she was to be the lead opposite Kevin Costner in *Robin Hood*. But she had to drop out because she was having a baby.

I remember, when I read that, thinking: Barbra Streisand does not get pregnant at such a time . . .

A. R. Roussimoff was the other new kid on the block that rehearsal morning. Actually, he was not precisely *new* to any of us, he was just new as an *actor,* because as Andre the Giant he was the most famous wrestler in the world. I had become a lunatic Andre fan, would go to the Garden to watch him entertain the masses. I became convinced that if there ever was to be a movie, he should be Fezzik, the strongest man.

Andre was always still. When he entered a room he would look for a place in a corner and go there. A man with a great and good heart, I suspect he had grown weary of the strange ways humans reacted to him. They either took to him immediately, as we all did—Andre was by far the most popular figure I have ever been around on a movie set—or they panicked.

Andre came from France and his voice came from the basement, so he was not always a thrill to understand. When Reiner gave him the part, he also gave him a tape that had his part recorded on it. Reiner, a wonderful actor, had done the line readings himself. He hoped Andre would take the time to memorize his role. Which in point of fact he had. But his readings that morning, to be honest, had a certain rote quality to them.

After the script was read, Reiner broke some scenes down and had the actors work on them. One such occasion involved Andre and Cary Elwes rehearsing their talking fight scene. They stood in front of us, went through it very slowly, said the words, and it was cool in the room as Andre began to perspire. We are not talking a little *shvitz* here. As we watched we were all stunned to see Andre's shirt become, suddenly, sopping. We kept watching. In a few moments more the shirt was dry. You turn your head away—soaked. It was simply the first physical manifestation of how different giants are from the rest of us. There was never any odor to the perspiring. It just became part of the day, "Oh, Andre's wet again."

It was a beautiful afternoon when we broke for lunch and we found a nearby bistro with outside tables. It was perfect except the chair was far too small for Andre—the width was for normal people, the arms far too close. There was a table inside that had a bench and someone suggested we eat there. Except Andre wouldn't hear of it. So we sat outside, and I can still see him pulling the arms of the chair wide apart, managing to squeeze in, then watching the arms all but snapping back into place, pinioning him for the rest of the meal. He ate very little. And the utensils were like baby toys, dwarfed by his hands.

After lunch we rehearsed again, and now Andre was working with our Inigo, Mandy Patinkin. They were doing one of their scenes and Mandy was trying to get some information out of Andre and Andre was giving one of his slow, rote memory readings. Mandy, as Inigo, tried to get Fezzik to go faster. And Andre gave back one of his slow, rote memory readings. They went back and tried it again and again, Mandy as Inigo asking Andre as Fezzik to go faster—Andre coming back at the same speed as before—

—which was when Mandy went, "Faster, Fezzik"—and slapped him hard in the face.

I can still see Andre's eyes go wide. I don't think he had been slapped outside a ring since he was little. He looked at Mandy and it was all so sudden and there was a brief pause . . .

And Andre started speaking faster. He just rose to the occasion, gave it more pace and energy and you could almost see his mind going, "Oh, this is how you do it outside the ring, let's give it a try." In truth, it was the beginning of the happiest period of his life.

It was my happiest movie experience, too. I am almost never around the set, mainly because it is so boring. Now, Andy Scheinman, the producer, and I would arrive late morning and stay through dailies. There were the standard tensions caused by weather, budget, and ego—*all* movie sets are plagued by weather, budget, and ego—but beyond that, the shoot went wonderfully well. Postproduction was difficult for the same reason the whole project was difficult, why so many bright and talented men had wanted to make it and ultimately failed—*just what was the movie?* Was it a comedy? Fingers crossed, yes. Action flick? Fingers crossed again. Spoof? I don't do spoofs, but a lot of people thought it was. Romance? Believe it.

We were in dangerous terrain—*because whenever you mix genres in a movie, that's where you end up.* I remember George Hill calling me in despair the day after the first *Butch Cassidy* sneak. Because the audience hadn't liked it? The reverse. They had loved it—they just thought it was so *funny.* And George was convinced that the balance had to be right, because if it was too funny, the shootout at the end wouldn't be moving. And if it was too dour, the whole beginning third—the fun and games part—would just lie there. So he set out the next morning going through the flick and taking out laughs until he got the balance right.

Reiner fought the same battle and eventually, like Hill, won. When we started having sneaks, the audience *loved* us. The test scores were sensational, among the top results of that year. Fabulous. We were flying. And we should have been.

I was talking once to a famous critic's darling director and he said this: "People talk about movies in three parts: preparing, shooting, and postproduction. That's wrong. There are really only two parts: the *making* of the movie and the *selling* of the movie." I'm not sure he isn't right.

The studio did not know how to sell us. (No criticism intended here. Heartbreak sure, but everybody was behind the movie.) *But what the hell was it?* They never figured it out. Our trailer—one of the more crucial selling tools—was so confusing I was told it was pulled from theaters, something I had never heard of before. The ad campaign was changed and changed again. We had nothing to sell us, no stars. The book, successful, was a cult success, but no King, no Grisham.

We came out and were a mild hit: $30 million, would have been $60 today. A double, to use their terminology. (A home run today is over $100 million in box-office gross—although your children will live to see the day when *that's* a flop.) Audiences loved us once we got them in. They just didn't see any reason to come. When we came out on cassette, word of mouth had caught up with us and we were the hit we should have been in theaters.

It had been a difficult wait, a decade and a half. I had started writing something for my kids when the '70s started. The movie hit the theaters in 1987. It's the new millennium now and your kids can see it on tape. When you say that, smile.

Andre died in early '93. I hadn't seen him but once since the movie was done, but I was terribly upset. I spoke to Rob, Andy, Billy Crystal, all the same. We told Andre stories, made ourselves feel better. We were shocked, you see, but not surprised. Andre, who was turning forty when the movie was made, knew it was coming soon. Here is what I wrote when I heard the news.

REQUIEM FOR A HEAVYWEIGHT

PARIS. Jan 30 (AP) — The professional wrestler Andre Rene Roussimoff, a native of France who was known to fans as Andre the Giant, died this week, apparently of a heart attack. He was 46.

He was handsome once. I remember a photo he showed me, taken at a beach with some friends. Dark, good-looking kid, maybe 17. Big, sure—he said he was around six foot eight then and weighed 275—but that was before the disorder really kicked in. Acromegaly. Something goes haywire with the growth hormones. He was working as a furniture mover during the day, taking wrestling lessons at night, sleeping when he could.

At 25, he topped out, but I don't think he ever actually knew his size. I met him in England when he was playing the rhyme-loving Fezzik in *The Princess Bride*. I had written the novel and now the screenplay. This was in the summer of '86 and Andre's publicity listed him at seven foot five, 550 pounds. Close enough. All he was sure of was that he'd had pneumonia a little while earlier and had lost 100 pounds in three weeks in the hospital.

Gone now at 46, he was the most popular figure on any movie set I've even been on.

He was *very* strong. I was talking to an actor who was shooting a movie in Mexico. What you had to know about Andre was that if he asked you to dinner, he paid, but when you asked him, he also paid. This actor, after several free meals, invited Andre to dinner and, late in the meal, snuck into the kitchen to give his credit card to the maitre d'. As he was about to do this, he felt himself being lifted up in the air. The actor, it so happens, was Arnold Schwarzenegger, who remembers, "When he had me up in the air, he turned me so I was facing him, and he said, 'I pay.' Then he carried me back to my table where he set me down in my chair like a little boy. Oh yes, Andre was *very* strong."

When Arnold Schwarzenegger tells me someone is *very* strong, I'll go along with it.

Andre once invited Schwarzenegger to a wrestling arena in Mexico where he was performing in front of 25,000 screaming fans, and, after he'd pinned his opponent, he gestured for Schwarzenegger to come into the ring.

So through the noise, Schwarzenegger climbs up. Andre says, "Take off your shirt, they are all crazy for you to take off your shirt. I speak Spanish." So Schwarzenegger, embarrassed, does what Andre tells him. Off comes his jacket, his shirt, his undershirt, and he begins striking poses. And then Andre goes to the locker room while Schwarzenegger goes back to his friends.

And it had all been a practical joke. God knows what the crowd was screaming, but it wasn't for Schwarzenegger to strip and pose. "Nobody gave a shit if I took my shirt off or not, but I fell for it. Andre could do that to you."

Andre never knew what reaction he might cause in people. Sometimes children and grown-ups would see him and be terrified. Sometimes children would see him, shriek with glee, and begin clambering all over him as if the greatest toy imaginable had just been given them. And he would sit, immobile, as they roamed around him. Sometimes he'd put a hand out, palm up, and they'd sit there, for what they hoped would be forever.

Andre would never come out and say that wrestling might not be legit. He fought 300 plus times a year for about 20 years, and all he ever admitted was that he didn't like being in the ring with someone he thought might be on drugs. When he was in his prime, men who weighed 250 or 300 pounds would hurl themselves on him from the top rope and he would catch them and not budge.

But even seven years ago his body was beginning to betray him. There is a scene at the end of *The Princess Bride* where Robin Wright—and yes she is that beautiful—jumped out of a castle window, and Andre was to catch her at the bottom.

The shot was set up for Robin to be lifted just above camera range and then dropped into Andre's arms. Maybe a foot. Maybe two. But not much and Robin was never that heavy.

The first take, she was dropped and he caught her—and gasped, suddenly white like paper, and almost fell to his knees. His back was bad. And getting worse, and soon there would be surgery.

Andre once said to Billy Crystal, "We do not live long, the big and the small."

Alas.

McKee

Can you learn how to write movies?

No easy answer, but I would say if you have zero facility for the form, no. If you have some, writing courses can sure help a lot. At the very least, you will not write something like this, which I recently had to wade through. (Names changed to protect the innocent.)

```
OPEN UP ON A HALL IN A CASTLE.  Medieval
times.  Footsteps are heard.


                    KING
        Where are my troops?


                    PRIME MINISTER
        Mounting up, sire.


CRIES ARE HEARD FROM SOMEWHERE.


                    PRIME MINISTER
                (to a guard)
        See what that was.


THE GUARD DEPARTS.


                    KING
        I did not like that sound.
```

I think I made it to the top of page four before surrendering. When I pick up something like that, I feel sadness. Someone spent months on it. Someone has dreams of how the manuscript will change his life.

Personally, I must have had considerable facility for the form. I never saw a screenplay until I was thirty-three, and when I did, wrote one that got me fired (*Charly*). But my second screenplay, *Harper*, was a hit and is still shown today. *Butch* came two screenplays later.

Facility, hell—I could make a case—I don't want to but I could—that it's been downhill all the way since then.

The main thing to remember is this: you have to *try* to *know*. You have to grind one out and have it read before you can chance a guess. You may know you can't write poetry or novels, but this is so different, you have to give it a shot if you even think it's what you want to do with your life.

And an awful lot of you are taking that shot. The number of writing applications to one of the nation's top film schools, NYU, for example, has close to tripled in the last decade.

You may not have the time for that kind of thing. Or the amazing amounts of money required. There are still an awful lot of people teaching courses in screenwriting. I hope they're all terrific, but the one I audited is the most famous: Story Structure by Robert McKee.

He's a tireless speaker, knowledgeable and passionate—it's three full days over a single weekend and no one feels cheated when he's done. He started doing just Saturday mornings at a small school in California, but as interest in screenwriting has risen, so has he, and he is now all over the world. No matter what continent you live on, if you look outside and see a group of writers and movie nuts gathering, probably Robert McKee is in town.

I don't know if he can teach screenwriting, or if anyone can. But I do know this: after listening to him, I wish he'd been around when I started writing CUT TO for a living.

Misery
[1990]

Misery came about like this.

I got a call from Rob Reiner saying he was interested in this book by Stephen King and would I read it. He became interested when Andy Scheinman, Reiner's producer, read it on a plane and wondered who owned the movie rights. The book had been in print for a while, was a number-one best-selling novel, standard for King.

They found out it hadn't been sold—not for any lack of offers but because King wouldn't sell it. He had disliked most of the movies made from his work and didn't want this one, perhaps his favorite, Hollywooded up. Reiner called him and they talked. Now, one of the movies made from his fiction that King *did* like was *Stand By Me,* which Reiner directed. The conversation ended with King saying sure, he would sell it, but he would have to be paid a lot of money and that Reiner would have to either produce or direct it.

Reiner, who had no intention of directing, agreed. He would produce. He called me. I read *Misery.* I had read enough of King to know this: of all the phee-noms that have appeared in the past decades, King is the stylist. If he ever chooses to leave the world that has made him the most successful writer in memory, he won't break a sweat. The man can write anything, he is that gifted.

Misery is about a famous author who has a terrible car crash during a blizzard, is rescued by a nurse. Who turns out to be his number-one fan. Who also turns out to be very crazy. And who keeps him prisoner in her out-of-the-way Colorado home. It all ends badly for them both (worse for her). I was having a fine old time reading it. I'm a novelist too, so I identified with Paul Sheldon, who was not just trapped with a nut, but also trapped by his own fear of losing success. And Annie Wilkes, the nurse/warden, is one of King's best creations.

When I do an adaptation, I have to be kicked by the source material. One of the ways I work is to read that material again and again. So if I don't like it a lot going in, that becomes too awful. I wasn't sure halfway through if I would write the movie, but I was enjoying the hell out of the novel.

Then on page 191 the hobbling scene began.

Paul Sheldon has managed to get out of the bedroom in his wheel-chair, and he gets back in time to fool Annie Wilkes. This is more than a little important to him, because Annie is not the kind of lady you want real mad at you.

Except, secretly, she does know, and in the next fifteen pages, takes action.

I remember thinking, Jesus, what in the world will she do? Annie has a volcanic temper. What's in her head? She talks to Paul about his behavior and then she eventually works her way around to the Kimberly diamond mines and asks him how he thinks they treat workers there who steal the merchandise. Paul says, I don't know, kill them, I suppose. And Annie says, Oh no, they hobble them.

And then, all for the need of love, she takes a propane torch and an ax and cuts his feet off, says, "Now you're hobbled," when the deed is done.

I could not fucking believe it.

I mean, I knew she wasn't going to tickle him with a peacock feather, but I never dreamt such behavior was possible. And I knew I had to write the movie. That scene would linger in audiences' memories, as I knew it would linger in mine.

The next half year or so is taken up with various versions, and I work with Reiner and Scheinman, the best producer I have ever known for script. We finally have a version they okay and we go director hunting. Our first choice is George Roy Hill, and he says *yesss.* Nirvana.

Then Hill calls and says he is changing his mind. We all meet. And Hill, who has *never* in his life done anything like this, explains. "I was up all night. And I just could not hear myself saying 'Action' on that scene. I just haven't got the sensibility to do that scene."

"What scene?" (I am in agony—I desperately want him to do it. He is tough, acerbic, brilliant, snarly, passionate.)

"The lopping scene."

What madness is this? What lopping scene?

"The scene where she lops his feet off."

"George, how can you be so wrong?" (After *Butch Cassidy* and *Waldo Pepper,* we have been through a lot together. The only way to survive with George is to give him shit right back.) "That is not a *lop-ping* scene, that is a *hobbling* scene. And it is great and it is the reason I took this movie and she only does it out of love."

"Goldman, *she lops his fucking feet off*. And I can't direct that."

"It's the best scene in the movie when she *hobbles* him. It's a character scene, for chrissakes."

He would not budge. And of course, since it was the most important scene and the best scene, it had to stay. A sad, sad farewell. We were about to send the script to Barry Levinson when Rob said, "To hell with it, I'll direct it myself."

And so the lopping-scene poll came into my life.

Because Hill has a brilliant movie mind and you must pay attention. Rob had no problem directing the scene. But what if George was right? I, of course, scoffed—the *hobbling* scene was a character scene, unlike anything yet filmed, and it was great and it was the reason I took the picture and it had to stay.

Still, we asked people. A poll was taken at Castle Rock, informally, of anyone who had read the script. "And what did you think of the lopping scene?" Rob would keep me abreast in New York. "A good day for the hobblers today, three secretaries said leave it alone." That wasn't exactly verbatim, but you get the idea.

Enter Warren Beatty. Beatty understands the workings of the town better than anyone. He has been a force for forty years, has been in an *amazing* number of flops, and whenever his career seems a tad shaky, he produces a wonderful movie or directs a wonderful movie and is safe for another half decade.

Beatty was interested in playing Paul. Rob and Andy met with him a lot and I spent a day there when the lopping scene came up. Beatty's point was this: he had no trouble losing his feet at the ankles, but know that if you did that the guy would be crippled for life and would be a loser.

I said nonsense . . . it was a great scene . . . a character scene . . . was the reason I took the movie . . . Beatty waffled, casting continued. As did the lopping queries. I went on vacation as we were about to start, and while I was gone, Rob and Andy wanted to take a final pass at the script. I was delighted. They wanted it shorter, tighter, tauter, and are expert editors. When I got back, I read what they had done.

It was shorter, tighter, tauter—

—only the lopping scene was gone, replaced by what you saw in the movie—she breaks his ankles with a sledgehammer.

I scrreeamed. I got on the phone with Rob and Andy and told them they had ruined the picture, that it was a great and memorable scene they had changed, it was the reason I had taken the job. I was incoherent (they are friends, they expect that) but I made my point. They just wouldn't buy it. The lopping scene was gone now, forever replaced by the ankle-breaking scene. I hated it but there it was.

I am a wise and experienced hand at this stuff and I *know* when I am right.

And you know what?

I was *wrong*. It became instantly clear when we screened the movie. What they had done—it was exactly the same scene except for the punishment act—worked wonderfully and was absolutely horrific enough. If we had gone the way I wanted, it would have been too much. The audience would have hated Annie and, in time, hated us.

If I had been in charge, *Misery* would have been this film you might have heard of but never have gone to see. Because people who had seen it would have told you to ride clear. What makes a movie a hit is not the star and not the advertising but the word of mouth. So in the movie business, as in real life, we all need all the help we can get. And we need it every step of the way.

———

Casting Kathy Bates

"I'm going to write the part for Kathy Bates."

"Oh, good. She's great. We'll use her."

I was the first speaker, Rob Reiner the second. And lives changed.

I had seen Kathy Bates for many years on stage. We had never met but I felt then what I do now: she is simply one of the major actresses of our time. I'd seen her good-heartedness in *Vanities,* where she played a Texas cheerleader. I'd seen the madness when she played the suicidal daughter in *'Night, Mother.* I had no sure sense that her talent would translate—a lot of great stage performers are less than great on film; Gielgud, Julie Harris, Kim Stanley will do as examples—but there is an old boxing expression that goes like this: *Bury me with a puncher.* And it was a moment in *Frankie and Johnny in the Clair de Lune* that made me know she was the lady I had to be buried with. She plays a waitress who has a fling with a cook and at one point she is wearing a robe and he wants to see her body.

The scene was staged so that he saw her naked body and the audience saw her face, and there was such panic in her eyes and at the same time, this wondrous *hope*. (Casting note: when Michelle Pfeiffer, who I think is a brilliant character actress, played the same part in the movie, the same moment was there, but it didn't work for me because Pfeiffer is so loved by the camera that all I kept thinking was, Why was she worrying when the worst that could happen would be a pubic hair maybe out of place?)

Anyway, Kathy got the part.

It was really almost that simple because Reiner had seen her on Broadway and thought she was as gifted as I did. We could have had almost any actress in the world. Obviously it's a decent part—Kathy won the Oscar for it—but the main reason so many women were inter-ested is there is almost *nothing* for women out there nowadays. Sad but very true. Rob had lunch with Bette Midler, who would have been fine and would have helped open the picture. But she did not want to play someone so ugly, and Rob realized she would be wrong for the part. *All* stars would be wrong for the part, he decided. Annie is this unknown creature who appears alone out of a storm. We know nothing about her. Stars bring history with them, and I believe, in this case, that would have been damaging.

Example: there is a scene where Annie asks Paul to burn his most recent book in manuscript. It is the last thing on earth he wants to do and he says no. They argue but he is firm.

Fine, Annie says, I love you and I would never dream of asking you to do anything you didn't want to do. Forget it. I never asked. But—

—big but—

—while she is saying forget I ever asked, what she is doing is walking around his bed, flicking lighter fluid onto the sheets. She is threatening, in Annie's sweet, shy way, to fry him.

Rob and Andy and I talked so much about that scene. Was it enough? Did she have to do more? We decided to go with it. But my feeling is that even with as brilliant a performer as Streep in the part, it would not have worked, because sitting out there in the dark, some part of us would have known that Meryl Streep wasn't really going to incinerate Jimmy Caan.

But no one knew who Kathy Bates was. And because of that, not to mention her skill, the scene held. One of the advantages to working with an independent—which Castle Rock was in those days—is that they have more freedom in casting. No way Mr. Disney or the Brothers Warner would have us go with an unknown in the lead of what they hoped would be a hit movie. And you know what? If I had been the head of a large studio, I wouldn't have cast her either . . .

———

Casting Jimmy Caan

It was as simple and discouraging as this: no one would play the part.

We knew the role was less flashy. Had to be, the guy's in the sack most of the movie. We also knew he was under the control of the woman, something stars *hate*. But we also felt the movie was essentially what the Brits call a "two-hander." The Paul Sheldon character is not only the hero, he's in almost every scene. Wouldn't *anyone* say yes?

We went to William Hurt—

—didn't want to do it.

We rewrote it, went back to William Hurt—

—didn't want to do it yet again.

Kevin Kline—

—didn't want to do it.

Michael Douglas—

—met with Rob, didn't want to do it.

Harrison Ford—

—didn't want to do it.

Dustin Hoffman was called in London—

—liked Castle Rock, liked Rob, didn't want to do it.

Understand, this entire casting process took maybe six months, and we are well into it by now and this is where my respect for Mr. Reiner reached epic size. Because you must understand that well before this point, *all* the major studios would have had me in for rewrites or fired me, because they would have known the script stank. It had to stink. Look at those rejections.

Reiner simply got more and more bullheaded.

And, secondly, he *needed* a famous face as Paul Sheldon, because Paul Sheldon *was* famous, just as Annie Wilkes was unknown. On he trudged.

DeNiro—

—didn't want to do it.

Pacino—

—didn't want to do it.

Dreyfuss—

—WANTED TO DO IT.

Yes, Lord.

You see, Rob and Richard Dreyfuss had gone to high school together. And more than that, Rob had offered *When Harry Met Sally* to Dreyfuss, who said no. Biiiig mistake.

This time when Rob called him, Dreyfuss said this: "Whatever it is, I'll do it." Rob was, of course, amazingly relieved. But he felt it was silly for Dreyfuss to take a part without first at least reading it. Rob gave him the script. Dreyfuss read it—

—oops—

—didn't want to do it.

Hackman would have been wonderful—

—didn't want to do it.

Well before this point, Mr. Redford was sent the script. He would have been extraordinary. He met with Rob. He felt the script would make a very commercial movie.

Long regretful pause—

—didn't want to do it.

How many is that? You count, it's too painful. Understand, this is not the order of submission. My memory is that William Hurt may have been first but his second rejection came well after a bunch of others had passed. Anyway, it is all a swamp to me now.

Enter Warren Beatty.

Kind of wanted to do it. Met and met with Rob and Andy. Had a number of wonderful suggestions that helped close holes in the script. He was definitely interested. But there was this wee problem with *Dick Tracy,* which he was producing, directing, and starring in and which conflicted. To this day, I don't think Warren Beatty has said no.

Andy one day mentioned Jimmy Caan. Who had been in the wilderness. Rob met with him, asked about his supposed drug problem. Caan replied that he was clean. "I will pee in a bottle for you," he said. "I will pee in a bottle every day."

He didn't have to.

The reason for detailing the above is because there is a lesson here. Two, actually. First is this: *we will never know.* Would Kevin Kline have made it a better flick? We will never know. Would any of the skilled performers listed? We will never know. They never played the part. They might have been better or worse, all that we can be sure of is that they would have been different. Jimmy Caan did play it and he was terrific.

One special thing Caan brought to the party is that he is a very physical guy, he is like a shark, he has to keep moving, he cannot be still in a room. And playing Paul, month after month trapped in that bed, drove him nuts. That pent-up energy you saw on screen was very real. And it was one of the main reasons, at least for me, the movie worked.

Second point. When we read about George Raft turning down *The Maltese Falcon* because he didn't trust one of the great directors of all time, John Huston, it seems like lunacy. The movie, of course, went on to make Mr. Bogart a star. But Bogart was a nothing then, a small bald New York stage actor who was going nowhere. And Huston had never directed. The same is true when we read of all the people who were offered the lead in *East of Eden* or *On the Waterfront* or *Raiders of the Lost Ark*.

Careers are primarily about timing.

Paul Sheldon is an attractive, sensitive man in his forties, a writer of romance fiction. If you ask me what star best describes that guy I would answer with two words: Richard Gere.

Why didn't we go with him?

Wrong question.

The real question is this: How is it possible for us to spend six months looking for an actor for a part for which Richard Gere would have been perfect and never once, *not even one time mention his name*? That's how dead he was at the time we were looking. We were looking before *Internal Affairs* revived him and *Pretty Woman* put him back on top. We were looking in 1989, seven years since *An Officer and a Gentleman*. And in those seven years, these were his choices: *The Honorary Consul, Breathless, The Cotton Club, King David, No Mercy, Miles from Home*.

He was not just dead, he was forgotten. Happens to us all. Remember my leper period? There's a good and practical reason Hollywood likes Dracula pictures—it's potentially the story of our lives . . .

————

The Author Sees His Children

Misery was Stephen King's baby. He made it up. And we wanted very much that he like what we had done with it. He was in California and a screening was arranged, hundreds of people, and he sat unnoticed in the middle of the audience. (King, in case anyone is interested, is amazingly unpretentious. And real smart.)

Anyway, the screening starts and we are pacing around in the back or sitting in corners, because this book meant a lot to him. Near the climax, Annie Wilkes is bringing some champagne into Paul Sheldon's room, supposedly to celebrate, but as in the novel, she is planning to kill him. She puts a gun into her apron.

Now, by total accident, the person sitting next to King is involved with Castle Rock. And reported the following. As Annie takes the tray down to Paul's room, an edgy Stephen King is hunkered down in his seat, muttering to himself. And this is what he is saying: "Look out . . . don't trust her . . . she's got a gun in her ayy-pron . . ."

(He liked it fine. As did we all.)

Talent Tends to Cluster

I think the '90s are by far the worst decade in Hollywood history.

Many reasons, starting with the possibility that, being an old fart in good standing, I hate anything new. Let me throw in a couple of other possibilities.

Talent tends to cluster. We know Aeschylus was not the only guy hacking out plays in Athens. We know that Balanchine had Robbins, that Placido had Luciano, that Chekhov and Tolstoy and Dostoyevsky and a bunch of other Russians all walked a similar earth.

And today, in every single art I can think of, is a time of low talent. When I took a modern novel course at Oberlin in 1951, we studied people who had published between 1900 and 1950 but who all had written something in the year 1927. So we read Dos Passos and Wolfe and Steinbeck and Faulkner and Hemingway and Fitzgerald—not, alas, the same today.

Not for painters or singers or writers or screenwriters.

But no discipline makes my point more than movie directors.

We had *one* great one until very recently—Mr. Kubrick.

What I came to town, in 1953, such was not the case. And remember, there are a lot of directors I am not counting, because they were not involved with Hollywood financing or Hollywood sensibility—Bergman, Buñuel, Clair, Fellini, Kurosawa, Renoir, to pick a quick half dozen.

And I am also not counting some old guys who were still capable of thrilling us—Capra, Chaplin, De Mille.

Following is a list of top directors and my favorites of their movies.

Cukor	*The Philadelphia Story, My Fair Lady*
Curtiz	*The Adventures of Robin Hood, Casablanca*
Donen	*Seven Brides for Seven Brothers, Singin' in the Rain* (codirected with Gene Kelly)
King	*Twelve O'Clock High, The Gunfighter*
McCarey	*The Awful Truth, Going My Way*
Minnelli	*An American in Paris, Gigi*
Reed	*Odd Man Out, The Third Man*
Siegel	*Invasion of the Body Snatchers, Dirty Harry*
Siodmak	*The Killers, The Crimson Pirate*
Walsh	*High Sierra, White Heat*

Pretty impressive. Ten terrific directors, all of them operating at the same time. Are we agreed? Hope so.

Now here's the shocker: **none of these guys made my first team.** I'm talking Ford, I'm talking Hawks and Hitchcock, Kazan and Lean, plus Mankiewicz and Stevens, not to mention Wilder and Wyler and Zinnemann.

All these brilliant guys turning out one film after another, some of them glories, some of them not—

—and don't you wish they were around today?

But they're not, and what we see suffers as a sad result.

It wasn't just the directors, either. Here is a list of a bunch of young performers who all were in the **same acting class.** New York City, 1947. Robert Lewis was the teacher and these were the faces he looked out on.

Marlon Brando	E. G. Marshall
Montgomery Clift	Kevin McCarthy
Mildred Dunnock	Patricia Neal
Tom Ewell	William Redfield
John Forsythe	Jerome Robbins
Anne Jackson	Maureen Stapleton
Sidney Lumet	Eli Wallach
Karl Malden	David Wayne

The talent in that room was enough to change the entire world of acting. To this day.

I would like to throw in one more reason why movies are what they are. If you were to ask me, more than anything else, this is the reason: *studio executives.*

Not that they are not bright—they are. Not that they're not hardworking—they are. But from my point of view, precious few of them bother to read screenplays. They are far more interested in saving their asses with a deal than with a quality flick.

Here's what's far worse than the fact that they don't read screenplays: **precious few of them know how.**

What we have is a world, as former studio head David Picker so wisely stated, where Hollywood is no longer making movies, they are selling a product. And the product they are selling only happens to be movies.

Ask not for whom the bell tolls . . .

Sequels

In the summer of 1999, the most hyped art object in history (well, since Viagra, anyway) said "Here I am" to the world: George Lucas's money machine, *The Phantom Menace.* And the reviews were mainly two things: surprised and bad.

Lucas countered that the critics have never liked him, that *Star Wars* got unfriendly reviews, too. (This pronouncement was reported as fact, another reason to wonder about the hardworking entertainment media, since *Star Wars* was nominated for eleven Oscars, won seven. Personally, I would like to get hammered like that each and every time at bat.) I *knew* the movie would be bad, so I was not at all surprised. Why?

Because sequels are whores' movies.

And always will be. Understand, there is zero criticism of Lucas intended, nor should there be. Probably you didn't see the *Butch and Sundance* prequel. I was kind of the producer. And that, too, was a whore's movie.

Steven Spielberg, the most successful figure of our time, has six sequels to his credit so far: one *Jurassic Park,* one

Gremlins, two *Indiana Jones*es, and two *Back to the Futures*.

With *Phantom Menace*, Lucas has tied him: one *American Graffiti*, two *Indiana Jones*es, and three *Star Wars*. But when the next two *Star Wars* sequels are in the can, he will have undisputed possession of the championship.

So the two richest film guys have the most whores' movies. Class, take a minute and think real hard: Is there maybe just possibly some teenie-weenie connection between those two facts?

Let me talk about beginners for a second, which we all were. When that is who and where you are, and your prayer is someday to be in the movie business, your fantasies cannot stop going into overdrive. You're going to meet Bergman or Fellini or Lean (or fill in your own master). And you're going to be loved by the critics and the public. And Cameron Diaz will fold herself into your strong arms. (Or Marilyn or Audrey or Kate. For me it was always Jean Simmons.)

Our talent will fucking stun the civilized world. And when we start out to write our screenplay, it must be so original and dazzling, so different and glorious, people will have no choice but to love us. And why?

Because we are so wonderful.

The pulse of what we write *then* is always this: *creative*. The pulse for a sequel is always this: *financial*. So they are never of a similar quality.

Are there exceptions? I was on the Cannes jury a decade back, wandering with the Australian director George Miller, the doctor. (So designated because there were two Australian directors named George Miller and the other one didn't go to med school.)

Forgetting his credits, I gave him my whore theory just as I have to you.

Such a cry of outrage you have never heard. I had forgotten George had done *Mad Max* as his first flick, *Mad Max 2* (*Road Warrior* here) two years later. "I had no money for the first one," he said. "I did the second one because I wanted, hopefully, to get it right this time."

He did—it's the one sequel that's better than the original.

A lot of people will argue for the second *Godfather,* terrific, but I think the first is the one that echoes.

In Lucas's case, I think there are precious few on the planet who preferred *Return of the Jedi* to *Star Wars.* Well, why, pray tell, should *The Phantom Menace* be any less boring and flawed than the last of the first trilogy?

People will come up with all kinds of bullshit for whoring. I remember telling people, Well, there was just so much great stuff about Butch and Sundance I couldn't fit in the first one. Wonderful interesting new material.

Bullshit. That was a whore talking.

And whatever Lucas tells us today about why he did the deed, whatever excuse he comes up with, it will be bullshit. If you disagree, then answer this: Why didn't he finance a sequel to *Howard the Duck*?

The Year of the Comet
(Alas)
[1992]

One of the moments that screenwriters can never obliterate from our memories is when we realize that, now and forever, we have written a flop.

And when I say "flop," I am not referring, not even remotely, to a "*succès d'estime,*" i.e., a film that maybe doesn't make back *all* its money but has its passionate admirers. And I don't mean an effort, however worthwhile, that has perhaps "come a cropper." Not an effort that "falls short," that "misses the mark," that "runs aground." Not the "ill-judged," or its cousin, the mighty struggle that went "in vain."

No, lads. I am talking about the whiff, the stiff, the stinker, the all-out fucking fiasco.

I am talking, alas, of my original screenplay, *The Year of the Comet*.

If you write screenplays for a living, there are really only three choices. The adaptation of someone else's writing is one, and I think the easiest, because someone else has done the brute work, made the people, invented the story. The adaptation of your own work is much harder—I've done it several times—*Magic, Marathon Man, The Princess Bride* (also *Heat*—no, not the Pacino-DeNiro one, the Burt Reynolds one; and the reason you will not learn more about this baby in these pages is simple: to my knowledge, lawsuits are still flying). What makes this kind of adaptation complicated is that we have gone through so much failure trying to get the novel to work, we tend to cling to our favorite scenes and sequences when we come to make the movie. "Oh, no, I can't cut that sequence, it almost *killed* me to write that."

We have forgotten, in other words, Faulkner's great dictum: in writing, you must **kill all your darlings.**

But I doubt anybody doubts the original is the hardest of all, presents the greatest problem. Simply because you are, duh, making it up. What saves you in this kind of enterprise is this: your passion. In *Butch,* I needed to try and tell that story of the two guys, moving through decades and countrysides, who become legends a second and glorious time. In *The Ghost and the Darkness,* the lions were my passion. I wanted to write about brute power and horror and fear, and at the heart of it, the existence, even for nine months, and even in Tsavo, of evil moving among us.

What made *The Year of the Comet* possible was this: my passion for red wine.

Now, what kind of tale could I try? Answer: *anything.* There are no rules when you start in. I could have written a heart-wrenching drama—Ray Milland *deux,* if you will. A Jimmy Cagney gangster flick, set in Prohibition, about who owns Chicago. I could have made it a George Lucas job, set in the future when scientists have discovered that if you substitute blood for Bordeaux, people will stagger around a lot but they'll also live forever.

One of the things you probably aren't aware of is that *Easy Rider* cost Hollywood hundreds of millions of dollars. Oh, not the movie itself. That was a tremendous success. I am talking about all the idiots who decided to rip it off and capture the suddenly exposed "youth market."

Charade was another money-loser. A great success by itself, it unleashed a stream of other idiots who decided to do their own romantic-comedy-thrillers. Forget that they didn't have Peter Stone's wonderfully stylish script, Stanley Donen's equally stylish direction. Plus those two ugly clods toiling in the vineyards, Cary Grant and Audrey Hepburn.

I was one of the leading idiots, and for my sins I decided to write a romantic-adventure-comedy-thriller about a bottle of red wine.

The settings were pretty much preordained by the nature of the material. Sing Sing somehow seemed wrong. Devil's Island, too. So I wrote it to take place in the most romantic places I knew—London, the Scottish Highlands, and the French Riviera.

Now, those places pretty much dictated that the story be a chase. I had to get from one to the next. With at least some semblance of logic.

My movie would be a chase, then, after a bottle of wine.

But it couldn't be Hearty Burgundy. Had to be a wine worth the travel. So I invented what surely would have been, had such a thing ever existed, the most valuable wine ever. 1811, known in Europe as "The Year of the Comet," is generally thought of as being the greatest year for wine, if not ever, certainly of that century.

And if it was great then, and in a sufficiently large bottle, it might be drinkable in 1978, the year I wrote it (or indeed, 1992, the year the movie got released). So I decided on a bottle of the most famous red, Chateau Lafite Rothschild. And I made up a celebratory bottle—Napoleon had been having some good years in that era—that was bigger than any ever made, a bottle equal to two regular cases of wine.

I liked that for a lot of reasons. The bottle would have been worth many millions, so its breaking might be useful. It would still possibly taste as good as anything yet found on Planet Earth. And it would be heavier than shit, helpful if I could figure out how to use that for comedic moments.

For my lovers I thought it might be wonderful to write a role for Glenda Jackson as my wine lady. (We are a quarter century back when I am fiddling with the idea.) Can't remember who I thought of for the man, but Cary Grant must have been in my heart.

Remember, this was the second of a three-picture deal I had signed with Mr. Levine, following *A Bridge Too Far* and *Magic*. It was finally released by Castle Rock in 1992—and if you think that time leap is unusual, well, it isn't. You only need one person who has the wherewithal to make your movie to make your movie.

Nothing had happened to the notion—it was still a romantic comedy about a chase after a legendary bottle of wine. Wine's still around and there is some evidence that romance has survived too, if you look hard enough. But no one wanted it back in the '70s. Castle Rock, just starting out, did. If God wanted to punish me and made me take a job as a studio head, the first thing I would do is hire all the bright young film-school students and movie nuts I could find and have them read *every* script my studio owned. I am guessing, but thousands is probably low. And since the studio heads are what they always have been, hardworking and imperfect, I am betting I could find a bunch that slipped through the cracks. All that it takes for the worst screenplay of all time to become the best screenplay of all time is the news that Tom Cruise wants to do it.

Anyway, the wine picture disappeared for over a decade. And then, suddenly, it was a movie. What I want to talk about now was our first public screening.

I don't think even a phenomenon like Mr. Spielberg knows for sure what he has until he sees it in front of strangers. Oh, sure, he has the most amazing commercial track record of all time. And sure again, *Jurassic II* probably was not much of an angst-maker. But for the rest, he is like the rest of us, at *your* mercy.

There is an amaaaazing amount of bullshit that you read in the print media or hear on the tube about why movies are hits or flops. *Titanic* was this, that's why it turned out the way it did. *The Postman* was that, that's why it turned out the way it did. Everybody wanted to see the young lovers on the big ship. Nobody wanted to see Kevin Costner in a movie about an apocalyptic mailman.

Well, that's only true *after* it opens.

I was with one of the top executives at one of the studios that was involved with *Titanic* and this person said to me, with fingers very much crossed—this is the week it opened, remember—*"If it just does a hundred million at the box office, we'll be okay."* Now this is a very bright fellow. And had seen the screenings and pored over the results. He had heard and seen the audience reaction—

—**and he had no idea what it would do.**

Here is the truth about *Titanic: people wanted to see it.*
Here is the truth about *The Postman: people didn't want to see it.*
Everything else is mythology.

I felt pretty good about *The Year of the Comet.* I mean, I felt pretty good *for me.* I mean, I wasn't slashing my wrists. Any number of reasons, but chief, I think, is that I had been around the shoot. Peter Yates, the fine English director, is a friend, has been for many years, and he runs a very pleasant set.

I knew we were not Bergman, but I also knew we had delivered what we set out to do, a romantic-adventure-comedy-thriller, this one about a legendary bottle of wine. How big a hit we might be, of course I had zero idea. We could fail, too.

But no way we could be a disaster.

I remember the evening of the sneak very well, still, almost a decade later. I sat where I like to sit, all the way back, rear corner, left or right. I watched the audience come in. They were young Californians, and kind of excited to be there in the test audience. Usually, people at these test screenings are excited. It's something most of them have never done before, never will again.

And they can be, at least I think they can be, wonderfully helpful. Especially when they are confused about something. Very often those of us involved with the effort think we have made something clear, when in fact, we have not. I love test screenings for that kind of help.

By far the best screening I ever saw or will see—not a test, but the first time the movie was shown in New York—was *Jaws.* A lot of people do not remember what a disaster it was in the making, but it was comparable to *Godfather I* and *Tootsie*. No one remembers what disasters those two were, either, before they were released. But they were. Nightmares the media glommed on to, ridiculed constantly, only to shut up when the final product was shown.

Jaws went wildly over budget, had a director in diapers who was clearly helpless, unable to deal with those pesky little problems that cropped up, like disastrous weather and a monster that didn't work. Then it went into the silence all movies enter—postproduction. (Not a lot of famous funny editing-room stories.) Anyway, there we are in the theater, a thousand people maybe, some famous, most not, all curious.

Lights down, time to fish or cut bait.

I never remember any music hitting an audience like those first guttural notes of John Williams's great score. There were gasps two seconds in. And nobody spoke for two hours. Laughed a little. Screamed a lot. And 124 minutes later, when the lights came up, we all knew something remarkable was about to go out into the world.

I was there because Richard Zanuck and David Brown, the producers, had been heads of Fox when *Butch Cassidy* was purchased and made. And if *Jaws* was the best, *Butch Cassidy and the Sundance Kid* was the worst.

I had never seen it all put together. Director George Roy Hill had been in despair after the first sneak, because, as I said earlier, the audience had laughed too much, which made the ending a problem. So he set about taking out laughs.

Example: the movie opened with these words:

> Not that it matters,
> but most of what follows is true.

Got a laugh, so he cut the first words, "Not that it matters, but." Laugh gone.

Unlike *Jaws*, *Butch* had been a splendid shoot. But there was controversy because my very late great agent, Evarts Ziegler, had secured $400,000 for the screenplay. A lot of money today. Back then, record-shattering. It made all the papers, not just *Variety*. And a lot of people wondered what the world was coming to, a western selling for that.

It's my belief that the reason the reviews were so shitty is because of the money I got. A lot of people were pissed, a lot of those people were critics. For them the title of the movie really turned out to be this: *Butch Cassidy and the Sundance Kid $400,000*.

All the New York and national magazine reviews were mixed to terrible. You could not have reprinted one in its entirety. The reviews in the rest of the country were terrific, and in the rest of the world we soared. But I had no idea of any of that as I sat in another large theater in New York for the first major screening. A similar audience to the *Jaws* gathering.

And *Butch* just *died*.

No one left, but no one laughed either. Or was moved. Just a bunch of opinion makers sitting on their hands, and as I fled up the aisle all I heard were remarks about why would anybody open a western in late September, and would Redford be a star, and would the movie make money, and why would anybody pay that much for a screenplay in the first place.

I didn't see the movie for years after that. I went during one of its reissues—they did that in those days—and by that time the movie had become sort of the *Forrest Gump* of its day, in terms of audience reaction, anyway, and I sat happily munching my popcorn as the audience muttered, "Who *are* those guys?" along with Redford and Newman.

Way better time was had by all.

Going from glorious to crushing to sheer horror, the worst I ever saw was when I was a judge at Cannes and I saw this movie at night when you had to get all dressed up in your tuxedo and it started late, I want to say after ten, and it turned out to be an opera—in Portuguese, yet—and all the creative people were there, hopeful, nervous, and the lights went down in that greatest of all movie palaces, and once the audience ascertained they were going to be sung to and it was dinnertime, well, they fled. A thousand fled.

We didn't have that many people at our sneak for *Comet* in Sherman Oaks. It was at a mall, and the theater held a flat five hundred.

For those of you who don't know, here is what generally happens today at test sneaks.

The audience comes in. They have been recruited by whatever company is running things. And usually the people selected are moviegoers who have been to this kind of story before.

They sit down and get comfortable.

Somebody from the focus group goes to the front and greets them, thanks them for their help. Then the usual excuse about the quality of what they will be seeing: there are no credits, the print is scratchy, etc., etc. Then the test leader asks them a favor—when the movie is done will they all *please stay in their seats and fill out a short survey*.

A focus group of twenty-five or so has already been selected and will stay after the theater is empty and talk to the group leader, answering more specific questions.

Final thanks for coming.

Lights out.

Magic time.

And it is exciting. When I'm involved and when I'm not. Because so much is riding on this special evening.

Not that these groups are without flaw. The highest-rated film I've been involved with was *The Princess Bride*. I was told by the man who runs these things that it was the second highest movie of its year. That would indicate a huge hit, which *The Princess Bride* was not.

But these nights, as well as draining you, tell you a lot. *Have you got a shot?* That's what you know by the end of the night and your head hits the pillow.

Okay. *The Year of the Comet.*

What you do at the start when you write a movie is this: *you set up your universe.* The audience needs to know what world it's entering. Comedy, drama, horror, what.

I was very careful with this baby. So I opened in London—gorgeous romantic London—at a wine tasting.

I did it for several reasons. Get the people familiar with where we were going, of course that. But also to set up my lady. Penelope Anne Miller played a brilliant but loveless wine expert at a family auction house. Her father treated her with coldness—this was London, after all, and she was a woman. And her older brother treated her with disdain— she was smarter than he was and he was frightened she might inherit.

Not only am I properly setting up the world of the movie, I am also adroitly setting up this fact: we have a maiden here who sure as shit could use a Prince Charming.

This was not ever intended to be a blockbuster beginning—I was a long way from *Sunset Boulevard*. But I knew it was solid. That Yates had directed it well. And it looked terrific.

Only now I begin to catch sight of really the most amazing thing: a couple is walking out. Not ninety seconds into it, and a couple is leaving. Probably baby-sitter problems, I told myself. Perhaps one or the other has an upset stomach.

That must have been it.

Now in the far aisle, *four more* are up and about.

Even I could not believe it was an epidemic of food poisoning.

I am gripping the seats now, because the nightmare was just beginning. A dozen are now up. Now a dozen more. Waves of people. In the first five minutes, *fifty people left the theater.*

Left a *free movie.*

Left a chance to be a part of a big Hollywood *sneak.*

Hated what I had written so much they would rather face the reality of their own lives than what I had to offer.

Death. Death. Death.

We tried to fix it. We quickly did a new opening scene where we meet the hero first, in a steam bath, as his boss shows up and drags him off to the wine tasting, which the hero *hates*—and says so and calls them boring and phony.

Guess what?

Death. Death. Death.

There was nothing we could do.

Here's why: when I saw a wonderful failure called *Searching for Bobby Fisher,* you would have thought you were seeing *E.T.* Wild and constant applause. You could feel the adoration in the room.

So how come the movie stiffed?

Because *Bobby Fisher* was a movie about chess, and the audience I saw it with was made up entirely of *an invited group of chess experts.* My God, they even applauded the *moves* on the chess board during games. Fucking surreal. You see a hand take a knight, move it here or there, and "Bravo!" from all around me. But there weren't enough chess players on earth to make the movie work for a mass audience.

Maybe if you had seen *The Year of the Comet* at a sommeliers' convention you would have thought you were seeing *E.T.* too.

There was nothing we could do because no matter how we fussed, this was a movie about red wine and the moviegoing audience today has zero interest in red wine. They felt ignorant and they hated us.

Now, no one knew that before we went into production. And if we had done a study that showed as much, we would have gone right ahead anyway. Because the studio who originally developed *E.T.* did a survey that showed—without doubt—that there was no audience that would want to see that movie.

Those five minutes of that first screening will be with me forever. If you ask me on my deathbed, have I ever been to Sherman Oaks, I will rise up and cry, "How could those bastards choose real life over meeee?"

But hope, as I wish I had said, is the thing with feathers.

Because after the test screenings and the audience reaction that never climbs out of the nether world, after the early reviews that do not mistake my screenplay for Kit Marlowe or the movie for anything worth anything, you still have hope.

Other people have gotten lucky, you tell yourself. A couple of summers ago, the Farrelly brothers' glorious comedy *There's Something About Mary* didn't reach the top box-office slot till the *seventh* week. Amazing. And *Bonnie and Clyde* stiffed at first, later found glory.

It is *not* a flop, you tell yourself. Oh, others may scoff at you, may turn away from your glorious and talented presence, but you know this: miracles happen every day.

Maybe—the odds are against it, but just maaaaybe—the gods will smile on you.

The movie opens around the country. Business is not anyone's definition of robust. But you refuse to admit the possibility that you, in all your splendor, have written a flop.

Here is when I finally gave up all hope.

The movie has been out about a week, maybe a little more. I am talking to my eldest, Jenny, a Philadelphian now. We blab about the usual family stuff, the Knicks and the Sixers. Next, a pause. Then I hit her with the biggie; casually, I inquire: "So what did you think of the movie?"

Her reply was said with such sadness: "Oh, Dad, I meant to see it, I really did, but when I looked, it was gone from all the theaters."

Final knife in the heart—because when your own kids don't see your stuff, now that's a flop.

Maverick
[1994]

The Linda Hunt Part

I thought Linda Hunt was wonderful as The Magician in *Maverick*. Crazy and weird and tough and different and if you wonder what it is that I am smoking as I write this because you saw the movie and don't remember Linda Hunt being in it, well, we are both right. She was in it. She was wonderful. She was cut out of the finished film.

Shit happens.

Sometimes movies are amazingly difficult and time-consuming to get going. *Maverick* couldn't have been easier. It went like this: I met Mel Gibson and his partner Bruce Davey, they said they had rights to the character and would I like to write the screenplay and I said, "Sure." Truly as seemingly simple as that.

But I have secrets. I think all writers do. There are very few projects that I have been offered that I would always say yes to. My interests change, needs change, confidence ebbs and flows. A year earlier I night have not done *Maverick*. I said yes for four small reasons and one big one. Here are the four: (1) I loved the old TV show with James Garner; (2) I felt the material was in my wheelhouse; (3) I had never met Gibson but after five minutes I knew he could play the hell out of the part; (4) I had not written a western in twenty-some years, was glad for the opportunity to try again. And the one big reason? Shamefacedly, here it is:

I knew it would be easy.

That is actually the main reason I came aboard so fast. Because I had been writing originals, and them are hard. The last thing in life I wanted was to try another original. This adaptation had to be a breeze—all I needed to do was pick one of the old TV shows that had too much plot, expand it, and there would be the movie.

One of the shocks of my life happened in my living room, where I spent many hours looking at the old *Maverick* shows I'd been sent. Because, and this was the crusher, *television storytelling has changed.* These old shows had shitloads of charm, most of it supplied by Garner. But not only was the Garner character generally passive, there was almost no plot at all. *Nothing for me to steal.* I essentially had to write, sob, another original. It was not going to be easy money at the brick factory again (as it always is).

I set to work trying to figure out a story.

All I really had was that wonderful main character. A con man and gambler. Now, if you are given the job of writing a movie about an Olympic gymnast, you know going in that the movie has to climax with her going for the gold. *Rocky* had to end with The Big Fight.

So Maverick had to end with a poker game.

For some reason, the first visual I got was of Gibson sitting on a horse, hands tied, a noose around his neck. Rattlesnakes are thrown to scare the horse. As he is about to die, he says, in voice-over, "It had just been a shitty week for me from the beginning." I liked that because I hadn't seen it before and it also told us a lot about the feel of the movie and about the man. He wasn't going to die, it said that much. He was humorous, it said that, too. For me, it set the style of everything that followed.

So Maverick would begin with him getting hanged.

To fill in the rest I made this assumption: *Maverick would be a movie about a guy who needed money.*

Why the assumption? Well, this is a movie that has to stand alone, not as one of a thirty-nine-episode (they were in those days) TV season. So the poker-game climax couldn't be just *any* game, it had to be the most important game of his life. (Had it been just one of thirty-nine episodes, the game would not have needed any particular weight.) Now, if the game is important, it must require important money to enter. And if he already has it, what's the big deal? He would just have to lose it and spend the bulk of the movie getting it back. I didn't like the feel of that. He would be tracking, avenging, and the essence of the TV character is that he is acted *on.* I decided he needed the money, so he could meet various people and have adventures, all building to The Big Game. My problem was to make getting there half the fun.

There is no mathematical logic to any of this, it's just how I decided what the narrative might be against what you might decide. No right or wrong storytelling answer exists. *Ever.* I went with my answer for many reasons, but chiefly this: it gave me my spine for the movie. And until I have that, I am essentially helpless. Once I have it, I have the confidence to start to write.

In the first draft Maverick meets a banker friend who gives him some money and an Indian friend who gives him the rest. Then I figured a change had to happen—you couldn't just have him going from success to success, this is a movie hero, he has to win but he should sweat a little along the way.

So I had him robbed by the bad guy.

By solving that problem, I presented myself with another: Maverick needed money to get in the game and I didn't have a lot of time for anything elaborate. I needed something oddball and had no idea what, when I got this idea: What if somebody owned those rattlesnakes that are tossed from a sack at the start to scare his horse? Who, though? It had to be someone with a lot of money, obviously, because he'd end up giving a lot to my guy. But it also had to be somebody who lived in a desolate place, because that's where the hanging took place.

I decided on a nut hermit. (Think of Elisha Cook, Jr.) It seemed logical in a lunatic way. A hermit *might* live in this terrible area, and since hermits are strange, he *might* also have pots of money to give to a wandering movie hero in a pickle. Following is the meeting between Maverick and The Magician. This might give you a sense of what I was after. Okay. Mel Gibson is hanging in space. He struggles. He can't make it. His body hangs motionless. His eyes start to close . . .

CUT TO

An arrow, slicing through the air--

--it hits the rope--

--splits the rope--

--MAVERICK crashes to earth amidst the rattlesnakes.

They hiss at his still body, begin to curl.

It's impossible to tell which one will strike first.
Now--

CUT TO

A GNARLED HAND. That's all we see at first, just the
hand. Or rather, TWO GNARLED HANDS. One of them grabs
a burlap sack, the other starts scooping up the rattlers, putting them back inside. No fear of consequences. One-two-three-four-five-six, and the
rattlers are gone from view. And once they are--

PULL BACK TO REVEAL

THE MAGICIAN, for that we will find is the name of the
MAN we are looking at.

LITTLE OLD MAN, more precisely.

WEIRD-LOOKING LITTLE OLD MAN, more precisely still.
He is dressed in clothing that neither fits nor
matches. One more thing--

--when he talks, HE TALKS VERY LOUDLY. Clearly, he
does not have a lot of company.

Now he takes a foot, pushes MAVERICK so that he's
lying face up.

Next he takes an arrow from his quiver, puts it in his
bow, pulls it back to fire, aiming at MAVERICK'S
HEART.

(MAVERICK, it might be noted here, is wearing a shirt
that is many many sizes too small.)

                    THE MAGICIAN
    I'm a gonna kill you.

CUT TO

MAVERICK. Barely able to speak. Still, this piece of
news is not so much depressing as it is strange.

> MAVERICK
> (whispered)
> ...if you were going to kill me...why didn't
> you just let me hang...?

CUT TO

THE MAGICIAN, coming closer.

> THE MAGICIAN
> 'Cuz then you wouldn't have knowd your crime.

> MAVERICK
> (Blinking up)
> ...who are you...? and what's my crime...?

> THE MAGICIAN
> I'm the Magician--and your crime--
> (bigger)
> --the crime you're gonna die for--
> (huge)
> --the crime that's gonna condemn you to Hell
> is this:
> (roaring)
> YOU STOLE MY RATTLESNAKES.

CUT TO

MAVERICK. He's just in terrible shape but he didn't
think he was going mad.

> MAVERICK
> ...do I look like a rattlesnake thief?

                    THE MAGICIAN
             (studies MAVERICK a long while,
              the arrow still ready.
              Finally he nods)
        That's exactly what you look like.

                    MAVERICK
        You're wrong--I play cards.

                    THE MAGICIAN
             (shakes his head)
        A gambler? Not in that shirt.

CUT TO

MAVERICK. He closes his eyes, tries to laugh--

--but he can't. Not just because he hasn't the
strength but because he is far beyond exhaustion. His
body begins to shake, as if with fever. HOLD ON MAVER-
ICK.

   Now we're back into the story, which is where I needed The Magician
to give Maverick the money to enter the game. Why would he have
money in the first place? I figured he'd been out there forever, it wasn't
illogical for him to have found valuables from people over the decades
who had died in this rough ground.
   Why would he give it, though? Couldn't be sympathy. Maverick had
to earn it. The hermit didn't have a name then. I decided to call him The
Magician because I decided he wanted some magic in his life. Not totally
illogical—he's a weird old guy coming to the end, clearly his life hasn't
had a lot of ups. Okay. He wants magic. I sold the notion to myself.
   Problem: Maverick is a gambler, what can he do that's magical?
   The great sleight-of-hand artist John Scarne did something that I read
about once which almost cost him his life. Scarne, after thousands of
hours of practice, had taught himself to cut to the ace of spades *at will*.
He pretended it was a trick but all he did was riffle the cards, spot where
the spade ace was, and instantly count how many cards into the deck it
was and then cut to it.
   Just writing that seems amazing. Scarne almost got killed when he

pissed off a major Prohibition-era gangster who saw him cut the ace and wanted to know the trick. He wanted to be able to do it too. And he thought Scarne was putting him on when he claimed he couldn't. So he was going to kill Scarne. Fortunately for one and all, the gangster was finally convinced.

I decided Maverick could also cut to the ace of spades at will. He has, built into his character, marvelous skill with cards. The Magician says he wants to see magic before he dies and if Maverick can do something magical, he will let him go and give him the money for the entrance fee. Maverick begins his con, comes up with a story, told sincerely, that he once had magic, the day his mother died he had it, and The Magician says, You can do it again, but Maverick is reluctant, says he's convinced he will fail. The Magician forces him to try and of course he cuts to the ace of spades, gets the money, and goes off to the poker game. Now this was all done straight, the audience did not know it was a trick, and at the end of the movie, in the first draft, Maverick is about to tell how he did it, then changes his mind, saying that life's always a little better when there's just a touch of mystery in the air. In other words, he tells us it was magic, not a con.

Okay, exposition's over.

The first draft is accepted, Dick Donner comes on to direct, and we start the first of endless months of revisions. Donner likes The Magician, and what he likes about it is the magical aspect, the sense of something strange. He likes it so much he wants more of it.

And I never told him what I just told you—that it was a con.

He did not know the Scarne story. (I've used this material twice so far, as any of you who saw *Magic* know.)

I never told him for this reason: *because he never asked.*

In the second draft it's the same setup, only everything else is different. Maverick cannot cut to the ace of spades at will, and he really did have magic the day his mother died. This time around, Maverick cuts what we think at first glance is the ace of spades but it turns out to be the ace of clubs—in other words, he fails. But The Magician gives him the money anyway because Maverick has come close and given The Magician hope that the next guy he finds will actually be able to do it. "Hermits need hope," The Magician says, one of the truer lines I've written in my life.

The third draft stays the same, with just the amount of money changing. I must explain that I am willing and happy to do any changes here because I am not threatened by anything that's happening—nothing is altering the spine of the movie. It is still about a guy needing money. I get very crazy if you mess with the spine. Otherwise I am totally supportive.

And I think the reason I never told Donner about the Scarne story was because writers need secrets just as much as hermits need hope. Also, I think I was afraid if I told him the truth, Donner would hate it. And want other changes that *would* alter the spine.

Marion Dougherty, who is fabulous, is casting the movie, and it is Marion who gets this notion: *make The Magician a woman.* She felt it would add a new dynamic. Donner went for it, and, as I said, I didn't mind, I was just trying to service the director. The spine was safe. And once Marion's notion was taken, there was nobody else, really, who would have been as good in the part as Linda Hunt.

In the fourth draft, the dynamic changes again: now she gets into his life to give him back confidence, to send him on his way knowing he has a chance to win. She says he came close and next time he'll come closer, all of which leads, of course, to the big card game when the ace of spaces *is* cut and wins the game for Maverick. Donner liked that because he wanted to get the encounter to be as mystical as possible—by that time Tom Sanders, our production designer, had come up with some startling and beautiful notions of what the hermit's home might look like.

The fifth draft is essentially the same as the fourth, except now The Magician is convinced Maverick has magic inside him. He cuts to the ace of clubs again, but this time the *next card* is the ace of spades. It was, hopefully, a stronger version and was intended to be both different and emotional. This is how the concluding moments read in rehearsal, starting with the reveal of the spade ace as the next card. Henry, it should be noted, is The Magician's pet rattlesnake who was been watching the sequence with great interest.

CUT TO

MAVERICK AND THE MAGICIAN.

                    THE MAGICIAN
     Next time you'll get it right--maybe the next
     time after the next time. But you got magic
     inside you--knew it all along--that's what
     makes me a great hermit.
              (beat)
     I know things.
              (throwing more money at MAVERICK)

```
Buy yourselves some clothes that fit--thank me
or I'll kill you--
        (she grabs up HENRY)
--now get out of my life.
        (sweetly, to HENRY)
Yes...there's a good baby...yes...
```

We leave her there. And that's where I left the sequence after rehearsal. Linda Hunt and Gibson were terrific. No question it was different from anything else in the movie. Donner still liked the notion, still wasn't happy with the scene, but he couldn't verbalize what more he wanted. And frankly, I was tired. I had delivered the first draft in March, it was now August, and after that kind of time with this many changes, you lose not only your zest but your objectivity.

I was out of the loop for the next many months. Donner brought in Gary Ross, who wrote the excellent *Dave,* for another whack at The Magician. I wasn't even remotely upset—I didn't have it in me for another go.

It was, apparently, a happy shoot. Which, as I've said, has nothing whatsoever to do with the quality of the film. We don't like to believe that but it's true. I was called out to see the first showing of the film. It wasn't a true sneak. There was an audience of a couple hundred people but it wasn't in a large neutral theater somewhere in Pasadena; rather, they chose a place without air conditioning—without *working* air conditioning—on the Warners' lot on a hot afternoon.

There was a lot of tension—there always is at such a moment—there should be, my God, if you're not tense then, get out of the picture business—but the time pressure *Maverick* was under made it unendurable. I delivered the first draft on March 12, 1993. That week Gibson said he liked it, so we were a "go" project.

And that same week I was told that the movie would open—would *definitely* open—on the weekend before Memorial Day, May 20, 1994. Ready or not. I have never been around a flick that went so fast. Thirteen months from first draft without director to being in 2,000-plus theaters. This is a terrible gamble to take—there was no time for mistakes.

We all saw the movie on March 13. The picture had to be totally locked and ready to go to the lab for printing by early May. This was not, obviously, a low-budget art film. There was no time for tinkering. The picture had to work.

It did and it didn't.

The audience loved Jodie Foster, loved *loved* Gibson—more importantly, loved *them*. Great affection for James Garner, too. Not to mention the crucial ending card sequence. (What always gives you hope at such a time is if the ending holds. If that's happening, even if you're in rough shape, you have a solid chance.)

The Linda Hunt scene was a train wreck.

Sure, this was a rough cut, two and a half hours long. Yes, the air-conditioning malfunction was a factor. And Linda Hunt was wonderful.

It still stopped the picture dead.

Gibson was fine in the scene, too. And it sure was gorgeous to look upon. But it was dead wrong. I don't know why. A different style, maybe. Maybe what was once a simple con to get money had become too convoluted. We'll never know. It just did not work. The audience was confused at first, then, more dangerously, they began to lose interest. When you have a sag like that it can cripple everything that immediately follows.

We met afterwards. The early thoughts were of how to save it but soon we all knew the entire sequence had to be jettisoned. This was a major chunk of film we were eliminating, and opening day could not be delayed. Reshoots were scheduled for the next weekend. Instead of The Magician blasting Maverick out of the hanging tree—from the second draft on, the original bow and arrow had become sort of an elephant gun—a providential blast of lightning saves him.

But without someone to give him money, guess what? He couldn't be robbed. So the moments when the bad guy robs him were edited out, and Graham Greene as the Indian friend had to be brought back to set up that his money is in his boot. And then after he is saved you see Gibson hobbling along after his horse, showing us his money is safe.

I think we sort of kind of got away with it. It was a loosely plotted movie anyway, so no one noticed. And Donner was able to get the movie down from two and a half hours to two hours ten. I think he could have gotten it down to under two hours, had he been given time. Maybe it would have worked better. We'll never know. It pleased a lot of people just as it was in the summer of '94. Which is all it was ever meant to do. Let's leave it at that.

One of the great truths of the movie business is that movies are *fragile*. And even the most successful are only a step away from disaster. Every step of the way . . .

Courtroom Scenes

There are no rules to screenwriting, as we all know, but one of them is this: you must never ever open your first draft screenplay with a courtroom scene.

What we are talking about here is this: limitations of the form.

If you will look at Ephron's Harry and Sally scene or what the Farrellys did to poor Ben Stiller, I would argue that those scenes are better in a movie than anyplace else. I don't care how talented the poet, his version of the zipper madness is not going to be as wonderful as the flick was. And no novelist's orgasm scene is going to be as wonderful as what Billy and Meg did in the Carnegie.

I don't think those scenes work as well on the stage either. Oh, they would get laughs, but you would not have the immediacy, you would not see the horrible embarrassment of the two chief men in the movies.

No, these are movie moments, great ones, and best left there.

But the screenplay, like any other form, cannot come close to doing everything. Let me write a little of the courtroom scene and I think the problem becomes clear.

```
FADE IN ON

A majestic courtroom.  You sense decades and
more of history here, you feel the tears of
those who lost, the exultation of the winning
side.  You sense, more than anything, that
this is a place where justice, that rare and
valued commodity, could actually breathe.

CUT TO

The Defense Team.  Half a dozen lawyers, led
by one solid man.  This is MELVIN MARSHALL, a
bulldog in the courtroom.  Short, powerful,
he seems almost to be bursting out of his
custom-made suit.
```

Seated beside him is The Defendant, and if
MARSHALL is the beast in this story, then WA-
VERLY DIAMOND is the beauty. She has never
had a day in her adult life when men did not
turn in her direction, study her eyes wondering how anything could be that blue. Watching her now, it seems inconceivable that she
could have knifed her husband to death in
cold blood.

CUT TO

The one man alive who seems most intent on
proving that she did kill wealthy WALTER DIA-
MOND. This is the most famous prosecutor in
recent San Francisco history, the legendary
TOMMY "THE HAT" MARINO.

MARINO has come a long way from his Mafia-
ridden boyhood. The son of the famous HARRY
"THE HAT" MARINO, the terrifying waterfront
boss of all bosses, TOMMY has spent his life
trying to prove that a man can come as far
from his childhood as he so desires.

TOMMY "THE HAT" stands now, as does everybody
else in that great room, for here he comes,
and we see him close as we

CUT TO

JUDGE ERIC WILDENSTEIN himself. Here is what
you must know about him--

Okay, enough. You must see by now that in spite of all
my dazzle, your eyes are glazing over. You have been given
too much information in too short a time about which you
don't give a shit, no wonder you're bored.

You can open a *movie* with a courtroom scene—easy,
because we see the faces of the actors so their identities register.

And you can open the shooting script—after you are in production—with a courtroom scene. You aren't trying to sell quite so hard when you're in production.

I guess what I'm trying to say is don't ask the screenplay to do what it has trouble with. Information overload is one of those trouble spots. There are *many* others and if I made a list of all those that I know, it would do you no good at all. You will want to find your own disasters . . .

The Ghost and
the Darkness
[1996]

I have been a professional writer for over forty years now. (I began my first novel, *The Temple of Gold,* on June 25, 1956.) And in all that time, I have come across but two great pieces of material. The first, dealing with Butch Cassidy and his adventures with the Sundance Kid, became a famous movie around the world. But it was unknown material before that.

The second is the tale of the man-eating lions of Tsavo, which was well known around the world, just not in the United States. In Africa, it is *the* most famous story of high adventure. A hunt for wild animals is called a "stalk," and no less an aficionado than President Theodore Roosevelt termed it "the greatest stalk of which we have any record."

More recently, in his splendid book *Millennium: A History of the Last Thousand Years,* the Oxford historian Felipe Fernandez-Armesto has written over seven hundred pages on what's been going on Down Here for the last ten centuries.

Well, *two* of those pages are about the lions of Tsavo.

Why were Butch and Sundance unknown for so long? I think because they ran away to South America when the Superposse came after them, instead of shooting it out, which is what western heroes always did, since westerns are based on confrontations.

I think the reason the Tsavo lions are unknown here is because, when Americans go to the movies, they want solutions to questions, not more questions. The Tsavo story, something that never happened before and has not happened since, is still, at its dark heart, a mystery.

And always will be . . .

I first heard about them in July of 1984, my initial trip to Africa, at one of my favorite spots on earth, the Masai Mara Plains (it is in Kenya, and when the land becomes Tanzania, the name becomes the Serengeti). It was night, a bunch of people were sitting by a fire. And then, in that magical semidarkness, someone began telling the story of what happened at Tsavo back in 1898. I clearly remembered that I turned to Ilene, my good wife of twenty-some years, and said something I had never said before: "That's a movie."

My plan then was simple—to research the story back in America, to return to Africa at the proper time for further work, and then to write it as an original screenplay. Life, however, as most of us are continually shocked to discover, has plans of its own which tend to take precedence. I did a lot of research when I returned home, yes. But our marriage ended, the further trips to Africa never took place, and the lions found a small corner of my brain, growled, and went to sleep.

Dissolve: five years later. It's 1989.

I got a call from my agent, Robert Bookman at CAA. "You remember that lion story?" I said I sure did. "Well, there's some interest in the project at Paramount. Do you have a problem flying to L.A. to try for the job?"

I said I had zero problem flying to L.A.

But there was indeed a problem.

I have a bad back and it tends to go into spasm when it chooses—crippling me, usually for a week or two. And it had gone out just before Bookman called. When that happens, the worst thing is having to sit in a car for a long time. Having to sit in an airplane for a long time also isn't so terrific. But I made the trip the next day, met with the Paramount Guys. The usual bullshit grunts of hello. Then it was my turn to sell.

This is not something for which I am noted. I have only tried one "pitch" in my life, and that was for friends, and I was so awful I quit halfway through. Now I was sitting in a room with a bunch of strangers. More precisely, *they* were sitting in the room.

Me, I was lying on the floor.

Pretty much in spasm.

Looking up at them.

I said I had no idea how to write the movie. I said I had no idea yet what the story was. But I also said I knew what the story *should* be: a cross between *Jaws* and *Lawrence of Arabia*.

I said they could doubt my talent to be able to successfully write that movie, but they could never doubt my passion for wanting to try. I mean, shit, I was flying six thousand miles more or less doubled over—that had to be indicative of *something*. (I was told that the meeting, because of my position, achieved a certain brief notoriety.)

At any rate, I was hired.

I delivered the first draft on April Fool's Day, 1990. I always aim for that date—after all, we *are* talking about the movie business. Shortly afterwards, we met again, the Paramount Guys (PGs) and *moi*. Here is what they said: Yes, we like the script. Yes, we think it's a movie. But it is also going to be a very very expensive movie. So we will make it only if we can get one of these three stars to play Patterson, the main character:

Costner
Cruise
Gibson

Well, those happen to be wonderful performers, and all three were good casting for the role. Serious about their careers and their choices of material. And huge stars.

The problem is, you just don't get people like that for pictures like this (neither O'Toole nor Scheider nor Dreyfuss nor Shaw were huge stars) because stars know they inevitably are going to be dwarfed by the desert or munched by the monster. In the case of *The Ghost and the Darkness,* I knew that none of Paramount's holy trinity would sit around while the lions stole the movie. So while I said "Terrific" to the studio about their casting choices, I've been at this a while and I have a certain sense for failure when it is coming down the track at me. I knew, old hand that I am, that none of the three would do it. The movie was dead in the water.

A week later, Kevin Costner said yes.

One of the points to keep in mind when talking about movie stars is this: not only do *we* change, *they* change. So today when people disparage the lovely Miss Roberts and wonder why she isn't that smiling star of *Pretty Woman,* the answer is pretty easy: that child is gone. Julia Roberts was twenty-two then, we knew nothing much about her, and we all fell in love. Well, she's in her thirties now, we know *everything* about her, some of it a bit disquieting. Our ardor has cooled.

The Kevin Costner of today, we know about: the divorce, the *Waterworld* budget, the fact that no one breathing saw *The Postman,* all that good stuff. But we're still in 1990, remember, and *Dances with Wolves* is about to explode across the world, catapulting Costner into an orbit few stars ever attain. Remember how we rooted for him, putting his career on the line to do an, ugh, western? A three-hour, ugh, western at that. And not just to star but, for the first time, to direct?

Well, he gambled and won and we didn't just love him, we carried him through our village shoulder-high. He had become, in front of our eyes, the new Gary Cooper. We could not find sufficient superlatives.

So as I flew out to the next meeting with the PGs, I knew that after half a dozen years, the gods were smiling.

"We know what we said last week," the PGs began. "We know we said we would only do it with Costner or Gibson or Cruise. And we are thrilled that Kevin wants to do it so badly. That only proves what we felt about the value of the material. And since Costner agreed so quickly, we now know what we have to do."

And then a pause.

Not just any pause. This baby hovering on the horizon was one of the longer lulls of my young life. I knew I was about to die, but I could not guess the method, poison or sword.

Then the PG spoke that most dreaded of all terms: **"special relationship."**

There is something you must understand about studio executives (and these guys were absolutely standard: bright, decent, hardworking—and shortly to be fired for helping run the company off a cliff). *Studio executives love stars.* Because these are the executive's two eternal verities:

1. they all know they are going to get fired, but
2. they also know that if they can just sign enough stars to enough flicks, they will delay their beheading.

Perfectly understandable behavior. I'd do it too. Where it gets dangerous is here: it is not enough that they love stars; *in their continually fevered brains, they want to believe that the stars also love them.* And so over the decades I have heard that "Sly and I have a special relationship" and "Dusty and I have a special relationship" and Arnold and I and Clint and I and Marlon and I and Paul and I and Steve and I and . . . backward reeleth the mind.

The truth is this: stars do not now and never have given even the remotest shit for studio executives. Stars only care, *legitimately and correctly,* about the material and the deal.

But studio executives, poor, put-upon, terrified, underappreciated like the rest of us, dream of being loved.

"We have a *special relationship* with Tom Cruise," the head PG said that day. "We are doing a picture with Tom now and we want this to be his next. He has a lot on his plate at the moment, yes, but we are prepared to wait for him. Because we know he'll love this. And we know he loves working with us."

"Because of your special relationship," I said.

Heads nodded all around.

We waited six months for an answer. The movie he was starting was indeed a plateful. It was called *Days of Thunder* and it was not the easiest shoot ever undertaken, and not only that, he was also producing.

Cruise passed.

Costner had taken off five months and three weeks before, very pissed off, and with very good reason. We never went to Gibson. No point. There was now no movie. And honestly, I felt, there never would be.

The Tsavo lions curled up inside my brain again, growled again, and slept for five more years . . .

Which is not to say there was zero action. Michael Douglas, who has a remarkable record as a producer (he won an Oscar for his first try, *One Flew Over the Cuckoo's Nest*), and his partner, Steve Reuther, came aboard. And Stephen Hopkins was selected to direct. Stirrings, sure. But lots of movies get producers, bring directors on, then disappear. We needed a male star. Optimist that I have always been, I knew we would never get one.

But as the sadly missed Mr. Williams once wrote for Miss DuBois, "Sometimes there's God so quickly." Because our salvation was taking place across town, on the Warner Brothers lot, where the actor Michael Keaton had what I can only call the most helpful fit of madness of my screenwriting career. (No, I meant that sentence just as I wrote it.)

Understand this about stars: *they do not want to appear in commercial films.* Oh, some will put up with them. Harrison Ford owes his entire fabulous career to three series: *Star Wars, Indiana Jones,* and Tom Clancy. Stallone exists because of *Rocky* and *Rambo.* Mel Gibson also had two, *Mad Max* and the *Lethal Weapons*. But these are not the norm.

Michael Keaton chose to ignore the ecology of Hollywood—you do one for me, I'll do one for you. He had been in the first *Batman,* which Jack Nicholson stole. He had done the second, this time bowing to Pfeiffer and DeVito. And that, apparently, was enough. He did not want to wear the dreaded Bat suit again. He felt the part of Batman wasn't terrific. And you know what?

Dead right. Batman was and always has been a horrible part, a stiff the others got to be flashy by playing off of.

So Keaton walked.

And Val Kilmer replaced him.

Val Kilmer, who, it turned out, *loved* Africa.

Once more the phone rang from Hollywood. The lions answered it with me. We were alive again. Because the new Paramount people had always liked the Tsavo script. And suddenly there was this hot new star who wanted to play Patterson. *Batman Forever* had not opened yet. But the advance word was sensational.

Suddenly we were a "go."

A dozen years passed between that first night on the Masai Mara and when we got released. We might have come out in '91, in place of *Robin Hood,* riding the Costner love fest. And if we had, I think we would have owned the civilized world. We also might *never* have come out, because if Keaton had stuck with Batman, Val Kilmer wouldn't have gotten his blink of sunshine, and no way any studio would have sent us into production without a star.

Anyway, that's how movies get made.

The Lions

The real ones are—right now, as they have been for over half a century—in Chicago. The Field Museum of Natural History. I went to see them with Ilene soon after we got back from the Africa trip.

There they crouch in their exhibit, probably not as big as in your imagination. Partly because they were maneless males. (Not uncommon in certain parts of Africa. If they live in an area rich with thorn trees, as these did, the thorns rip the manes off them over time.)

But here is what you must know about them, and I mean this—

—**they are scary.**

There is clearly a madness at work, some raging insanity; I have never seen anything like them. I felt when I first heard about them just exactly what I felt that day when I saw them and what I feel now: that **they were evil.**

I called one The Ghost, the other The Darkness, for several reasons. I could differentiate the two in the screenplay, characterize them, if you will. More than that, the names were evocative, they would read well on the page; and more than that, if the movie ever happened, they would look good on the screen, these giant killing machines, with such easily identified manes.

Why were they so remarkable?

A few basic facts you should know about man-eating lions:

1. They are always *old*. Because they cannot hunt their rightful food (wildebeest, etc.), they are forced to go after something all lions are repelled by, *us*. Our smell tends to disgust them. To kill and eat humans is something only a close-to-decrepit lion would be forced to do.

2. They are always *alone*. Because they have been forced out by their pride. They can't keep up, so out with them.

3. *They return to the scene of their last kill.* Again, perfectly logical. If they are lucky enough to get a snack at say, Seventy-seventh and Madison, why not go right back there again, and as soon as possible.

Okay. Old, alone, return for more goodies.

For reasons of greed, the British decided to build a railroad across East Africa. This was simply a giant undertaking, rating not far below the Pyramids. Thousands of men were employed. Brutal brutal labor.

In 1898, John Henry Patterson, the hero of the story, a thirty-year-old Scottish engineer, was given the job of building a bridge across the River Tsavo—thorn tree *heaven*—approximately 130 miles inland from the coast town of Mombasa.

Patterson faced problems, varied and serious: a shortage of material; surly natives who threatened to rebel (and on at least one occasion, tried to kill him); malaria; lack of food; insufficient medical supplies. Not a whole lot of fun, but he was stubborn and it was going well enough.

Until March of that year and the first lion attack.

No big deal at first; a lion jumped out at a coolie on a donkey, then ran away.

Yawn.

Patterson spent all night in the trees waiting for the lion to come back to the spot, and when it did, he nailed the sucker.

Back to the bridge.

Then, slowly, like acid dripping, bad things happened. A lion attacked a coolie, dragged him into the bush, you could hear the coolie's scream and his bones breaking. More of that. Then the awful realization that there were *two* lions. And they were young and they were fearless and they began attacking large groups of men in broad daylight. They also began leaping nine-foot thorn fences and dragging coolies out of their tents, and the coolies began sleeping in the trees, which was fine except there were so many of them sometimes the trees bent and the coolies fell to the ground, where the lions were waiting for them. During all these days, Patterson was working on the bridge when it was light, spending his nights alone in the trees.

Now the natives began to think the lions were not normal. Natives always do that in Tarzan pictures: "Bwana, these beasts are not of our earth," and Tarzan always proves them wrong. Well, Tarzan wasn't around in Tsavo, and as the months went by, some militia were sent from Mombasa—not many, there weren't many, and they couldn't be spared long, and they saw nothing. And when they departed, back came the lions. And now professional hunters came, and they killed a lot of baby lions and stayed until the big two began eating them, and now Patterson was dying from fatigue but he came up with a plan. He stuck three of his best shots in a railroad car, protected them with metal bars across the middle, put some meat on the far side from them—a ridiculous plan really—the killers were to enter on the far end and when they did they would trip a wire and the door would close behind them and they would be helpless as the three shooters blew them away—

—ever hear anything so moronic?

Well, it *worked*.

Kind of.

One of the lions came, and it was trapped, and these three great shooters blasted the shit out of it at close range—

—and missed—

—yes, missed; they couldn't but they did—

—and they blasted a hole in the car and the lion got away.

The workers began to leave, going back to other parts of Africa, back to India; and Patterson was killing himself, days on the bridge, where work was slowing, nights trying to stay awake in the trees.

Then another plan, this time a great one: move the hospital in a day, leave the old one smelling of blood and sheets and take the sick and the wounded to a clean, odorless one, while Patterson waited for them to attack in the blood-smeared hospital. He even spread cattle blood all around to make it irresistible—

The attack came, he could hear them outside—

—then silence—

—then horrible death screams in the night as the lions savaged the new clean perfect hospital, killing on and on. The natives took off after that, the railroad came to a dead halt.

Back in London, Parliament was having these screaming matches because they ruled the world, the sun never set, etc., etc., and here in Africa this great railroad had been stopped—

—dead—

—no work was being done—

—by two *lions*.

—and why can't somebody do something?

Patterson finally did.

It took him nine months, but he got the first. Then, Christmas week of '98, he was in a tree when the second came by, and he shot him, but the lion came up after him and he jumped down, broke his leg landing, and when the lion got back to earth Patterson shot him again—

—but it would not stop—

—Patterson could only watch, no bullets left—

—the lion took a huge hunk out of a tree limb, died six inches from Patterson's body.

I still think an amazing and great piece of narrative material.

Plus this: lions have never behaved like that again. Never have two young males joined to savage the countryside. No accounting for it. How can you explain nine months of miraculous escapes, of knowing what the enemy will do before the enemy did it? Patterson later found a cave where they took their victims. Bones forever. They didn't eat their victims a lot of the time. Sometimes they licked the skin off, drank the blood.

One hundred thirty-five men dead, the most of any lions in history.

I still hold with evil . . .

The Hero

Patterson's life was never quite the same. He wrote a book about his experiences that sold extremely well. He fought in many battles as his life went on, a strong figure in the battle to found Israel. But wherever he went, he was the man who killed the lions.

I don't think anyone can doubt his bravery.

I have seen the trees he spent his nights in—fifteen or eighteen feet up, sometimes less—trying to stay awake, while out there somewhere he knew they were watching him, waiting for him.

I have seen lions kill, seen them shred slaughtered and dying animals, been shocked not just at the blood, but at their speed. When they are moving in for a meal, they are not the bewhiskered cuddly things the Disney Organization would have us believe them to be.

I have been to Tsavo, though not for long—it is not a place for your dream house. Looked at where Patterson went. Night after week after long bloody month. As the total of dead mounted. As the sense of the enemy's power mounted. As the bridge slowed, stalled, stopped. As his fatigue began to drive him toward Lord only knows what madness.

And I don't know how the man did it. For me, that is genuinely heroic behavior.

And I hope you agree. I need that from you now.

The Willie Mays of Firemen

I once had the opportunity to spend an afternoon with a wonderful old New York City fireman. Retired. Irish, of course. Father had been a fireman, both his sons were too.

When I meet someone out of the ordinary for me, someone I am not likely to come across again, I ask a lot of questions. Pester them if they don't mind. I guess looking for material. Because all I know is my ordinary life, college, army, grad school, wife, kids, writing.

"I worry for my sons," I remember him saying.

Why?

"The life."

I waited.

"Well, when I went in, there was no choice. Not just because my father had been one but because, well, yes, you knew every day you went off to work you might not come home, yes, you remember all the funerals, but you also remember the sense of doing something glorious, you remember the people on the streets cheering the wagon as the siren screamed and traffic got out of the way. People knew you were risking your life and there was a sense of appreciation. I always worked in slum areas, always wanted to work in slum areas, more action there, I loved that." Now he was silent, I suppose in reverie, back where the action was.

"And your sons?" I prompted.

"People throw shit at wagons now. Bricks, garbage—my boys are going out on the job, looking to save a building, save a life, and what do they get? Shit. *They get shit.* They're both taking early retirement and I'm glad of it."

Back to his reveries for a while.

Then I asked it: "Did you ever know a great fireman?"

He looked at me. "I don't know what 'great' means here."

"Somebody better than anybody else. More talented than anybody."

No reply.

"Okay. Willie Mays was the greatest and most talented baseball player I ever saw. Was there anybody like that?"

Now this great Irish smile. "The Willie Mays of firemen? Know what you mean—know what you mean." Thinking. "The Willie Mays. Never been asked that. Never been asked it but I know what you mean." Still the smile, still the thinking. "Better than anybody, did I ever know somebody who was—" And then he looked at me. Said this: "Yes. One."

"What made him better?"

"He's still alive, y'know. We used to bet about that. I knew the flames would get him."

"What did he do that was so special?"

Now the old man looks at me. "Bravest thing I ever saw. We're getting out of a building, old tenement, about to explode, we're on the second floor, one more to go and we've got no time, y'see, and he's the same as me, wife, boys—and then he stops dead."

"What?" I say.

" 'Heard a baby,' he says. He points to this apartment door that's closed, of course, and flames are all around us, you must believe that, it was so loud and so hot and so horrible.

"And I say, 'Get out, Johnny,' and he doesn't answer, just turns and kicks the door off the hinges, then shouts 'Go' but of course I couldn't do that to the man. He grabs the door by the handle and uses it as a shield as he makes his way through this blazing apartment in this terrible old place that's about to die, and on he goes till he gets to another closed door, and of course he kicks that open too and, my God, there *is* a baby inside, screaming to wake the dead. He tucks her away under one arm, uses the first door as a shield again and comes back running through the flames, and then we all get the hell out of the place just before it goes."

I remember thinking in that quiet moment: How does someone know he can do that? Or I guess more important, where does it come from that he *must*? I knew one thing for sure—that baby was lucky I was not the guy outside the door that terrible day.

"Bravest thing I ever saw," the old man said finally.

I hope you agree with that too.

Because now I am going to tell you among the saddest and most important things I have in my arsenal. That incredible act of heroism the Willie Mays of firemen did?

That is what Sylvester Stallone does in an action picture before the

opening credits start to roll. That is what Arnold Schwarzenegger does in an action picture before breakfast. That is what Harrison Ford and Mel Gibson do in their action pictures before they've brushed their teeth!

Stars do not—repeat—*do not play heroes*—

—stars play *gods*.

And your job as a screenwriter is to genuflect, if you are lucky enough to have them glance in your direction. Because they may destroy your work, *will* destroy it more often than not—

—but you will have a career.

Plus one more thing to remember: what is genuinely heroic in life may not work for film. It simply, as they say, *won't shoot*.

In *Adventures in the Screen Trade* I wrote about trying to translate to film what many military experts feel was the single most heroic action of the entire war. It involved a river crossing.

My problem, Doctor, was that what the experts were talking about as incredibly brave was not the soldiers who made the first crossing—the normal group glorified in a movie—it was the *next* wave of soldiers, the ones who saw the first group get slaughtered, who knew they were mostly going to die, and who made the second crossing anyway.

I saved someone from drowning once. I was in a pool here in New York, no one else in the water, an Indian kid, maybe five years old, on the diving board, his parents chatting off to one side. The kid dove in, came up, went down, came up, whispered "Help," and I got him before he died.

Sorry, folks, that doesn't raise the hackles. It won't shoot. In real life, it's extraordinary. On film, nothing.

(It got even worse when I took the kid back to his parents, told them what had happened. They thanked me, went back to their chatting and when I left the pool, the kid was playing alone, getting close to deep water again. This was *so* fucking surrealistic I have doubted since that day if anything happened at all.)

Why am I telling you all this?

Because Patterson, wonderful heroic John Henry Patterson, famous throughout his lifetime as the man who killed the lions?

Sorry folks, *it doesn't shoot*.

For nine months he sits in a tree?

Wow.

For nine months his plans mostly suck?

Whoopee.

For nine months he *fails*?

What are you smoking, this is a Hollywood movie.

Look, when I wrote that Butch and the Lions were the only two great pieces of narrative I ever came across? Absolutely true. Which is not to say they were *perfect*.

Everything needs helping along.

To help the move to South America, I invented the half-hour Super-posse chase. (In real life, as soon as Butch heard about who was arraying against him, he fled to South America. That was of less than no use to me at all.)

Remember that—it was to help the story.

And I realized that Patterson, my hero's story, needed help too. So, with a pure heart, I invented Redbeard.

Redbeard

Redbeard was always and forever only this: a plot point. I needed, for today's audience, to make Patterson, my hero, more heroic. So I came up with what I thought would be a suitable device.

Redbeard would be a professional who came, did his job, moved on when the job was over. There were, in point of fact, people who lived that way. Hunting was popular among the very rich, and there were men for hire if you were a Russian prince and wanted to shoot in America. Or Africa. Or the mountains of India. You hired them for weeks or months, and they saw you got the best chance at game. Protected you in the bargain.

What made Redbeard different was he was a legend even to other professionals. In other words, the greatest hunter in the world.

In the very first draft, his part was relatively small. Patterson was in terrible trouble. The lions had stopped the railroad. Redbeard entered, sized up the situation. Now, I couldn't have him win immediately, because that would have denigrated the lions. So his hospital idea failed. That helped me, because it gave a chance for even *him* to be impressed by the greatness of the lions. Then he came up with the notion of putting Patterson high up, all alone, in a clearing, on a rickety wooden support. (It was called a "machan," and in real life it was Patterson's idea. He had used one before, in India.) Patterson is alone and helpless. Redbeard is in the area. The Ghost comes. (In real life it circled Patterson for hours and hours, before it struck. Couldn't use that in the movie, it wouldn't shoot well.) Then The Ghost attacks, Redbeard wounds it, together they kill it and triumph.

The point now was for the audience to relax. The cavalry had come to the rescue.

Then, the next morning, when Redbeard is eaten, Patterson, poor helpless fellow, would be alone against The Darkness, what chance could *he* possibly have if even Redbeard had failed?

The fact is this: Redbeard worked as a device.

My problem, Doctor, was he worked *too well.* In all the succeeding drafts, the powers that be wanted *more* of him. Obviously, they saw a costarring part. Fine for them.

Biiiig problem for me.

Let me try and explain why.

One of the great exchanges in movie history—I don't mean "great" in the sense of Shakespearean, because screenwriting isn't about that; I mean "great" in the sense of being supremely helpful, of defining character—anyway, it's in *Casablanca,* by the Epsteins and Howard Koch. Probably you remember the moment. Bogart is talking to Claude Rains in front of his club.

> RAINS
> And what in heaven's name brought you to Casablanca?

> BOGART
> My health. I came to Casablanca for the waters.

> RAINS
> Waters? What waters? We're in the desert.

> BOGART
> I was misinformed.

Let's talk about this for a moment. First of all, it is wonderfully elegant dialogue. Witty, plus it makes you laugh out loud. I wish to God I'd written lines as glorious as "I was misinformed."

But what does it tell us? Well, it could be telling us that Rick is geographically challenged, coming to the desert for a water cure. But I think "I was misinformed" tells us he knew exactly where he was.

What it tells us is this: *Don't ask.* What is tells us is: *Bad things happened, it's dark down there, and I will die before I tell you.* A lot of that comes from the dialogue, a lot from the speaker of the dialogue. If the Hansons are in Casablanca, you know it's because they have a gig there. Or some high school girl they like is taking summer school. But Bogart—Bogart *then*—forty-four years old, with the gravel voice, the sad wrinkled face, that man understands *pain.* And no power on earth will make him talk about it, it's that awful.

The character of Rick, of course, is very old—he is the Byronic hero, the tall dark handsome man with a past. Most movie stars—actors, not comedians—have essentially all played that same role. And they have to always face front, never turn sideways—

Because, you see, *there's nothing to them.* Try and make them full, try and make them real, and guess what? They disappear.

They are not well-rounded figures. No one in that kind of movie is. Paul Henreid is playing Honor and wonderful Ingrid is playing Anguish and my adored Bogie is playing Wounded Bravery. (When he died, I was working in my really awful pit and one of my roommates knocked on the door and said, "I have to tell you, Humphrey Bogart just died." I was done with writing for that day. Just before he died, I was riding a bus uptown and passed a movie theater and there was an old Jewish couple sitting behind me and the man said, pointing at the marquee, "Look, it's a Humphrey Bogart," and the woman said, "He's so wonderful." I wish I'd known him at that moment. So I could have told him. Even Byronic heroes don't mind a bit of good news.)

Let me rewrite that exchange for you now. Let's say Rains is talking not to Bogart, but to Dooley Wilson.

                    RAINS
     And what in heaven's name brought Rick to
     Casablanca?

                    DOOLEY
     You don't want to know.

                    RAINS
     But I do, I asked the question.

DOOLEY

His life turned to shit, Claude. He hated his
job, but he should never have sold insurance
in the first place. And then his wife, she died
having their kid, who died too. He got so depressed, y'know? He felt so goddam *failed*.
Here he was, forty-five going on a thousand.
Then he knocked up his mistress and she
cleaned him out of all his savings, and then it
turned out she'd faked the whole thing and run
off with his best friend from high school. He
just couldn't get his shit together, y'understand? So he took a course in nightclub management and when this spot opened up, he came
here.

Think about what that does to one of the greatest of all Hollywood
movies. **It makes Rick a wimp. It makes him a loser.** Kills the flick, ruins
it, destroys it, makes it an Adam Sandler flick. Never forget the following:

Hollywood heroes must have *mystery*.

Okay, back to Billy's little Redbeard problem. I had written a Byronic
hero. He's Shane. The village is in trouble, he rides in, saves it, rides out.
For that very great western directed by the very great George Stevens, it
is crucial that we know *nothing* about the guy. Ever.

The bigger Redbeard's part became, the more risk for me, because the
more you expose that character to the sunlight, the more he starts to
fade. Redbeard, in ensuing drafts, kept appearing earlier and earlier. In
the finished film, he's half the picture. I did the best I could, gave him
action to do. And did my best to always keep him in shadow, but . . .

Michael Douglas the Producer

As good as the game. If I speak of his producing life first, it is because
that is what he was on *The Ghost and the Darkness* first (the performing
decision came later). Here are a few of his producing credits:

One Flew Over the Cuckoo's Nest
The China Syndrome

I have worked with Redford. I have been in a room with Beatty. They are brilliant men, passionate about what they produce, and boy are they not dumb.

Well, Michael Douglas is their equal.

And Douglas did something no other actor ever did with me—he spent *time*. On the script. Going over it and over it. Actors just don't do that. They are simply too busy.

But Douglas spent literally *days* locked in a room with me and with Stephen Hopkins, who did a wonderful job directing the movie. Good days they were too. Michael understood the story, understood Patterson and had ideas of how to improve him, understood Redbeard, the man with no past. I remember saying to Hopkins after, say, six hours in a room, just the three of us, that I had never had that before.

In that room, you forgot he was this Oscar-winning producer and actor. He was just this other, well, *guy* who wanted to improve things. Lots of his ideas were terrific. Lots of them weren't. But unlike so many stars, you could call it on Douglas. You could tell him his suggestion sucked. And when he would ask why, if you could explain it well enough, he would just make some self-deprecating remark and on we went to the next problem.

If you get the feeling I cannot say too much about Michael Douglas the producer, you are on the money.

Michael Douglas the Star

In the beginning, a quarter of a century back, I tended to think of him as either this TV sidekick working the streets of San Francisco, or Kirk's son. But then this unusual thing happened before our eyes: he started getting good, then he *was* good, then he was better than that. Most of the time, stars arrive full-blown.

Douglas was okay in *Coma*, back in '78. And he was overshadowed by Jack Lemmon and Jane Fonda in *The China Syndrome*, the year following. Between '79 and '84, he was only in three flicks, none memorable. Then in '84 came *Romancing the Stone,* where he was just terrific, the same in the sequel, *The Jewel of the Nile,* in '85.

It was 1987 when he exploded. *Wall Street* and *Fatal Attraction.* He won the Oscar for the former, deservedly, but I thought he was even better in the other.

After that, *The War of the Roses, Basic Instinct, Falling Down, An American President.*

Who's better?

My answer is: at what he does, no one. And just what does Douglas play so brilliantly? This: *the flawed, contemporary American male.*

I now repeat something I wrote earlier in this book. It bears repeating: by the first day of shooting, *the fate of the movie is sealed.* The point, once again, is that if you have prepared the script right, if you have cast it right, both actors and crew, you have a shot. If you have made a grievous error in either script or casting, you are dead in the water.

Val Kilmer was set as Patterson. All the other parts, except Redbeard, were to be played by the best actors we could get who were not going to be prohibitively expensive. A good decision because the lions were also expensive costars.

Redbeard was limited as to number of weeks. We wanted a star at least the size of Kilmer. Ahh, but who?

I will get into this in detail some other time, but personally, I write my star parts for dead or old stars. It helps me define in my head the character I am trying to write. I use Cary Grant a lot, Cagney a lot, and for the women, for years I wrote everything for Jean Simmons.

Gable would have been fine as Redbeard—he'd played a hunter, and well, in *Red Dust,* later in the remake, *Mogambo.* And since he died so rarely, his death would have been terrific. John Wayne would have been good too, and he died even less than Gable.

But Burt Lancaster was my man.

Who did I want today? Eastwood, obviously, who got famous thirty-five years ago playing The Man With No Name in his spaghetti-western period. But I knew that was ridiculous, because he never plays supporting roles. And though Redbeard clearly was the star in his time on screen, he was also clearly a supporting role.

Connery would have been perfect.

We went to Connery, had high hopes, made a good offer—but Jerry Bruckheimer made a much better one, grabbed him for *The Rock.* (And a great move it turned out to be—I don't think the movie works nearly as well without Connery.)

Back to square one.

Tony Hopkins came next. For me, along with Morgan Freeman, the two best movie actors of the era. I had no idea what Hopkins would have done with the part, but it would have been fascinating.

He had, I think, agency problems at the time, and was not in a position to accept anything when we needed him. (Understand that if I am not as accurate or juicy in these paragraphs as you want me to be, it is because of this: screenwriters tend not to know this kind of stuff.)

Square one again.

My memory is we were thinking very seriously about going to the French star Gerard Depardieu when the earth moved.

Michael decided to play the part himself.

My initial reaction was delight. He is a major star, he gave the movie all the weight it would need. He also ensured against any catastrophe that the movie would get made.

More than that, I knew the script would be protected because I had spent hours and days with him going over it and I knew he understood where the strengths were.

But shit, as we all know, has a way of happening.

The first thing that went was the name.

No big deal, you are probably thinking, and of course, you are correct. It is not a big deal. Except writers are *nuts*—that is a law in the State of California as you no doubt know—and we *love* the names we give our made-up friends and acquaintances. A lot of us can't even *start* until we know our people's names.

I loved "Redbeard." I thought it was a terrific name; and I thought it was helpful in trying to make the guy mythic. Just that single word, those two syllables and you were talking about someone whose exploits had filled the nights beside a thousand campfires.

I lucked into the name Remington pretty quickly. Sold myself that if not as good, at least it didn't suck. Still the one word, and there was the echo of the gun that was so famous in settling the Wild West.

Sigh of relief.

Then, sharply, I was into nightmare.

Michael wanted Remington to have a history.

This next scene is one of the worst things I've ever written. I actually remember my stomach cramping when I did it. It comes the first night Michael Douglas has arrived to save the day. In the background, a bunch of warriors are getting ready to jump around and give themselves courage. Douglas is talking to Kilmer and Samuel, who is the narrator of the film, a native helping Patterson as best he can. Another native comes up and indicates to Remington that they are ready. Remington leaves and the camp doctor, who has also been present, comments that Remington is indeed a strange man. Here is what Samuel replies to that—get ready, hold your noses.

                        SAMUEL
        Two great tribes of his country fought a ter-
        rible civil war for many years.

                        VAL KILMER
        And his side lost?

                        SAMUEL
        Everything. Land and family. The very young
        ones and the very old ones. All lost. He
        buried his family and left his country for-
        ever. Now he hunts all over the world but he
        always returns here. He says Africa is the
        last good place.

Remember my made-up speech about Bogart taking a course in night-club management? Same thing here. This is what that speech and ensuing references to Remington's past do to this legendary figure: **They make Remington a wimp. They make him a loser.** He's just another whiny asshole who went to pieces when the gods pissed on him. "Oh, you cannot know the depth of my pain" is what that seems to be saying to the audience. Well, if I'm in that audience, what I think is this: *Fuck you.* I know people who are dying of cancer, I know people who are close to vegetables, and guess what—*they play it as it lays.*

This little speech may not seem like much but not only does it cast a pall over everything that follows, it destroys the fabric of the piece. Every ensuing mention of Remington and children and loss is all so treacly you want to whoopse. Never forget the following:

Movie stars must have mystery.

By now you must be thinking this:

Well, Bill, why did you do it? I will answer that for you, but the bigger point is this:

What does a screenwriter do when he is asked to damage his own screenplay?

This is not an isolated incident. It happens to us all. And it happens a lot, usually because of star insecurity, but directors can fuck things up pretty good, too.

I did what Douglas wanted. The alternative, of course, was to leave the picture. Which would have been stupid, I think, because the instant I am out the door, someone else is hired to do what I wouldn't.

In this case I did it for another reason: Douglas's intelligence. I know he must have known what he wanted was horseshit, was damaging to a project in which his name was going to be billed in several places. From those hours in the room with him, I just knew he would see the lack of wisdom in his ways and we could cut it all out in the editing process.

If you saw the movie, you know it didn't get cut out. His past and his pain is there for all to see. (When the screenplay was printed in a collection, I got rid of all this. Too late, of course, but I felt a little better.)

Did Michael Douglas suddenly get stupid?

Nosir. What happened, I think, was that in that room he was a *producer,* and later he became a performer, a *star*—with all those terrible feelings of fraudulence stars live with, with all those different insecurities.

Michael wanted the audience *moved* when Remington died. That's what I think was at the heart of the changes. And the best way to do that was to win sympathy for Remington. What he succeeded in doing was destroying him.

Another thing. In *Adventures in the Screen Trade* I wrote a lot about Dustin Hoffman's less than ideal behavior during *Marathon Man.* Hoffman always felt he had a problem with himself in the part, which was that he was far too old to be playing a graduate student at Columbia. And of course he was dead right, being close to forty at the time. Well, remember what I wrote about Douglas, what he plays so brilliantly? The flawed, *contemporary* American male? I underline "contemporary" because I think that might have been the problem for Douglas—playing a man from a different century.

I think he did not feel he could play it as written, so changes were made to make him more comfortable. To make his character one the audience would care about and be moved by.

Guess what—when we had our first sneak, one of the questions the audience was asked was to rate the characters in order of how they liked them. And the audience rated Michael Douglas **fourth.**

Panic Out There.

A lot of cuts and pads were made to be sure he was more sympathetic the next sneak. The audience wasn't buying it—they still rated him fourth. Kilmer was third. Now, fellow scriveners, remember this advice—when your two stars are rated *below* two supporting players, do not put a down payment on that beach house in Malibu.

The Shoot

Brutal, as expected.

I was only in South Africa a couple of times, but a few memories:

(1) Two of the lions were gay. The bigger of the two was dominant, the male. The smaller (we're talking comparatives here), the lady. Now, they traveled a long way to get to the location, and on the journey, one of the lions took sick. The bigger one. He lost so much weight that he became the smaller of the two. And when this happened, the smaller, now the larger, became the dominant, the male. I offer this anecdote to any sociologists amongst you.

(2) One afternoon we were screen-testing lions. No, not right and left profile, but what kind of expectations could we have in behavior. We had giant mechanical lions that had been built, but what we wanted to find out was what, if anything, the real beasts could do.

We are in a bare soundstage that we built. Primitive, obviously; imagine a high school gym and you get the picture. There is a tiny set—some long grass, actually. And the camera crew is all ready; they are also in a thickly barred cage. I am watching from another thickly barred cage. Because this lion we are testing is *savage.*

A door slides open and in comes a circus-cage kind of thing on wheels with a single lion inside. The tension in that large room was immediate and terrifying, because here was something primitive in with us now. The trainer, an elegant and well-dressed French man, unlocks the cage—he is the only thing on earth the lion responds to. He brings the lion to his spot. Stephen Hopkins, directing from behind bars, asks for a few basic things. The trainer speaks to the lion in French, and the animal does surprisingly well.

Back they go to the circus cage and as they get there, this wondrous thing happens. The trainer in his lovely suit bends slightly, puts his arms out wide. And the lion goes up on its hind paws and for a moment, they dance.

Hours later I ran into the trainer and talked about how touching the moment was. I asked if the lion cared for him. He said this: "Mr. Goldman, I feed him." But it was so gentle, I went on, I got the sense he *cared* for you. "Mr. Goldman, I feed him," he said again. I was persistent. "But he wouldn't ever hurt you, would he?"

He came next to me and took off his glasses and pointed to what the thick-rimmed glasses had hidden—his entire eyebrow covered a long and very frightening scar. "I made a mistake once," was all he said.

(3) Michael Douglas arrived when we were many weeks into shooting. His first day was a scene with a thousand extras, where Val Kilmer was trying to convince the leader of the workers not to leave, that he needed them.

Val couldn't get it.

I don't know if he hadn't learned his lines or if he hated his lines. Or if, as the character of Patterson, he didn't want to ask for help. This is important stuff: stars *hate* asking for help.

(Shhh—they're afraid their fans will find them wimpy.)

A lot of bad things have been written about Val Kilmer's behavior. I will not add to them here. I will say he was going through a terrible time. His marriage had fallen publicly and painfully apart a few weeks before. He had come directly to us from a nightmare, *The Island of Dr. Moreau.* (How much he contributed to that nightmare is a subject much debated.) He was exhausted and not, I think it's safe to say, at his best on our shoot.

As I said, Douglas arrives and Kilmer cannot get his lines right in front of a thousand extras. His producer hat very much on, Douglas takes Kilmer aside and asks, approximately, the following: Do you want a career like Eric Roberts? Do you want a career like Mickey Rourke? Well, you can have that if you don't shape up.

I am not telling this to you because it is such great gossip, because obviously it isn't that. But there was clearly not a whole lot of chemistry between these two stars as the movie unfolded.

And does that matter? It's certainly not the reason the movie didn't do what I had hoped. If you were to ask me those reasons I would begin with this: *the script was not good enough*. I always think that on every movie I'm involved with if it doesn't work.

I also think the time was wrong. Not the time of year when it was released, I mean the *time for lions*. In our long history, perhaps no other animal has had such graph changes. From being vermin to being gods.

Now is a cutie-pie stage. *Born Free* and *The Lion King*. I don't think the audience wanted much to hear about these two monsters that shredded so many lives.

But I also feel that if Douglas and Kilmer had been in *Butch Cassidy* instead of Redford and Newman, you would not remotely be listening to anything I might have to say about Hollywood . . .

Killing Gatsby

I don't think anyone out of the business realizes (nor should they) just how fragile movies are, how even the greatest successes run, at least for a while, neck and neck with failure.

As an example, nothing in my experience equals one of the major overhyped disasters of the '70s, *The Great Gatsby*.

In my entire life dealing with the madness Out There, there was no project I wanted to write as much as Gatsby. It is as great as any American novel ever and I love it. So when there was a whisper of the rights becoming available, I got into it, told everybody of my undying passion.

Francis Ford Coppola got the job. Not to direct, just to write. I'm not sure where in his career he wrote the script, but I wouldn't be surprised if it was before *The Godfather* made him famous.

I was a huge fan of his writing in those days, *You're a Big Boy Now*, *The Rain People*, *Patton*. But nothing prepared me for the Gatsby script. I still believe it to be one of the great adaptations. I have never met him (still haven't) but I called him and told him what a wonderful thing he had done.

If you see the movie, you will find all this hard to believe.

Gatsby, for those of you who don't know, is a bootlegger who, one summer on Long Island, gives the most glamorous parties imaginable, mainly to impress his great love, Daisy, who is married to a prig. These are the parties that today the magazines and newspapers would kill to cover. All the perfumes in Arabia-type deals.

Well, the director who was hired, Jack Clayton, is a Brit,

and like most Brits we fawn over, less talented than you might think. But he had the one thing all of them have in their blood: a murderous sense of class. All they need is to hear you speak a few words and they know everything they need to know about you. It is their least appealing trait.

Well, Clayton decided this: that Gatsby's parties were shabby and tacky, given by a man of no elevation and taste.

There went the ball game.

As shot, they were foul and stupid and the people who attended them were foul and silly, and Robert Redford and Mia Farrow, who would have been so perfect as Gatsby and Daisy, were left hung out to dry. Because Gatsby was a tasteless fool and why should we care about their love?

It was not as if Coppola's glory had been jettisoned entirely, though it was tampered with plenty; it was more that the reality and passions it depicted were gone. I was in a rage when I left the theater, because we have so very few chances in our careers of doing things so well.

Writers can screw things up, actors too, directors certainly. Even as great a flick as *Chinatown* was almost destroyed by the wrong score, but it was changed in time. I've written this before and please tattoo it behind your eyeballs: **we are all at one another's mercy . . .**

Absolute Power
[1997]

Absolute Power is the hardest screenplay I have ever written. Eventually, it stopped me cold—for the first time I was faced with an assignment that I simply could not complete. And would never have been able to had Tony Gilroy not come to save me.

The Novel

November '94.

Martin Shafer, who runs Castle Rock films, called and said he was sending me *Executive Power*, a first novel by a young Washington lawyer, David Baldacci. Shafer mentioned nothing specific pertaining to the plot but he did tell me this: that Baldacci, in the last three weeks, had sold the worldwide book and movie rights for *five million dollars*.

Better than a sharp stick in the eye.

The next day a 466-page typed manuscript arrived. I had never read a novel with that kind of early success. (Few ever had.) Curious as hell, I started reading, wondering what magic potion Mr. Baldacci had come up with. It broke down as follows:

Chapter 1, pages 3–17

A great old thief, LUTHER WHITNEY, breaks into a deserted mansion belonging to eighty-year-old WALTER SULLIVAN, one of the more powerful billionaires around. It is very tricky and tense, the break-in, pitting sophisticated burglary tools against a top-of-the-line security system.

LUTHER makes his way to the master bedroom, takes what looks like a VCR remote from a nearby table, points it at what looks like an ordinary mirror, and clicks. The mirror swings open to reveal a room-sized vault—a vault with a chair in it, the chair *facing the door.*

LUTHER enters and starts bagging the goodies—cash, jewelry, coins, bonds, stamps, millions of dollars' worth.

During this, a limo and a van are approaching the mansion. In the limo are two women and a man. One of the women is trying to undress the man, who is good-naturedly trying to fend her off. Both are drunk. The other woman sits opposite, watching with some distaste and dealing with a large appointment book.

LUTHER hears the cars, realizes he is in trouble because it's too late to escape. So he hides in the vault, shuts the door, sits in the chair.

Footsteps come closer and closer and the bedroom light is turned on and LUTHER is shocked and blinded and for a moment, he thinks he's been found out. Then he realizes this: *the door is a two-way mirror.*

From the bedroom, it's just a mirror. But from where he sits, it's a window on the room—he has a life-sized view of what's happening in the bedroom just a few feet beyond—

—and what's happening is this: two very drunk people are clearly going to fuck.

LUTHER recognizes the two people: THE WOMAN is the gorgeous twenty-five-year-old CHRISTY SULLIVAN, wife of WALTER SULLI-VAN, the ancient billionaire. THE MAN is clearly not her husband—and LUTHER is stunned when he realizes who he is . . .

Pretty terrific start.

I had no idea where the story was going, but I knew I wasn't about to stop reading. I also had no idea who the main characters would be, but I guessed this trio would be around:

LUTHER WHITNEY, the great old thief
CHRISTY SULLIVAN, the philandering blonde
THE WELL-DRESSED MAN whom she was philandering with

A total of three.

The reason for the detail here is because of one simple truth: movies are not Chekhov. You have your star part, that's essential. And depending on what kind of flick it is, you have your love interest or your villain. Or often, both. Those are your key roles.

But you cannot have even half a dozen main characters. *The Big*

Chill, sure. *Peter's Friends, Return of the Secaucus Seven*. But the glory days of the all-star MGM movie is, because of budget primarily, as removed as the Ice Age.

Chapter 2, pages 18–26

That same night, JACK GRAHAM, an attractive, athletic young Washington attorney, returns home from a fancy party. JACK has pretty much everything going for him, but be careful what you wish for, you might get it.

JACK is engaged to JENNIFER BALDWIN, who is gorgeous and the heiress to the Baldwin fortune, run by her father, RANSOME BALD-WIN. JACK has a job at one of the top Washington law firms, which happens to handle the Baldwin interests. JACK is new there, having taken the job at JENNIFER's urging, and because of his connection with the Baldwins he will become a partner at the next review.

JACK goes to bed, where he takes down a picture of his former fiancée, KATE WHITNEY. They have not seen each other in four years but he knows she is now a State's Attorney. JACK loved KATE, still misses her, but also misses, and almost as much, her father, LUTHER, with whom he was very close.

JACK decides to call KATE, dials her, then hangs up after the beep sound on her phone machine as he loses his nerve . . .

Short, helpful, very tense—because while you are reading, what you are thinking is this: *Get back to the bedroom*. There were also several new characters I knew I would be meeting again.

JACK GRAHAM, clearly to be the hero
KATE WHITNEY, even though she hasn't done much yet
JENNIFER BALDWIN, the rich and beautiful fiancée

Along with, please remember—

LUTHER WHITNEY, the great old thief
CHRISTY SULLIVAN, the philandering blonde
THE WELL-DRESSED MAN whom she was philandering with

Bringing the total to *six*. Six *major* characters.
So far.

Chapter 3, pages 27–57

Back to the vault.

LUTHER, helpless, watches as the sex begins, heats up, gets violent, gets bloody. THE MAN tries to strangle CHRISTY but she slashes him in the arm with a letter opener and is about to stab him in the heart when he screams and TWO WELL-DRESSED MEN race in and blow her brains out.

Now to a new place.

At this same time, KATE WHITNEY is working late in her office. She thinks momentarily of her hated father, LUTHER, calls her home for messages but there is only a breather who hangs up. She goes back to work, watched by a photo of herself and her mother from which LUTHER has been unmistakably ripped away.

Back in the bedroom.

The naked and bleeding ALAN RICHMOND, THE PRESIDENT OF THE UNITED STATES, is staring dumbly at the bloody letter opener in his hand that almost killed him. BILL BURTON, the older of the two Secret Service men, who did the shooting, is almost sick at the sight of blood and brains. His partner, TIM COLLIN, steadies him. PRESIDENT RICHMOND passes out as Chief of Staff GLORIA RUSSELL, the other woman in the limousine, races in.

COLLIN reports the facts to RUSSELL. RUSSELL plans a coverup. The room is sanitized and they all leave. But unknown to RUSSELL, the letter opener, which she commandeered, has fallen from her purse behind the bed.

THE PRESIDENT, RUSSELL, BURTON, and COLLIN hurry down to the waiting cars, preparing to get the hell gone—

—which is when RUSSELL realizes the letter opener isn't in her purse.

LUTHER, who has left the vault, has taken it with him as he uncoils a rope and goes out the window.

THE SECRET SERVICE chase him on foot, almost catch him in a thrilling footrace, but he manages to make it to his car and zooms off.

RUSSELL, BURTON, and COLLIN return to the bedroom, realize two facts, neither of them good for the Jews: (1) the letter opener is gone, complete with fingerprints of both the PRESIDENT and the murdered CHRISTY SULLIVAN on it; and (2) there was an *eyewitness*.

They know they are in very deep shit indeed. And will be until they have murdered the eyewitness and have the letter opener back.

LUTHER knows the power of his enemies—he returns to his home, packs, flees into the night . . .

Whew.

It was clear at this point why $5 million had been spent. I thought it was just about the best opening of a commercial novel I had ever read. It was also clear that I was not reading the book strictly for pleasure. Sure, that's present and crucial—

—but I was also being asked to turn it into a movie. And clearly, it was not going to be easy money at the brick factory.

More new characters who weren't leaving soon:
GLORIA RUSSELL, the Chief of Staff
BILL BURTON, the veteran Secret Service guy
TIM COLLIN, the young hotshot

And let us not forget—
JACK GRAHAM, pretty clearly to be the hero
KATE WHITNEY, even though she hasn't done much yet
JENNIFER BALDWIN, the rich and beautiful fiancée
Along with, please remember—
LUTHER WHITNEY, the great old thief
CHRISTY SULLIVAN, the philandering blonde
THE WELL-DRESSED MAN, now revealed as PRESIDENT ALAN RICHMOND, whom she was philandering with

Nine characters now.
And counting.

I finished the book and then did something I have never done before when offered an assignment—I read the whole thing again. And as I did, I became convinced that more and more characters who appeared were crucial to the story. Here are some of them:

SETH FRANK, the detective trying to solve it all, *maybe the lead*
WANDA BROOME, who conceived the break-in with LUTHER
WALTER SULLIVAN, the good billionaire and wronged husband
SANDY LORD, SULLIVAN's lawyer and a power in Washington
LAURA SIMON, SETH's top aide, who ties LUTHER to the crime
MR. FLANDERS, a bystander who photographed the attempt on LUTHER's life
MICHAEL McCARTY, world's top assassin, hired to kill LUTHER

And just in case you went to the kitchen for a snack—

GLORIA RUSSELL, the Chief of Staff
BILL BURTON, the veteran Secret Service guy
TIM COLLIN, the young hotshot

And let us not forget—

JACK GRAHAM, pretty clearly to be the hero
KATE WHITNEY, even though she hasn't done much yet
JENNIFER BALDWIN, the rich and beautiful fiancée

Along with, please remember—

LUTHER WHITNEY, the great old thief
CHRISTY SULLIVAN, the philandering blonde
THE WELL-DRESSED MAN, now revealed as PRESIDENT ALAN
RICHMOND, whom she was philandering with

You add it up, it's too horrible.

You simply cannot have that many characters in a movie today. It's confusing, it's a turnoff, and in terms of movie storytelling, it's just wrong.

And wrong more than ever *now,* when the hunger for a vehicle role, a locomotive (as they sometimes refer to the male lead Out There), has reached hysterical heights.

Even worse than the number of characters was this: *there was no star part.*

LUTHER was the best character, but he could not be the star, for many reasons, chiefly this: in a great shocker, he is murdered halfway through by order of the President.

No to LUTHER.

JACK GRAHAM, the young lawyer, was maybe the biggest part. But he didn't come into the story till very late, and the star must enter early.

No to JACK GRAHAM.

SETH FRANK was the cop on the trail. But he didn't solve all that much.

Couldn't be SETH FRANK.

What's a mother to *do* . . . ?

I called Shafer and said I would like to try it, and I would try to write ten good roles—because that was what the material called for. Shafer said this: "It's okay. We'll go with ten one-million-dollar actors rather than one ten-million-dollar one."

All I had to do now was write the bastard.

Why did I say yes?

Because I had not done a flat-out thriller since *Marathon Man*, twenty years earlier, and was anxious to try another. Because it was Castle Rock, the best movie studio for writers in my third of a century of writing screenplays.

And because Baldacci, bless him, had written *three* sensational sequences. The opening sixty-page rough sex with the PRESIDENT OF THE UNITED STATES; the double assassination attempt to kill LUTHER, with both COLLIN and McCARTY having point-blank shots at the old guy, and, maybe most moving of all, LUTHER's shocking murder by COLLIN, which comes at a time when the reader thinks LUTHER is finally safe.

Wonderful stuff.

These three, I felt—they had to run a total of fifty pages at least—were so strong they would support the remainder of the screenplay, no matter how badly I might screw things up.

Aside to young screenwriters: no, I am not bullshitting when I say this last. I am always terrified I am going to screw everything up. The most hideous advice—and at the same time the most releasing—was given to me by George Roy Hill, still and always the greatest director I ever worked with. I had just taken on the job of trying to make the famous Woodward-Bernstein Watergate book somehow translate to screen. Hill, a world-class sadist, looked at me, and these were his words: "*All the President's Men*? Everybody's going to be waiting for that one." And here he smiled. "Don't fuck it up."

At a Knicks game recently I ran into Ben Stiller, who has his own demons trying to figure out the glorious Budd Schulberg book *What Makes Sammy Run?* Naturally I was kind, told him this: "Don't fuck it up."

He kind of smiled . . .

The First Draft

May, 1995.

I called this draft *Not Executive Power,* because I thought Baldacci's title so damaging—there were already several other movies ahead of us in the pipeline that also were called "Executive" something or other.

Even more important, at least to me, was this: I kept forgetting the name of the novel when people asked me what I was working on.

The first script ran 145 pages—too long, I knew that, but I also knew that the crucial thing for me in this initial pass was to get the story written. And then read it.

I never read anything I've written till I'm done. If I did, I would be so appalled at the crimes I'd committed, I would never be finished rewriting the first scene.

I wrote it.

I read it.

Ugh.

It looked like a screenplay. If you lifted it up, it hoisted like a screenplay.

But it just kind of laid there.

No one to really root for—

—except old LUTHER, who died halfway through.

Not having someone to root for is a terrible problem.

But an even bigger problem was this: the story didn't end, it just stopped.

Endings are just a bitch. (Tattoo that behind your eyelids.)

The best ending of mine, I think, is *Butch Cassidy*. And I like the "As you wish" in *The Princess Bride*.

Endings in thrillers are particularly brutal. At least they have been for me. I've tried several—*Marathon Man, No Way to Treat a Lady, Magic, Control, Brothers*. If you read any of them, chances are, if you remember them at all, it's not for the way they concluded.

Maybe it's because the initial pulse for the story was played out before the ending came. *Marathon Man,* at least as I remember, came from two ideas: (1) What if someone in your family whom you knew and loved wasn't remotely what you had thought? (Babe—Dustin Hoffman in the movie—has no idea his beloved brother, Doc—Roy Scheider—is a spy and not a businessman); (2) What if the world's most wanted Nazi came to Manhattan? (Szell—Olivier, *yesss*—has to come here to retrieve his diamond fortune from a bank, if it was safe for him to go there.)

Well, by the time blood had been spilled, by the time Olivier had slaughtered Scheider and Hoffman had cornered Olivier, it was just a matter of mixing and matching. I had nothing much more up my sleeve.

David Baldacci (curse him) didn't have a sleeveful either. The manuscript I read ended like this: in the last chapter, SETH FRANK, the detective who's been in charge of the CHRISTY SULLIVAN murder case, comes to the White House along with a bunch of law enforcement officials and arrests PRESIDENT ALAN RICHMOND. RICHMOND says that as President, legally he can't be served with anything. SETH replies that after his impeachment he'll be plain ALAN RICHMOND again and when that happens, he's going to trial.

Not heart-pounding, but solid enough.

The epilogue is the quagmire.

JACK GRAHAM, KATE's onetime lawyer fiancé, has gone on a trip and come back to Washington and *knows nothing* of recent events, such as the murder trial of the PRESIDENT OF THE UNITED STATES. "Inconceivable," as Vizzini used to say. SETH FRANK comes to visit him and fills JACK in on what's been happening. COLLIN got twenty years to life, GLORIA RUSSELL got 1,000 hours of community service, RICHMOND lied on the stand, was torn apart on cross, was found guilty and given the death penalty.

Clearly, I had to come up with an exciting ending.

My brain chose this time to go on holiday.

So did I, and on Christmas afternoon of 1994 I found myself walking around a polo field in Barbados with John and Alyce Cleese, whining about my ending problem. One of them, I think it was Alyce, said, "Why doesn't another woman kill him?"

I wrote it as soon as I got home.

Not Executive Power ended this way: SETH the detective hero and JACK the lawyer hero go to the White House and meet with the PRESIDENT, who denies everything and has letters (false but sworn to) backing up his case. He then explains why they can't touch him. And indeed, they can't. He has too much power, too many who will lie for him. JACK and SETH leave in wild frustration.

Then we cut to the exterior of another mansion. Then inside, to the corridor outside the master bedroom. COLLIN paces, RUSSELL works on her appointment book.

Now a woman's cry comes from inside. They glance at each other, shrug. Nothing they haven't heard so many times. Then another feminine cry, louder. They go on as before.

Then *gunfire* from the bedroom.

COLLIN and RUSSELL rush inside to see a naked, drunk blonde holding a gun. "He dared me," she says.

And RICHMOND lies alongside her, shot in the heart.

Finally and briefly, a cemetery. We hear Bernard Shaw telling CNN viewers that RICHMOND's sudden fatal heart attack has shocked the nation but we've been through worse and we'll come through this, too.

We're at LUTHER's grave now. JACK and KATE, LUTHER's daughter, pay their last respects to the old guy.

Final fade-out.

Stephen Sondheim once said this: "I cannot write a bad song. You begin it here, build, end there. The words will lay properly on the music so they can be sung, that kind of thing. You may hate it, but it will be a proper song."

I sometimes feel that way about my screenplays. I've been doing them for so long now, and I've attempted most genres. I know about entering the story as late as possible, entering each scene as late as possible, that kind of thing. You may hate it, but it will be a proper screenplay.

This first draft was proper as hell—you just didn't give a shit.

I met with the Castle Rock people. They still wanted to make *Absolute Power* (by now, Baldacci had come up with the better title). They just didn't want to make *this* version of the story.

Yes, they knew they had said write ten terrific parts, we'll be fine. But the problem with doing it the way I had done it was this: there was no one to root for. Couldn't I write someone we could care about besides LUTHER, who dies so soon? In other words, was there somewhere in the material—please, God—a star part? Because that's what the movie needed.

I agreed with them.

But the same problem still haunted me—

—*there was not now and had never been a star part.*

The Second Draft

October, 1995.

I must explain something about the way I work. I have always only done movies I wanted to do—which means caring for *and being faithful to* the source material.

I had never changed a story this much.

If I could figure out how to do it at all. I pored over and over my three star-part choices.

1. Luther

Still by far the best character in both the book and the movie. *But he had to die.* Not just because of a wonderful chance for a strong scene. LUTHER's death provided the impact the story needed to sustain itself. Morally and viscerally.

Definitely could not be LUTHER.

2. Jack Graham

The logical choice, really. He ends up with the girl, LUTHER's daughter, KATE, so he carries that emotion with him. Also, he is close to LUTHER—he's the one LUTHER turns to when he decides to try and expose PRESIDENT RICHMOND.

Problem: That happens literally halfway through the novel (and on page 71 of my 145-page first draft).

Could I bring JACK in earlier?

Sure. This wasn't a documentary, I could do anything I wanted. There *was* no JACK. He was a character in a novel, for chrissakes. I could open the damn movie with JACK being born if I wanted to.

But if I did bring him in earlier, he would have just stood there. He had nothing really to do till LUTHER came to him for help.

So could I *really* bring JACK in earlier?

Not without totally changing everything and making it JACK's movie—but it *couldn't* be, because *JACK wasn't in the goddam vault,* and what was seen from that vault, and its consequences, *had* to be the story.

Definitely could not be JACK.

3. Seth Frank

SETH, the detective trying to solve the murder, might seem even more logical. Detectives are traditionally there from the uncovering of the crime till the solution.

But not here.

The crime itself is not only a high point of the whole story, it also takes thirty pages of the first draft. And and and—SETH doesn't detect all that much. JACK solves his share too.

Definitely could not be SETH.

A double hero would be best.

Problem: I'd already tried it that way in the first draft. With JACK and SETH. And failed.

"Sheeesh," as Calvin used to tell us.

I went over them again and again.

LUTHER? No.

JACK? No.

SETH? No.

If you happened to be walking near Seventy-seventh Street and Madison Avenue during the early fall of 1995, that sound you heard was me screaming.

Finally, blessedly, I remembered Mr. Abbott.

One of the great breaks of my career came in 1960, when I was among those called in to doctor a musical in very deep trouble, *Tenderloin*. The show eventually was not a success. But the experience was profound.

George Abbott, the legitimately legendary Broadway figure, was the director of the show—he was closing in on seventy-five during our months together and hotter than ever. All in all, Mr. Abbott was connected with more famous and successful shows than anyone else in history, as producer, director, writer, or star. (We are talking about one of those careers—if you are a sports fan, think of the Babe or Wilt.)

Mr. Abbott was a big man, six-two maybe, ramrod straight. Someone once wrote of him: "If he's ever late, you figure there's been an accident." The most totally professional man that ever walked the earth.

And as I was going through my second draft of *Absolute Power* madness, I remembered a Mr. Abbott moment. He was coming from backstage during rehearsals, and as he crossed the stage into the auditorium he noticed a dozen dancers were just standing there. The choreographer sat in the audience alone, his head in his hands.

"What's going on?" Mr. Abbott asked him.

The choreographer looked at Mr. Abbott, shook his head. "I can't figure out what they should do next."

Mr. Abbott never stopped moving. He jumped the three feet from the stage to the aisle. "Well, have them do *something*!" Mr. Abbott said. *"That way we'll have something to change."*

The choreographer got off his ass, started moving the dancers.

As I remembered Mr. Abbott, I got off *my* ass, too. We were not going to shoot the second draft, I reminded myself. *So just write something so we'll have something to change.*

LUTHER could not be my guy for reasons of death.

JACK could have been—his love affair with LUTHER's daughter made that appealing. Except for this: in the novel and in the first draft, too, *LUTHER and KATE never once talked to each other.* She betrays him, arranges for his capture; but that moment when she serves as decoy is their only contact in the Baldacci story. (They are estranged and have been for years when the story begins and stay that way after the murder; LUTHER is terrified to *ever* talk to her, for fear the Secret Service might kill her on the theory that she might know something.)

I didn't want to mess with that.

No to JACK.

So SETH, by elimination, became my star.

There was still the problem of his not solving all that much. But I figured I could help that by having him do stuff that had belonged to other characters in the novel and the first draft.

One of the ways I did this was by giving him a family. I have two daughters, Jenny and Susanna, who loved Nancy Drew when they were kids. Guess what? SETH now had twin daughters with those names who were fifteen, had outgrown Nancy but not the notion of being detectives.

The family was a way to keep SETH around, and also to get rid of exposition that other characters carried earlier. And it made SETH vulnerable, so that, near the end, when he is closing in on RICHMOND, the PRESIDENT has BURTON and COLLIN "send him a message" by instructing them to hurt his family. Which they do, driving them off the road, putting ELAINE and the TWINS in the hospital. So SETH has a huge emotional score to settle when, in the last scene, he visits the White House and brings RICHMOND down.

Not Shakespearean. But maybe an improvement over the first draft. And SETH was now at the center of pretty much everything possible. I had certainly written a star part, which was primarily what I meant to do.

I sent it out. Fingers very much crossed.

Because this draft was going to Clint Eastwood.

His agent had called while I was writing this draft and indicated he wouldn't mind taking a look at it when it was done. And I was desperate to work with Eastwood, had been for decades. He is quietly having one of the very greatest careers. He and John Wayne are the two most durable acting stars in the history of sound. Plus plus plus the directing.

Eastwood as SETH set the blood racing.

I had given them *something.* So at least we had something to change. Little did he know . . .

Third Draft

December, 1995.

The second draft got out to Castle Rock around the twentieth of October. Their reaction was good—not terrific, but certainly good—and they were very appreciative about the amount of work that had gone into changing it.

Now, nothing to do but wait for Eastwood.

On the first of November Martin Shafer called to report that Eastwood definitely was reading it.

Then he called later that day and this is what he said: Eastwood had already read it. He thought it was absolutely okay.

But—

—big but—

—he had already played detectives like SETH before, and didn't want to play that character again—

—now Shafer dropped the shoe—

—Eastwood *was* interested in playing LUTHER. He thought LUTHER was a terrific character but—

—amazingly huge but—

—**but Eastwood wanted LUTHER to live and bring down the PRESIDENT.**

I was rocked.

During these days of waiting, my fantasies of writing a movie for Clint Eastwood grew out of control. I grew even more desperate to work with him—

—but I simply didn't know if I could write what he wanted.

I asked Shafer if he would commit in advance. I was terrified of changing everything so totally—always assuming I could figure out how—only to have him say no.

The answer was he would not. He would have to read it first. (I knew that, of course. I was just frightened and floundering.)

One other problem—it was now November, I was literally starting from scratch again and I knew this: *I had to get it in before Christmas.* His agent had indicated as much, because Eastwood had taken time off after *The Bridges of Madison County* and was ready to go to work again. After Christmas he would be gone to something else, leaving me dead in the water.

I told Shafer I would have to let him know.

These were the words I wrote in my journal that night:

HOW, GOD?

I spent the next days trying to come up with anything at all that might spark me, give me the confidence (always the greatest enemy) to plunge ahead.

A few days later I wrote this thought down: "LUTHER could use his street contacts—beggars who work the streets—to find out where CHRISTY SULLIVAN spent the day before she was murdered."

Baldacci is kind of vague on what CHRISTY, the billionaire's wife who gets murdered, did earlier that day of her tryst. I figured maybe if I could think of something exciting, it would be a way LUTHER could get incriminating evidence on PRESIDENT RICHMOND.

Snooze.

Andy Scheinman, one of the heads of Castle Rock, came to spend a couple of days with me. We got some stuff, but not a lot, and none of it splendid.

On the tenth of November I told Andy that one of three things would happen: (1) I would figure out how to do it and write it, or (2) I would realize I couldn't write it and bow out and they could bring in someone fast to replace me, or (3) we bring in someone now to help me figure out a way to make it work.

I was floundering terribly.

The Ghost and the Darkness was going and I had to get to South Africa, and part of the remains of my brain was trying to deal with changes for that.

I knew, generically, my problem: *I simply was too familiar with ABSOLUTE POWER*—I could not free my imagination.

And I was going nuts—every empty day meant Christmas was that much closer and I had to get it to Eastwood before then or lose him. Here is something most people don't understand: *you never get the fucking actor you want.*

I had a chance for Clint Eastwood in the Clint Eastwood part. *And I wanted that.*

November 15 and good news—maybe Frank Darabont would spitball with me. (Darabond had one of the great directing debuts with *The Shawshank Redemption* and wrote that remarkable script.)

Close—but he had other commitments.

November 25 and I haven't started.

And I am drowning.

That night the Knicks beat Houston. (I am—not even arguably—one

of the four all-time great Knicks fans.) But even better than the victory
was this: I took Tony Gilroy to the game.

Tony *(Dolores Claiborne, Extreme Measures)* is someone I have
known for thirty years, since he was ten, which was when I met and
interviewed his father, Frank, the Pulitzer Prize–winning playwright
(The Subject Was Roses) for a book I was writing about Broadway, *The
Season.*

"So what's with *Absolute Power*?" he asked politely; Tony had read
the first draft months and months before.

I know Tony well, so I unloaded. I told him I was panicked. I told him
of the impossibility of my ever sleeping again. I told him it was doubtful
I would live beyond the weekend. And all because this, you should pardon the expression, *actor* had come up with the idea of having Luther
live and bring down the President.

"That's great," Tony said.

At the moment, death by thumbscrew would have been letting him
off easy. "Why?"

"It's so obvious why—Luther's the best character. He's always been the
best character—and when he dies, he takes the movie down with him."

Kind of casually I asked, "You think you could figure out how to do
what Eastwood wants?"

He was intent on the game. "Haven't thought about it," he shrugged.
Then this: "But it shouldn't be hard."

That night I called Shafer and Tony was hired for a week.

The next morning he came blasting in—"I know where Luther goes
right after the robbery—he goes to see his daughter."

"Can't."

"Why do you say that?"

"They never talk. Baldacci is very clear on that in the novel. They
don't talk before the murder because they are estranged, and they can't
after because he's afraid the President will kill her—"

**"Forget about the novel—I haven't read the novel—my main strength
is that I haven't read the novel—*the novel is killing you.*"**

"They can't talk and that's that!"

"Think about it, for chrissakes."

Later that day, I not only thought about it, I wrote it. Here's the first
LUTHER-KATE scene:

CUT TO

A YOUNG WOMAN PARKING HER CAR--a high rocky area above

the Potomac. Below, a jogging path is visible, full
of runners.

THE YOUNG WOMAN gets out, locks her car, starts down a
narrow walk toward the joggers.

SHE'S IN HER MID-THIRTIES. Pretty. And there's something familiar about her.

CUT TO

LUTHER, standing by the edge of the jogging path,
studying the runners. Now he registers something: and
smiles.

CUT TO

THE WOMAN IN HER MID-THIRTIES as she comes jogging
along. She runs well.

CUT TO

LUTHER. An imperceptible straightening of his
clothes.

CUT TO

THE JOGGER. Now we realize who she is: the little girl
in the photo on LUTHER's dining room table. His
daughter, all grown up. Now her face registers something: his presence. And the instant she realizes
this, her eyes go down to the path, she increases her
speed, and runs right past him.

CUT TO

LUTHER.

                    LUTHER
        Kate.
                (she runs on)

Kate.
          (she slows, hesitates, stops.)

CUT TO

KATE, hands on hips, breathing deeply, moving to the
edge of the path as he approaches. The river flows behind them. Runners pass by.

Beat.

                    LUTHER
          Probably too late for me to take it up.
               (she says nothing--he
                gestures toward the path)
          The jogging.

                    KATE
          Ahh.

Beat.

                    LUTHER
          Dumb way to start this, I guess.

                    KATE
          For a man of your charm.

                    LUTHER
          Wanted to talk.

                    KATE
          About?

                    LUTHER
          Believe it or not, the weather.
               (she waits)
          Nights are starting to get cold.

                    KATE
          That happens this time of year.

CUT TO

LUTHER. He speaks quickly now, his voice low.

> ### LUTHER
> I was thinking of maybe relocating. Someplace
> with a kinder climate.
>> (nothing shows on her face)
>
> I just wanted to check it out with you first...
>> (still nothing)
>
> ...you're the only family I've got.
>> (and on that)

CUT TO

KATE. She speaks quickly now, her voice low.

> ### KATE
> Luther, you don't have me.

The last words he wanted to hear--

--but you can't tell from looking at him.

> ### KATE (cont'd)
> You were never there. Remember? You're talk-
> ing to the only kid during show-and-tell who
> got to talk about visiting day.

> ### LUTHER
> I'm talking permanent, you understand.

> ### KATE
> We don't see each other anyway--we haven't
> seen each other since Mom died and that's a
> year--
>> (a step toward him)
>
> --look, you chose your life. You had that
> right. You were never around for me. Well,
> fine. But I have no plans to be around for
> you.

And now she stops, turns away toward the path--

--LUTHER can say nothing, watches her--

--then she spins back--

>   KATE
>   (louder now)
>   --wait a minute--have you done something?--

>   LUTHER
>   --no--

>   KATE
>   --is that why you're here now?--are you active
>   again?

>   LUTHER
>   --<u>no</u>--

KATE moves in close now--

>   KATE
>   --I think you're lying--
>   (big)
>   Christ, Father, <u>what have you done</u>?--
>   (and on her words--)

CUT TO

CHRISTY SULLIVAN'S BODY in the bedroom of the mansion--

I don't think I can ever explain how freeing that scene was for me.

These two characters, whom I had been thinking about for six months and who had never been allowed to talk to each other, were suddenly ripping at each other. And there's all that emotional father-daughter stuff working under, because *you* know LUTHER knows if he doesn't run, the PRESIDENT will kill him—but he's willing to risk all that just to hear his only child ask him to stay.

I am aware we are not talking about a scene that will change the course of film history. But I was grateful to be able to write it. I think what I was dealing with was this: I started as a novelist, was a novelist for a decade before I ever saw a screenplay, and in part of my head at least, even though I haven't tried one in a dozen years now, I'm still a novelist. And I guess I never thought I would do that to another novelist, change everything. God knows it's been done to me—the novel *No Way to Treat a Lady,* for example, was based on this notion: What if there were *two* Boston Stranglers, and what if one of them got jealous of the other?

Guess what? In the movie, there's only one strangler. And I hated that they had done that.

Now here I was doing it.

And thank the Good Lord.

Tony came over for the next few days, always bringing ideas with him. LUTHER should have a safe house. If LUTHER is one of the great thieves of the world—and he is—there can't be too many like him, and law enforcement agencies must keep track of him—which meant SETH and LUTHER could meet without SETH doing a great deal of time-wasting detective work.

Most of all, Tony solved the ending—because the only person in the story who has the right to take revenge against PRESIDENT RICHMOND is the wronged husband, WALTER SULLIVAN. SULLIVAN is the reason RICHMOND made it to the White House, after all. In earlier versions, as in the novel, SULLIVAN is murdered by the Secret Service.

Guess what—not this time. He lives and he kills the PRESIDENT. SULLIVAN and LUTHER, two previously dead characters, bring down the most powerful man on earth. And JACK GRAHAM, the hero of the first draft?

Gone. Totally out of the picture.

On the fifteenth of December I was exhausted. But I was done. I sent the third draft of *Absolute Power* to California.

On the twenty-eighth of December, Eastwood said "yes" to playing LUTHER.

And right after that, I smashed my thumb.

I was closing the refrigerator door and forgot to pull my thumb away in time and I creamed myself and a blood blister formed beneath the nail and it took six months for the blister to work its way up, to finally disappear.

Every time I looked at it, I was glad—because it reminded me of two things: first, of my most difficult time as a screenwriter. Because I know if I don't take Tony to the Houston game, or if he can't come, maybe the movie of *Absolute Power* never happens. Certainly, I would no longer have been involved.

And second, and most important of all: the fragility of writing careers.

———

Working with Eastwood

First Meeting

Not entirely true. I had interviewed him nearly a decade earlier, for a book I was writing, *Hype and Glory,* about my experiences judging the Cannes Film Festival and the Miss America Contest. Eastwood's flick that year, *Bird,* was the outstanding directing achievement of the fortnight and I tried to win that honor for him, was outvoted. (*Bird,* in case you don't know, is one of the genuinely underrated films of the '80s and as good a movie about music as any. Ever.)

He was, as he is, gracious, gave me the time I needed. He was, as he approached sixty, very much a legend—

—and then here's what happened to him—

—*he got hot!*

In the Line of Fire, Unforgiven, A Perfect World, The Bridges of Madison County. Starred in all four, directed three, got a directing Oscar for one, all of them enormous successes, in America, yes, even more in the rest of the world.

Never a career like it. (Others have been up there longer, but not without gigantic career dips and slides.) Having said that, it still doesn't score to outsiders as it should. Maybe this will put it in perspective. He has been ranked the biggest box-office star five different times. Here are the performers who ranked second to him each year.

1993	Tom Cruise
1985	Eddie Murphy
1984	Bill Murray
1973	Ryan O'Neal
1972	George C. Scott

What I'm trying to tell you is this: we are not dealing with the guy who plays the butler.

He had decided in early January he would also direct *Absolute Power*. I fought mightily against this, lost the battle. (That was a joke, for any of you just in from distant lands.)

February was when we had our first script meeting. A couple of Castle Rock people and I drove over to Malpaso's offices on the Warner Brothers lot, Malpaso being Eastwood's production company. A lot of hits have come from there, and Hollywood people tend to be just a little ego-ridden about the positioning and size of their offices—sort of the West Coast equivalent of penis enlargement.

We walked into Malpaso. Tasteful. Fine. But by no means a spot where Jack Warner or Harry Cohn would have been happy. We were greeted by a young couple, Tom and Melissa Rooker. I assumed the rest of the Malpaso staff was elsewhere. Turned out I was wrong. *They* were the rest of the Malpaso staff. "He's in there," one of them said and pointed to a small office. And in there he was.

Better-looking somehow with age. In great shape—he watches what he eats, works out constantly. Hello hello hello, and we're ready to hack away at the script.

And I am, frankly, terrified. Because directors—even though we all know from the media's portrayals of them that they are men and women of wisdom and artistic vision, masters of the subtle use of symbolism—are more often than not a bunch of insecure lying assholes.

Over the decades I have been with so many who sniveled and crawled to get the job to do the movie I'd written and who once they got the job ditched everything and went to work on their own version.

Tattoo this behind your eyeballs: *directors have no vision.* Directors are like the rest of us—storytellers trying to get through the day, and somehow stay close to the fire.

One of the reasons the media gushes about them is this—they don't know shit about the movie business. They are filling columns or minutes for circulation or ratings. And since they want to feel important, the people they interview have to be fabulously important. The *hottest* young star, the *most brilliant* director. That kind of madness.

Let me tell you why I think there is this idiotic bilge that goes on about film directors—we think they are Merlin. And why? **Because they turn paper into celluloid.** Surely only a magician could do that.

In case you've forgotten, dear reader, I am still in the presence of my director and still terrified. Waiting for him to rip my script apart.

Silence.

"I guess I killed you," he says. "But it's good work."

I mutter something to the effect that I'm glad he felt it came out all right, then wait for the other shoe to drop. No screenwriter is unfamiliar with bullshit.

"The President's wife," Eastwood says then. "Could she be on a fact-finding mission while we're telling our story, so we don't have to wonder about her? That a problem?"

I shake my head. Not even close to being a problem. I wait.

"Could Kate be put in some jeopardy?" he asks then. "Might help. I thought they might try to get to Luther through his daughter."

I nodded. Kate, now and forever, would be in jeopardy.

Then there is this pause. And what I don't realize is this: the meeting is *over.*

Someone mentions casting thoughts and he grimaces. He *hates* casting. In fact he hates it so much he doesn't do it anymore. He just calls up people whose work he admires and asks if he could send them a script and would they read some part or other because he would like them in this picture he's directing. "If I saw actors, I sympathize with them so much I'd hire everybody. If an agent has someone new, I ask them to send me a tape. It seems to work out okay."

Now the grimace is gone and there is suddenly—for no reason—this great smile on his face. The reason I don't know the reason is my back is to the door and from behind me, this *baby* has pushed the door open, and come in. It is the Rookers' son, Jack, all of one, whom they bring to the office because Eastwood likes the kid wandering around. Jack holds out his arms, Eastwood lifts him, carries him along out to the car, where we say goodbye.

Every screenwriter should have one of those meetings before they die.

Shooting in Baltimore

I don't like being on the set for any number of reasons:

(1) it's just amazingly boring if you have nothing to do, and I have nothing to do because

(2) my work is done, not to mention

(3) I make the actors nervous, a serious problem but not as serious as

(4) I fuck up shots.

I am not trying to ingratiate myself with you here. This is not "colorful" behavior on my part. It's embarrassing, considering how long I've been at this and how many sets I've visited.

I always try to get out of the way. Usually what I manage is this: to get in the actors' sight line and destroy their concentration. When actors are performing in a movie, the last thing they need is additional distractions, like seeing a strange face staring back at them.

I also have a remarkable knack for hiding exactly where the shot is going to go. Example. As you read this, look straight ahead of you for a sec. Okay, that's where the actors are acting. So what I do is head in the opposite direction, usually a corner behind the camera—

—forgetting, of course, that the actors are going to move on this shot. And the camera, of course, will move along with them.

To where I'm hiding.

It is so awful when this happens. And I am not pretending it happens on every shot. But it's rare I don't do it at least once every morning.

The worst thing I've ever done was on *The Princess Bride*. During the Fire Swamp sequence.

For those of you who don't know, and how dare you not, Buttercup and Westley are being pursued by her fiancé, Prince Humperdinck. They are forced to go through the Fire Swamp, not easy—no one has ever come out of it alive.

One of the dangers in the Fire Swamp is the flame spurts.

These unexpected streaks of flame happen there and when I wrote the novel, well, Buttercup and Westley are making their way through the place, and suddenly flames—her dress is on fire.

Westley saves her.

In all the endless screenplay versions, same deal. Buttercup and Westley are making their way through the place, and suddenly flames—her dress is on fire.

Westley saves her.

Okay. Pinewood Studios. The glorious Norman Garwood Fire Swamp set. This is my dream come true, watching this baby happen, and you can bet I am tense, but for me, kind of almost happy.

Okay. Roll of drums, please.

Rob Reiner says "Action" and now here comes Cary Elwes as Westley leading my beloved Robin Wright as Buttercup into the Fire Swamp and they are making their way through the place—

—and suddenly flames—

—and *I* scream out loud, "Her dress is on fire!"

The shot is obviously ruined. Rob says "Cut," Robin's dress is made flame-free, the actors go back to their positions. And Andy Scheinman, Rob's partner, sidles over to me and says quietly, "Bill, try and remember this time—*her dress is supposed to be on fire.*"

———

I made no mistakes watching Eastwood. I think he might have killed me if I had. With a look. But there was another reason I was safe—

—*the speed of it.*

It was the fastest, the most professional operation I've ever seen. You couldn't get ahead of it to screw it up. His crew has been with him since *Birth of a Nation* and if one of them drops by the wayside, well, either his son or his assistant or someone else familiar with how it works moves into place. He had brought *Bridges of Madison County* in way under budget. We were talking of that once and he said, "Don't tell anybody that—they don't want to hear about efficiency out here."

I had watched him and Ed Harris do a take of their cat-and-mouse scene over coffee, which they got through in one take. Not surprising with him. He is noted for saying to performers, "Would you try to just do your speech and don't mind us, we're just trying to get the lighting right." So the actor does the speech, only the camera has been rolling so the rehearsal is the take and then quickly on to the next.

They were setting up for another angle of the cat-and-mouse scene and Harris went off by himself, sipped coffee, while Eastwood just walked here, there, always glancing back to his crew to see if they were ready yet and *how much longer*?

As I watched him pace I went back thirty years to the other great professional star of my career, Paul Newman, and we were shooting a scene from *Butch Cassidy*. We were halfway through the schedule, the Old West part finished and fine, now a week in Los Angeles before heading down to Mexico for the South American sequences.

There was a wonderful feel in the air.

Shooting up in Utah had gone well, on schedule, and here in Los Angeles, right after lunch, the crew was setting up for the scene, I don't remember which exactly, maybe Newman's close-up where he tells Redford how he always wanted to be a hero and Redford says too late now and Newman is hurt because he knows it's true.

Doesn't matter, the point is that it's after a long lunch, on a movie where everyone is feeling pretty loose, and the crew is taking its time getting things set for the next scene, getting the lighting right, getting everything in just the right position—

—and *slappp*—

—and the crew is taking its time, making sure the lighting is right and everything is where it should be—

—and *slapppp!*

Now the crew hears this sound, and a few of them stop, trying to trace what it is, where it's coming from—

—and *slappp!*

—and *SLAPPP!*

And now we all saw him. Pacing as Eastwood paced. Newman, that least demanding of the great stars. He is **clapping his hands sharply,** and he does not do that to draw attention to himself, and you can see from his face he is trying to concentrate on what he has to do and this is an important scene for him and he wants to get it right, but his concentration is leaving him—

—not one fucking sound on the set now.

And quietly, this: "Could you help me, please, I'd like to get this done."

And the crew, roadrunners all now, finished their work, watched while he nailed his take.

The crew was ready. A nod from the cinematographer. Back Eastwood and Harris went. This shot included the lady serving them coffee from behind the counter.

Before they start, Eastwood turns to the lady, who has no lines, and he asks if she is comfortable, is this okay for her.

She was comfortable indeed.

Now lunch break.

The shooting was in a museum and lunch was a block away, in an empty store the company had rented for the duration of the stay and turned into a cafeteria.

Eastwood exited the museum, where a car was waiting to drive him the block. He shook his head, crossed the street, started alone up the sidewalk. I followed. I do that. I once saw Jimmy Cagney get off *the crosstown bus* on East Fifty-seventh Street and start walking with a friend. I forget what I was doing there but whatever it was, nothing on earth was as important to me right then as seeing that man in the flesh, with that walk, the lilt, the whole great package.

I am not alone in following my favorites. Years back—we are in the '50s now—a young girl had finished college and had come to Magic Town and was given the most incredible bit of information—

Greta Garbo's address.

This is incredible because of something you don't know—this young woman is the world's great Garbo fan. I remember her telling me, the night she found out, that she was going to follow her dream the next morning.

The next night when I saw her she was in terrible shape—exhausted, arms scratched, legs too. What happened was this: she had been told that Garbo took a walk every morning at such and such a time, but what she had not been told was that when Garbo walked, she *walked*.

Long strides to Central Park and then she really let it go. And this friend, small and totally unprepared, chased after her, up hills and down, through thickets and out, until she sank to a bench, crushed, never to traipse after the great Swede again.

I saw Garbo twice myself. Once at Christmas near Eighty-sixth and Second Avenue. Late afternoon. A bunch of us were waiting to cross when I glanced around, saw her. She saw me, too. And then her eyes *flashed* and there was an imperceptible shake of her head and I knew she meant please don't make a commotion. I nodded, watched her walk on, unnoticed in the Manhattan crowd.

The other time I was with a young woman and it was on a side street near Garbo's apartment and she was walking along with a woman with an eyepatch. Garbo and her friend moved by, and once they were gone I said to the lady I was with, "Did you see that?" and she said, "Yes, wow, a lady with an eyepatch."

Anyway, there is Clint on the Baltimore sidewalk, lunch hour, people streaming past him. Me a half dozen steps behind. Now this thing starts to happen. A real-life double take. Numberless Baltimoreans move past this lone mid-sixties guy. No reaction. Another step. They look at one another, start to say something like, "That guy remind you of . . . ?"

Naww.

Another step. Now they are staring at one another, turning quickly back. Then they stop.

Dead on the sidewalk.

Holy shit.

Then they spin.

It's *him*. He's *here*. *Dirty Harry walks amongst us.*

Back they all scurry and he is gracious, always that, soft-spoken, that too, and he nods to them and smiles back at them and if they give him something to sign, why, of course, he signs it—

—*but he never stops walking.* They would have had him then.

He reaches the cafeteria, nods courteously a final time, then goes inside, gets in line for his tray—

—let me say that again for those of you new to the entertainment business—*he gets in line for his tray*—waits in line for his food, then goes to a table and has his meal, just like anybody else.

I believe what has kept Eastwood (and Newman) on top all these years is somehow they have clung to the truth: that in spite of their fame, in spite of our millions of spins toward them, they *are* just like anybody else.

Shooting in Los Angeles

It is the first of August now and I am Out There with Stephen Hopkins, on the mixing stage for *The Ghost and the Darkness*. (Every time I am near anything remotely resembling a mixing stage, I am so glad I decided, decades past, when offers started coming, that I never wanted to be a film director.)

And then, casually, I asked him if he wanted to go to the next stage. Why would he want to do that? he asked, and I told him that Mr. Eastwood was directing there. We hotfooted it over, said our hellos. I hope you will forgive me for this totally punch line-less anecdote but I thought it was pretty neat, having two movies grinding forward on contiguous stages.

Hopkins had to go back to his torment and I found myself talking, for the first time in my life, with Gene Hackman. (I had written his previous movie, *The Chamber*—a total wipeout disaster, although not his fault or mine, and the reason I left it out of this *Adventures* section is, while it was a terrible experience, it wasn't a very interesting one, and besides, I never saw the movie and neither did anyone else, so no one would give a shit. This kind of thing happens in the picture business—meeting someone even though you "worked together" before—where not only do writers get fired by failed directors, but the relay-race nature of the operation means that you only meet people who work the same time you do. And since writers are there at the start, and composers, say, are there at the end, I am not all that familiar with anyone who has ever scored a film I've been involved with.)

At any rate, Hackman and I are talking and then Eastwood comes over. I note, meaninglessly, that we are all kind of tall, unusual in Hollywood. Eastwood says, quietly, "We're ready for you, Gene." Hackman leaves us and Eastwood says how much he loves working with Hackman. I ask why Hackman in particular. "Because I never have to give him direction," Eastwood replied. Then he said this:

"I like working with actors who don't have anything to prove."

Wonderful line, that.

The shot has been set up. Hackman, as President Richmond, is still blind drunk in the bedroom. Scott Glenn plays the Secret Service man,

Burton, who, along with his partner, Collin, has just shot the woman dead. The scene was written like this:

```
              RICHMOND
     Kill her?
              (COLLIN, by the body, nods)


               BURTON
     No choice in the matter.
              (His words are efficient but
               clearly, he has been rocked.)

CUT TO

RICHMOND, staring stupidly at the letter opener.  He
drops it back to the floor, tries to stand, can't.

BURTON helps him back to bed.

Which is when he passes out cold.
```

Hackman is getting comfortable, lying on the bed. Scott Glenn waits in position. Hackman is the Gene Hackman we all know—then, suddenly, with nothing happening at all, he is blind drunk. Which is when Eastwood says softly, "Go when you want, Gene."

A pause.

Then he gets it dead solid perfect.

Eastwood says softly, "Thank you very much," and we are on to the next setup.

Look, I'm not praising his speed here. (We were nine days ahead of schedule at this point.) That's just the way he works. Partially because he can't stand waste, partially because what he wants more than anything on earth is to finish and get out to the golf course.

But what was so wonderful for me, after all these years, was the sheer professionalism. He is really the Mr. Abbott of the movie business. Being around the atmosphere he creates, I actually felt good about being in the picture business.

It can be so awful. The ego-ridden stars inflicting their inadequacies on the rest of us. (John Cleese, a friend, once made this observation: "Stars seem to think that their problems are more important than anything else on earth and must take precedence over everything.") The terror-stricken executives, in whose mouths the truth is so often a foreign object. The directors, panicked that you will find out how truly small their talent is. So they punish and fire, confident that the executives are too paralyzed to do anything about it.

Absolute Power is not a great movie.

But for me it was a great experience.

II.
Heffalumps!!!

"I saw a Heffalump today, Piglet."
"What was it doing?" asked Piglet.
"Just lumping along," said Christopher Robin.

For reasons lost to time, I have always thought of screenplays as being like Heffalumps, these strangely shaped *things* that no one really knows much about, such as what they look like, or are *supposed* to look like, or actually what they *do* (especially if aroused).

I think most people are intimidated by the way screenplays look when they first see them. (I know I was.) Now I read them as easily as fiction, as do most people in the business. It just requires a little familiarity.

In this section, you're going to look at six movie scenes you already know, starting with Peter and Bobby Farrelly's Zipper Scene from *There's Something About Mary* and Nora Ephron's Orgasm Scene from *When Harry Met Sally*. These, and the others you'll come to, are in different styles and come at different points in their respective movies, but what they all do, brilliantly, is thicken and improve the story.

I picked these scenes because I find them among the best I've read. I also talked to most of the writers about their scenes, how they came about, all kinds of good stuff.

Enough. We are now going to examine some Heffalumps.

And try not to be intimidated by how they look. Maybe even, if we're lucky, get comfortable having them around.

First, I'm going to ask a favor from you now, and this is it:
(1)—turn to the next page, glance at it—but *don't read it*.
(2)—then go right on to the page after that.
Got it? Turn. Glance. Go on. Okay, show me what you're made of.

Whose woods these are I think I know.
His house is in the village, though;
He will not see me stopping here
To watch his woods fill up with snow.

My little horse must think it queer
To stop without a farmhouse near
Between the woods and frozen lake
The darkest evening of the year.

He gives his harness bells a shake
To ask if there is some mistake.
The only other sound's the sweep
Of easy wind and downy flake.

The woods are lovely, dark, and deep,
But I have promises to keep,
And miles to go before I sleep,
And miles to go before I sleep.

All right, class, what was it?

A description of a snowy place somewhere? I think that's a proper answer, but it's not what I'm looking for. A dissertation on loneliness by Robert Frost? I won't argue, but still, not for me. One of the literary masterpieces of the century? I'd go along with that, too, but here's the answer I want:

It's a poem.

And why?

Because it looks *like a poem.*

Read it again. Here it is:

> Whose woods these are I think I know.
> His house is in the village, though;
> He will not see me stopping here
> To watch his woods fill up with snow.
>
> My little horse must think it queer
> To stop without a farmhouse near
> Between the woods and frozen lake
> The darkest evening of the year.
>
> He gives his harness bells a shake
> To ask if there is some mistake.
> The only other sound's the sweep
> Of easy wind and downy flake.
>
> The woods are lovely, dark, and deep,
> But I have promises to keep,
> And miles to go before I sleep,
> And miles to go before I sleep.

Still a (wonderful) poem, isn't it? Why are we so sure? Because we're *familiar* with the form. We have been looking at poems our entire life on earth.

> Mary had a little lamb
> Its fleece was white as snow.
> And everywhere that Mary went,
> The lamb was sure to go.

The Frost poem rhymes. So does the story of Mary and her lamb. Many poems do. But they don't have to.

Here's one of my favorites, an all-timer, Johnny D. on a hot streak.

No man is an island, entire of itself; every man is a piece of the continent, a part of the main; if a clod be washed away by the sea, Europe is the less, as well as if a promontory were, as well as if a manor of thy friends or of thine own were; any man's death diminishes me, because I am involved in mankind; and therefore never send to know for whom the bell tolls; it tolls for thee.

The Donne, besides being so gorgeous, says a lot, at least to me, about the human condition, or, if that's too phony for a book on screenwriting, then about the way we live now. The creating of beautiful images is a huge weapon for any poet. But Sappho says a good deal about life on earth in just six words, none of them lush with imagery.

> Pain penetrates
>
> Me drop
> by drop

Tough to be heartbreaking in six words. How did she do it? Here's another strange-looking poem, somehow just as heartbreaking. (My father drank.)

> I want to go on the wagon. Really
> I want to, but I like it,
> I like it, and I can't, really,
> I mean I can but
> I won't.

Not all poems are heartbreaking, obviously, and obviously not all are short. (Peek at Dante if you want proof.) But all poems have one thing in common. Probably you've forgotten from your courses in Basic Lit.

POETRY IS COMPRESSION.

Long, short, doesn't matter, rhyming, not, the same. All the rest, the same. Except if you can tell me *everything* a poem says more briefly than the poem does, then it isn't much of a poem.

This next is a poem by E. A. Robinson that had a devastating effect on me. I think I was probably ten or eleven when I came across it, and I didn't know poems could do this, y'see, tell a story I'd be interested in, because I was a sports nut then and only interested in games. You probably know "Richard Cory," but if you don't, let the last line surprise you, as it did me. If you want to read it out loud, that's not a bad idea.

> Whenever Richard Cory went down town
> We people on the pavement looked at him:
> He was a gentleman from sole to crown,
> Clean favored, and imperially slim.
>
> And he was always quietly arrayed,
> And he was always human when he talked;
> But still he fluttered pulses when he said,
> "Good morning," and he glittered while he walked.
>
> And he was rich—yes, richer than a king—
> And admirably schooled in every grace:
> In fine, we thought that he was everything
> To make us wish that we were in his place.
>
> So on we worked, and waited for the light,
> And went without the meat, and cursed the bread;
> And Richard Cory, one calm summer night,
> Went home and put a bullet through his head.

That last line, the suicide, is a big moment in my life. I was going along, reading the story about this Cory, and he was a rich guy, and I figured he lived in a big house near this town he walked in, but he wasn't some snob, he spoke to anybody and everybody he met along the way, and I liked that about him.

I didn't know what "fine" meant when it says "in fine," but I didn't let that bother me. It was probably an assignment in school and I knew it couldn't take too long because I could see the end of the poem when I started reading it—still a huge plus for intellectual me.

Anyway, I knew it was a bad time in the town, money scarce, but this Cory was such a terrific guy *they didn't resent him.* They wanted to *be* him, sure, but who wouldn't, this wonderful guy born to money but not conceited or anything, in a time of pain and suffering, who wouldn't want to be him? You could do what you wanted if you were him, you could leave your lights on all night long in every room of your house if you were him, you could eat the best of whatever the grocer or the butcher had to sell, not just bread and bread and more bread and—

—and then the suicide.

Whoa.

I'm this kid, remember, and what I did was, I knew I had gotten it wrong somehow, missed his pain, so I went back up to the first line and I put my finger under the words and went verrrrry slowly, saying them out loud as my finger moved, and I read that first sentence and what it told me was that Cory was a very big deal when he took his walks. Everybody looked at him, he was so rich and so well dressed and so, well, gorgeous.

So this great guy takes a walk. I had the first sentence nailed.

Second sentence, more of the same, talked to people, a decent down-to-earth millionaire who was so special he *glittered.*

Third sentence, we find out he wasn't just rich, he was richer than a king. And we know he's human and kind but by now I get it: he's *perfect.* No wonder we want to be that guy.

I'm ten or eleven, remember, looking for where I goofed, and I start the last stanza—but now I knew the kicker—this Cory is going to blow his brains out. And first line, no clue, we're working and waiting for light; second line, it's worse, we're cursing our bread, which is what life has chosen for us, and then those last two lines, boom, end, and I thought, that's the most amazing story I ever heard, this wonderful fabulous guy who had everything, every-single-thing, and couldn't take it anymore.

I don't think I knew I wanted to be a storyteller then—Irwin Shaw was the sea change for me a few years down the line. But later, when Shaw gave me the guts to think I might somehow possibly give it a try, one of the thoughts I had then was, Jesus, to be able to tell a story as great as Richard Cory's, what a thing that would be. I still think that. Hope you do too.

Poems can also, thank God, make us laugh. Here's Nash's "Reflections on Ice Breaking." One of the famous short poems of the century.

> Candy   But liquor
> Is dandy   Is quicker.

Here's another not so famous but for me, funnier. Dorothy Parker, bitching about life as only she could.

> A single flow'r he sent me, since we met.
>   All tenderly his messenger he chose;
> Deep-hearted, pure, with scented dew still wet—
>   One perfect rose.
>
> I knew the language of the floweret;
>   "My fragile leaves," it said, "his heart enclose."
> Love long has taken for his amulet
>   One perfect rose.
>
> Why is it no one has ever sent me yet
>   One perfect limousine, do you suppose?
> Ah no, it's always just my luck to get
>   One perfect rose.

You will be thrilled to know that poetry class is now over. But I have another favor to ask—*glance back at them.*

Really take a minute and I think you'll be surprised again at the way they look on the page, how different from one another. But we're not afraid of them, we know they won't hurt us, they're just, well, these words put down in a particular way to have a particular effect.

Well, so are screenplays.

They won't hurt you either. Screenplays *can* make you laugh *and* cry, they can shock and soothe and frighten the shit out of you and make you ache for the love always just out of reach. Screenplays can make a studio head reach for his checkbook and spend a hundred million dollars. Screenplays can make directors and production designers erect entire cities. They can make stars say yes and thereby change forever the lives of the writers who made the story come alive.

But too many of us are still way too wary. We were *not* read them as children trying to go to sleep. (And if your family *did* read them to you, I don't want to know about it.)

Get ready now. Here comes the Zipper Scene from *There's Something About Mary*. Why did I rate *Mary* so highly? Because it's so funny, sure, but more than that, because it made me care more than anything else in '98. And these days, caring more is all I care about . . .

There's Something About Mary

by Ed Decter & John J. Strauss and Peter Farrelly & Bobby Farrelly

We ended with a couple of funny poems, so we're starting with a couple of funny scenes. I wrote in a *Premiere* article that I thought *There's Something About Mary* was the best movie of 1998. The Academy, in its infinite wisdom, ignored it totally, partially because it has always ignored the two kinds of movies that are hardest to get right—comedies and adventure films.

Peter and Bobby Farrelly are the youngest of the screenwriters in this section. Their credits, prior to this, were *Kingpin* and *Dumb and Dumber* and lots of TV they sold that was never shot. I have read their latest effort, *Me Myself and Irene,* which stars Jim Carrey as a cop with a split personality and Renee Zellwegger as a girl trying to deal with her boyfriend(s) problems. I don't make predictions, but if it is not a tremendous success it will mean the world will have ended.

Brothers, early forties, the Farrellys live and work in Providence, about a mile from each other. Married with families, they meet five days a week around noon, work till six or later, alternate on who types.

Ed Decter and John J. Strauss, TV writers and friends of theirs, had written the original screenplay of *Mary,* suffered through endless years in development hell. The earlier script began with a guy wondering what had happened to his high school love, then hiring a detective to find out. The detective finds her, falls in love with her too, and lies that she is fat with many children. That notion was something to hang on to, the Farrellys felt.

And they took it from there.

When they were wondering what kind of tragic thing could happen to the guy who hires the detective, help came from an unexpected source. Years before, one of their sisters had given a party, and a cool guy who

was there got his dick caught in his zipper. We are talking twelve-year-
olds, remember, and after an hour or so, their father, who is a doctor,
and their mother, a nurse, were aware that a guest had been in the
upstairs bathroom for a very long time.

They went in, the father freed him, and they drove the kid home,
telling everyone he had taken sick.

And never told anyone.

Then, a couple of years ago, their father came clean, and they realized
that someday they would have to try and work that into a movie.

The character of Ted was Ben Stiller, playing seventeen, with braces
Szell would have been proud of. Cameron Diaz—do I have to tell you
Cameron Diaz played Mary?—well she did, also at seventeen. Ted has
come to pick Mary up for the prom, there's been a scuffle with her
brother, Warren, who is retarded. Mary needs a strap fixed so she heads
upstairs with her mom. Ted has a bleeding lip that needs tending. So he
makes the famous request to Mary's dad about using the bathroom.

A few final explanations. Screenplays are written, like plays, in a kind
of shorthand. Stage directions, that kind of stuff. We all tend to settle on
our own *particular* stuff. The few you might not know are these:

INT. means we are looking at something interior.

EXT. means we are outside.

POV. means point of view.

(O.S.) means offscreen. You are hearing someone talk, but not seeing
the speaker.

SNAP FOCUS. I never used it but I assume it means when something
vague suddenly goes to a very sharp image.

The rest you can figure out for yourself.

The Zipper Scene

                    TED
               (to Mary's Dad)
         May I use your bathroom?

INT. BATHROOM--TWILIGHT

TED dabs his head with a tissue, then moves to the toilet. As he TAKES A LEAK he glances out the window to
his left.

TED's POV--two LOVEBIRDS are perched in a branch,

Ted smiles...

...at the SOUND of these beautiful tweeties singing their love song for themselves, for the spring, for Ted and Mary, and suddenly they fly away and we...

SNAP FOCUS...

...to reveal MARY in the bedroom window DIRECTLY BE-HIND WHERE THE BIRDS WERE, in just a bra and panties, and just then her mother glances TED's way and MAKES EYE CONTACT with what she can only presume to be a leering Peeping Tom.

ON TED...

...loses the smile and ducks his head back into the bathroom, HORRIFIED.

PANICKING NOW, he hastily zips up his fly and

                 TED
    YEEEOOOOOWWWWWW!!!!!!!!!!!

TED GETS HIS DICK STUCK IN THE ZIPPER!

CUT TO:

EXT. BATHROOM DOOR--NIGHT

A concerned MARY, her MOM, DAD, and WARREN are huddled outside the bathroom.

                MARY
         (knocking gently)
   Ted, are you okay?

                    TED (O.S.)
              (pained)
         Just a minute.

                    MARY'S MOM
         He's been in there over half an hour.
              (whispering)
         Charlie, I think he's masturbating.

                    MARY
         Mom!

                    MARY'S MOM
         Well, he was watching you undress with a silly
         grin on his face.

                    TED (O.S.)
              (pained)
         I was watching the birds.

They all look at each other.

                    MARY'S MOM
         Charlie, do something.

                    MARY'S DAD
         All right, kid, that's it, I'm coming in.

INT. BATHROOM--CONTINUOUS

A whimpering TED huddles in the corner as MARY'S DAD
enters.

                    MARY'S DAD
         What seems to be the situation here? You shit
         yourself or something?

                    TED
         I wish.

TED motions for him to close the door and MARY'S DAD
obliges.

>   TED (CONT'D)
>   I, uh...I got stuck.

>   MARY'S DAD
>   You got what stuck?

>   TED
>   It.

>   MARY'S DAD
>   It?
>   (beat)
>   Oh it. All right, these things happen, let me
>   have a look, it's not the end of the world.

MARY'S DAD moves closer and puts his reading glasses
on.

EXT. BATHROOM DOOR--CONTINUOUS

As MARY, her MOM, and WARREN listen in.

>   MARY'S DAD (O.S.)
>   OH FOR THE LOVE OF GOD!

>   TED (O.S.)
>   Shhhhhh!

INT. BATHROOM--CONTINUOUS

>   MARY'S DAD
>   (calls out)
>   Shirley, get in here! You gotta see this!

>   TED
>   What?! No please, sir--

                    MARY'S DAD
         She's a dental hygienist. She'll know what to
         do.

MARY'S MOM comes in and closes the door behind her.

                    MARY'S MOM
         Teddy, hon, are you okay?
                    (moving closer, seeing the
                     situation)
         OH HEAVENS TO PETE!

                    TED
         Would you shhh! Mary's going to hear us.

                    MARY'S MOM
         Just relax, dear. Now, um...what exactly are
         we looking at here?

                    TED
                    (dizzy)
         What do you mean?

                    MARY'S MOM
                    (delicate)
         I mean is it...is it...?

                    MARY'S DAD
                    (gruff)
         Is it the franks or the beans?

                    TED
         I think a little of both.

Suddenly we hear WARREN from outside the door:

                    WARREN (O.S.)
         Franks and beans!

Ted hangs his head.

EXT. BATHROOM DOOR--CONTINUOUS

MARY and WARREN are huddled outside the door.

> MARY
> (to WARREN)
> Shhhh.

> MARY'S DAD (O.S.)
> What the hell's that bubble?

MARY reacts to this.

INT. BATHROOM--CONTINUOUS

> TED
> One guess.

> MARY'S DAD
> How the hell'd you get the beans all the way up
> top like that?

> TED
> I don't know, it's not like it was a well
> thought-out plan.

> MARY'S MOM
> Oh my, there sure is a lot of skin coming
> through there.

> MARY'S DAD
> I'm guessing that's what the soprano shriek
> was about, pumpkin.

> MARY'S MOM
> I'm going to get some Bactine.

> TED
> No, please!

Suddenly a POLICE OFFICER sticks his head in the bathroom window.

> POLICE OFFICER
> Ho there.

> TED
> (humiliated)
> Oh God.

> POLICE OFFICER
> Everything okay here? Neighbors said they
> heard a lady scream.

> MARY'S DAD
> You're looking at him. C'mere and take a look
> at this beauty.

> TED
> No. That's really unneces--

But the OFFICER's already climbing in the window.
Once inside, he turns his flashlight on TED and WHIS-
TLES.

> POLICE OFFICER
> Now I've seen it all. What the hell were you
> thinking?

> TED
> (frustrated)
> I wasn't trying--

> POLICE OFFICER
> Is that bubble what I think it is?

MARY'S PARENTS nod.

>   POLICE OFFICER (CONT'D)
> But...how...how'd you get the zipper all the
> way to the top?

>   MARY'S DAD
> Let's just say the kid's limber.

The POLICE OFFICER makes a face, then rolls up his sleeves.

>   POLICE OFFICER
> Well, there's only one thing to do.

>   TED
> No, no, no, I'll be fine. I'll just hang my
> shirttail out and work on it in the morning.

>   POLICE OFFICER
> Look, son, this will only hurt for a second.

The OFFICER reaches down and takes hold of the zipper.

>   TED
> No, no, please!

>   MARY'S MOM
> Teddy, be brave.

>   WARREN (O.S.)
> Beans and franks!

>   MARY (O.S.)
> Warren, shhh.

Defeated, TED holds his breath and braces for the worst.

>   POLICE OFFICER
> It's just like pulling off a Band-Aid. A-one
> and a-two and...

CUT TO:

                        PARAMEDIC
     We got a bleeder!

EXT.--MARY'S HOUSE--NIGHT

TWO PARAMEDICS rush TED out the front door on a
stretcher. MARY runs alongside him, holding a towel
on his crotch, while a THIRD PARAMEDIC dabs at his
crotch with a towel. MARY'S MOM and DAD are out front
along with two FIRE TRUCKS, four POLICE CARS, and a
crowd of about thirty NEIGHBORS.

                        PARAMEDIC
                    (To MARY)
     Keep pressure on it!

MARY does as she's told.

                        MARY
                    (running along)
     Ted, I'm so sorry. Are you going to be okay?

                        TED
                    (irrational cockiness)
     You betcha!

He gives her two thumbs up as they slide him into the
ambulance.

INT. AMBULANCE--CONTINUOUS

The doors SLAM shut and as the ambulance pulls away,
TED starts to WHIMPER and we can see MARY fade into the
night...

                    _____

  A great comedy scene.
  Let me ask you something—what's *your* favorite moment? Here are
three of mine. This for openers:

                              TED
          YEEEOOOOOWWWWWW!!!!!!!!!!

And this:

                         MARY'S MOM
          I'm going to get some Bactine.

She's a dental hygienist, right, of course she'd head for the Bactine.
Do you know how much that would hurt?
And:

                              TED
          I don't know, it's not like it was a well
          thought-out plan.

I just love the character for being able to come up with, in that situation, a line of that quality.

I think this is the scene that makes the movie.

Look, there is, as we all know, no "best" anything. Never forget that
in the eighteenth century, the leading literary critics felt the greatest
writers *of all time* were Homer, Sophocles, and Richardson.

This movie hits me as hard as it does because I am—as so many of
us are—Ben Stiller. Taller, sure, and I never wore braces, but my high
school days involved living with a deaf mother who told me I caused her
deafness, only releasing the truth, that I had nothing to do with it, when
she was dying, and a drunken father who stayed in his second-floor
room for four years, only venturing out to pledge sobriety, a ruse for his
driving to the liquor store for another long supply. And you get through
that fine, you tell yourself you're lucky, a lot of people have it worse.
And, boy, do they. I had a nice house, there was Minnie who worked for
my family and cared if I survived, and how many people get to go to
Bears games or camp in the summertime? But I couldn't bring friends
home, not with that secret on the second floor, and I didn't date, because
who would go out with me, and my schoolwork went to shit and I
stayed home a year faking sickness and as I lay there what I thought of
was how beautiful *she* was going to be, and how good our life together.

You think I didn't root for Ben to win Cameron Diaz?

The Farrellys think it's *another* scene that makes the movie.

Peter Farrelly says, "It was where Matt Dillon comes back and he
says—wow, she's grown heavy and she's on welfare and she's got kids

and she's got all sorts of problems and we show Ben go home that night and he thinks about it and comes back the next day and says, '*I still want to meet her.*' And he says maybe he can help her out, I can't let it go.

"Because that's true love. Anybody could fall in love with Cameron Diaz. Come on, you see Cameron Diaz and you'd want to chase her fifteen years. Why root for that? You know, who wouldn't? But even when he thought she was a whale and she was on welfare, and had a bunch of kids out of wedlock, he *still* wanted her because he was in love with her. And so at that point, the audience says—*he deserves it.* And that, I think, is why it works."

Understand something—movie scenes, like scenes from plays, are not finally intended for the page. They were written with actors and directors very much in mind. In fiction, the novelist or short story writer is your sole companion and you view his world through his eyes. Same with a poet.

On the printed page, the explosive quality of the Zipper Scene can never totally come across. (The second time I saw it, I thought the man in front of me was literally going to die before it was over.)

But you can tell on even one reading that the quality is there.

Most brilliant movie writing tends to be ignored by the critics.

For many reasons, the writer traditionally has been ignored when it comes to kudos. Very few of us get away with it. Callie Khouri did on *Thelma and Louise*, Bob Towne with *Chinatown*, me with *Butch*. But we are not favored by the media. We do not get sent out to do television talk shows. That you expect. What's hard is when stars—who for the most part write as well as most six-year-olds—say they make up their parts. (I would love to have Conan or Jay ask to see a star's screenplay, then read it on the air.) And directors rarely take less than all the credit they can get.

You must deal with that as your career goes on. It ain't gonna change. But the media must love someone. If Steven Spielberg had directed the Zipper Scene, all the critics you've ever heard of would have written something along these lines: "After all these years of thrilling us with dramatic adventures, who would have guessed his genius could move so easily to farce. There is no end to the man's talents. You can feel his touch behind every line of dialogue. More, Steven, please."

If James Cameron had been behind the camera, the huzzahs would have been of this order: "Of course he is a master of size, of special effects, but who would have guessed the man was also a comic genius. There were hints of this wit in some earlier work—especially *Aliens*—but here he just lets it fly. Next, George Bernard Shaw? Please, James."

The fact is that both these wonderfully gifted directors are as helpless as Jo-Jo the Dog-faced Boy when given anything remotely connected with laughter. But the *Mary* scene is so good, someone has to get credit for it. Couldn't have been the writer, could it now?

Why Do We Write?

I write out of revenge.

I write to balance the teeter-totter of my childhood. Graham Greene once said one of the great things: **an unhappy childhood is a writer's gold mine.**

I have no idea if my early years were unhappy or not, since I have childhood amnesia (not as uncommon as you might think). Zero memories of my first six years of life. Oh, I've been told things that happened, there are family photos of this or that, but it's all secondhand.

I once went to see a shrink who specialized in regression. I am, it turns out, surprisingly hypnotizable. But we decided there was no reason to proceed, since my life was going along without more than the usual amount of bad stuff.

But I'll bet if I had gone visiting, it would have been dark down there.

I was a novelist for a decade before I began this madness known as screenwriting, and someone pointed out to me that the most sympathetic characters in my books always died miserably. I didn't consciously know I was doing that. I didn't. I mean, I didn't wake up each morning and think, today I think I'll make a really terrific guy *so I can kill him.* It just worked out that way.

I haven't written a novel in over a decade—although I hope to have a hand in *Buttercup's Baby* soon—and someone very wise suggested that I might have stopped writing novels because my rage was gone. It's possible.

All this doesn't mean a helluva lot, except probably there is a reason I was the guy who gave Babe over to Szell in the

"Is is safe?" scene and that I was the guy who put Westley into The Machine.

I think I have a way with pain. When I come to that kind of sequence I have a certain confidence that I can make it play. Because I come from such a dark corner. I wonder if there is any connection between why you write and what you write well.

Anyway, you know my m.o., think about yours.

When Harry Met Sally

by Nora Ephron

I have known Nora Ephron a quarter century, but it was not love at first sight. She was dating Carl Bernstein when I first met her, in Washington in '74, and I was trying to figure out the story for the movie of Bernstein and Bob Woodward's Watergate book, *All the President's Men*.

What Nora and Carl did was write their version of my screenplay and present it to Robert Redford, the producer, without my knowledge. It was the worst experience of my movie career (see *Adventures in the Screen Trade* for the gorier details). We both live in New York, didn't cross paths often, but once, a few years after her betrayal, we happened to be at the same dinner party, one with placecards yet, and I still remember my feeling of triumph when I caught her shifting cards so she and I would not be near each other.

Then, I don't remember really, a decade back, maybe a few years more, we were again at a gathering and she came over and said, "I'm really sorry," and I hugged her and that was forever that.

She is very famous now, perhaps the most successful woman director in the world (*Sleepless in Seattle, Michael, You've Got Mail,* among others). But she has *always* been famous, odd for a writer. Before movies, her novel *Heartburn* headed all the lists. She was well known when she first came to town, as a journalist. *Wallflower at the Orgy,* her first book of essays, established her, thirty years back.

Her folks were in the business, too, Phoebe and Henry Ephron, a top screenwriting team—*Carousel, The Desk Set,* among many others. They also wrote plays about her infancy—*Three's a Family* and *Take Her, She's Mine*—based on her letters from college.

Her first screenwriting credit—with Alice Arlen—was for *Silkwood,* a marvelous movie. Probably her most famous work, now and maybe forever, is going to be *When Harry Met Sally*.

It was a total sleeper, the first movie made by Castle Rock films. Rob Reiner had never had a commercial hit. Meg Ryan—and how did she miss getting an Oscar nomination for this work?—had never costarred in a hit. Billy Crystal had costarred in a couple of films, but a romantic lead?

And everyone fell in love with it. Good as it was then, it's much better now, because the quality of movies—not counting special-effects flicks—has dropped so low.

Ephron's screenplay does the heavy lifting, so all the others can twinkle. A bubble of a film, stylish as hell, filled with short witty scenes about the impossibility of love, gorgeous montages of New York as we all want it to be, and little vignettes of older couples talking to the camera of their love experiences—try getting that past a studio executive today.

Crystal's character fucks everything that moves. Ryan's, though she claims sexual knowledge, is mocked by him. He is the stud, she the professional virgin. Then, forty-four minutes in, they go to the Carnegie Deli for a snack. And this happens.

The Orgasm Scene

INT.--CARNEGIE DELICATESSEN--DAY

HARRY and SALLY are seated at a table, waiting for
their sandwiches.

>   SALLY
>   What do you do with these women? Do you just
>   get up out of bed and leave?

>   HARRY
>   Sure.

>   SALLY
>   Well, explain to me how you do it. What do you
>   say?

A waiter brings their order.

                    HARRY
I say I have an early meeting, an early hair-
cut, an early squash game.

                    SALLY
You don't play squash.

                    HARRY
They don't know that. They just met me.

                    SALLY
        (rearranging the meat on her sandwich)
That's disgusting.

                    HARRY
I know. I feel terrible.
        (takes a bite of sandwich)

                    SALLY
You know, I am so glad I never got involved
with you. I just would have ended up being
some woman you had to get out of bed and leave
at three o'clock in the morning and go clean
your andirons. And you don't even have a fire-
place.
        (quite irritated now, slapping the meat
         over quickly)
Not that I would know this.

                    HARRY
Why are you getting so upset? This is not
about you.

                    SALLY
Yes it is. You're a human affront to all
women. And I'm a woman.
        (bites into sandwich)

                    HARRY
Hey, I don't feel great about this, but I don't
hear anyone complaining.

                    SALLY
Of course not. You're out the door too fast.

                    HARRY
I think they have an okay time.

                    SALLY
How do you know?

                    HARRY
How do you mean, how do I know. I know.

                    SALLY
Because they...?
        (she makes a gesture with her hands)

                    HARRY
Yes, because they...
        (he makes the same gesture back)

                    SALLY
How do you know they're really...
        (she makes the same gesture)

                    HARRY
What are you saying? They fake orgasm?

                    SALLY
It's possible.

                    HARRY
Get outta here.

                    SALLY
Why? Most women, at one time or another, have
faked it.

                    HARRY
Well, they haven't faked it with me.

                    SALLY
How do you know?

                    HARRY
Because I know.

                    SALLY
Oh right.
          (sets her sandwich down)
That's right. I forgot. You're a man.

                    HARRY
What's that supposed to mean?

                    SALLY
Nothing. It's just that all men are sure it
never happens to them, and most women at one
time or another have done it, so you do the
math.

                    HARRY
You don't think I can tell the difference?

                    SALLY
No.

                    HARRY
Get outta here.

HARRY bites into his sandwich. SALLY just stares at
him. A seductive look comes over her face.

                    SALLY
Oooh!

HARRY, sandwich in hand, chewing his food, looks up at
SALLY.

                    SALLY (CONT'D)
Oh! Oooh!

                    HARRY
    Are you okay?

SALLY, her eyes closed, ruffles her hair seductively.

                    SALLY
    Oh God!

HARRY is beginning to figure out what SALLY is doing.

                    SALLY (CONT'D)
    Oooh! Oh God!

SALLY tilts her head back.

                    SALLY (CONT'D)
    Oh!

Her eyes closed, she runs her hand over her face, down
her neck.

                    SALLY (CONT'D)
    Oh, my God! Oh yeah, right there.

HARRY looks around, noticing that others in the deli
are noticing SALLY. She's really making a show now.

                    SALLY (CONT'D)
        (gasps)
    Oh!

A man in the background turns to look at her.

                    SALLY (CONT'D)
    Oh! Oh!
        (gasps)
    Oh God! Oh yes!

HARRY, embarrassed, looks at her in disbelief.

                    SALLY (CONT'D)
              (pounding the table with both hands)
        Yes! Yes! Yes!

HARRY looks around, very embarrassed, smiles at cus-
tomers. An OLDER WOMAN seated nearby stares.

                    SALLY (CONT'D)
        Yes! Yes!

By now, the place is totally silent and everyone is
watching.

                    SALLY (CONT'D)
        Yes! Oh!
              (still thumping table)
        Yes, yes, yes!

SALLY leans her head back, as though experiencing the
final ecstatic convulsions of an orgasm.

                    SALLY (CONT'D)
        Yes! Yes! Yes!

She finally tosses her head forward.

                    SALLY (CONT'D)
        Oh. Oh. Oh.

SALLY sinks down into her chair, tousling her hair,
rubbing her hand down her neck to her chest.

                    SALLY (CONT'D)
        Oh, God.

Then suddenly, the act is over. SALLY calmly picks up
her fork, digs into her coleslaw, and smiles inno-
cently at HARRY.

```
A WAITER approaches the OLDER WOMAN to take her food
order.  The woman looks at him.

                    OLDER WOMAN
        I'll have what she's having.

FADE OUT.
```

What you cannot imagine now is the shock value of that scene. Yes, huge laughs, all that, but people simply could not believe that Meg Ryan FAKED AN ORGASM! When people talked about the flick, there was the usual *have you seen?* and then the bleed into *didn't you love?* and from there, quickly, **could you believe it?** And then the babble babble babble, *is it true?*

For those who could not resist this book because of my justly famous writings on sex in the twentieth century, here is what a famous therapist told me: Yes, all women do, and should. (To make the man feel, well, more manly, or when they are tired and want to get to sleep quickly.) Also, yes, all women deny they have ever done such a thing. They will admit they have heard of such behavior, perhaps even some of their friends have done it, but, no, they have not. And, alas, no, men cannot tell. Sorry, guys, no matter how magnificent our studliness, we cannot tell. The only change in a woman is this: for reasons known only to God, there is a slight rise in the temperature of the roof of her mouth. (Who else but me and Suzy tell you these things?) And if you can figure out how to measure that, I don't know what it is you're interested in, but it sure isn't sex.

One of the most unusual things about the scene is this: it ends on the biggest laugh of all, the Billy Crystal–inspired line, spoken by Rob Reiner's mom, Estelle, "I'll have what she's having." (Crystal is also responsible for one of my favorite lines in *The Princess Bride*. Miracle Max and his wife have just made this gigantic chocolate-covered miracle pill to bring Westley, the hero, back to life, and then they say that Westley shouldn't go swimming for at least a good hour.)

Love that.

Which is not to say I like it a whole lot when performers ad-lib over my lines. Because few do it well. Most suck. I am more aware than you are of my limitations, but I am a waaaay better writer than just about any actor you can mention (just as they outclass me in their discipline).

The problem comes when the *star* decides to ad-lib. Actually, this is as much the director's problem as mine, since hopefully I am not on the set. But if the director forces a smile and encourages the star, guess what—

—the star, feeling loved, which is all he wants to feel, will ad-lib forever. And if the director squelches the star, guess what—the star may well soon be sulking in a nearby trailer.

As you must realize by now, screenplays are not just dialogue. So does it matter, really, if a star misbehaves? Just to *us,* mainly. But there is nothing, spelled n-o-t-h-i-n-g, that a writer can do about it.

Most comedy scenes reach a peak somewhere in the middle and then it's a race to try and get out fast. The orgasm scene in *Harry* builds, then builds some more, and then takes off.

Clearly, Ephron and the Farrellys write in somewhat different styles; overall, she relies more on wit, they are more at ease with physical comedy. But both these scenes have one crucial thing very much in common—

—the core of the comedy is based on embarrassment. A great deal of the laughter comes from the figure who is really doing nothing. Billy Crystal just sits there, first confused, then intrigued, then stunned at Meg Ryan's behavior. Ben Stiller gets huge laughs just standing, huddled, facing the corner of the bathroom as nightmares swirl all around him.

One of the reasons these are classic screenwriting scenes has to do with the skill of the writers in making those moments play so strongly. The funny moments shout out at you when you read the scenes. I think one of the reasons I admire these scenes so much is that I can't write them. There are occasionally funny things in *Butch* and *The Princess Bride,* but I did not set out to write a comedy scene. The laughs happened to be there.

I wish I could write funny, I think we all wish we could, but when I read stuff like this, here's what I think: Thank God somebody can.

Spitballing

People who know me well are well aware that my view of myself is less than Olympian. There are certain fields in which I can and do hold my own. No one is a greater sports nut, for example. (Not counting hockey.) Few are more passionate eaters. I will give anyone you know a run on their love for red wine. (Provably so—what other wine aficionado has written as big a disaster as your correspondent? viz: *The Year of the Comet*.)

But what I do better than anyone else on earth is spitball.

If you are a young screenwriter and for some reason unfamiliar with the term, write it down. You will be doing it for the rest of your life. It is possible to spitball on the phone, by e-mail, etc. But it is my view that it is best done in person. And it should not be done in a hurry. Spitballing sessions should run, at the least, several hours.

Spitballing is this: two or more people trying to find a story.

It's understood that the writer, the one who is drowning, is trying to tell a tale that at present is just lying there like toothpaste. Inert, barely breathing.

There is almost nothing better for me than when another writer, in agony of course, helpless of course, comes to me and we spitball. I tell you, I am sublime at such moments.

Now, when *I* am the one in trouble, all sublimity goes out the window. For one of the sad truths about the act is that you may be a whiz when the problems belong to others; nevertheless, you are totally helpless when they are your own. That is true for all of us—we are trapped in our own skins.

I guess it's like group therapy, which I did for years, and *loved*—what a joy to be able to say to another tormented soul, "Ed, Ed, don't you see, this girlfriend who is killing you is exactly the same as all the others. They just change hair colors." But when their visions are turned on you— "Jesus, Bill, this one is exactly the same kind of crazy destructive bitch as they all are"—you are stunned at the revelation.

There is only one rule to spitballing, and it is crucial: **you must be able to suggest anything and make a total asshole of yourself at all times, secure in the knowledge that no one outside the room will ever know.**

I remember once being in an office with a studio guy and a couple of people were sitting around, fighting the story. And one of the people said this: "What if they're all women?" Now the story, as I remember, was a male adventure flick. And this studio guy commented on that—"This is an adventure movie here, how stupid a suggestion is that?" Naturally the writer was finished for that day.

The truth?

It was a *great* spitballing notion, and the studio guy—gasp of surprise, right?—was the asshole.

Because making them all women opened up the world. I use it myself a lot now. Or what if the story is about a high-tech robbery and you suggest that it take place a hundred years ago? What if we make it a tragedy instead of the comedy we're stuck on?

What those ideas do, of course, is this: *they make you think about why they are wrong.* You have to defend and explain. And sometimes, out of one weird spitballing idea comes another idea that is also weird but less so, and then out of some divine blue, someone is shouting, "No, no, listen to me, I've got it—*listen to me*—"

—and there it is, the spine of the story, with all the sludge ripped away. You can see it and it's going to be such a great movie you wouldn't believe it. At its best, what spitballing does is give you the illusion that just this once you have slain hunger and beaten death.

One final note: I have never in forty-six years of writing used the word "viz" before. I don't even know if I used it correctly—I was coming to the end to the first paragraph and there it was, buzzing around, so I put it in. And I promise you this: Even if it is wrong, I won't change it, no matter what the copyeditor says . . .

North by Northwest

by Ernest Lehman

My first trip to Hollywood for work was in 1965, when *Harper* went into production. I remember a lot of things from the experience (see *Adventures in the Screen Trade*), but one particular moment stands out.

A trim figure had come onto the set whom I did not know, but there seemed to be great goodwill in his being there—a lot of people flocked around. I had no idea who it was till, believe it or not, one of the camera crew said this: "That's Ernie Lehman the screenwriter—*even his flops are hits.*"

We later met, became friends. But I never quite forgot the words of the camera guy. Because in that land of horseshit hyperbole, his remarks about Lehman were, if anything, an understatement. Here is what Lehman wrote from 1954 through 1966:

1954	*Executive Suite*
1954	*Sabrina*
1956	*The King and I*
1956	*Somebody Up There Likes Me*
1957	*The Sweet Smell of Success*
1959	*North by Northwest*
1960	*From the Terrace*
1961	*West Side Story*
1963	*The Prize*
1965	*The Sound of Music*
1966	*Who's Afraid of Virginia Woolf?*

Amazing to me, still now. It may be unmatched in Hollywood history, maybe in any discipline. Because these weren't just, some of them, insanely commercial films, they were honored, fifty-some nominations in all, four flicks up for Best Picture, two of them won. More than that, most of them are *good*.

Even more incredible than the success are the screenwriting Oscars. Think a moment before you take your shot. How many wins? Go over the list and concentrate.

Zeee-ro.

Sabrina lost to *The Country Girl; Somebody Up There Likes Me* didn't get a nomination, but it would have lost to *The Red Balloon; North by Northwest* lost to, wait for it—*Pillow Talk* (barf). But my favorite is *West Side Story,* which got *eleven* nominations, won *ten* Oscars. (Guess which one it *didn't* win.)

He was nominated, sure, and he won a bunch of Writers Guild Awards, but I'm still pissed for him.

North by Northwest, briefly, is a mistaken-identity flick. Cary Grant plays an ad executive who is mistaken for a man named Kaplan, kidnaped, interrogated by James Mason as if he were Kaplan, then gotten drunk and stuck behind the wheel of a car on a mountain road.

He survives, goes to the UN to try and find out who Mason is, gets involved in a murder there, hotfoots it to Grand Central, takes a train for Chicago on which he meets the oh-so-lovely Eva Marie Saint, who works for Mason and tells him, once they are in Chicago, where he can at last meet Kaplan—a desolate Indiana spot filled with cornfields.

What follows is one of the very best pieces of action-adventure I have ever read.

The Crop-Dusting Scene
(written directly for the screen by Lehman)

```
DISSOLVE TO:


HELICOPTER SHOT--EXT. HIGHWAY 41--(AFTERNOON)


We START CLOSE on a Greyhound bus, SHOOTING DOWN on
it, and TRAVELING ALONG with it as it speeds in an
easterly direction at 70 m.p.h.  Gradually, CAMERA
DRAWS AWAY from the bus, going higher but never losing
sight of the vehicle, which recedes into the distance
below and becomes a toy-like object on an endless rib-
bon of deserted highway that stretches across miles of
flat prairie.  Now the bus is slowing down.  It is
```

nearing a junction where a small dirt road coming from
nowhere crosses the highway and continues on to
nowhere. The bus stops. A man gets out. It is Thornhill. But to us he is only a tiny figure. The bus
starts away, moves on out of sight. And now Thornhill
stands alone beside the road--a tiny figure in the
middle of nowhere.

ON THE GROUND--WITH THORNHILL--(MASTER SCENE)

He glances about, studying his surroundings. The terrain is flat and treeless, even more desolate from
this vantage point than it seemed from the air. Here
and there patches of low-growing farm crops add some
contour to the land. A hot sun beats down. UTTER SI-
LENCE hangs heavily in the air. Thornhill glances at
his wristwatch. It is 3:25.

In the distance the FAINT HUM of a MOTOR VEHICLE is
HEARD. Thornhill looks off to the west. The HUM GROWS
LOUDER as the car draws nearer. Thornhill steps
closer to the edge of the highway. A black sedan looms
up, traveling at high speed. For a moment we are not
sure it is not hurtling right at Thornhill. And then
it ZOOMS past him, recedes into the distance, becoming
a FAINT HUM, a tiny speck, and then SILENCE again.

Thornhill takes out a handkerchief, mops his face. He
is beginning to sweat now. It could be from nervous-
ness, as well as the heat. Another FAINT HUM, coming
from the east, GROWING LOUDER as he glances off and
sees another distant speck becoming a speeding car,
this one a closed convertible. Again, anticipation on
Thornhill's face. Again, the vague uneasiness of in-
definable danger approaching at high speed. And
again, ZOOM--a cloud of dust--a car receding into the
distance--a FAINT HUM--and SILENCE.

His lips tighten. He glances at his watch again. He
steps out into the middle of the highway, looks first

in one direction, then the other. Nothing in sight.
He loosens his tie, opens his shirt collar, looks up
at the sun. Behind him, in the distance, another vehicle is HEARD approaching. He turns, looks off to
the west.

This one is a huge transcontinental moving van, ROAR-
ING TOWARD HIM at high speed. With quick apprehension
he moves off the highway to the dusty side of the road
as the van thunders past and disappears. Its FADING
SOUND is replaced with a NEW SOUND, the CHUGGING of an
OLD FLIVVER.

Thornhill looks off in the direction of the approaching SOUND, sees a flivver nearing the highway from the
intersecting dirt road. When the car reaches the
highway, it comes to a stop. A middle-aged woman is
behind the wheel. Her passenger is a nondescript man
of about fifty. He could certainly be a farmer. He
gets out of the car. It makes a U-turn and drives off
in the direction from which it came. Thornhill
watches the man take up a position across the highway
from him. The man glances at Thornhill without visible interest, then looks off up the highway towards
the east as though waiting for something to come
along.

Thornhill stares at the man, wondering if this is
George Kaplan.

The man looks idly across the highway at Thornhill,
his face expressionless.

Thornhill wipes his face with his handkerchief, never
taking his eyes off the man across the highway. The
FAINT SOUND of an APPROACHING PLANE has gradually come
up over the scene. As the SOUND GROWS LOUDER, Thornhill looks up to his left and sees a low-flying bi-
plane approaching from the northwest. He watches it
with mounting interest as it heads straight for the

spot where he and the stranger face each other across
the highway. Suddenly it is upon them, only a hundred
feet above the ground, and then, like a giant bird, as
Thornhill turns with the plane's passage, it flies
over them and continues on. Thornhill stares after
the plane, his back to the highway. When the plane has
gone several hundred yards beyond the highway, it
loses altitude, levels off only a few feet above the
ground and begins to fly back and forth in straight
lines parallel to the highway, letting loose a trail
of powdered dust from beneath its fuselage as it goes.
Any farmer would recognize the operation as simple
crop-dusting.

Thornhill looks across the highway, sees that the
stranger is watching the plane with idle interest.
Thornhill's lips set with determination. He crosses
over and goes up to the man.

>   THORNHILL
> Hot day.

>   MAN
> Seen worse.

>   THORNHILL
> Are you...uh...by any chance supposed to be
> meeting someone here?

>   MAN
>   (still watching the plane)
> Waitin' for the bus. Due any minute.

>   THORNHILL
> Oh...

>   MAN
>   (idly)
> Some of them crop-duster pilots get rich, if
> they live long enough...

                         THORNHILL
          Then your name isn't...Kaplan.

                         MAN
               (glances at him)
          Can't say it is, 'cause it ain't.
               (he looks off up the highway)
          Well--here she comes, right on time.

Thornhill looks off to the east, sees a Greyhound bus
approaching. The man peers off at the plane again,
and frowns.

                         MAN
          That's funny.

                         THORNHILL
          What?

                         MAN
          That plane's dustin' crops where there ain't
          no crops.

Thornhill looks across at the droning plane with growing suspicion as the stranger steps out onto the highway and flags the bus to a stop. Thornhill turns
toward the stranger as though to say something to him.
But it is too late. The man has boarded the bus, its
doors are closing and it is pulling away. Thornhill
is alone again.

Almost immediately, he HEARS the PLANE ENGINE BEING
GUNNED TO A HIGHER SPEED. He glances off sharply,
sees the plane veering off its parallel course and
heading towards him. He stand there wide-eyed, rooted
to the spot. The plane roars on, a few feet off the
ground. There are two men in the twin cockpits, gog-
gled, unrecognizable, menacing. He yells out to them,
but his voice is lost in the NOISE of the PLANE.

In a moment it will be upon him and decapitate him.
Desperately he drops to the ground and presses himself
flat as the plane zooms over him with a great noise,
almost combing his hair with a landing wheel.

Thornhill scrambles to his feet, sees the plane banking and turning. He looks about wildly, sees a telephone pole and dashes for it as the plane comes at
him again. He ducks behind the pole. The plane heads
straight for him, veers to the right at the last
moment. We HEAR two sharp CRACKS of GUNFIRE mixed
with the SOUND of THE ENGINE, as two bullets slam
into the pole just above Thornhill's head.

Thornhill reacts to this new peril, sees the plane
banking for another run at him. A car is speeding
along the highway from the west. Thornhill dashes
out onto the road, tries to flag the car down but the
driver ignores him and races by, leaving him exposed
and vulnerable as the plane roars away and another
series of SHOTS are HEARD and bullets rake the ground
that he has just occupied.

He gets to his feet, looks about, sees a cornfield
about fifty yards from the highway, glances up at the
plane making its turn, and decides to make a dash for
the cover of the tall-growing corn.

SHOOTING DOWN FROM A HELICOPTER about one hundred feet
above the ground, we SEE Thornhill running toward the
cornfield and the plane in pursuit.

SHOOTING FROM WITHIN THE CORNFIELD, we SEE Thornhill
come crashing in, scuttling to the right and lying
flat and motionless as we HEAR THE PLANE ZOOM OVER HIM
WITH A BURST OF GUNFIRE and bullets rip into the corn,
but at a safe distance from Thornhill. He raises his
head cautiously, gasping for breath, as he HEARS THE
PLANE MOVE OFF AND INTO ITS TURN.

SHOOTING DOWN FROM THE HELICOPTER, we SEE the plane
leveling off and starting a run over the cornfield,
which betrays no sign of the hidden Thornhill. Skim-
ming over the top of the cornstalks, the plane gives
forth no burst of gunfire now. Instead, it lets loose
thick clouds of poisonous dust which settle down into
the corn.

WITHIN THE CORNFIELD, Thornhill, still lying flat, begins to gasp and choke as the poisonous dust envelops
him. Tears stream from his eyes but he does not dare
move as he HEARS THE PLANE COMING OVER THE FIELD
AGAIN. When the plane zooms by and another cloud of
dust hits him, he jumps to his feet and crashes out
into the open, half blinded and gasping for breath.
Far off down the highway to the right, he SEES a huge
Diesel gasoline-tanker approaching.

SHOOTING FROM THE HELICOPTER, we SEE Thornhill dashing
for the highway, the plane leveling off for another
run at him, and the Diesel tanker speeding closer.

SHOOTING ACROSS THE HIGHWAY, we SEE Thornhill running
and stumbling TOWARDS CAMERA, the plane closing in behind him, and the Diesel tanker approaching from the
left. He dashes out into the middle of the highway and
waves his arms wildly.

The Diesel tanker THUNDERS down the highway towards
Thornhill, KLAXON BLASTING impatiently.

The plane speeds relentlessly toward Thornhill from
the field bordering the highway.

Thornhill stands alone and helpless in the middle of
the highway, waving his arms. The plane draws closer.
The tanker is almost upon him. It isn't going to stop.
He can HEAR THE KLAXON BLASTING him out of the way.
There is nothing he can do. The plane has caught up
with him. The tanker won't stop. It's _got_ to stop.

He hurls himself to the pavement directly in its path.
There is a SCREAM OF BRAKES and SKIDDING TIRES, THE
ROAR OF THE PLANE ENGINE and then a tremendous BOOM as
the Diesel truck grinds to a stop inches from Thornhill's body just as the plane, hopelessly committed
and caught unprepared by the sudden stop, slams into
the traveling gasoline tanker and plane and gasoline
explode into a great sheet of flame.

In the next few moments, all is confusion. Thornhill,
unhurt, rolls out from under the wheels of the Diesel
truck. The drivers clamber out of the front seat and
drop to the highway. Black clouds of smoke billow up
from the funeral pyre of the plane and its cremated
occupants. <u>We recognize the flaming body of one of
the men in the plane. It is Licht, one of Thornhill's
original abductors</u>. An elderly open pickup truck with
a secondhand refrigerator standing in it, which has
been approaching from the east, pulls up at the side
of the road. Its driver, a farmer, jumps out and hurries toward the wreckage.

                    FARMER
          What happened?

The Diesel truck drivers are too dazed to answer.
Flames and smoke drive them all back. Thornhill, unnoticed, heads toward the unoccupied pickup truck.
Another car comes up from the west, stops, and its
driver runs toward the other men. They stare, trans-
fixed at the holocaust. Suddenly, from behind them,
they HEAR the PICKUP TRUCK'S MOTOR STARTING. The
farmer who owns the truck turns, and is startled to
see his truck being driven away by an utter stranger.

                    FARMER
          Hey!

He runs after the truck. But the stranger--who is
Thornhill--steps harder on the accelerator and speeds
off in the direction of Chicago.

I suppose, along with the shower scene from *Psycho,* this is the most famous sequence Hitchcock ever shot. When you see the movie, it all seems so seamless it feels like the creation of it must have been pretty much the same way.

But no.

Lehman and Hitchcock knew each other a little, wanted to work together. MGM had just bought their first property for Hitchcock, a Hammond Innes best-seller, *The Wreck of the Mary Deare.* Briefly, the plot concerned a ship floating in the English Channel with nobody aboard, followed by a huge naval inquiry.

For weeks, Lehman would drive to Hitchcock's house on Bellagio Road in L.A. and they would spend the day talking. Which was when Lehman noticed that every time he brought the conversation around to *The Wreck of the Mary Deare,* Hitchcock would look anxious and change the subject.

Soon it was obvious neither of them wanted to do it, but they liked the time they spent together, so, without telling MGM, they decided to find something else they wanted to do together. Hitchcock had a lot of stuff he wanted to shoot, and he would spitball them to Lehman.

One of them was the longest dolly shot in history, without any cuts, which would take place at a Detroit auto factory and you would start at the beginning of the assembly line and slowly watch the car being put together and when the car is completed and ready to be driven off the assembly line there is a dead body inside.

Lehman in those days was very tough and famous for leaving projects as soon as he could. He was constantly quitting (he quit *North by Northwest* twice), only to be brought back soon after.

The car shot does me no good, he said.

Another Hitchcock moment: we are in Banff, Lake Louise, a religious group having its annual spiritual retreat—and a twelve-year-old girl takes a gun out of her baby carriage and shoots someone.

Does me no good, Lehman said.

Okay—this: in Alaska, two men who *hate* each other, sworn enemies, walk toward each other across a frozen lake where a hole has been cut. They walk slowly, closer and closer, and when they get close, they fall into each other's arms and hug.

Wonderful bits, sure, but no more than that.

One day Hitchcock says, "I've always wanted to do a chase across the face of Mount Rushmore."

That was the start of everything.

Hitchcock had also always wanted to do a sequence at the United Nations where somebody's addressing the General Assembly and he stops and says, "I will not continue until the delegate from Peru wakes up." The page taps the delegate from Peru on the shoulder—and he's dead.

By now, Hitchcock has to leave to shoot *Vertigo*—for me, the most overrated movie of all time—but Lehman is aware that whatever the story is, it's moving in a northerly direction.

As well as being famously pessimistic, Lehman is also not the fastest writer around. He constantly criticizes himself, ditches stuff, but eventually sixty pages are shipped off to Hitchcock, who sends Lehman a rave four-page handwritten letter of approval, and they meet again.

With both Cary Grant *and* Jimmy Stewart anxious to come aboard.

(Can you imagine what that must have been like—two of the very greatest stars *ever* panting to join the team. Personally, I cannot. I don't believe we have stars like that anymore. Probably we know too much about them now. Anyway, I haven't spotted a lot of them in the movies I've seen lately.)

Lehman is writing this with no knowledge of what comes next but he's got Cary Grant on the train where he meets Eva Marie Saint. He and Hitchcock are spitballing again.

Hitchcock muses: Do you know what I've always wanted to shoot? What?

I always wanted to shoot a scene where a man is alone. Totally alone. No matter where you shoot, all 360 degrees, nothing.

Lehman listens.

And then the villains try and kill him.

How? asks Lehman.

With a *tornado,* Hitchcock says then.

And Lehman is dying, he's got half a sensational script, and he says, Hitch, how do they get a *tornado* to kill him at that moment?

Hitchcock grumbles, goes silent.

Lehman too.

More silence.

They were used to it. They would sit through these incredibly long silences, staring at the walls.

Then Lehman says these words: *maybe a plane. A crop-duster plane.*

And suddenly they were both jabbering away, and then they were both acting out the scene, and then Lehman went home and wrote the scene faster than he ever wrote anything before.

———

Remember that—Lehman wrote it. It is an Ernie Lehman scene, filmed *exactly* as he wrote it. Hitchcock shot it—and not that well. Look at the shot when the plane hits the truck. Awful.

Lehman gets insufficient credit for it now and, I suspect, will get less in the future. It *feels* like such a great Hitchcock scene. And it is. And that is a great tribute to Lehman.

We all have limitations. We all have confidence with stuff that's in our wheelhouse. When I work with a director for the first time, here's what I do: look at every movie he's ever made. So I can have a sense of what he does well, where he is helpless. And I will never willingly write a scene I know he can't shoot.

Hitchcock, elevated to God these days (though I have my doubts), was terrific with funny/scary. He could deal with a few people in a room. Period. But you could not give him size.

David Lean, yes, you could give him size. But I doubt Lean would have been happy shooting *North by Northwest*. I think he would have found it uninteresting. As Hitchcock might have snoozed through Bolt's great script for *Lawrence*.

Did Lehman "create" the crop-dusting scene? Yeah, for the most part. He wrote the shit out of it. He *handed* what you read to Hitchcock. And the next time some failed professor's learned book comes out detailing Hitchcock's Symbolic Use of Catholicism in the Crop-Dusting Scene, of course don't buy it. But you might check the index. I'll bet Ernie Lehman's name isn't there.

Action-adventure and comedy are brutal to make work. And the easiest to make badly. As the saying goes, "Dying is easy, comedy is hard," but action-adventure runs right alongside.

I think because you are placing the character into situations where mere mortals never tread. And that can become ludicrous so easily. Great ones, like Errol Flynn as *Robin Hood* or *North by Northwest,* are diamond-rare.

These days, we are happy (I am, anyway) with two-thirds of a terrific action-adventure flick. *The Fugitive*—saw it twice, but please forget the last part, when you're at the doctor's convention. *Men in Black*—loved it, even if Act III was in very deep shit indeed. Critics rarely honor these two genres. "Oh," they might say, "*The Fugitive* will certainly pass a pleasant evening for you." But that's as far as they go.

I think if someone could figure out a way to make a medicinal action-adventure flick, one the critics could say was "important," they would own the world.

One of the amazing things about the crop-dusting scene is that it ran *eight minutes* on film. Not possible today. I once read a quote from David Lean who had just been shown a fresh print of *Lawrence of Arabia* and was asked what he thought. Lean said he was surprised at how brave he was, holding so many shots for so long.

If you've seen that greatest of epics, you know immediately what he means. And no one would shoot that way today.

I think, because of MTV.

I think movies changed—*not* the storytelling but the manner of it— *not* with the coming of MTV but with the talent in the room at the time.

Meaning this—if MTV had come along in the thirties, when the great music stars could actually, gasp, *perform,* what you would have seen was Fred Astaire doing, say, "Dancing in the Dark," and it might have been done in one take, or more likely, a few. And you would have seen both his head and his feet in the same shot, something he insisted on as often as possible.

Well, what the fuck can you do with Elton John? Fat and funny-looking and totally without performing instinct. Here's what you do— *you hide him.*

How?

By cutting so fast no one will realize he is a studio creation. By roaring in for close-ups of glasses, or feet working the pedals, of his face mouthing words, or his hands on the keyboard, or dancing girls behind him, or God knows what—

—but the relentlessness of the cutting pattern keeps us from seeing that John, a wonderful piano player, and a decent enough singer, can't *move.*

Michael Jackson can move, but I'm not sure for how long, because what you see are snippets of him in action, five seconds here, fifteen there. And then all the filler shots to hide the star.

MTV was meant clearly for teens, and teens go to the movies, and what happened was this: they got bored with longer shots, no matter how logical or helpful they may have been.

Movies today are too often a blizzard of cuts—just another reason why the '90s are the worst decade. Sad, because I think there are occasions when fast cutting is terrific. But there are many many other occasions when pre-MTV styling would help the story much more.

And I think the crop-dusting scene, if you could write something as exciting and see it up there today, would still knock your socks off.

And look all fresh and shining and young and original. And thrill us all anew . . .

Adaptations

When I am offered an adaptation, the initial two questions are always the same. And I take them seriously because we are talking about six of the ever-declining number of months I have left. It will take me that long from the time I say yes till the first draft is done.

The writing itself takes maybe a month.

The thinking, figuring out the story, will take twice that (research fits into this period).

The remaining half is simply a matter of building up my confidence.

This is always the first and foremost question:

Do I love it?

Followed hard upon by this:

Can I make it play?

I have turned down three great hits, and I would make the same decisions today, even though I liked the resulting movies a lot.

The Godfather, for moral reasons. (Only time ever for that.) This is still mystifying to me. The reason I turned it down was I did not want to glorify the Mafia. Even though *Butch* glorifies outlaws, I know. I loved the book so—it's still the great novel read for me of the last few decades (Tommy Thompson's *Blood and Money* is of the same quality in nonfiction). I wanted to do the Puzo. In the end, could not. The movie sure did okay without me.

The Graduate, because I just didn't get the book.

Superman, I was most anxious to do.

I was a comic-book nut when I was a kid, and a huge collector. This was during the Golden Age, 1937–43. I mean, I had the first *Superman,* the first *Batman,* the first *Robin the Boy Wonder,* the first *Captain Marvel.* No way of remembering how many, hundreds, obviously. I remember, growing up, I had a washing machine container in my bedroom and it was filled with my comics.

Mint condition, you understand.

I still see the me of then, this miserable fucked-up kid, and when schoolwork was done, I would go to my treasure trove and kneel down and go through and take my time deciding which glorious adventure land did I want to visit then. I needed places to get to just to get through those years. Books? Sure, I was a compulsive reader. Movies? Absolutely, when I was allowed to walk up to the Alcyon. *But these adventures were in my room with me.*

Jesus Christ, I still know what "Shazam" stands for.

Superman was to be one of those European money deals. They had the rights, we talked. I had no idea which story I would tell from so many. The Krypton stuff, the early years, first day on the job—who knew? But I knew I could make it work. A villain would be a problem, sure, I mean a legitimate one, Supe being all-powerful. But lead me to it.

And in the meeting this came out: they needed a star.

As Superman.

Because of their financial needs, they had this one requirement.

Dead I was.

They talked of Eastwood's interest.

Dead.

They spoke of Jimmy Caan.

Still and forever dead.

Because I knew this: *no star would play the part.* (I really *knew* it.) No star would wear the costume. No star would risk looking that stupid. Years later I spoke with Warren Beatty, *very* smart, about when his turn came to be offered the title role. He had been given the costume, had taken it home, had put it on, had run around his swimming pool, as I remember, had looked at himself for a very short moment before taking it off.

Eventually, they did what they had to do to get the movie made: went for a wonderful unknown and surrounded Chris Reeve with stars. I would have written that. Never had the chance.

Okay, you want me to adapt something and you have given me something to read—book, article, whatever. Guess what I do? I read it. As a traveler, as someone who might be on a trip and has just picked up something he hopes he loves—*not* as a screenwriter (that comes later).

I'm pretty fast in my decision making, I think I always have been. I almost always know before I'm done. And if I can answer the two crucial questions in the affirmative—do I love it, can I make it play?—you pretty much own the next six months of my life.

Then lawyers and agents fire guns across the water.

Once that is past—and it doesn't take long, or shouldn't with men of goodwill—there may be meetings. Usually only with the producer. (In my experience, we are always the first wave in the battle; that is the blood of screenwriters splattered all over Omaha Beach.)

Usually the producer has shit to say. My favorite is when someone says, "We can have a lotta fun with this." Then he takes his tan and his smile and goes. And then you are alone with you, the screenwriter.

Here is one of the main rules of adaptation: you *cannot* be literally faithful to the source material.

Here's another that critics never get: you *should not* be literally faithful to the source material. It is in a different form, a form that does not have the camera.

Here is the most important rule of adaptation: you *must* be totally faithful to the *intention* of the source material.

In *All the President's Men,* we got great credit for our faithfulness to the Woodward-Bernstein book.

Total horseshit: the movie ended *halfway through* the book. What we were faithful to was their story of a terrible hinge in American history. In other words, we didn't Hollywood-it-up.

Look—something moved you when you said, Yes, I want to try and adapt this. (If you didn't feel that, then you are just another hooker and I will not weep as you go down.) And whatever it was that the original writer put down—whatever it was that made you, for a moment, say "omigod"—that feeling has got to be translated from the book to the script. *And you must protect that to the death.*

In the later stages of movie making, when I am working with producers or directors or stars, and they put in for their needs, fine, that's that process. Lose those wars if you must, not crucial.

But if they begin to encroach on your emotional core, if you let them take that ground, you lose everything.

Here is how I adapt and it's very simple: I read the text again. And I read it this time with a pen in my hand—let's pick a color, blue. Armed with that, I go back to the book, slower this time than when I was a traveler. And as I go through the book word by word, page by page, every time I hit anything I think might be useful—dialogue line, sequence, description—I make a mark in the margin.

A blue one.

I put the book away, fiddle, panic, if there's research to be done, I start in on it.

Then maybe two weeks later, I read the book a third time, this time with a different color pen.

Let's go with a red one.

And I repeat the same marking process—a line in the margin for anything I think might make the screenplay.

Then more research, more thoughts, and maybe—but only maybe—a few notes. I am doing two things, of course, during these months—

—building up my confidence for the actual writing—

—desperately trying to find the spine of the flick.

Now another reading of the text.

A brown pen, maybe.

I hope you see why I have to care for the source material. Because I am going to live with it. If I had to reread and reread something I didn't like, I would more than likely have gone out the window long ago.

What follows now is pages 204–205 of my copy of Stephen King's wonderful *Misery*. It's the scene where Kathy Bates saws through Jimmy Caan's ankles (breaks them in the movie; check out the *Misery* essay). It's pretty obvious that whatever the spine of the piece was, I knew from the start it had to pass through this sequence.

What follows after that are two more pages from the same book, a blink further on (pages 211–212). It's after the violence, Paul is writing and the "t" has just fallen out of his typewriter (the "n" had already fallen out). One line is circled—King has bees buzzing and I wrote the word "sound" in the margin. One line is underlined—it's the first day of summer.

In other words, I did *not* think the typewriter breaking would make the movie, whatever that movie might turn out to be.

When I am done with all my various color-marked readings—five or six of them—I should have the spine. I should know where the story starts, where it ends. The people should be in my head by now.

So I make a list and tape it to the wall in front of my Mac. On my wall I put these five words for the start of *Misery*—

1. finishing
2. leaving
3. driving
4. storm
5. crash

Hopefully, the whole movie, the entire story would be thirty shorthanded words. They could tell me about something as short as a single cut. Or a ten- or twelve-page sequence. Which I hope is in my head. Then, always checking out the list, all I have to do is write the movie.

just because of a broken spring. If they caught them they made sure that they could go on working . . . but they *also* made sure they would never run again. The operation was called *hobbling*, Paul, and that is what I'm going to do to you. For my own safety . . . and yours as well. Believe me, you need to be protected from yourself. Just remember, a little pain and it will be over. Try to hold that thought."

Terror sharp as a gust of wind filled with razor-blades blew through the dope and Paul's eyes flew open. She had risen and now drew the bedclothes down, exposing his twisted legs and bare feet.

"No," he said. "No . . . Annie . . . whatever it is you've got on your mind, we can talk about it, can't we? . . . please . . ."

She bent over. When she straightened up she was holding the axe from the shed in one hand and a propane torch in the other. The blade of the axe gleamed. Written on the side of the propane torch was the word *Bernz-O-matiC*. She bent down again and this time came up with a dark bottle and the box of matches. There was a label on the dark bottle. Written on the label was the word *Betadine*.

He never forgot these things, these words, these names.

"*Annie, no!*" he screamed. "*Annie, I'll stay right here! I won't even get out of bed! Please! Oh God please don't cut me!*"

"It'll be all right," she said, and her face now had that slack, unplugged look—that look of perplexed vacuity—and before his mind was completely consumed in a forest fire of panic he understood that when this was over, she would have only the vaguest memories of what she had done, as she had only the vaguest memories of killing the children and the old people and the terminal patients and Andrew Pomeroy. After all, this was the woman who, although she'd gotten her cap in 1966, had told him only minutes ago that she had been a nurse for ten years.

She killed Pomeroy with that same axe. I know she did.

He continued to shriek and plead, but his words had become inarticulate babble. He tried to turn over, turn away from her, and his legs cried out. He tried to draw them up, make them less vulnerable, less of a target, and his knee screamed.

"Only a minute more, Paul," she said, and uncapped the Betadine. She poured a brownish-red muck over his left ankle. "Only a minute more and it's over." She tipped the blade of the axe flat, the tendons standing out in her strong right wrist, and he could see the wink

of the amethyst ring she still wore on the pinkie finger of that hand.
She poured Betadine on the blade. He could smell it, a doctor's-
office smell. That smell meant you were going to get a shot.

"Just a little pain, Paul. It won't be bad." She turned the axe over
and splashed the other side of the blade. He could see random
flowers of rust blooming on this side before the goop covered it.

"Annie Annie oh Annie please please no please don't Annie I swear
to you I'll be good I swear to God I'll be good please give me a chance to
be good OH ANNIE PLEASE LET ME BE GOOD—"

"Just a little pain. Then this nasty business will be behind us for
good, Paul."

She tossed the open bottle of Betadine over her shoulder, her
face blank and empty and yet so inarguably solid; she slid her right
hand down the handle of the axe almost to the steel head. She
gripped the handle farther up in her left hand and spread her legs
like a logger.

"ANNIE OH PLEASE PLEASE DON'T HURT ME!"

Her eyes were mild and drifting. "Don't worry," she said. "I'm
a trained nurse."

The axe came whistling down and buried itself in Paul Sheldon's
left leg just above the ankle. Pain exploded up his body in a gigantic
bolt. Dark-red blood splattered across her face like Indian war-
paint. It splattered the wall. He heard the blade squeal against bone
as she wrenched it free. He looked unbelievingly down at himself.
The sheet was turning red. He saw his toes wriggling. Then he saw
her raising the dripping axe again. Her hair had fallen free of its
pins and hung around her blank face.

He tried to pull back in spite of the pain in his leg and knee and
realized that his leg was moving but his foot wasn't. All he was
doing was widening the axe-slash, making it open like a mouth. He
had time enough to realize his foot was now only held on his leg
by the meat of his calf before the blade came down again, directly
into the gash, shearing through the rest of his leg and burying itself
deep in the mattress. Springs boinked and squoinked.

Annie pulled the axe free and tossed it aside. She looked absently
at the jetting stump for a moment and then picked up the box of
matches. She lit one. Then she picked up the propane torch with
the word *Bernz-O-matiC* on the side and twisted the valve on the
side. The torch hissed. Blood poured from the place where he no
longer was. Annie held the match delicately under the nozzle of

1

CHAPTER 32

"Oh blessed Jesus," Ia moa ed, a d made a co vul-
sive moveme t forward. Geoffrey grasped his frie d's arm.
The steady beat of the drums pulsed i his head like some-
thi g heard i a killi g delirium. Bees dro ed arou d
them, but o e paused; they simply flew past a d i to the
cleari g as if draw by a mag et--which, Geoffrey hough
sickly, hey

2

Paul picked up the typewriter and shook it. After a time, a small
piece of steel fell out onto the board across the arms of the wheel-
chair. He picked it up and looked at it.

It was the letter t. The typewriter had just thrown its t.

He thought: *I am going to complain to the management. I am going
to not just* ask *for a new typewriter but fucking* demand *one. She's got
the money—I* know *she does. Maybe it's squirrelled away in fruit-jars
under the barn or maybe it's stuffed in the walls at her Laughing Place,
but she's got the dough, and t, my God, the second-most-common letter
in the English language—!*

Of course he would ask Annie for nothing, much less demand.
Once there had been a man who would at least have *asked*. A man
who had been in a great deal more pain, a man who had had nothing
to hold onto, not even this shitty book. That man would have *asked*.

Sequel

Hurt or not, that man had had the guts to at least *try* to stand up
to Annie Wilkes.

He had been that man, and he supposed he ought to be ashamed,
but *that* man had had two big advantages over this one: *that* man
had had two feet . . . and two thumbs.

Paul sat reflectively for a moment, reread the last line (mentally
filling in the omissions), and then simply went back to work.

Better that way.

Better not to ask.

Better not to provoke.

→ Outside his window, bees buzzed.

Sequel   It was the first day of summer.

3
_____

had been.

    "Let me go!" Ian snarled, and turned on Geoffrey,

his right hand curling into a fist. His eyes bulged madly

from his livid face, and he seemed totally unaware of who

was holding him back from his darling. Geoffrey realized

with cold certainty that what they had seen when Hezekiah

pulled the protective screen of bushes aside had come very

close to driving Ian mad. He still tottered on the brink,

and the slightest push would send him over. If that happened,

he would take Misery with him.

    "Ian --"

    "Let me go, I say!" Ian pulled backward with

furious strength, and Hezekiah moaned fearfully. "No boss,

make dem bees crazy, dem sting Mis'wess--"

    Ian seemed not to hear. Eyes wild and blank,

he lashed out at Geoffrey, striking his old friend high on

The Seventh Seal

by Ingmar Bergman

I know, or have interviewed, the other screenwriters in this section. And when I began thinking about just what this section might be, I thought I would try and meet Bergman, even went as far as to contact a representative of his in America. I sort of envisioned it like this: casual, you know, have something set up that would fit his plans, fly over, say, from London, when I was there, go to whatever island he is presently inhabiting, talk for a few minutes.

I think Bergman is the greatest screenwriter. I think a hundred years ago he would have been a great novelist, Balzac maybe. And the more I thought about our meeting, the more I realized something: I was **nuts** to contemplate such a thing. And why? Because I did meet my great writing hero, the man who changed my life, Irwin Shaw.

I was in my teens once, wanting to write, not really knowing what it meant, if I could, not dating, certainly not dating the girls I dreamed of, a shitty student, C average, used to be tops in school but then all kinds of family madness came crashing down and I was in trouble, and I think I probably knew that.

Which was when a cousin of mine, who did not read much, out of some mystic blue, gave me a copy of *Mixed Company,* a collection of Shaw's stories.

I didn't know his stuff, picked up the book, glanced at the first story, "The Girls in Their Summer Dresses," read it, then on to the next, "The Eighty-Yard Run," then "Act of Faith," and that day spun into tomorrow and probably it was the tomorrow after that before I'd finished "Sailor off the Bremen" and "Welcome to the City" and "The Dry Rock" and all the others and I don't think I knew it at the moment of putting the book down—

—but my life was never the same—

—because I had read these wondrous *things,* these vignettes and tables, told with such ease and style—for me, Shaw and Fitzgerald are the great American stylists—and I knew this: *I could do that.*

Okay, it's decades later, and my publisher at Delacorte is Ross Claiborne, wonderful Ross, and he knows of my feelings for Shaw and one day he says this: "Irwin's going to be in town, *would you like to meet him?*"

What a thing.

Which is not to say the day dawned without apprehension. I knew I'd be okay—my God, all I had to do was tell what happened and he had to like that—

—but what if he turned out to be an asshole? What if he was embarrassed by his early work, felt he had moved past it? Some of the stories were forty years old. What if he pissed on them, said they were just starters, juvenile stuff, those words that had been everything for me.

We had lunch at the Four Seasons, and as I walked in, I was terrified our time together would be a disaster.

It was.

Not because of him, no, he was just what I wanted him to be, this tough and feisty warrior, grizzled and funny, passionate, who loved sports and loved New York. He was wonderful that day.

I was the horror show.

I knew this was my one shot, and I needed to tell him what he meant; y'see, I might never meet him again; before the meal was over, *he had to know.* But all the rehearsals I'd done in my mind dried up, and I didn't know what to say, how to tell him, and at the very start I sensed it was not going to be one of my good days and that only made me panic more, so I gushed and blubbered and embarrassed the man, and I could feel myself slipping down the iceberg and I couldn't stop. This was the one day when I wanted to be wonderful and it was a fucking nightmare and when it was over I thought, well, thank God, I can't be any worse—

—and then I did it. We were walking along Park Avenue just before parting and I was talking about how he never made me stop reading, never used the wrong word, that great simplicity of the storytelling, and I heard myself saying these terrible words: **It's easy for you, isn't it, the writing?**

I still see this sad look in his eyes as he turned to me. And I don't know what he was thinking but I knew I had disappointed him so badly. I had trivialized the man, *I had ignored his pain.*

"It wasn't easy," he said very softly.

He went his way, I mine, and I guess that was the worst lunch of my life, because the one thing we have, everyone who writes or paints or composes, is our pain—pain that we deal with by huddling away in our pits and getting through it as best we can.

I remember in 1957 literally reeling out of a now-dead movie theater on Eighty-sixth Street—because I had just seen *The Seventh Seal*. And I knew I had never seen anything like it.

No one else has told this kind of story on film, at least not this well. The kinds of narratives that interest Bergman don't have a lot of roles for Sylvester Stallone in them, or very happy endings. His movies tend to be short, without an ounce of fat, and they are peopled with decent human beings trying to make sense of the madness down here. And usually failing.

The reason I never want to meet Bergman should be pretty clear to you by now: What if I said, **"Was it a lot of fun writing *The Seventh Seal*?"**

This is the opening of the movie. I can't come up with many better.

The Playing Chess with Death Scene

The night had brought little relief from the heat, and at dawn a hot gust of wind blows across the colorless sea.

The knight, Antonius Block, lies prostrate on some spruce branches spread across the fine sand. His eyes are wide-open and bloodshot from lack of sleep.

Nearby his squire, Jons, is snoring loudly. He has fallen asleep where he collapsed, at the edge of the forest among the wind-gnarled fir trees. His open mouth gapes toward the dawn, and unearthly sounds come from his throat.

At the sudden gust of wind the horses stir, stretching their parched muzzles toward the sea. They are as thin and worn as their masters.

The knight has risen and waded into the shallow water, where he rinses his sunburned face and blistered lips.

Jons rolls over to face the forest and the darkness. He moans in his sleep and vigorously scratches the stubbled hair on his head. A scar stretches diagonally across his scalp, as white as lightning against the grime.

The knight returns to the beach and falls on his knees. With his eyes closed and brow furrowed, he says his morning prayers. His hands are clenched together and his lips form the words silently. His face is sad and bitter. He opens his eyes and stares directly into the morning sun, which wallows up from the misty sea like some bloated, dying fish. The sky is gray and immobile, a dome of lead. A cloud hangs mute and dark over the western horizon. High up, barely visible, a sea gull floats on motionless wings. Its cry is weird and restless.

The knight's large gray horse lifts its head and whinnies. Antonius Block turns around.

Behind him stands a man in black. His face is very pale and he keeps his hands hidden in the wide folds of his cloak.

>   KNIGHT
> Who are you?

>   DEATH
> I am Death.

>   KNIGHT
> Have you come for me?

>   DEATH
> I have been walking by your side for a long time.

                    KNIGHT
That I know.

                    DEATH
Are you prepared?

                    KNIGHT
My body is frightened but I am not.

                    DEATH
Well, there is no shame in that.

The knight has risen to his feet. He shivers. Death
opens his cloak to put it around the knight's shoulders.

                    KNIGHT
Wait a moment.

                    DEATH
That's what they all say. I grant no re-
prieves.

                    KNIGHT
You play chess, don't you?

A gleam of interest kindles in Death's eyes.

                    DEATH
How did you know that?

                    KNIGHT
I have seen it in paintings and heard it sung
in ballads.

                    DEATH
Yes, in fact I'm quite a good player.

                    KNIGHT
But you can't be better than I am.

The knight rummages in the big black bag which he
keeps beside him and takes out a small chessboard.
He places it carefully on the ground and begins setting
up the pieces.

                    DEATH
    Why do you want to play chess with me?

                    KNIGHT
    I have my reasons.

                    DEATH
    That is your privilege.

                    KNIGHT
    The condition is that I may live as long as I
    hold out against you. If I win, you will re-
    lease me. Is it agreed?

The knight holds out his two fists to Death, who
smiles at him suddenly. Death points to one of the
knight's hands; it contains a black pawn.

                    KNIGHT
    You drew black!

                    DEATH
    Very appropriate. Don't you think so?

The knight and Death bend over the chessboard. After
a moment of hesitation, Antonius Block opens with his
king's pawn. Death moves, also using his king's pawn.

The morning breeze has died down. The restless movement of the sea has ceased, the water is silent. The
sun rises from the haze and its glow whitens. The sea
gull floats under the dark cloud, frozen in space.
The day is already scorchingly hot.

```
The squire Jons is awakened by a kick in the rear.
Opening his eyes, he grunts like a pig and yawns
broadly.  He scrambles to his feet, saddles his horse
and picks up the heavy pack.

The knight slowly rides away from the sea.
```

———

Why do I think Bergman's so great? Five reasons.

1. Because he is.
2. Because I think Chekhov is *the* playwright of the last hundred years and Bergman works the same side of the street. Heartbreaking, sure, but sometimes laughter. Funny/sad. Think it's easy? Good luck.
3. Because I just spent a weekend looking at five flicks—*The Seventh Seal, Wild Strawberries, Persona, Winter Light, Through a Glass Darkly.* Sure, there is the occasional tendency to want to jump out the window, but once you get past that, you enter his world. He takes you places you've never been, never knew existed, and you know you'll never be quite the same after.
4. I wrote a line for Butch once when they are in South America and Sundance wonders what they are going to do if the Superposse keeps on tracking them: "We'll outlast the bastards."

Hollywood is so full of short-time wonders. Welles and Sturges, and all these other great talents who got sucked up by their own egos, began to think they knew what they were doing. Welles worked for decades, but his great work lasted really two years, *Kane* and *Ambersons.* Sturges was around for close to twenty, but there is only real quality for five.

Bergman is not your everyday flash in the pan. He was at it in '44, was still great *forty* years later with his last masterpiece, *Fanny and Alexander.* For me, that's a career. (Oh, he's still at it. His latest screenplay just went into production.)

5. But all of the above reasons are nothing compared to the one thing that sets him apart from all the rest—**Ingmar slugged a critic.**

I don't remember all the details but I'm sure I didn't make this up—I mean I have no thoughts that Frederico biffed the guy from *Il Mundo.* Here's what I'm pretty sure happened.

In Sweden, Ingmar is at least as famous for his stage work as for his flicks. He was rehearsing a play one afternoon when a critic wanders in—a guy who had hammered our hero on more than one occasion.

Anyway, Ingmar sees him, temporarily stops rehearsal, leaves the stage, chases the critic up the aisle into the lobby, and *clocks the mother*.

Yessss!

Think Orson or Hitch could do that?

Entering Late

Here is reality.

```
FADE IN ON

A COLLEGE SCREENWRITING CLASS.

A DOZEN STUDENTS sit rapt, as at the front,
their lecturer inspires them.

WILLIAM GOLDMAN is that lecturer.  Known for
his modesty, GOLDMAN resembles a handsome
Cary Grant; his wit, charm, and incisive vi-
sion are known around the world.

                  GOLDMAN
      Why should we study poetry?  Or art?
      Or music or ballet?  Because each
      hour spent examining the other dis-
      ciplines makes us better screenwrit-
      ers.  Here is one of my favorite
      quatrains:

      "She lived unknown, and few could know
      When Lucy ceased to be;
      But she is in her grave, and, oh,
      The difference to me!"

      Why should we be aware of those words
      by William Wordsworth?  Listen now
      with great care, as I recite it to
      you again.  And pay complete atten-
```

tion to the simple word "oh." I
should tell you this: it comes at the
end of the third line, and it is entirely surrounded by commas, one
follows the preceding word, "grave,"
the next following the crucial "oh"
itself.

"She lived unknown, and few could know
When Lucy ceased to be;
But she is in her grave, and, oh,
The difference to me!"

Did you hear? It is not possible to
read or hear that poem without giving
particular emphasis to that simple
two-letter word. You have to land on
it hard. Now think. What is
Wordsworth doing? First, of course,
he is making us aware of the depth of
his pain. And **oh**. And ***oh***...!
          (beat)
But what else is he doing that relates to screenwriting? Class?

CUT TO

THE STUDENTS. And it's clear they revere
him, want to please him so much, but right
now, no one seems to want to raise a hand.
They are, by the way, a good-looking bunch
of twenty-year-olds. Silence from the assembled.

CUT TO

GOLDMAN, looking at each of them in turn.
Waiting silently.

CUT TO

THE PRETTIEST OF THE PRETTY GIRLS. Her name
is Susan and she has a wonderful mind, but
she's a Marilyn Monroe type, so who would
know? She raises a hand nervously.

           GOLDMAN
      (indicating she should speak)
Go ahead, Sarah.

           SUSAN
      (correcting)
Susan.

           GOLDMAN
Sorry, close only counts in horse-
shoes. What is Wordsworth doing?

           SUSAN
      (hesitantly)
Is he...controlling the reader?

CUT TO

GOLDMAN, all smiles

           GOLDMAN
In the words of Marv, yesss.

CUT TO

GOLDMAN. CLOSE UP.

           GOLDMAN
When we write our screenplays--more
than anything else this is what we
want--to control the reader's eye.
      (intently now)
We use all our tricks to make that
happen. We space a laugh on the page
differently than we space a shock--

```
        all in an attempt to make the reader
        hear our voice.
                (louder)
        --do we understand this?
                (before they can all answer,
                 the bell rings)
    More on this anon.


CUT TO


THE STUDENTS, rising slowly, heading out.


Except for SUSAN.  She grabs her books, waves
to the others, goes to GOLDMAN's desk.  One
final glance around--they're alone.  And you
can tell that even though she is twenty and
he is pushing seventy, they are more than
student and teacher.


                SUSAN
        Why the Sarah?


                GOLDMAN
        So no one would suspect us.


                SUSAN
        Gonna be hard to do that now.
                (beat)
        I'm pregnant.


HOLD ON THE TWO OF THEM.  He sits down hard
at his desk.  We can see some photos there
now--snapshots of his family, his smiling
wife, their four smiling little kids.


BLACKOUT.
```

I tried very hard to make that as interesting for you to read as I could. I put in stuff about how I'm handsomer than Cary Grant, how I'm so charming you want to throw up, all to keep you going. And I believe entirely in the central notion that Wordsworth did control our eye, which is what screenwriters want to do.

I said at the start it was reality, and I tried to make that as true as I could. It might be a college class somewhere. When I write a movie, I see every cut. I think we all do, and if we don't, I think we all should. When I wrote "fade in on" a classroom, I didn't describe it, but I could have, I kept a couple from my past in my head. I see the desk and me standing there and the students.

And I try to imagine that I am sitting there in the theater, watching.

Do you know what you would have done if you had, **in reality,** sat through a scene like that? Do you realize the pain you would feel? You would have been groaning. You would have thought some terrible trick was being played on you. That scene runs *three and a half minutes.*

I was at the Mount Kenya Safari Club years ago, late afternoon, gorgeous sunset, perfect beauty and silence, which is what you go there for—

—when suddenly this awful drumming began and I looked out to see the next cabin, where twenty Africans in native costume were banging away and chanting—and I realized some asshole must have paid them to do that, and maybe the people in the next cabin enjoyed it—

—me, I thought it was the worst practical joke ever. That's what you would have thought if you'd been in a theater and this awful droning about Wordsworth went on. You might have thought someone was trying to drive you mad.

I hope we understand this by now: movies have nothing to do with reality.

But that scene has enough dramatic material to make a valid movie scene. Here is how you would do it:

FADE IN ON

A COLLEGE SCREENWRITING CLASS

A DOZEN STUDENTS sit listening in various states of disinterest.

Their lecturer is a man in his mid-60's.
Knowledgeable, stiff.

                    LECTURER
    Wordsworth has many lessons for us as
    screenwriters--
           (the bell rings)
    --we'll start here next time.

CUT TO

THE CLASS, getting up, heading out.

One student, SUSAN, twenty and very sexy,
goes to the desk, glances around, sees they
are alone.

                    LECTURER
    Yes, Susan?

                    SUSAN
    I'm pregnant.

HOLD ON THE TWO OF THEM. He sits down hard
at his desk. We can see some photos there
now--snapshots of his family, his smiling
wife, their four smiling little kids.

BLACKOUT.

   Fifteen seconds. Do you have the requisite information?
Think so. Were you bored? Shouldn't have been. We are, at
this moment, at something I have written about before and
you know all about anyway, but since it is one of *the* crucial
facts of our work, I'm going to put it in very large type.

This has been about entering late.

We must enter all scenes as late as possible.

We must enter our story as late as possible.

Why?

Because of the camera.

Because of the speed.

I cannot think of exceptions. Not in proper screenwriting.

The story I used here could make, in the hands of a skilled novelist, an engrossing piece of work. It could be comic—the silly old fart forgetting his years. It could be heartbreaking—that's so easy I won't even bother.

And this could be the first page of a novel. Or it could come fifty pages in or a hundred and fifty. That is the decision the novelist must make. He does not have the camera literally looking over his shoulder. **He is the camera.**

You could do endless stuff on the professor, his coming to grips with a failed life, his loveless, or glorious, marriage, doesn't matter, *he* could still feel failed. You could do endless stuff with the girl. Maybe she has always been a hunk, maybe her father could not keep his hands off her, maybe her father was a saint who protected her from the potential evils of the world so when she saw this Cary Grant of a professor, she couldn't help falling for him.

Maybe she's a young Glenn Close, nutty as hell, who has hated the wife for years and has set out to destroy her and she ain't pregnant at all. Or maybe she is pregnant, but it's not the professor's child.

Any way you want to take this, feel free. And feel free to take all the time you want to develop whatever story you decide to tell.

But not in a screenplay.

There is no time in a screenplay.

Do you want to read a piece of *great* screenwriting? Not mine, alas. It comes from the mind of Raymond Chandler.

```
FADE IN ON
```

```
A married couple in an elevator.  They stand
silently.  The man wears a hat.
```

```
The elevator stops.

A pretty young woman gets in.

The man takes off his hat.
```

Do you understand that? You must understand **why that is great.** With that shot, you know *everything.* You know it's a crappy marriage, you know he wants better, you know there is sexual energy in that rising room now.

And you can do that in what, ten seconds?

That scene could be entered a minute before, with the married couple in the lobby, either bickering or staring daggers at each other.

Or a day or a month later.

Don't need it. Let Chandler show you the way.

Enuf, for the nonce, on this. (See "viz.")

You know all the nutty stuff people find on the Net? Here are two that were sent to me yesterday, one related to what we're doing, one not, but I love the "not" so much I have to tell you. Also, I'm getting carried away on this point, never the best thing to do.

Okay. This is from a supposed U.S. Government Peace Corps manual. It is given to volunteers who work in the Amazon jungle. It tells what to do if an anaconda attacks you. In case you don't know much about them, maybe this will help: they are the largest snakes in the world, they can grow to thirty-five feet, can weigh four hundred pounds.

This is what the manual said:

1. If you are attacked by an anaconda, do not run. The snake is faster than you are.

2. Lie flat on the ground. Put your arms tight against your sides, your legs tight against one another.

3. Tuck your chin in.

4. The snake will come and begin to nudge and climb over your body.

5. **Do not panic.**

6. After the snake has examined you, it will begin to swallow you from the feet. Permit the snake to swallow your feet and ankles. **Do not panic!**

7. The snake will now begin to suck your legs into its body. You must lie perfectly still. **This will take a long time.**

8. When the snake has reached your knees, slowly and with as little movement as possible, reach down, take your knife and very gently slide it into the snake's mouth between the edge of its mouth and your leg. Then suddenly rip upwards, severing the snake's head.

9. Be sure you have your knife.

10. Be sure your knife is sharp.

I guess I could relate this to screenwriting. My question would be this: How do you do that and not make it a comedy scene? I mean, do you have the volunteers reading it aloud? How, without laughing?

When you've got the answer, I'd sure like to know about it.

The next e-mail is just for us. Pay close attention.

Ten Things We'd Never Know Without the Movies

1. It is always possible to park opposite the building you are visiting.

2. When paying for a taxi, don't look at your wallet as you take out a bill—just grab one at random and hand it over, it will always be the exact fare.

3. Television news bulletins usually contain a story that affects you personally at the precise moment that it's aired.

4. It is not necessary to say hello or goodbye when beginning or ending a telephone conversation.

5. Any lock can be picked by a credit card or a paperclip in seconds—unless it's the door to a burning building with a child inside.

6. The ventilating system of any building is the perfect hiding place no one will ever think of finding you in and you can travel to any other part of the building undetected.

7. All bombs are fitted with electronic timing devices with large red readouts so you know exactly when they are going to go off.

8. Should you want to pass yourself off as a German

officer, it will not be necessary to speak the language—a German accent will do.

   9. Once applied, lipstick will never rub off—even while scuba diving.

   And my favorite

   10. You can always find a chainsaw when you need one.

Pretty neat, I thought, And there is one crucial point about all ten, and while you are pondering just what it might be, a story. Concerning number 3, about TV news always affecting you personally.

That actually happened once. To someone I know. Here it is:

Almost thirty years ago now, two young actors were in their twenties. Their names were Penny Marshall and Rob Reiner and they were both on TV shows. *Huge* hit TV shows. (Think *Seinfeld* and *Friends* today.) Rob was Meathead on *All in the Family,* she Laverne in *Laverne and Shirley.*

They met. And the Gods smiled down. They fell in love. And got married. And were just so happy. But the home they were living in was not to their liking, nothing ever got finished, the place was a mess.

They went to New York to star in a TV movie Rob wrote, *More Than Friends.* They would be gone little more than a week.

And in that week, the decorator promised, everything would be made right. Their home would be exactly as they wanted it to be.

Back they come after the shoot. Together, suitcases in hand, they go to their Dream House. They unlock the front door and, very nervous now, enter. They peek into their living room.

As in their dreams.

The dining room.

Yes again.

The kitchen.

Ideal.

Now slowly, up the stairs they go to their bedroom. They put their suitcases down in silence. It's beyond belief perfect.

Like schoolchildren they sit on the end of their bed, turn on the TV and the *instant* they do, what they see is Jean Dixon saying these words: "Jeane Dixon predicts: **Penny and Rob will split.**"

See, life can imitate art. (The marriage did not last.)

Enough. Did you think about the ten things? Fine. Then tell me the one crucial thing about them all—

—I'm waiting.—

—Want a hint?—

—Forget hints, here's the answer:

They're all the same.

They're all about what the camera does.

They're all about speed.

To show you what I mean, I'll talk about the first couple. Here's numero uno—

1. It is always possible to park opposite the building you are visiting.

Well, we've all sure seen that baby. (Or its corollary: the star raises his hand in New York and a cab stops *instantly*.) Here's how you might write it:

```
FADE IN ON

Wall Street.  High noon.  MEL GIBSON tools
along in his Ferrari, spots a parking place
across from City Hall, and as he heads toward
it--

CUT TO

MEL, hurrying up the steps of that ornate
building.
```

Maybe the entire enterprise takes, what, twenty seconds at the outside? Fine. Now let's try it another way. Same set-up.

CUT TO

Wall Street. High noon. MEL GIBSON tools
along in his Ferrari, looking for a place to
park.

CUT TO

THE STREET. Jammed. Cars wedged in right
beside one another.

CUT TO

MEL. Hmm. He glances at his watch, bites
his fingernail for a moment--then, as his
face lights up--

CUT TO

An empty spot--just up ahead around the corner and

CUT TO

MEL, doing his best to maneuver in heavy
traffic that seems to thicken and--

                    MEL
        Son of a bitch!

CUT TO

A CLUNKER driven by a heavyset woman with a
mustache has snared the empty spot, starts to
park.

CUT TO

MEL, glancing at his watch again as he turns
the corner--up ahead now is the woman, trying

to maneuver her car into the spot. Clearly
she'll never be able to make it fit. MEL
pulls up, stops, waits.

CUT TO

THE WOMAN WITH THE MUSTACHE, trying like hell
to make her clunker fit the small spot. No
way.

CUT TO

MEL, biting his fingernail again, watching,
waiting.

CUT TO

THE WOMAN WITH THE MUSTACHE. She is now
backing her clunker into the car behind her,
trying to make space. The brakes are on in
the rear car, and she has no success. Now
she stops, sits there frustrated, her car
half-in half-out of the space.

                    MEL
               (calling out to her)
          Doesn't look like it's going to fit.

                    WOMAN WITH THE MUSTACHE
          Thanks for sharing, you Australian
          asshole--

--and as she gets out of the car, leaving it
just as it is, gives him a final finger--

CUT TO

A SIGN WITH AN ARROW INDICATING A GARAGE.

CUT TO

MEL, a little rattled now, seeing the sign,
driving up to it--

CUT TO

A GARAGE ATTENDANT shaking his head sharply.

PULL BACK TO REVEAL

MEL in his Ferrari, trying to drive into the
garage. THE ATTENDANT points to a sign: <u>No</u>
<u>Space</u>.

CUT TO

MEL, driving ever more slowly around the
block--it's clear now--<u>he will never find a</u>
<u>parking space</u>.

   2. When paying for a taxi, don't look at your wallet
as you take out a bill—just grab one at random and
hand it over, it will always be the exact fare.

FADE IN ON

Wall Street. High noon. MEL GIBSON sits in
a taxi as it pulls up in front of City Hall.
He pulls out a bill, hands it over, and as he
starts to get out--

CUT TO

MEL, hurrying up the steps to that ornate
building.

   That takes even less time than finding a parking space
did. Terrific. Mel is on his way inside *to where the real
scene is about to begin*. In other words, just as the earlier
sequence was more than likely not a movie about Mel Gib-

son finding a parking space, this one is not about Mel Gibson getting out of a cab. But let's try it again.

```
FADE IN ON

Wall Street. High noon. MEL GIBSON sits in
a taxi as it pulls up in front of City Hall.
He pulls out a bill, hands it over to the CAB
DRIVER, and as he starts to get out--


                    CAB DRIVER
          This is a single.


                    MEL
          What?


                    CAB DRIVER
          You gave me a single--I brought you
          in from JFK, it's thirty-two bucks,
          plus tolls.


                    MEL
          Sorry.
                    (He doesn't look at his wallet
                     this time either, just hands
                     over another bill.)


                    CAB DRIVER
          This is another single.  That's two.


                    MEL
          Must be jet lag.
                    (Hands over another bill, still
                     without looking at his wallet)


                    CAB DRIVER
          Three singles don't cut it, Mister.
                    (beat)
          Why don't you ever look at your wal-
          let?
```

                        MEL
          Look, I'm in a hurry--

                        CAB DRIVER
          --does this scam work where you come
          from, you Australian asshole?--
                    (calling out)
          <u>Officer</u>?

     CUT TO

     ONE OF NEW YORK'S FINEST, moving to the
     DRIVER.

                        POLICEMAN
          Problem?

                        CAB DRIVER
          This guy owes me from JFK and all he
          does is hand over three singles--
                    (big)
          —and he never looks at his wallet.

                        POLICEMAN
          Don't get you.

                        CAB DRIVER
          Watch.
                    (to MEL in the back)
          I'd like my money, mister.

                        MEL
          Here, take it.
                    (he hands over another bill
                     without looking at his wallet)

                        POLICEMAN
          Damndest thing I ever saw. What'd he
          give you?

                              CAB DRIVER
        Progress--a five.

                              POLICEMAN
                    (to MEL)
        Mister? You owe the man. Now, why
        don't you just look in your wallet,
        take out the money, and <u>hand it over</u>.

CUT TO

MEL sitting there, the wallet in his hands.
He tries to raise it up to eye level so he
can see it. His arms won't move. He tries
to drop his head to chin level so he can see
it down there. His head won't move.

                              MEL
                    (soft)
        I don't...seem to be...able to
        do...that.

                              POLICEMAN
        This is not funny--you don't pay the
        man, you go to jail. <u>You want to go
        to jail</u>?

Let's leave Mel pondering that question. And pardon my
riff about Mel's not being able to look at his wallet—I was
in a *Last Action Hero* mode, **and this scene would have
worked there.** Because that movie was about an action hero
in a movie who didn't know he was in a movie, he thought
he existed in our world.

All the ten clichés in the list are about trying to save time.
Because the alternatives are too gruesome for the movie-
goer: sitting there with nothing happening that relates to
the story.

Get on with it—that is what the camera demands, and
when we write movies, we have no choice but to obey.

Here's a shot that's a favorite of mine—it's when I can

tell a movie is in trouble. When a car drives up to a house and you see the whole long drive, you just know the movie is going to suck. Because there is only *one reason* to show the drive.

There better be a monster in the house . . .

Chinatown

by Robert Towne

and

Fargo

by Joel Coen & Ethan Coen

I'm not sure, really, why I linked these two great Oscar-winning screenplays. I could fake you out with a lot of reasons. They both form the basis for among the best detective movies ever made, both are funny and savage and filled with shocks and surprises, both are literate and surprisingly witty.

Both have wondrous detectives at their core. Gittes (Jack Nicholson), armed with his juvenile cynicism, thinks he know everything but is totally unprepared when he meets a man (Noah Cross, played by John Huston) who is *really* willing to do anything.

Marge (Frances McDormand), the pregnant police chief, is a lot smarter than Gittes but amazingly unprepared for the strange and terrible things people do to one another.

Both movies are dazzlingly complicated until you know their truths, and then they are clear and inevitable, as all wonderful storytelling must eventually be.

I think what links them in my mind is the placement of their two great scenes. The *Fargo* detecting scene starts half an hour in, the *Chinatown* confrontation begins twenty-five minutes before the end. (I have gone to Bergman for an example of a beginning, and, modestly, said he, I am going to use *Butch Cassidy* as an example of an ending.)

These two scenes both have the same effect on their respective movies. When you read them you know this: *the work is done.* A magician's phrase for that part of a trick—it can come close to the start or near to the end—when the magician's crucial work is finished. All that remains is the unfolding of the inevitable.

In both movies, after these two scenes, the remainder, for me, is inevitable. The writers have us in their power, at their mercy; they can do with us what they will.

———

The Coens drive me nuts a lot of the time.

Example: I cannot explain too often how crucial it is for you to know your story before you start. For me, if I don't know how a story is going to end, I don't know how to enter each individual scene preceding. I am not saying you must know each cut, obviously, but it is essential that you know the story you are trying to tell. I asked them how they know they are ready to start a screenplay.

                    JOEL
     To start it? Well, since we started writing we
     don't do an exhaustive outline--

                    ETHAN
     --or any outline. The rule is, we type scene A
     without knowing what scene B is going to be--
     or for that matter, we type scene R without
     knowing what scene S is going to be.

                    JOEL
     What happens with us is mostly that we tend to
     write fast at the beginning, then get very
     slow, then speed up once we really have to con-
     front the structure.

                    ETHAN
     And also, because we're doing our own thing,
     we can get stuck and literally grind to a halt
     and put it aside for a year even.

In other words, everything I feel you must do, they don't. Obviously, there is no correct way to work. I think the one thing writers are all interested in is how others do it. (Maybe looking for, at last, the right way—who knows?)

I have a theory as to why it works for the Coens. Peter and Bobby Farrelly have equally bizarre ways of getting things done. Listen to this madness:

                    PETER
     Bill, you said once you were in a spot where
     you didn't know what was going to happen next.

>   BOBBY
> Well, that's what we do. We write ourselves
> into a corner purposely--
>
>   PETER
> Because we think if we can go into a corner
> where there's no way out, and then we take a
> week or a few days or a month even, and find a
> reasonable way out without making it absurd,
> then nobody in the audience is going to sit
> there and get it within a minute and get ahead
> of us.

And what do they do in that "week or a few days or a month even"?

>   PETER
> We just drive. You know, it frees everything
> up. We just get in the car and drive. I drove
> across country fifteen times but together
> we've only done it five times.

Okay, my theory as to why it works for them is simplicity itself: *numbers*. Not because they are brother writing teams, although that doesn't hurt. They certainly know each other so well, and can deal with each other's idiosyncracies. But it's because there are two of them. I can't do it that way—if I get into a dark place, I can't say to my writing partner, "Here, fix the fucker." There's only me, trapped helpless in my pit, no way out.

Another example of why the Coens drive me nuts: *The Big Lebowski*. This nutball mélange of a flick takes place a lot of the time in a bowling alley, where John Goodman, who is nuts, is taunted by another bowler named Jesus (John Turturro). A tournament is mentioned several times.

And I know this: that is going to be some fucking bowling match. I don't know if either Goodman or Turturro is going to survive the thing, but *I cannot wait*.

Guess what? Not only is there no bowling contest, the Coens never even *thought* of having one. For them, it was just background for character. Well guess what?—they're *wrong*, because I want to see Goodman kick Turturro's ass.

The Coens, whatever their billing says, both do everything—write, produce, direct. They show up pretty much every day at their office on the West Side, do a kind of nine-to-five thing, but most of the time they wouldn't glorify what they do by saying it's writing.

They often set scripts aside, as they did *Fargo,* after about sixty pages were done. They wrote a stage direction—"Interior. Shep's apartment. Carl is banging an escort." There it stood for a year and a half. They may have as many as half a dozen scripts stashed away around their office. I don't know about you, but if they're close to being *Fargo,* I wish they'd get cracking.

Fargo is the story of a complicated crime that goes very wrong.

An automobile dealer needs money. What he decides to do is have his wife kidnapped and split the ransom money—courtesy of his father-in-law—with the kidnapers. (His wife is wealthy, he is not, and his father-in-law openly despises him.)

The kidnappers do not know each other well, and when they spend time together, it turns out they despise each other, too.

The dealer gives the kidnappers a car as the first installment of what they will eventually receive. In the meantime, he is harassed at work by people trying to buy cars from him, and at home, where he is trying to put together a deal with his father-in-law that will render the kidnapping unnecessary. He strikes out.

The kidnappers abduct his wife. They are driving through the area of Brainerd, Minnesota, with the wife in the backseat. They are in their new car. A cop stops them—the chattier of the two has forgotten to put tags on the car. The cop leaves his motor running, his lights on, and comes over to the car where the wife is lying on the floor in the rear. The chatty one tells the silent one that he will handle things. He tries to bribe the cop, who will have none of it, and when the officer asks the chatty kidnapper to please step out of the car, the silent one shoots him dead.

The chatty one is stunned at this, but he gets out of the car in the snow and starts to drag the dead cop off the road.

At this moment, another car drives by, slows, sees the chatty one dragging the cop away, and then takes off.

The silent kidnapper pursues them, and after the car chase has gone on a while, realizes they have pulled off the road. He does the same, finds them, kills two more.

Blackout.

We hear a phone ringing, a couple are in bed, it's the middle of the night. The woman answers, says she'll be right there. The man, her husband, says he will fix her some eggs, she needs her strength.

We see, as she gets out of bed, that whoever she is, she is pregnant.

Now, in a quick breakfast scene, we see she is also a police officer. And it's clear she is going to the crime scene. Where she has zero chance of ever solving the madness we have just seen unfold.

The Barfing in the Snow Scene

HIGHWAY

Two police cars and an ambulance sit idling at the side of the road, a pair of men inside each car.

The first car's driver door opens and a figure in a parka emerges, holding two Styrofoam cups. His part-ner leans across the seat to close the door after him.

The reverse shows Marge approaching from her own squad car.

                    MARGE
    Hiya, Lou.

                    LOU
    Margie. Thought you might need a little warm-
    up.

He hands her one of the cups of coffee.

                    MARGE
    Yah, thanks a bunch. So what's the deal, now.
    Gary says triple homicide?

                    LOU
    Yah, looks pretty bad. Two of'm're over here.

Marge looks around as they start walking.

                    MARGE
    Where is everybody?

                         LOU
      Well--it's cold, Margie.

BY THE WRECK

Laid out in the early morning light is the wrecked
car, a pair of footprints leading out to the man in a
bright orange parka face down in the bloodstained
snow, and one pair of footsteps leading back to the
road.

Marge is peering into the car.

                         MARGE
      Ah, geez. So...Aw, geez. Here's the second
      one...It's in the head and the...hand there, I
      guess that's a defensive wound. Okay.

Marge looks up from the car.

      ...Where's the state trooper?

Lou, up on the shoulder, jerks his thumb.

                         LOU
      Back there a good piece. In the ditch next to
      his prowler.

Marge looks around at the road.

                         MARGE
      Okay, so we got a trooper pulls someone over,
      we got a shooting, and these folks drive by,
      and we got a high-speed pursuit, ends here,
      and this execution-type deal.

                         LOU
      Yah.

                         MARGE
          I'd be very surprised if our suspect was from
          Brainerd.

                         LOU
          Yah.

Marge is studying the ground.

                         MARGE
          Yah. And I'll tell you what, from his foot-
          print he looks like a big fella--

Marge suddenly doubles over, putting her head between
her knees down near the snow.

                         LOU
          Ya see something down there, Chief?

                         MARGE
          Uh--I just, I think I'm gonna barf.

                         LOU
          Geez, you okay, Margie?

                         MARGE
          I'm fine--it's just morning sickness.

She gets up, sweeping the snow from her knees.

          ...Well, that passed.

                         LOU
          Yah?

                         MARGE
          Yah. Now I'm hungry again.

                         LOU
          You had breakfast yet, Margie?

                          MARGE
        Oh, yah. Norm made some eggs.

                          LOU
        Yah? Well, what now, d'ya think?

                          MARGE
        Let's go take a look at that trooper.

BY THE STATE TROOPER'S CAR

Marge's prowler is parked nearby.

Marge is on her hands and knees by a body down in the
ditch, again looking at footprints in the snow. She
calls up the road:

                          MARGE
        There's two of 'em, Lou!

                          LOU
        Yah?

                          MARGE
        Yah, this guy's smaller than his buddy.

                          LOU
        Oh, yah?

DOWN IN THE DITCH

In the foreground is the head of the state trooper,
facing us. Peering at it from behind, still on her
hands and knees, is Marge.

                          MARGE
        For Pete's sake.

She gets up, clapping the snow off her hands, and
climbs out of the ditch.

                    LOU
How's it look, Marge?

                    MARGE
Well, he's got his gun on his hip there, and he
looks like a nice enough guy. It's a real
shame.

                    LOU
Yah.

                    MARGE
You haven't monkeyed with his car there, have
ya?

                    LOU
No way.

She is looking at the prowler, which still idles on
the shoulder.

                    MARGE
Somebody shut his lights. I guess the little
guy sat in there, waitin' for his buddy t'come
back.

                    LOU
Yah, woulda been cold out here.

                    MARGE
Heck, yah. Ya think, is Dave open yet?

                    LOU
You don't think he's mixed up in--

                    MARGE
No, no, I just wanna get Norm some night
crawlers.

INT. PROWLER

Marge is driving; Lou sits next to her.

                    MARGE
    You look in his citation book?

                    LOU
    Yah...

He looks at his notebook.

    ...Last vehicle he wrote in was a tan Ciera at
    2:18 A.M. Under the plate number he put DLR--I
    figure they stopped him or shot him before he
    could finish fillin' out the tag number.

                    MARGE
    Uh-huh.

                    LOU
    So I got the state lookin' for a Ciera with a
    tag startin' DLR. They don't got no match yet.

                    MARGE
    I'm not sure I agree with you a hunnert percent
    on your policework there, Lou.

                    LOU
    Yah?

                    MARGE
    Yah, I think that vehicle there probly had
    dealer plates. DLR?

                    LOU
    Oh...

Lou gazes out the window, thinking.

    ...Geez.

>   MARGE
> Yah. Say, Lou, ya hear the one 'bout the guy
> who couldn't afford personalized plates, so he
> went and changed his name to J2L 4685?
>
>   LOU
> Yah, that's a good one.
>
>   MARGE
> Yah.

THE ROAD

> The police car enters with a whoosh and hums down a
> straight-ruled empty highway, cutting a landscape of
> flat and perfect white.

––––––––

Why did I say that the work is done in this movie about one-third of the way through?

No logical reason, but I remember that when I saw *Fargo* the first time, after that scene I felt a sense of peace. I have seen everything the Coens have done, and I know they are perverse. But I could not conceive that even the Coens could kill Marge. (My God, Frances McDormand is *married* to Joel. No way he offs his wife.) Which means I have faith I can give her my heart.

And that whole insane opening? I thought the whole *movie* was going to be about unraveling that baby. So when she nails it right out of the chute, you bet I relaxed. How could I not? I was going to spend another hour with one of the major movie characters of the decade. And I didn't *care* if at times she was less dazzling than here. I just wanted to be along on the ride.

So, yes, for me, here, even this early, the work is done.

––––––––

Decades past, Bob Towne and I had the same agent, the late and very great Evarts Ziegler—we are in the '60s now—and Towne was already *the* script doctor. He was this mysterious figure and he seemed to have fixed *everything,* but his cover was blown at the Oscars in '72 when Francis Ford Coppola thanked him from the microphone for his help with *The Godfather.*

The odd thing about his writing—I can still hear Ziegler trying to

make sense of this—was that when he doctored, he was *fast*, met dead-
lines, etc., but on his own stuff, death. Paint dried more quickly.

Chinatown took a while.

Towne had the two rapes from the start—the rape of the land and the
rape of the woman. His problem was which to lead with, how to knot
them together, and that was hard.

The scene that follows, the confessional if you will—one of the most
famous in modern films—amazingly enough *did not work*. It was in a
couple of different places in the script. And one day Towne was meeting
with the director, Roman Polanski, and they both knew there was something wrong, it was no fucking good, and suddenly they both realized
that a confession of this depth is not casually spoken, it is bled, battered
out of someone, and the force of revelation struck Towne: Nicholson
would have to beat the truth out of Dunaway. The moment he knew
that, the scene was written in half an hour.

Remember that no film, before it comes out, is a classic. We fantasize,
sure. But usually only in the privacy of our own rooms. I remember
when George Roy Hill and I were working on *Butch;* during a break we
started talking about our hopes for the film. One of us, could have been
me, said, "I just want it to be remembered as being as good as *The
Gunfighter.*" (Check it out at your video store.)

And when you luck into a classic, as *Chinatown* turned out to be, certain moments and actors take your memory. Here, obviously, you think
of Nicholson with his cut nose, Dunaway trying to control her crum-
bling world. But the great performance in the movie, for me anyway,
and the greatest role, is neither of those.

                    TOWNE
Noah Cross <u>is</u> the center of the story. Without
Noah Cross the story goes to shit. I mean, his
character is absolutely the center of it all,
and I've often reflected that it's Huston's
performance, which is so uncompromising. He
doesn't blink or hesitate in the fact that he
is an evil man. Most people won't have to face
the fact that at a certain time and a certain
place, they're capable of evil. And his ra-
tionale was that he faced the fact that everybody has it in them, and that he just did it.

Take a look at the ending Chinatown scene, where Huston is taking his younger daughter from the car. Ecstasy on his face. Evil triumphant. And even though he is not present in the earlier confession scene, boy is he *there*.

Before our interview, I had only talked to Towne once. It was right after I first saw *Chinatown,* was bowled over by the story he told, the way he told it, got his number from our agent, called and raved.

Towne was not, at that moment, a happy camper.

> TOWNE
>
> Looking back at it now, I'm somewhat chagrined
> at my anger at Polanski. There were a lot of
> things. There has been a lot of talk about his
> ending, which is what's in the movie now, and
> what I wanted, which was virtually as dark and
> maybe, I think, a little more literary. Eve-
> lyn Mulwray killed her father. And had to go
> to jail. And Gittes was going to talk about
> it. She was going to be fried, because the
> identity of her daughter had to be protected.
> So it made a mess of it anyway. But, in retro-
> spect, Roman was right. The movie needed a
> stark ending after such a complex story.

I wondered if Towne had any idea, at the first showing, what the movie would become. I figured on a "yes"—having seen the movie so many times, I could not see where the trouble might come from.

> TOWNE
>
> The first sneak? It did not go well. We had a
> horrendous score on the picture. By some guy
> that Roman knew. It was dissonant, weird,
> scratchy. Roman was momentarily enamored of
> it. He said the score was perfect. He was
> going off to direct an operetta at Spoletto,
> when mercifully, he ran into a grand old gen-
> tleman named Bronislau Kaper, who won an Oscar
> for his score of <u>Lili</u>, and he said, "Roman,
> that score is killing your picture." Roman had
> great respect for him and he said, "Okay, we

better get the score changed." Jerry Goldsmith
came in then, and did that great score. I was
on the set when Jerry spotted it, and it was at
that time when you could see the movie come to
life. It was like you couldn't see the movie
with the other score, and now you could, and I
thought, "Omigod, we may have a chance..."

I love movie stories like that. They let us know so much the media
doesn't. The media really is interested in cute stars and hits and occasionally (*The Postman*) disasters. But most movies come so close to disaster. Remember two things:

1. It is so hard to get a movie *made*.
2. It is so much harder to make a movie of quality.

In the great studio era, when MGM was churning out a movie a
week, not such a problem. I'm thirty-five years into it and maybe I average one movie made per year. That's counting *everything*—stuff I've
written and stuff I've doctored and stuff I've consulted on—and I've
been *lucky*.

And of all those, I love only two. *Butch* and *The Princess Bride*. For
the rest, some good parts, but all I see are where I should have been better. Got a phone call from Rob Reiner three years after *Princess Bride*
came out. In despair. He had just that night figured out where he should
have placed the camera in a scene to make it better. Nuts? Sure. But a lot
of phone calls like that get made.

The "She's My Daughter, She's My Sister" Scene

EXT. BUNGALOW-HOUSE, ADELAIDE DRIVE

Gittes pulls up in Mulwray's Buick. He hurries to the
front door, pounds on it.

The Chinese servant answers the door.

                         CHINESE SERVANT
          You wait.

                            GITTES
                (short sentence in Chinese)
          You wait.

Gittes pushes past him. Evelyn, looking a little worn
but glad to see him, hurries to the door. She takes
Gittes' arm.

                            EVELYN
          How are you? I was calling you.

She looks at him, searching his face.

                            GITTES
          --Yeah?

They move into the living room. Gittes is looking
around it.

                            EVELYN
          Did you get some sleep?

                            GITTES
          Sure.

                            EVELYN
          Did you have lunch? Kyo will fix you some-
          thing--

                            GITTES
                (abruptly)
          --where's the girl?

                            EVELYN
          Upstairs. Why?

                    GITTES
          I want to see her.

                    EVELYN
          ...she's having a bath now...why do you want
          to see her?

Gittes continues to looks around. He sees clothes
laid out for packing in a bedroom off the living room.

                    GITTES
          Going somewhere?

                    EVELYN
          Yes, we've got a 4:30 train to catch. Why?

Gittes doesn't answer. He goes to the phone and
dials.

                    GITTES
          --J.J. Gittes for Lieutenant Escobar...

                    EVELYN
          What are you doing? What's wrong? I told you
          we've got a 4:30--

                    GITTES
               (cutting her off)
          You're going to miss your train!
               (then, into the phone)
          ...Lou, meet me at 1412 Adelaide Drive--it's
          above Santa Monica Canyon...yeah, soon as you
          can.

                    EVELYN
          What did you do that for?

                    GITTES
               (a moment, then)
          You know any good criminal lawyers?

> EVELYN
> (puzzled)
> --no...

> GITTES
> Don't worry--I can recommend a couple.
> They're expensive, but you can afford it.

> EVELYN
> (evenly but with great anger)
> What the hell is this all about?

Gittes looks at her, then takes the handkerchief out
of his breast pocket, unfolds it on a coffee table,
revealing the bifocal glasses, one lens still intact.
Evelyn stares dumbly at them.

> GITTES
> I found these in your backyard--in your fish
> pond. They belonged to your husband, didn't
> they?...didn't they?

> EVELYN
> I don't know. I mean, yes, probably.

> GITTES
> --yes positively. That's where he was
> drowned...

> EVELYN
> What are you saying?

> GITTES
> There's no time for you to be shocked by the
> truth, Mrs. Mulwray. The coroner's report
> proves he was killed in salt water. I want to
> know how it happened and why. I want to know
> before Escobar gets here. I want to hang on to
> my license.

                    EVELYN
        I don't know what you're talking about. This
        is the most insane...the craziest thing I
        ever...

Gittes has been in a state of near frenzy himself. He
gets up, shakes her.

                    GITTES
        Stop it!--I'll make it easy--You were jealous,
        you fought, he fell, hit his head--it was an
        accident--but his girl is a witness. You've
        had to pay her off. You don't have the stomach
        to harm her, but you've got the money to shut
        her up. Yes or no?

                    EVELYN
        ...no...

                    GITTES
        Who is she? And don't give me that crap about
        it being your sister. You don't have a sister.

Evelyn is trembling.

                    EVELYN
        I'll tell you the truth.

Gittes smiles.

                    GITTES
        That's good. Now what's her name?

                    EVELYN
        --Katherine.

                    GITTES
        Katherine. Katherine who?

                    EVELYN
        --she's my daughter.

Gittes stares at her. He's been charged with anger,
and when Evelyn says this, it explodes. He hits her
full in the face. Evelyn stares back at him. The blow
has forced tears to her eyes, but she makes no move,
not even to defend herself.

>   GITTES
> I said the truth!

>   EVELYN
> --she's my sister--

Gittes slaps her again.

>   EVELYN (CONT'D)
> --she's my daughter.

Gittes slaps her again.

>   EVELYN (CONT'D)
> --my sister.

He hits her again.

>   EVELYN (CONT'D)
> My daughter, my sister--

He belts her finally, knocking her into a cheap Chinese vase that shatters and she collapses on the sofa,
sobbing.

>   GITTES
> I said I want the truth.

>   EVELYN
>   (almost screaming it)
> She's my sister and my daughter!

Kyo comes running down the stairs.

                    EVELYN (CONT'D)
     For God's sake, Kyo, keep her upstairs. Go
     back!

Kyo turns after staring at Gittes for a moment, then
goes back upstairs.

                    EVELYN (CONT'D)
     --my father and I, understand, or is it too
     tough for you?

Gittes doesn't answer.

                    EVELYN (CONT'D)
     ...he had a breakdown...the dam broke...my
     mother died...he became a little boy...I was
     fifteen...he'd ask me what to eat for break-
     fast, what clothes to wear! It
     happened...then I ran away...

                    GITTES
     ...to Mexico...

                    EVELYN
     ...Hollis came and took...care of me...after
     she was born...he said...he took care of
     her...I couldn't see her...I wanted to but I
     couldn't...I just want to see her once in a
     while...take care of her...that's all...but I
     don't want her to know...I don't want her to
     know...

                    GITTES
     ...so that's why you hate him...

Evelyn slowly looks up at Gittes.

                         EVELYN
          --no...for turning his back on me after it
          happened! He couldn't face it...
                    (weeping)
          I hate him.

Gittes suddenly feels the need to loosen his tie.

                         GITTES
          --yeah...where are you taking her now?

                         EVELYN
          Back to Mexico.

                         GITTES
          You can't go by train. Escobar'll be looking
          for you everywhere.

                         EVELYN
          How about a plane?

                         GITTES
          That's worse. Just get out of here--walk out,
          leave everything.

                         EVELYN
          I have to go home and get my things--

                         GITTES
          --I'll take care of it.

                         EVELYN
          Where can we go?

                         GITTES
          ...where does Kyo live?

                         EVELYN
          --with us.

                         GITTES
        On his day off. Get the exact address.

                         EVELYN
        --okay.

She stops suddenly.

                         EVELYN (CONT'D)
        Those didn't belong to Hollis.

For a moment Gittes doesn't know what she's talking
about. Then he follows her gaze to the glasses lying
on his handkerchief.

                         GITTES
        How do you know?

                         EVELYN
        He didn't wear bifocals.

Gittes picks up the glasses, stares at the lens, is
momentarily lost in them.

EVELYN

from the stairs. She has her arm around Katherine.

                         EVELYN
        Say hello to Mr. Gittes, sweetheart.

                         KATHERINE
                   (from the stairs)
        Hello.

GITTES

rises a little shakily from the arm of the sofa.

                         GITTES
        Hello.

With her arm around the girl, talking in Spanish, Evelyn hurries her toward the bedroom. In a moment she
reemerges.

                    EVELYN
               (calling down)
          --he lives at 1712 Alameda...do you know where
          that is?

REACTION—GITTES

He nods slowly.

                    GITTES
          --sure. It's in Chinatown.

                    ————

I just saw *The Matrix,* which has the best special effects I've ever seen,
and one of the things I wondered was this: How long will they hold?
How long before they look just as dated as *King Kong* seems to us
today?

A friend of mine just saw, on television and for the very first time,
Titanic. And are you shocked if I tell you he was disappointed? I don't
think you can see *Titanic* anywhere today and have it work as it once
did. (I know, I know, the talk scenes were an embarrassment.) But when
I went, just after it opened, I was surprised and moved by the last forty
minutes. It was this very troubled movie that turned out well. Now, with
all the hype and honors, I wonder. We know too much about it—how
they did the effects, what a miserable shoot it was, how cute Leo is, what
an asshole James Cameron turned out to be—anyway, I think its time is
over, in the sense of surprise.

And I wonder about these two movies in the same way. Towne thinks
if Faye Dunaway had had sex with her pop, John Huston, today they
would end up on Oprah Winfrey, or, if Oprah wouldn't have them, then
Geraldo. Towne feels there is so little shame in our world now, it dam-
ages the possibility of drama at this level.

Take Littleton, an uncontested nightmare, but is it any more lunatic
than the fact that several of the networks sent out press releases afterward proudly announcing their rise in ratings since they started covering
the massacre?

What's so awful about this is that people are taking the insanity for
granted.

A news event like Littleton, well, of course, that must be written about. What is so terrible is that after the news has been given, after all the pictures shown, they keep on showing them again and again. OJ, Di, Monica. Katie flies out for the interviews and Diane sheds such tears and Reba flies out—first telling the world what she is doing—to sing "Amazing Grace" at the *second* funeral.

Hey, what about the dead kids, anybody give a shit about them?

And I assume you must be wondering, Why am I telling you all this? I guess the answer is, I wonder if it is affecting screenwriting. Is the second-rateness of the world right now going to drag us storytellers down?

The answer is, I don't know, but I do know we have to try harder. It's easier, as the audience dumbs down and expects less, to be satisfied with less than our best work.

I hope Towne is wrong in his feelings about our lack of shame. When I look at this great scene, when I feel the awful pain of the Dunaway character looking at Nicholson and saying, after the revelation, "My father and I, understand, or is it too tough for you?"

Or is it too tough for you? Those words still echo inside me every time I watch the scene, and I go to my own life and wonder, could you have faced *this*? What would you do if *that* happened? My mind goes spinning away, visiting all kind of dark places we all have and hide.

And what about Marge? Where did she come from? And how wonderful that we have, at last, an American Sherlock Holmes, though ours is a woman. And pregnant. And kind.

Mr. Ziegler, referred to earlier, was once told that technology was going to change everything. He shook his head no. "I don't care," he began, "what you say. I don't care if your fucking technology figures out a way to beam movies from the moon directly into our brains." And here he paused a moment before finishing with this: "People are still going to have to tell stories."

Hear, hear.

La Vida

As I was walking out of my building yesterday, a doorman signaled for me to stop. I did. Then he opened the *New York Daily News,* indicated something for me to read.

It was a cartoon. It showed a man sitting at a computer. Ordinary nerdy writer-type guy with one unusual physical attribute: the top of his head was open and his brain was gone. On further inspection, he had taken his brain, stuck it in an ashtray. The caption was something like this:

How to be a successful screenwriter.

That was yesterday.

Today I am having morning coffee in a little place out on Long Island. I pick up a weekly newspaper, come awake reading an obit of Alan Pakula, who had a house in this area, was a true gentleman, and died in a freak car accident. Something fell off the vehicle ahead of him, and, as if aimed by Lucifer, came through his windshield and killed Pakula.

Okay. I am reading the article and I am thinking of the line I heard spoken by Walter Payton, one of my heroes, and it is this:

Tomorrow is promised to no one.

(I managed to sneak that into *Absolute Power*, the Eastwood–Ed Harris scene in the coffee shop. Made the scene for me.)

Okay, back with the obit, talking of the many achievements of Pakula's career. (A lot of people don't realize what a wonderful producer he was. You love *To Kill a Mockingbird*? If you don't, seek help immediately. Well, Alan produced that.) Now the obit is coming to an end. Here is the last paragraph.

"Two such characters are present in what is likely to emerge over time as Pakula's greatest triumph, *All the President's Men*. Adapted from the Robert Woodward–Carl Bernstein account of their investigation into the Watergate break-in, Pakula's movie has so many elements necessary in a first rate movie that it's a virtual how-to manual. Into it, Pakula has packed a convoluted yet clear narrative, suspense, the grit of the best documentaries, mystery (the shadowy appearance of Deep Throat), sound and editing finesse and colorful characters played—even in the smallest roles—by fine actors."

Okay, working backwards now.

"colorful characters played—even in the smallest roles—by fine actors." Full marks to Pakula here. He not only had final say on who played what, he coaxed splendid work from all concerned. I don't think Redford has topped it since. Robards won the Oscar for Best Supporting Actor. Jack Warden, John McMartin, Martin Balsam, Hoffman remarkably unmannered. Super ensemble work.

"sound and editing finesse"—That is a phrase written by someone who read it someplace and knows zip about movies. I have no idea what it means. Sound guys are off in their own world. But I would certainly credit Pakula with working with his editor to give terrific pace to what is essentially a talk piece.

"the grit of the best documentaries, mystery (the shadowy appearance of Deep Throat)"—Sorry, that is Gordon Willis you're talking about here. Directors have little to do with the actual look of a flick. You say to your cinematographer, "I want this to look like a Hopper painting," and you pray he can do it. The documentary look was always present in the Watergate material. Jo-Jo the Dog-faced Boy would have known it shouldn't look like a Doris Day musical.

And the Deep Throat appearances? All all *all* Gordon Willis, the prince of darkness among great cameramen. (An old joke was that Willis shot the only movie where you could not tell Paul Newman's eyes were blue.) One of the Oscar winners from this flick said in his acceptance speech that the main reason the movie worked was Gordon Willis. If Pakula did anything, he knew enough to shut up and watch a master and go along for the ride.

"Into it, Pakula has packed a convoluted yet clear narrative, suspense"—Total horseshit. That was from the book. Everything in the movie is from the book and there is a very good reason for that—it *had* to be. There were a lot of powerful men from Nixon on down who were not presented back-lit and beautiful. Warner Brothers was terrified of lawsuits, as they well should have been. It was a risky undertaking and the last thing they needed was to have the release delayed because of court dates. Woodward and Bernstein had not been sued for their book. Meaning, it was accurate. Now, as any lawyer will tell you, you can sue the Pope for bastardy. Doesn't mean you're going to win, but if you have the money in this great land of ours, nothing will stop you. And these powerful Nixonites sure could have sued the movie.

But since they didn't sue the book, their case was woefully weakened.

As long as the movie stayed strictly with the book. Which it did.

So to credit Pakula for story or look is simply wrong. He was a hired gun, certainly not the guy the producer wanted, and he came into a finished situation.

Let me make one thing perfectly clear—Pakula did a splendid job directing this flick. I am not in any way criticizing his *directing*—I think it was outrageous he didn't win the Oscar. (*Rocky* robbed the store that year.)

But to ever give a director credit for work he had nothing to do with is as damaging as not giving him credit for what he did do. I have written this before, but there are eight people that have to be at their best for a flick to reach its potential:

Actor
Cinematographer
Composer (if you don't believe me, rent *Chariots of Fire*)
Director
Producer
Production Designer
Sound
Writer

If you like a movie, praise us all.

Butch Cassidy and the Sundance Kid

If I seem to be more personal in what follows, it's for one reason: *because I remember*. I have no idea what the other writers went through in the course of their lives, leading to the production of the scenes you have now read; I don't know where they were or who they thought they were, any of that stuff. And if I know about me, it's because I couldn't block out all that I wanted to.

I had no idea when I sat down to write it, but I have come to believe that the jump off the cliff in *Butch Cassidy and the Sundance Kid* has turned out to be the most important scene of my life. I can argue that everything good that has come out of my relationship with Hollywood was because of this scene.

What did I know when I wrote it? About screenwriting, really very little. The first draft of *Butch* was done over the Christmas vacation of 1965–66, when I was, quite by accident, teaching creative writing at Princeton University.

My then-wife Ilene and I moved to Princeton early in '65, when our second daughter, Susanna, was about to be born. I remember, just as we were settling in, getting news of a start date for *Harper*, my first American film. (I had doctored *Masquerade* the year before.)

I think I may have done another screenplay around this time. *In the Spring the War Ended*, from the fine novel by Richard Zinackis. A marvelous piece of material, and as current now as then—it was about American deserters in World War II, thousands of them, all of them hiding out in Brussels. Their nightmare was simply that when World War II ended, their own private war was about to begin—ignored while the cannons blasted, now they were targeted, and how were they going to survive, somehow get back home?

I wrote the screenplay and the producer liked it, gave it to a top director, Martin Ritt, who climbed immediately onboard. But Fox, the studio that owned the material, buried the project because they needed all the Pentagon cooperation they could get, since they were about to enter production on *Patton*.

I don't remember if I swore off movies at the time, but I was more than a little frustrated, and very pissed. And certainly, for the time being, a novelist again.

The teaching came about this way.

We had moved, I had taken a room at an inn there where I planned to write. Then the writing professor came calling. Princeton had two in those days, the regular full-time guy, and a visiting guy.

It turned out it was the regular guy who contacted me, because he had suddenly gotten a shot at a year's sabbatical and in order to accept it he had to find another writer immediately to replace him. And since I was right there in town, I was asked.

And I was thrilled. Every piece of nonfiction I've ever tried has had, at its basis, teaching. I always wondered how I would like the life of a professor. I talked it over with Ilene and we agreed there was no downside. The job would be seven or eight hours a week of teaching and seminars, and for the rest, I would get to work on a novel. I had not attempted anything in over two years, having been wiped out by *Boys and Girls Together*. (I had wanted to write a long novel. Dumbest thing I ever did.)

It was finished in '63, published in '64 to brutal reviews. I was on the verge of tears for a month. The good thing that came out of it was that I decided never again to let the fuckers get to me. I have not read a review of anything of mine in thirty-five years now, and never will, good or bad.

Aside: I don't think that's a terrible idea for us. If there is a critic you love—and I don't care from what field—then you must read that critic, whether he is dealing with your work or anyone else's. If you detest them, as you should, if you find them poor sad inept creatures, as they are, if you feel that not only are they failures as critics—which goes with the job—but worse, failures in life, then why on earth would you bother to read them? End of aside.

A word about my work habits. I was a total writing failure growing up. By which I mean I could never get anything published, not even when at Oberlin I was fiction editor of the literary magazine. There were three of us who decided what got printed, two brilliant young women and *moi,* one of them the poetry editor, one the overall boss. All work was submitted anonymously, and each issue I would take my latest glory and stick it in with the other stories, and each time when the three of us met—I can still feel my heart pounding—oh God, I wanted someone here on earth to admit that I might, just might, please let me have just a fucking smidgen of talent.

"Well, we can't publish *this* shit." That's what my two lady friends would say. Each issue. "Well, we can't publish *this* shit."

I took a creative writing course at Oberlin. I was the only one in it who wanted to write. Got the only C. Everyone else, B-pluses or A's.

I remember my oldest friend on earth, John Kander, of Kander and Ebb the songwriting team (*Chicago, Cabaret, New York, New York*) was in the class and the day before each assignment was due—and I would have spent hours and hours and hours on my stories, working all week on them—Kander would look at his watch and say he better get started on a story.

Get started on a story. The fucker hadn't even begun, hadn't given it a thought. And each week when he got his A and I got my C, he couldn't help it, he would fight it, he apologized for his behavior—but he would just get helpless with laughter.

I took an essay-writing course. The half-dozen most brilliant girls at Oberlin—no place has more brilliant girls than Oberlin—and I was the class idiot. (I am not making this shit up.)

The teacher, wonderful Professor Roellinger, would always start with me. And these genius girls would sit there, nodding silently. Then Roellinger would say, "Who can help Bill out on this?"

And they would all raise their brilliant little hands.

And they were so nice. "That's some of your best work," they would assure me, "but perhaps it would make more sense, Bill, if you put your first point *before* your second point instead of after."

I took a creative writing course at Northwestern one summer. Worst grade in the class. Again. No sign of talent. Again.

And I so wanted to write. I had these stories and I wanted to tell them and I *was* telling them but everybody turned away.

I graduate Oberlin in '52, go into the Army, am sent to the Pentagon by mistake. (Since I am clearly as inept as I was back in essay-writing class, getting stuff out of order, I will now make sense of that last sentence.)

It is the fall of 1952, and I am at Camp Breckinridge, Kentucky, doing basic training. Basic training in those days was sixteen weeks' duration, the first eight military stuff—marching, firing, pulling pins, etc.—and the last eight a speciality.

Since I could type, I was sent, with gasping clarity, to clerical school, along, that same day, with six other guys. All of us college grads, none of us dumb. Immediately we are the teachers in the school.

The captain in charge of the clerical school knew one thing only: God had, for some reason, smiled on him. Because he was a crazed golfer and he realized that for the next twenty-two months—the remainder of our military commitment—he could do nothing but work on his golf game.

We seven could run the school without his presence.

How to keep us, though. Easy. He wrote a letter to the Pentagon, requesting that we be assigned to his clerical school until discharge. We were, he wrote, these fabulous, brilliant, and hardworking privates. The best.

The Pentagon got his letter and this was their reply: *Fuck you.* If these seven guys are as brilliant and fabulous, not to mention hardworking, as you say, *we want them here.* Great jobs await them here.

His request denied, his heart broken, the captain watched us run his place for the weeks remaining. And then, sob, he was alone again with the usual run of recruits one got in those days.

And we were sent to the Pentagon?

We were and we weren't.

During World War II, soldiers were sent overseas direct from basic training. I think the five Sullivan brothers—all killed aboard ship without a chance to say goodbye to their loved ones—were the reason things changed.

At any rate, all soldiers, at least in 1952, were given two weeks' leave *after* basic, *before* reporting. The seven of us went home, said our goodbyes to our families, then joined up again in Washington, a fortnight later, all of us wondering what our "great jobs" would be.

We never found out. Because during the two weeks that we were home the jobs were filled by others. So there we were, in Washington, with no jobs. What was the Army going to do with us?

We found out later that day—send us to Korea. They were going to ship our asses out immediately. On the next troop ship leaving for Korea.

Which never came.

The Korean War was winding down, there was no more use for us there. (We did not know this at the time, of course. The idea of getting "sent over" lingered with us. Providing not good thoughts. All those terrifying possibilities.)

So there we were, at the Pentagon, with twenty months to get through and no job. What we did not know was that to the ordinary Pentagon civilian boss, we were gold. The more people you have under you, the more power you have and the higher your rating.

We were sent to the basement. Where we did a lot of reading at our desks. And had an amazing number of rubber-band fights. This sounds childish, I suppose—suppose shit, it *was* incredibly childish—but we were going crazy from boredom. We got amazingly accurate with rubber bands and were the only office in Pentagon history—we are talking of the highlight of my military career, understand—that was *refused* a request for additional rubber bands.

Those twenty months were an amazing waste for us all. I remember once being given an entire sixty-page (or so) booklet containing abbreviations for every job title in the military. My job: improve them as I retyped them. I actually made the front page of *The Washington Post* when they discovered that one of my abbreviations had more letters in it than the job title it was abbreviating.

Another assignment was to copy an entire document of considerable length, and you must understand this, I am a fast typist but not an accurate one, and it took me weeks to do what my lady boss wanted, and when I finally *finally* was done, I gave it to her and she took it with two fingers and right in front of me dumped it in the wastebasket.

At night, after supper, I went back to the Pentagon, alone, went into my office, now empty, and night after night wrote my stories. I don't know how many, but I do know this—none of them were accepted by any of the magazines I sent them to.

The Army got rid of me in September '54—Corporal William Goldman if you please—and I went back to Highland Park, Illinois, for a couple of days before starting grad school at Columbia.

That first night home the phone rang and it was a friend who was about to get discharged from nearby Fort Sheridan. "Do you want to see *Gunga Din*?" he said.

I always want to see *Gunga Din*. It is, with no doubt whatsoever, the greatest movie ever made. And only an idiot (or a critic) would argue that point. Sure, I said, where?

"It's playing here on post."

Just tell me when, and I'm there, I told him.

"One problem," he explained. "You've got to be a soldier to get in." And that, sports fans, is how I spent my first civilian night—getting illegally back into my corporal's uniform, feeling guilty as shit, and terrified, lying my way back onto an Army base to see that joyous film.

Great as ever.

Columbia began terribly. My Oberlin record was so pathetic I could not get accepted on merit.

So dear departed friend Douglas Moore, the head of the Columbia Music Department, used his powers and I was accepted.

Registration day will always stay with me. Columbia was a big university, Oberlin was a small college. I had never seen so many students as that first morning. I went to the English Department, was given a form that had to be initialed by the professors whose classes I was taking, then bring the form back for authentication.

Hours and hours of standing in lines, getting some courses, not getting others, then finally, kind of triumphant, mid-afternoon, back to the English Department, where I gave the form to the secretary of the department. She looked at it—and boy is this etched in acid in my memory—said this: "But this is the wrong form."

I tried to explain: *she* had given it to me.

Did not faze her. "You'll have to do it all over again" was her reply, ripping it up, handing me another with this hate-filled smile. "You don't mind doing that, do you, Mr. Goldman? After all, you're lucky to be here."

As I type this I realize something—she kind of looked like Linda Tripp.

I studied my ass off, was tops in my class again, first time since eighth grade. I went on writing my stories during my two Columbia years—got a master's with honors, had the hours for a doctorate—got one job offer—Duluth University, teaching English comp, I think, for $3,200 a year.

But I didn't want to teach in Duluth. And I didn't want to go back to Chicago and get some job writing copy at an ad agency. I knew if I did I would die of alcohol.

Because I wanted to tell my stories.

I had over a hundred rejection slips by then. Never even *one* scrawled note of encouragement from some kind editor. It was getting harder for me to go to my desk. Confidence is everything and mine was going, going so fast.

So—and I don't know where the madness came from—in despair, twenty-four years old, a total failure in life, I went back home to Highland Park and, in my small bedroom, on the twenty-fifth of June, 1956, I sat down at my desk and started typing.

I had no idea what I was about to write, but I knew I had to write something, and so, for three weeks, I wrote, just sitting there, and this thing burst out of me, and I cannot tell you how strange that was, since

I had never in my life been even on a page 20 before, and suddenly there I was on page 45, and then 70, and what country I was visiting I had no idea, or how I got there, or was I going to get out alive.

As I write this, I can still see myself lying in bed those nights, having no idea what I was going to type the next day, but knowing I had to get something down—I left my body those nights, I was floating on the ceiling, looking down at the me thrashing and wondering what tomorrow could bring.

On July 14th, it was done. It had a title: *The Temple of Gold* (from the climb Gunga Din does to save everybody, never mind that he gets shot to death in the process, never mind that he *knew* it was going to happen).

So there I was with this 187-page thing, this heffalump, but what do you do next? What I did was this: contact a guy I had met in the Army who had met an agent once.

So off *The Temple of Gold* went to this agent, Joe McCrindle, who liked it, and who sent it off to a friend who was an editor at Knopf, who liked it too.

The acceptance call totally paralyzed me.

I was living on West Seventy-second Street in New York then, with John Kander and my brother, Jim, now dead, who wrote a wonderful musical, *Follies,* and a glorious play, *The Lion in Winter.*

Kander was out when the call came but he was back a little later and I told him and he was, of course, stunned and pleased and he asked who I had called to tell.

Nobody, was my answer. I was frozen.

So for the next, I don't know, hour, maybe more, Kander would call friends and say, "Billy's novel was taken by Knopf and he wanted you to know," and then he would hand me the phone and I would stumble through a few words, then Kander would take the phone back and explain that I was not too up for talking at the moment, and on he went to the next.

I know how strange this all must seem to you, and I did not know this then, but I was terrified of telling my favored brother, almost five years older, because he was the one who was programmed to succeed, but his writing career was still on hold then, no one wanted his plays then, but they would, that was the deal, and I was supposed to fail. It was like Greek crime for me to have done what I so unforgivably did: surpass my brother.

But running stride for stride was this: I knew I was a fraud.

And sooner or later, there was going to be a reckoning, and when it happened, I was going to suffer for my sins.

I think, in a way, I decided to forestall that punishment by working—if I could just write enough, the Fates might never catch up with me. I decided a novel a year would be fair, since I didn't have a real job. All I did was go to the movies.

And the next year I wrote *Your Turn to Curtsy, My Turn to Bow*—I am not much at titles, but this was my favorite, still holds pride of place. Two years later came *Soldier in the Rain* (I was involved in the theater is the reason it took so long—I was doctoring my first show on Broadway).

I had two original shows on Broadway the next year—not for long, alas, but the amount of time making things happen is the same, hit or flop. *Boys and Girls Together* came out in 1964, but so did *No Way to Treat a Lady* so I was still hustling, doing my best to keep the Fates from destroying me. Movies were starting to take up some time now too.

Now, dear reader, we are back at Princeton, I am a teacher and this terrible thing happens—*I cannot write a novel.* I wasn't blocked, as I had been when I was halfway through *Boys and Girls Together*. What happened was I became obsessed with my Princeton job.

A very few teachers had changed my life, had been so crucial and glorious for me, so *I wanted to be the best teacher these Princeton kids ever had.*

I wanted them to think of me as I thought of Miss MacMartin and Mr. Hamill, who got me through high school, and Mr. Murray at Oberlin and Miss Rogelski in second grade. I wanted the college kids to say, when they were full of sleep, "I had this writing guy at Princeton, and we used to talk—in seminar—and God, he was wonderful, he came at such a great time in my life."

All I wanted, not much, was to be remembered forever.

Well, there wasn't time for my own writing. I cared only about them. I started teaching in early fall, and I had my office, of course, and I went there some, to read the paper mostly, and the teaching got more and more exciting for me.

Suddenly, then, Christmas vacation.

And it had been three years since I'd written any fiction. Other stuff, sure, but in my heart I'm a novelist who happens to write screenplays—and at that moment I realized this: I had no novel pressing inside me. But I had to write *something* or the Fates would begin to close in.

So in a state of (I suppose) even more than the usual panic, I decided to try something I had never written before: an original screenplay.

———

When I begin a piece of writing, I know a lot but not enough. I know the pulse that makes me want to attempt whatever the piece is, article, novel, story, screenplay. (I just finished an article for the Sunday *Daily News*—this is early April of '99—about what is happening with my beloved Knicks this year. And what is happening is that the beat writers are trying to save the job of the inadequate head coach, Jeff Van Gundy. Their lack of truth-telling has driven me nuts this year—and that *rage* is what made me write the piece, what accompanied me every second I was thinking about it or writing it.)

I had no such rage when I sat down in my Princeton University office to tell Butch and Sundance's story. What I had was this: they moved me. These two guys, surviving for years together, and becoming legends *a second time*. Famous outlaws who never killed, who traveled with a beautiful young woman, who were remarkably popular with the ordinary people of their time—well, if I could get that down, maybe I'd have something.

Butch had been, in the Old West, one of the two legendary figures while still alive, the other being Jesse James. And then, in eight years of life in South America, Butch and Sundance became the *Banditos Yanquis*, legends *again*.

You have to know this about me now: I am moved more by stupid courage than anything else on earth. Have no idea why. But it has been with me for a very long time. Three examples from my childhood.

When I was probably seven or eight, I happened to read a book titled *Scarface, the Story of a Grizzly*. I remember next to nothing of it, except that Scarface was the biggest grizzly around, and tough enough to take all the crap life throws at you when everybody wants you dead. But my memory is, he was decent, didn't take advantage of being the toughest one around. And in the last chapter Scarface is old, but you still don't want to mess with him, and he is walking along this narrow mountain path, when, above him, an avalanche starts. And I figured he's escaped worse, he'll make it to a safe part of the mountain path.

But he didn't do that.

He turned and faced the oncoming avalanche. Then he stood up and as the giant rocks came down at him, he raised his giant paws and fought them, giving as good as he got until the boulders outnumbered him, carried him over the cliff to his death.

I remember Minnie's coming up and asking was I all right—Minnie is the woman who worked for my family and is the main reason I am still around—and I couldn't answer, couldn't do anything but sob my heart out.

The second example is when I am about the same age and the great Gershwin musical, *Porgy and Bess,* came to Chicago. My family went and we sat there and if you don't know the story, it's about this cripple, Porgy, who can't walk, he gets around on this pathetic goat cart, towed by a scrawny goat, and we're someplace in the Deep South. Porgy is hopelessly in love with Bess, a beauty but weak. Toward the end, Porgy is sent to jail (he murdered the village monster) and while he is there, Bess is wooed by a pusher, Sportin' Life, who, using drugs as a lure, steals her away, takes her to New York City, the other end of the universe as far as anyone in this town is concerned.

Porgy gets out of jail, and I am dreading the moment when he finds out Bess is gone. I mean, cripples don't win beauties in this world, not unless they are very rich indeed, and Porgy is a beggar. So he is out of jail and I am so scared for him, his life is over, how is he going to survive his loss, and he chitchats with the villagers and then he says it—where's Bess?

No one wants to answer but finally he finds out—Bess is gone, she is gone forever, gone to New York City.

Silence in the theater. Then Porgy says these three amazing words:

"Bring my goat."

And the music gets magical and here comes the goat and Porgy gets on his cart and the whole cast is singing "Oh Lord, I'm on My Way," one of the greatest songs ever—

—I was gone again.

The show ends and wild applause.

I am sobbing out of all control.

Curtain calls, more cheers.

You know what I'm doing.

Now, we had very good seats, near the front, and people started to put on their coats—

—and they cannot not notice me.

"Is he all right?" a gentleman asks my parents. Now, they didn't know what to answer, because they had no idea if I was all right or not. Soon other grown-ups began patting my head (I remember this humiliation, oh, do I ever) and the aisles are filled and movement is slow and the only sound is me trying to muffle my crying while I was figuring out— what was going to happen to Porgy? He didn't even know where he was going, that it was so far, that it would take him to places he had no experience of, that it was going to be so awful because what if his goat died, where was he going to get the money for another, or what was he going to do when one of the wheels came off his cart?

I cried all the way home, and we lived in the suburbs.

Now, neither of these outbreaks are close to what happened to me when I was eight and *Gunga Din* came to the Alcyon. Cary Grant, Victor McLaglen and Douglas Fairbanks, Jr., are all captured with knives to their throat while these evil Indian murderers are about to slaughter the entire British garrison, who do not know they are walking into a trap.

I figure Cary is going to save them, but he is wounded and Victor MacLaglen is the strongest of the bunch but he is in shitty shape too, and here come the British, deeper and deeper into the trap, and the Indian killers are waiting there, and suddenly, Cary Grant looks at Gunga Din, this joke of a water carrier, and whispers these words:

"The colonel's got to know."

By comparison, I was poised at *Porgy*. Gunga Din's all shot to shit, but he takes that bugle from a dead guy and starts this climb up this golden temple and when he gets there he blows the bugle and saves the British and is killed.

I have seen that movie sixteen times, and the last time—true, I tell you nothing but truths—I started crying in the *credits*.

Why am I telling you all this?

Remember me saying that when I started I knew a lot of things but not enough? Well, one of the things I knew was this: **I had, in my head, a moment of stupid courage.** And I knew if I could just get my story there, I'd be okay.

It comes at the very end. Butch and Sundance have done a payroll robbery, have been given away by a brand on the mule they used to carry the money. In a small Bolivian town, the word goes out, hundreds of armed troops come. (They really did.) Butch and Sundance run out of ammunition, Butch goes for more, a stash they left on their horses, Sundance giving cover. But it all goes badly and they are both of them mortally wounded. They are in a small shack, while outside the troops continue to gather. They both know this: they are going to die of their wounds. This is their farewell conversation.

The Australia Scene

CUT TO

BUTCH AND SUNDANCE, crouched close together by a window, peering out at the setting sun.

> BUTCH
> I got a great idea where we should go next.

> SUNDANCE
> Well, I don't wanna hear it.

> BUTCH
> You'll change your mind once I tell you--

> SUNDANCE
> Shut up.

> BUTCH
> Okay, okay.

> SUNDANCE
> It was your great ideas got us here.

> BUTCH
> Forget about it.

> SUNDANCE
> I don't want to hear another of your great
> ideas, all right?

> BUTCH
> All right.

> SUNDANCE
> Good.

                        BUTCH
     Australia.

CUT TO

SUNDANCE. He just looks at Butch.

CUT TO

BUTCH.

                        BUTCH
     I figured secretly you wanted to know, so I
     told you--Australia.

CUT TO

BUTCH AND SUNDANCE.

                        SUNDANCE
     That's your great idea?

                        BUTCH
     The latest in a long line.

                        SUNDANCE
                   (exploding with all he has
                    left)
     Australia's no better than here!

                        BUTCH
     That's all you know.

                        SUNDANCE
     Name me one thing.

                        BUTCH
     They speak English in Australia.

                    SUNDANCE
They do?

                    BUTCH
That's right, smart guy, so we wouldn't be
foreigners. And they ride horses. And
they've got thousands of miles to hide out
in--and a good climate, nice beaches, you
could learn to swim--

                    SUNDANCE
Swimming's not important, what about the
banks?

                    BUTCH
Easy, ripe and luscious.

                    SUNDANCE
The banks or the women?

                    BUTCH
Once we get the one we'll get the other.

                    SUNDANCE
It's a long way, though, isn't it?

                    BUTCH
              (shouting it out)
Everything's always gotta be perfect with you!

                    SUNDANCE
I just don't want to get there and find out it
stinks, that's all.

CUT TO

BUTCH.

                    BUTCH
Will you at least think about it?

CUT TO

SUNDANCE. He considers this a moment.

                    SUNDANCE
     All right, I'll think about it.

CUT TO

BUTCH AND SUNDANCE. CLOSE UP.

                    BUTCH
     Now after we--
               (and suddenly he stops)
     --wait a minute.

                    SUNDANCE
     What?

                    BUTCH
     You didn't see Lefors out there?

                    SUNDANCE
     Lefors? No.

                    BUTCH
     Good. For a minute there I thought we were in
     trouble.

CUT TO

THE SUN, dying.

PULL BACK TO REVEAL

THE SOLDIERS, tense and ready and

CUT TO

THE CAPTAIN, moving swiftly about the perimeter, gesturing his men forward, and as he does

CUT TO

ONE GROUP OF MEN, vaulting over the wall, then

CUT TO

ANOTHER GROUP OF MEN, vaulting over the wall, rifles
at the ready.

CUT TO

BUTCH AND SUNDANCE on their feet. Slowly they move
toward the door as we

CUT TO

MORE AND MORE SOLDIERS, vaulting over the wall.

CUT TO

BUTCH AND SUNDANCE, into the last of the sunlight and
then comes the first of a painfully loud burst of
rifle fire and as the sound explodes--

THE CAMERA FREEZES ON BUTCH AND SUNDANCE.

Another terrible barrage. Louder. Butch and Sundance
remain frozen. Somehow the sound of the rifles manages to build even more. Butch and Sundance stay
frozen. Then the sound begins to diminish.

And as the sound diminishes, so does the color, and
slowly, the faces of Butch and Sundance begin to
change. The song from the New York sequence begins.
The faces of Butch and Sundance continue to change,
from color to the grainy black and white that began
their story. The rifle fire is popcorn soft now, as it
blows them back into history.

   I can't do any better than that.
   It's the best ending I've ever been involved with. And of course, what

gives me the confidence to say this is I have such faith in the stupid courage part of the sequence—

—**they don't talk about their situation.**

That made them courageous for me. Here they were, bleeding and in increasing pain, surrounded, outnumbered, all that good stuff. They knew they were going to die, it was over. And they could have had memories, not necessarily soppy stuff, but other tough spots would have been okay, they had decades of life to go over. But once I knew they would never talk about the present, I had confidence that I, who had been wrecked by stupid courage over the decades, could finally have a moment of my own.

(I'm a total sucker for them. The one thing I can look at in *Marathon Man* is in the novel—God, I wished it had somehow been in the movie, too—when Babe, the marathon man, has been tortured and there's not a lot left and the three bad guys take him out to a car to finish things—

—and feebly, he breaks free, tries to literally run for his life, and he was never a great runner, never mentioned in the same breath as his two heroes, Nurmi and Bikila, the legends he has pictures of in his room, and while he runs he calls up all kinds of fantasies to spur himself, he tries to inhale through his damaged tooth, to make the pain even more horrendous, and nothing works, or works well enough—

—and then Bikila and Nurmi are flanking him, telling him the pain is part of being great, only real marathon men understand pain—

—and they bring him on home.)

Anyway, there I am at Princeton, looking for salvation, and that ending was one, if I could just get the story there.

I also felt confident about the beginning.

Wonderful real-life stuff. Butch Cassidy, unknown to the world in 1965, was a legend during his lifetime, so popular he would actually do this when followed by the law: he would ride up to farmhouses and say who he was, and that he was in kind of a pickle, and would it be all right if he hid out in their barn till the sheriff went by.

Sure, Butch. And they hid him.

Maybe it was because of the force of his personality, the universally remarked-on affability, the fact that he never shot or killed anybody until he became a payroll guard in South America, people just did what he asked them to do.

But nothing made me as confident as when Butch was in jail.

This is early in his career. The famous Hole in the Wall gang is not what it became. And I forget the state but let's say it was Colorado.

Okay. He is in prison and the governor calls him in. And says this: "Butch, if you'll promise me you'll go straight, I'll let you out."

And Butch's answer? "I can't do that."

Think for a second. Here he is, this young outlaw in prison. For God knows what reason, he is offered this: *freedom*. All he has to do is lie and say he'll go straight. And he answers thus:

"I can't do that."

I don't know about you, but for me, that's as brilliant an introduction to one of your heroes as any I've ever come across. *But it gets better*— Butch tells the governor this: "I'll make you a deal." Think for a second on that baby, too. The *convict* is offering the *governor* a deal. And here it was: "If you let me out, I promise never to work in Colorado again."

And the governor *takes* the deal.

And lets him out.

And Butch never worked in Colorado again.

Great great stuff. No wonder I was confident about the beginning.

Now, those of you who have seen the movie may be hard pressed to remember Paul Newman having any scenes with any governors. Because they were not there. Because I never wrote them. Because I could not figure how to get that great fucking scene into the story I was telling.

I tried, God knows. But my Butch was famous, he was not a kid, and in my story, the West was ending. And in order to get him out of jail, duh, I had to first get him *into* jail.

And there was no time for it.

It was wrong. Wrong at least for me. It would have screwed up my structure if I had put it in. I realized this while I was trying to get started with the screenplay. The one most confidence-building scene I had? Gone.

I had other reasons for feeling good about the start, stuff that did make the movie. The fact that Butch robbed two trains that had the same payroll guard, Woodcock, and blew him up twice. That happened. The fact that Butch put too much dynamite under a safe during another train robbery, and blew the safe apart so the money floated everywhere. Happened. Beautiful Etta Place, the Kid's girl. Existed. Trying to enlist and fight in the Spanish-American War. They did try. The bicycle scene was made up but at that time, bicycles really were a phenomenon, like rap today.

So when I set to work, back in the Princeton of thirty-four years ago, I was a lot younger, with enough confidence to get started. And I also knew the ending would keep me above the waterline.

My terror was this: the middle section was the one that would kill me.

———

Since the mid-sixties, the elements that make up a good story have not changed. But what has is the audience's knowledge. They are so much more experienced today. Cassettes have happened, cable has happened, the availability of flicks is so different from when I began.

My killer problem was that my guys had to do the unthinkable in a western: *run away*. It may not sound like much now, because *Butch* was such a hit, but then it was *the* block in my storytelling path.

Here is what happened in real life: E. H. Harriman, the railroad king, got sick of Butch robbing him, so he financed something new to the Wild West—a Superposse. He paid for half a dozen of the great lawmen to come together from all over the country to kill Cassidy.

Here is what happened then in real life: Butch took off for South America with Sundance and Etta.

He knew he had zero chance against an all-star team like that, so he left for sunnier climes till Harriman got bored paying all those guys and they disbanded. In other words, *they never chased him*. He fled.

Not the stuff of drama.

I had no great solution—I don't know that there is one—but here's what I decided to do with this: somehow try and make the audience *want* Butch and Sundance to run away. I had to make the Superposse so all-powerful, so impregnable to defeat, that people sitting out there in the dark would say yes, for chrissakes, **go to Bolivia.**

So what I did, hoping it would save me, was not invent the Superposse, but invent the Superposse *chase*. This *thing* had come from nowhere and was going to kill them and their world. This was my opening description:

> The Superposse consist of perhaps a half-dozen men. Taken as a
> group, they look, act, and are, in any and all ways, formidable.

They appear approximately half an hour into the story, leave close to half an hour later. And all they do is track our heroes. Outthink them at every turn. Butch begins reacting to them early on, "Who are those guys?" and soon it becomes a litany. The posse tracks them, never losing a beat, coming closer, always closer, shrinking the playing field until finally Butch and Sundance are trapped on a mountain ledge. This is what happens then.

The Jumping-off-the-Cliff Scene

CUT TO

The path, ending.

CUT TO

BUTCH AND SUNDANCE, standing there, just standing there gaping at the dead end the path has led them into.

                    BUTCH AND SUNDANCE
              (together)
       DAMMIT!

CUT TO

A long shot of the two of them standing there stunned, the sound echoing over and over and

CUT TO

BUTCH AND SUNDANCE, whirling, starting back the way they came and

CUT TO

THE SUPERPOSSE, moving toward them.

CUT TO

BUTCH AND SUNDANCE, watching them come.

                    BUTCH
       What I figure is we can fight or we give.
              (SUNDANCE nods)
       If we give, we go to jail.

CUT TO

CLOSE UP. Sundance shaking his head.

>   SUNDANCE
>   (with all the meaning in the
>   world)
>   I been there already.

CUT TO

BUTCH, nodding in agreement.

>   BUTCH
>   Me, too. If we fight they can stay right where
>   they are and starve us out--
>   (he glances up now and)

CUT TO

The mountain above them. High up, there are open flat
places where a man could fire down on them.

>   BUTCH'S VOICE (OVER)
>   --or they could go for position and shoot us--

CUT TO

BUTCH AND SUNDANCE.

>   BUTCH
>   --or they could start a little rockslide and
>   get us that way. What else could they do?

>   SUNDANCE
>   They could surrender to us but I don't think we
>   oughtta count on that.

CUT TO

BUTCH. He laughs, but the moment won't hold.

                    BUTCH
               (flat and down)
          What're we gonna do?

CUT TO

BUTCH AND SUNDANCE.

                    SUNDANCE
          You've always been the brains, Butch; you'll
          think of something.

                    BUTCH
          Well, that takes a load off; for awhile there I
          was worried.
                    (he looks back down the way
                     they came and)

CUT TO

THE SUPERPOSSE. The man in the white hat is gesturing
and now the Superposse begins to split, some of them
moving onto a higher path that leads above where Butch
and Sundance are.

CUT TO

BUTCH AND SUNDANCE, watching them climb.

                    SUNDANCE
          They're going for position all right.
                    (He takes out his guns, starts
                     to examine them with great
                     care)
          We better get ready.

                    BUTCH
              (getting his guns ready)
        The next time I say let's go someplace like Bo-
        livia, let's go someplace like Bolivia.

                    SUNDANCE
        Next time.

CUT TO

THE SUPERPOSSE. They continue to make their way up,
moving quickly and silently across the mountain.

CUT TO

SUNDANCE.

                    SUNDANCE
              (watching them get into
               position)
        You ready, Butch?

                    BUTCH (OVER)
        NO!
              (and as SUNDANCE turns)

ZOOM TO

CLOSE UP--BUTCH. He is smiling.

                    BUTCH
        We'll jump!

CUT TO

THE STREAM below. It is fifty feet down and going very
fast.

CUT TO

BUTCH AND SUNDANCE.

                    SUNDANCE
          Like hell we will.

                    BUTCH
                 (really excited now--all this
                  next is overlapping and goes
                  like a shot)
          No, no, it's gonna be o.k.--just so it's deep
          enough we don't get squished to death--they'll
          never follow us--

                    SUNDANCE
          --how do you know?--

                    BUTCH
          --would you make a jump like that if you didn't
          have to?--

                    SUNDANCE
          --I have to and I'm not gonna--

                    BUTCH
          --it's the only way. Otherwise we're dead.
          They'll have to go all the way back down the
          way we came. Come on--

                    SUNDANCE
                 (looking up the mountain)
          --just a couple of decent shots, that's all I
          want--

                    BUTCH
          --<u>come on</u>--

                    SUNDANCE
          --<u>no</u>--

                    BUTCH
--we got to--

                    SUNDANCE
--<u>no</u>--

                    BUTCH
--yes--

                    SUNDANCE
--get away from me--

                    BUTCH
--why?--

                    SUNDANCE
--I wanna fight 'em--

                    BUTCH
--they'll kill us--

                    SUNDANCE
--maybe--

                    BUTCH
--you wanna die?--

                    SUNDANCE
--don't you?--

                    BUTCH
--I'll jump first--

                    SUNDANCE
--no--

                    BUTCH
--o.k., you jump first--

                    SUNDANCE
--<u>no</u> I said--

                         BUTCH
                    (big)
          What'sa matter with you?--

                         SUNDANCE
                    (bigger)
          I can't swim!
                    (Blind mad, wildly embarrassed.
                     He just stands there)

CUT TO

BUTCH, starting to roar.

CUT TO

SUNDANCE, anger building.

CUT TO

BUTCH.

                         BUTCH
          You stupid fool, the fall'll probably kill
          you.

CUT TO

SUNDANCE, starting to laugh now and

CUT TO

The two of them. BUTCH whips off his gun belt, takes
hold of one end, holds the other out. SUNDANCE takes
it, wraps it once tight around his hand. They move to
the edge of the path and step off.

CUT TO

BUTCH AND SUNDANCE, falling through the twilight.

```
CUT TO


The biggest splash ever recorded.


CUT TO


The stream, going like hell.  Then


CUT TO


BUTCH AND SUNDANCE, alive in the water.  Music begins,
the same music that went on during BUTCH and ETTA's
bicycle ride, and as the music picks up, so does the
speed of the current as it carries them along, spin-
ning and turning and


CUT TO


THE SUPERPOSSE, frozen in the twilight on the moun-
tainside.
```

If you were in movie theaters back in those days, it was not hard to tell the scene worked—as Butch and Sundance jumped, as the cry of "Horseshiiiit" echoed. There were shouts of joy and surprise and laughter, and, yes, applause. Audiences loved the two guys so much now they would follow them anyplace. They wanted to know the crucial question from all audiences since we left the muck: **What happens next?**

They never questioned South America. And guess what—the movie runs a little out of steam halfway through South America. Didn't matter.

The people wanted to be there.

When that happens, and it happens rarely, at least for me, it's very hard to screw up your movie. I believe it would have been easy to screw it up if that scene had not worked. People might have felt uneasy about the trip the guys were taking, or might have said, well, the first stuff was fun but the rest of it wasn't as good. Might have said a million things.

But they didn't. They wanted to be there.

The movie became a phenomenon, changed a lot of lives. Redford, so marvelous, became, soon after, the biggest star in the world. Newman, already the biggest star in the world, and a joy to work with, had a terrific time, began a relationship with George Roy Hill that later encompassed both *The Sting* and *Slap Shot*. Hill, for me the most underrated director of the last thirty years, became one of the two Giant Apes in the world of moviemaking, along with David Lean.

And I became, well, you fill in the blank. Doesn't matter. All that does is: I'm still here . . .

Originals

An original screenplay? Nothing to it, really.

Just come up with a new and fresh and different story that builds logically to a satisfying and surprising conclusion (because Art, as we all know, needs to be both surprising and inevitable).

Do you know how hard that is?

I've tried a bunch and I'll talk about some of them briefly, but remember this—those two crucial questions that need answering for an adaptation? Well, they must both have already been answered positively by you before you embark. Yes, you love it and yes, you can make it play.

Butch—what I loved was the fun and games, the sadness, taking the girl with them, all that—but mostly I loved the becoming legends again. Plus, of course, the confidence their dying gave me.

I researched it for eight years before I'd sucked up enough. Articles on the west, books, etc. Basically what enabled me to go after it was my love of westerns. From *Stagecoach* on. To be able to write the guy who really *really* was the fastest gun in all our history, well, how often does that happen?

The Great Waldo Pepper—not something I would have written had George Roy Hill not loved old airplanes so much. It was his need that drove me, plus we had done *Butch*.

I made up this guy—Waldo—who looked golden and *was* golden except really he was a failure. And finally gave him his shot at having a dream come true, even if it killed him.

The other confidence builder was that it fell logically into three acts. The barnstorming first act, the air-show second act, the Hollywood-stunts third act. That was what happened to a lot of pilots in those days, and I followed along. I fucked up some and Hill and I had a huge falling-out for a year in the middle of the screenplay, but I can look at the movie now and feel glad that I went there.

The Year of the Comet—if *Butch* had its basis in my love for westerns, *Comet* was my shot at romantic comedy: Grant and Kate, Grant and Audrey, Grant and Roz, Fred and Ginger, dozens of others from the '30s into the '50s.

There aren't so many these years. Cleese's *Wanda*, Curtis's *Four Weddings and a Funeral* and *Notting Hill*, I think Ramis's *Groundhog Day*. Ephron's *Harry and Sally*, Peter and Bobby Farrelly's *Mary*. I think those are my main five for the last dozen years.

I love the form, I love red wine, I invented with plausibility what would logically be the most valuable bottle of wine in history. I had a decent-sounding mismatched pair of lovers, I set the chase in the most romantic places I know, London, the French Riviera, the Scottish Highlands.

I did everything right—and it all just lay there.

Conclusion? I did next to nothing right. That's why it all just lay there.

I can be very tough with my own work since I don't like it all that much—and I have thought a great deal about how I screwed this up. I cannot come up with a satisfactory answer.

I guess, to quote Frank Gilroy's great line from *The Gig*, where one character yearns to be a wonderful jazz musician but isn't: Passion ain't enough.

The Sea Kings—my pirate flick. The audience has to love those, and I don't think kids do today. Who could blame them? Errol's dead.

So what made me write it was the genre, plus this: as great a kernel for a movie as any I've known (see the "Leper" chapter for a recap of my passion for the idea).

And the script, you will have to take on faith, is not so terrible. But it never got made.

After Joe Levine failed with it in the '70s, Dick Donner took a run at it in the '90s.

I don't expect it to ever happen. Expensive as hell, and each time you think, well, just maybe, something like *Cut-*

throat Island comes along and you're dead for another decade.

Mr. Horn. If that title rings even a little bell, yes it was a four-hour miniseries starring David Carradine and Richard Widmark.

Hope it was good. Never saw it. Couldn't bring myself to.

Tom Horn. Bounty hunter. (A rock under a dead man's head was his signature.) Indian fighter. (Brought in Geronimo.) Sentenced to death for a murder he never committed. (Escaped at the last minute; it was impossible but he did.) Gave himself up. Finally got hanged. (He lost so much weight in jail that he hung alive at the end of that rope for half an hour.)

Just some of the high spots.

In terms of the talents that were needed to survive in the Wild West, this was the most talented man who ever lived there. Redford (wrote it for him) was going to do it, didn't.

This was one of my bad experiences. What I regret so terribly was that this great story never had its shot. I remember deciding that it would be the last original I'd ever work on. And I prayed I'd never come across anyone as blazing as Tom Horn again.

But it wasn't the last original I ever worked on, because we are all slaves to material, and when I heard the story of the Tsavo lions, I was hooked again. You can read the chapter on *The Ghost and the Darkness* to find out what happened. I think of all six, I regret most that this story never found its proper audience. No, I regret most that Tom Horn is still unknown to most of America. No, I regret—

—when we write scripts and they don't happen or happen less well than we want, we regret them all. And always will.

The last one really broke my heart. Danny DeVito came to me and wondered if I wanted to do a basketball movie he could direct. I lucked out, wrote *Low Fives,* for Danny and John Cleese. Danny was to play a down-and-out coach at the antithesis of an Ivy League school. (I think in Texas, but I remember it was somewhere hot.) Danny, on a recruiting trip in Africa, discovers an amazing basketball talent, enrolls him in his school.

John Cleese was to play the dean of this awful place, who was in deep agony there, and just as desperate to get out as Danny. A lot of nice stuff happened. We had a cast reading and Barry Sonnenfeld, now a star director, then with just *Addams Family* behind him, was set to direct. I remember a fabulous actor, now dead, J. T. Walsh, read the part of a racist basketball coach.

Was *Low Fives* perfect? Nope. Did it work? Bet your ass. One of my all-time movie afternoons, listening. Then Barry got offered a ton to do the *Addams* sequel, took it, Danny began to cool, it died.

I still have hope. Someone has to.

As I look back on these seven, I realize my age. If you are thirty or under, all you know about westerns might be David Peoples's glorious *Unforgiven*. (Aside: I remember reading the rave review given by Roger Ebert in *Cinemania*. He talks about Eastwood and Jack Green's shooting, mentions Hackman and Harris and Freeman and Fisher and Wayne and Ford and even gets around to Godard. Never mentions Peoples, though. Why should he? All Peoples did was *make it up*. Jesus, Roger, it was an original screenplay. You know why that's such a disgrace? Because you expect ignorance from most, but Ebert's supposed to be one of the good ones.

There are no good ones.)

Back briefly to my age. I doubt any of you would be interested in the genres that hooked me into films. But the basic pulse still must be there: if you want to write *The Matrix*—and I liked *The Matrix*—go with God.

Just care.

Pitching

There is a reason pitching comes right after original screenplays—people don't usually pitch adaptations.

(But how would you like to have been in the room when Van Zant pitched his vomitous *Psycho* carbon? *You must remember that*—because if some asshole executive can say,

"Gee, what a fresh and great idea *that* is, wait'll I get home tonight and tell the wife"—the point being that if *Psycho* got greenlighted, there's hope for us all.)

Okay, what do I know about pitching? First thing, find a teacup. Then barely cover the bottom with water. No, that's too much.

I know *nothing* about the subject. I have only, in a third of a century, pitched once—and this to friends—and I was so awful I quit halfway through.

But truth to tell, it doesn't matter what *I* know because you are not going to be pitching to me.

I think I would accept every pitch made to me. Because I remember my panic when I tried to do it. But it is a definite part of Hollywood now. A writer has an idea and in the old days, he might have written it. Sometimes he still does. But more and more, the agent gets his client a meeting with a studio exec in which the idea is discussed, i.e., pitched.

Hollywood, as we know, has zero sense of history and there is a feeling pitching is relatively new. Total nonsense. If you've read any history at all, you know it was invented by Torquemada to make his days pass more happily during the Spanish Inquisition. He would tell imprisoned playwrights that if they could interest him in an idea, he would let them live long enough to write it. If they didn't, he dropped the fellow into a large vat of boiling tar, which of course is where the term "pitch" comes from.

The Ten Commandments of Pitching

1. *Never forget whom you are talking to.* The studio executive views you as an impediment to either his lunch or his tennis game. But some part of him also knows you might help his career. He doesn't *want* to listen to you, he would rather he lived in a world where he didn't *have* to listen to you. So do not bore him. Rule one is this: *Be brief.*

2. Brief means this: *in and out in five minutes.* Unless the executive asks you to stay.

3. Remember you are not telling the story, *you are throwing out a hook.*

3a. *Keep it simple.*

3b. *Not a lot of detail.*

3c. *One or two lines.* What you tell the executive is this: "Here's the setup, boom." If they buy the setup, there is a real chance they will buy the movie.

4. *Grab them.* You want them to think, "Yeah, I get that."

5. *People are busy.* (Same as rule one but I thought you ought to be reminded.)

6. *Do not pitch more than one idea per meeting.*

7. If you can, *leave an outline.* Executives love this. Not a detailed shot-by-shot deal, but a couple of pages where you start with what you hit them with and thicken it a bit, embellish it; if you have any glorious scenes in mind, put those in. (Likewise, if your ending sucks, leave it out.) Giving them something to read can only be a plus. It helps them fill out your pitch. It also makes them think you actually care about the piece of shit you are selling. (Piece of shit, as you should know, is the way executives refer to screenplays Out There.)

8. *Never read a pitch.* Some writers are more comfortable doing it that way, but the meeting is about your future, not your comfort. *Learn to tell your story.* Practice it by yourself or on friends until you are comfortable. Executives like eye contact.

9. *Pitch the same idea ten times in one day.* Obviously, keep that news to yourself. Do not say to Mr. Fox, "I would love to talk more but I'm late for my meeting with Mr. Time Warner."

9a. *Be aware of the values of multi-pitching.* It is good to get your idea out there. Especially if you are new, because more people will know of your existence.

9b. *Be aware of the risks of multi-pitching.* It is not good if your goal is to have a relationship with a particular studio, which you might actually want. There are no secrets in the movie business. Everybody knows somebody. Be aware that your multi-pitch day will get out. Never tell anyone you are giving them an exclusive if you aren't. Your word actually has a certain value in Southern California. Even if theirs doesn't.

10. Never forget that even if they buy your pitch, *most studios are planning on firing you as soon as you hand them your first draft.*

Okay, let's try something. I will attempt to pitch for you a couple of the originals I talked about a few minutes before. See what you think.

Butch: "It's a western, it's about these two guys, one of them is the leader of this huge gang and the other is his sidekick who's a great shot and this millionaire forms this posse to stop them from robbing his railroads and—"

I'm gasping already.

Try again. "It's a western, kind of a modern-day Gable-Tracy adventure flick about these two guys who take off for South America with one of the girlfriends and—"

Worse. I'm dead now.

I don't think *Butch* lends itself to pitching. Doesn't mean it's good or terrible, just that the story doesn't compress easily.

The Sea Kings: "It's *Butch Cassidy and the Sundance Kid* on the high seas—these two great pirates who actually sailed together, one's the most dangerous in history, Blackbeard, and the other's the only rich pirate ever, kind of as if Bill Gates decided he was done being a computer nerd and wanted a life of adventure.

"See, Blackbeard has had all the adventure in the world and what he wants is to retire rich, and Bonnet, the rich guy, what he wants is to have all the adventure in the world. And when they meet and sail together, what I want this to be is the story of these two amazing guys who are each other's dream."

What do you think? I don't mind that so much. What I hope I did was **make you want to know more.**

The Year of the Comet: "A Cary Grant–Audrey Hepburn romantic comedy about this great couple who meet and just hate each other but they're both chasing a ten-million-dollar bottle of wine across London and the French Riviera, where they have wild adventures. And no, they don't hate each other at the end."

I don't think that's *too* terrible. Might hook someone.

(Maybe at the end of the day, if they were tired.) How's by you?

My personal feeling is that neither *The Great Waldo Pepper* nor *Mr. Horn* lend themselves easily to this process. They are more character studies, they are darker, their heroes die.

You pitch them for me, see how you do.

One last crucial thing: the better known your work is, the higher your reputation, the more likely you are to receive a positive response. This whole deal is a ridiculous crapshoot, thriving today because most executives do not know how to read screenplays. And hate having to read them.

But if you are starting out, it's a quick way to solvency. So get your story comfortably inside you. And tell yourself you're going to go into that office a nothing but you're coming back a star!

Stay in Your Genre

You must always be aware of the *kind* of movie you are telling: romantic comedy, high adventure, family drama, bloodbath action (don't), special-effects thriller, horror, farce, whatever.

Each genre has a set of unwritten constraints. If you're writing a farce, you must be skilled at basic plotting, because farce, to be really funny, has to be really real. The minute you stretch things in a farce, it shatters. If I am visiting my best friend and my wife is hiding in a closet because she's been having an affair with him, there must be a totally sound reason for me to be *needing* to get into that closet *right now*. The minute it's a frivolous reason, the farce dies.

I know you must be sick of the jump-off-the-cliff scene, and this is the last time I will mention it, but as terrific as it was with *Butch,* it would have totally destroyed a movie such as, say, *Casablanca.*

You could set it up in that picture very easily. At the end, the Nazi Conrad Veidt is chasing Bogie and Claude Rains.

They are in cars racing across the airfield. The cars crash into each other and they are forced to continue the chase on foot.

And Rains is old and let's say Veidt was a runner at Nazi school, and he's closing the gap, closing the gap—

—when up ahead is this cliff and down there is Vichy France and freedom and the chance to battle injustice and they shout *Horseshit* and over they go, splashing down into the river and the current carries them to safety while old Conrad can only snarl down from the top of the cliff.

Kills the movie, right?

When you are dying in the night trying to plot your screenplay, you might do well to remember Bogie and Claude, so ridiculous. And remember the *kind* of story you are telling.

And don't go wandering, you'll kill the babe while it's still in swaddling clothes.

The Two Hollywoods

Two war movies help us understand the duality of the movie business: one, *Saving Private Ryan,* written by Robert Rodat, directed by Steven Spielberg; the other, *Shame,* Ingmar Bergman handling both chores. (If you have never heard of *Shame,* sad for you, and please believe that.)

The Spielberg gets more and more awful for me the more I think about it; the Bergman is just what it was when I first saw it: shattering. It deals in eighty-eight minutes with a married couple, musicians (Max von Sydow and Liv Ullman) whose country has become a battlefield. Never mind which side is advancing or retreating, they don't know, why should we? In the course of their story, Von Sydow, the wuss of the duo, toughens up, kills. Ullman, the strength, weakens. The movie ends with the two of them trying to escape, in a crappy boat stuffed with other desperate people, going nowhere across an unforgiving sea.

War is, to coin a phrase, hell.

Saving Private Ryan, with its justly famous twenty-four-minute early battle sequence, its fine Homer-like *Odyssey* hour where Ryan is sought, becomes, once he is found, a disgrace. False in every conceivable way possible, including giving the lie to its great twenty-four minutes. That sequence told us war is hell, too. The last hour tells us that war can be a neat learning experience for little Matt Damon.

In other words, Hollywood horseshit.

I would like to explain what I mean by that phrase. I love Hollywood movies. I was brought up in the thirties and forties with Hollywood movies. I have spent half my life writing Hollywood movies.

There are really two kinds of flicks—what we now call generic Hollywood movies, and what we now call Independent films.

Hollywood films—and this is crucial to screenwriters—all have in common this: they want to tell us truths we already know or a falsehood we want to believe in.

Hollywood films reinforce, reassure.

Independent films, which used to be called "art" films, have a different agenda. They want to tell us things we don't want to know.

Independent films unsettle.

Understand, we are *not* talking here of art and commerce. Hollywood films can be, and often are, art. Independent films, most of them, for me anyway, are pretentious and boring.

And yes, I know my definitions are simplistic. Hollywood films can unsettle, Independent films can reassure. But in general, for this discussion, let's go with them.

One quick example to be mentioned here—*Shakespeare in Love,* art flick or Hollywood?

I might be tempted to say, my God, it's Shakespeare, how can it not be an art film? Plus those costumes, Dame Judi, all the other British accents. If ever there was an art film, doesn't it have to be this baby?

Not even close. Because what *Shakespeare in Love* tells us is that **the love of a good woman makes everything wonderful.** Well, I don't know about you, but I want to believe that. I want to have a shot at Gwyneth's sweet boobies, because I just know they can change the world.

If only t'were so. How many hopeless drunks are out there not married to Lady Macbeths but to a good woman? How many fucked-up people are clinging to their sanity with a good woman right alongside, helpless?

Listen, Bill Shakespeare and I both write for a living. And I have been blocked, too. Days when nothing happens, weeks when you just sit there, months when you storm around the city, cursing your lack of talent and your help-lessness.

And nobody's boobies are going to make God smile.

We *want* to believe. Life would be just so much happier a place if only that were so. But alas, it's Hollywood horse-shit. (Although I sure wanted to believe it when I was in the theater.)

Does the fact of the two Hollywoods affect screenwrit-ers? I have never waffled for you before and I sure won't start now—*it does and it doesn't.*

It does not remotely affect how we tell our stories.

It totally affects which stories we choose to tell.

Famous cartoon from fifty years back. A couple are at the original run of *Death of a Salesman.* The man turns to the woman, here's what he says: **"I'll get you for this!"**

The point is that most of us work all day, often at some-thing we don't much love anymore but we do it till we drop. At the end of our average days, we want peace, we want relaxation, maybe a bite of food, a few kind words. **We do not want to watch Willy Loman's suicide.**

What we are really dealing with when we talk of the two Hollywoods is **audience size.**

Most people want to be told nice things. That we really are decent human beings, that God will smile on us, that there is true love and it is waiting for you, just around the next corner. That the meek really will inherit the earth.

Most people want to be told nice things. I cannot repeat that too often to anyone who wants to screenwrite for a liv-ing. You can be Bergman if you have the talent, you can tell sad human stories—but do not expect Mr. Time Warner to give you $100 million to make your movie.

The studios are in business for only one great and proper reason: to stay in business. If you want to tell a reassuring story, no reason not to shoot for a studio flick with all the, yes, good things that entails. If you want to tell a different story, write it wonderfully but write it small. Avoid car chases and star parts and special effects.

Great careers are possible in Independent film. The Coens and John Sayles are as good as anybody operating anywhere.

Join them. God knows we can use you.

III.
Stories

I get movie ideas all the time. Stories just appear, sometimes from the papers, sometimes from some distant blue when suddenly a couple of connectives happen and there it is: a movie.

I am, alas, a totally instinctive writer, with—please believe this—next to no idea of what I'm doing. I do not think well, wish I did. That poetry section you read at the start of Part II ("Heffalumps!!!")—that's as deep as I get.

But yes, I am a veritable wellspring of movie ideas.

My friend John Kander, who laughed at me in short-story class? John has been a first-rank composer all his life. In the theater, no one has the melodic gift John Kander has. You have been humming him for decades, "All That Jazz," "New York, New York," "Cabaret," and on and on.

You know how Kander comes up with those melodies? He wakes up every morning of the world with music playing inside his brain. Every waking moment. And when he is given a lyric to set, all he does is dip into the constant flow of music, and there it is, a song.

Now the hitch is this, as Kander puts it: *"Sometimes the most awful horrible music you ever heard is going on inside my head all day."*

Same with me and stories: occasionally one will pass muster, but mostly, the next day, not even close.

You have already read the only two pieces of real material that seemed to me to be great and wondrous movie stories when I first came upon them, the Butch Cassidy saga and the tale of the killer lions I tried to make work in *The Ghost and the Darkness*.

One leaped to the head of the class, the other kind of slowly made its way along, never quite getting there. Glorious stuff of lion violence, but like any special-effects flick, when you can't care about the story, not enough.

I truly believe I did not tell that story as well as I should.

This part of the book is about figuring out what movie stories are, and trying to tell them as well as they should be told.

When I say ideas drop into my head, that's true. But only twice have they ever immediately become something. (That's in forty-five years plus of sitting here, a stat I always give young writers who wait around for inspiration.)

In 1963 I was living on Eighty-sixth and York, had a writing space in a guy's apartment two blocks north. And an article in the *Daily News* said that up in Boston, where the Strangler case was *the* crime of the decade, a new theory was evolving: *namely, that the murders might be the work of two different madmen.*

On the two short blocks' walk uptown that morning, *No Way to Treat a Lady* literally dropped into my head. Based on the premise that what if there were two stranglers, and what if one of them got jealous of the other. (This was changed in the movie totally, so I am not its biggest fan.)

In 1982, I was on a water bus in Venice with Ilene. We were leaning over the railing looking out at the fabulous street that is the Grand Canal and, as we passed a couple of gondolas with silent gondoliers working the oars I turned to Ilene and said these words: *"I know why the gondoliers don't sing."*

And then it was a mad rush trying to get off the vaporetto and back to the hotel so I could write down this story that had just suddenly appeared and I can still remember the race back because I knew if I didn't get it all down *right then*, it would leave me. The book, *The Silent Gondoliers,* written by S. Morgenstern, the great Florinese author of *The Princess Bride,* came out the following year.

The story involved this not even remotely handsome gondolier, who could make a gondola dance like no other gondolier in history, who loved music so much, but who, alas, was tone-deaf. He does everything to try and change his fate, but you can't do that, so finally he risks his life to save the Gondoliers' Church during the worst storm in the history of that great city.

We are talking here a fable, but not the simplest-plotted one on the block, and where it came from I will never begin to understand. Or what would have happened if we hadn't taken the water bus. Or if the gondoliers we had passed had been singing.

Suddenly in this case, connectives clicked in and two books were the result.

I am at the mercy of connectives. By which I mean, I guess, narrative bits that hook together, taking us deeper into whatever story we're struggling with. When I said before I am totally instinctive, I was serious. I cannot logic my way into making these connectives happen. (I can do it with other writers' work, just not my own.) Sometimes I will get x bits into a story, then a connective hits and I am twice as far along, twice x, say—

—and then it ends.

I have written a couple of novel beginnings—a hundred pages here, more there, and . . . nothing. And you change, time etches on us all, your pulses change and the story turns out to be . . . nothing. Soon you wonder, what the hell was *that* supposed to be? And who were you then . . . ?

Okay. The first of the three crime stories. Printed exactly as I read it in the *San Francisco Chronicle,* April 26th, 1999. You'll have to squint, but I think you'll find it worth the effort.

Story One:
The Old Guy

Last of `Rub-a-Dub-Dub' Fugitives
Florida cops arrest robber who escaped
from San Quentin 20 years ago in a kayak

Bill Wallace, Chronicle Staff Writer

A 78-year-old career bank robber, who once tweaked San Quentin guards by escaping with two colleagues in a prison- made kayak named ``Rub-a-Dub-Dub, Marin Yacht Club,'' is in trouble again.

Forrest Silva Tucker, a reputed member of the real ``Over The Hill Gang'' in Boston, is in custody on suspicion of robbing a Florida bank and later leading Broward County sheriff's deputies on a car chase.

In trying to avoid arrest Thursday, Tucker allegedly led officers on a chase, blundered into an enclosed schoolyard and was captured after he lost control of his vehicle and crashed into a palm tree.

Deputies said the chase ensued after Tucker, wanted for a bank robbery earlier that day in the town of Jupiter, was spotted visiting his girlfriend in Pompano Beach.

``You don't normally think of a 78-year- old man having a girlfriend, but apparently he had quite a way with the ladies,'' said Kirk Englehardt, a spokesman for the Broward County Sheriff's Department.

Tucker, a Miami native, may have that reputation in Florida, but he is best remembered in the Bay Area for engineering one of the most innovative escapes in San Quentin history.

With two other inmates, Tucker, a former boatyard employee who had a smattering of knowledge about marine design and construction, built a crude kayak and painted the blue prison caps

he and his accomplices wore a bright orange.

On Aug. 9, 1979, Tucker and fellow inmates William McGirk and John Waller launched their boat from a partially hidden beach on prison grounds.

Their flimsy craft, made of pieces of plastic sheeting, wood, duct tape and Formica, lasted just long enough for them to paddle several hundred yards to freedom right under the noses of several tower guards.

At one point, as they paddled frantically to keep the boat afloat, a tower guard called out to see if they needed help from the Coast Guard.

No problem, called back one of the kayakers: "My Timex is still ticking."

After the three turned up missing during the afternoon count, guards found the kayak beached beyond the prison walls. On one side was its name: "Rub-A-Dub-Dub, Marin Yacht Club." That side, the one facing the prison, had been painted bright blue; the other side was left unfinished.

Within a matter of months, McGirk and Waller were back at San Quentin. They were tried twice for escape, but both times amused jurors refused to convict them.

Tucker, meanwhile, remained free.

The next time he surfaced was a few years later in a Boston credit scam. The judge hearing the case freed him on his own recognizance after chagrined Marin County prosecutors said they did not want to try him for the San Quentin escape. Lost in the official correspondence between the two states was that Tucker still had years to serve on his original San Quentin sentence. Tucker walked out of the Boston court and never went back.

Tucker's connections to the Bay Area go back to the early 1950s when he and a crime partner, Richard Bernard Bellew, were arrested for a half-dozen East Bay banks robberies.

At the time of his arrest for the Bay Area robberies, Tucker already had a rap sheet going back to a 1936 bicycle theft. There were also two other convictions, including a Florida bust in which he had escaped from the jail ward of a South Dade County hospital by picking the lock on his leg irons.

After being convicted for the East Bay holdups, Tucker was sent to Alcatraz to serve his term. During a medical visit to Los Angeles General Hospital in 1956, he escaped and managed to get as far as Bakersfield before he was captured by the California Highway Patrol.

He was later transferred to San Quentin, where he engineered his

greatest escape.

Over the next few years, Tucker was identified by law enforcement agencies as a member of a group of elderly criminals in Massachusetts called the "Over the Hill Gang," which robbed supermarkets in Boston and its suburbs. He was suspected in 17 armed robberies over the years, most recently in a series of bank robberies in the part of southeastern Florida known as the Gold Coast.

Tucker's 20 years as a California fugitive came to an ignominious end against a palm tree last week. Deputies who searched the vehicle after the crash said they found burglary tools, weapons, police scanners and a large amount of cash.

He is scheduled for a court appearance later this week.

©1999 San Francisco Chronicle Page A1

Some pretty interesting stuff there, yes?

I think so, anyway, which leads me to this, which seems like the most important of all questions:

Is it a movie?

The operative word in that sentence is "seems." "Is it a movie?" is *not* even remotely a valid question. Here is what you must remember:

Anything can be a movie.

I'm not being cute. If *you* believe in a story, if *you* believe you can make the story play and make it interesting, then yes, it can be a movie. The question that should be asked, must be asked, before you start out to make a movie is:

Is it a movie I would like to write?

Lots of positives and negatives here. Tucker, the "old guy" of this chapter's title, has a lot of appeal, at least he does for me. Before I get to specifics, I'm going to show you what I do when I'm interested in a piece of material. *I reread it, and mark stuff that I find particularly interesting or usable.* Just a line or a check in the margins. Remember, we may be starting on writing a movie here.

What I want you to do now is this: go back and reread the article and *make your own marks.* Anything that you think might be appealing for a flick.

Turn the page now and you'll see what I liked.

Last of 'Rub-a-Dub-Dub' Fugitives
Florida cops arrest robber who escaped
from San Quentin 20 years ago in a kayak

Bill Wallace, Chronicle Staff Writer

A 78-year-old career bank robber, who once tweaked San Quentin guards by escaping with two colleagues in a prison-made kayak named "Rub-a-Dub-Dub, Marin Yacht Club," is in trouble again

Forrest Silva Tucker, a reputed member of the real "Over The Hill Gang" in Boston, is in custody on suspicion of robbing a Florida bank and later leading Broward County sheriff's deputies on a car chase.

In trying to avoid arrest Thursday, Tucker allegedly led officers on a chase, blundered into an enclosed schoolyard and was captured after he lost control of his vehicle and crashed into a palm tree.

Deputies said the chase ensued after Tucker, wanted for a bank robbery earlier that day in the town of Jupiter, was spotted visiting his girlfriend in Pompano Beach.

"You don't normally think of a 78-year-old man having a girlfriend, but apparently he had quite a way with the ladies," said Kirk Englehardt, a spokesman for the Broward County Sheriff's Department.

Tucker, a Miami native, may have that reputation in Florida, but he is best remembered in the Bay Area for engineering one of the most innovative escapes in San Quentin history.

With two other inmates, Tucker, a former boatyard employee who had a smattering of knowledge about marine design and construction, built a crude kayak and painted the blue prison caps

he and his accomplices wore a bright orange.

On Aug. 9, 1979, Tucker and fellow inmates William McGirk and John Waller launched their boat from a partially hidden beach on prison grounds.

Their flimsy craft, made of pieces of plastic sheeting, wood, duct tape and Formica, lasted just long enough for them to paddle several hundred yards to freedom right under the noses of several tower guards.

At one point, as they paddled frantically to keep the boat afloat, a tower guard called out to see if they needed help from the Coast Guard.

No problem, called back one of the kayakers: ``My Timex is still ticking.''

After the three turned up missing during the afternoon count, guards found the kayak beached beyond the prison walls. On one side was its name: ``Rub-A-Dub-Dub, Marin Yacht Club.'' That side, the one facing the prison, had been painted bright blue; the other side was left unfinished.

Within a matter of months, McGirk and Waller were back at San Quentin. They were tried twice for escape, but both times amused jurors refused to convict them.

Tucker, meanwhile, remained free.

The next time he surfaced was a few years later in a Boston credit scam. The judge hearing the case freed him on his own recognizance after chagrined Marin County prosecutors said they did not want to try him for the San Quentin escape. Lost in the official correspondence between the two states was that Tucker still had years to serve on his original San Quentin sentence. Tucker walked out of the Boston court and never went back.

Tucker's connections to the Bay Area go back to the early 1950s when he and a crime partner, Richard Bernard Bellew, were arrested for a half-dozen East Bay banks robberies.

At the time of his arrest for the Bay Area robberies, Tucker already had a rap sheet going back to a 1936 bicycle theft. There were also two other convictions, including a Florida bust in which he had escaped from the jail ward of a South Dade County hospital by picking the lock on his leg irons.

After being convicted for the East Bay holdups, Tucker was sent to Alcatraz to serve his term. During a medical visit to Los Angeles General Hospital in 1956, he escaped and managed to get as far as Bakersfield before he was captured by the California Highway Patrol.

He was later transferred to San Quentin, where he engineered his

greatest escape.

Over the next few years, Tucker was identified by law enforcement agencies as a member of a group of elderly criminals in Massachusetts called the ``Over the Hill Gang,'' which robbed supermarkets in Boston and its suburbs. He was suspected in 17 armed robberies over the years, most recently in a series of bank robberies in the part of southeastern Florida known as the Gold Coast.

Tucker's 20 years as a California fugitive came to an ignominious end against a palm tree last week. Deputies who searched the vehicle after the crash said they found burglary tools, weapons, police scanners and a large amount of cash.

He is scheduled for a court appearance later this week.

You'll notice, there's a lot of usable stuff I did not mark this time around. I concentrated on four.

The first mark deals with Tucker's capture. I think you've got to use it, though I'm not sure where it comes in the picture. Here's how it might work as an opening.

FADE IN

A POLICE VEHICLE, motor straining as it rockets down a
two-lane road, motor <u>screaming</u>. As it roars along--

CUT TO

ANOTHER POLICE CAR, and there are TWO COPS in the
front seat and THE DRIVER's gunning the car like crazy
and THE SECOND COP is getting a rifle ready to fire,
and the siren on this car is even louder and now, holy
shit--

CUT TO

A THIRD POLICE CAR, passing the first two like they
were standing still and the noise is getting painful
now as we

PULL BACK TO REVEAL

HALF A DOZEN POLICE CARS, all of them racing along
this road, all of them with rifles ready, sirens
screaming and whoever they're after stands zero chance
of survival, not with this bunch after him, but he
must be something, whoever he is, he must be a modern-
day Capone, and now, as THE POLICE CARS begin to bunch
together for the kill--

CUT TO

This crummy heap they're chasing, and it's old and it
was never meant to go as fast as it's going, and the
strain on the car is terrible, it's a miracle it's not

```
falling apart, but you just know if it keeps on at this
pace, it will, and now

CUT TO

FORREST TUCKER at the wheel, and maybe no one else
alive could do more with the pile of junk he's pilot-
ing, and this is our guy, folks, so get used to having
him around, not an ounce of fat on him, not an ounce of
fear inside, and what makes him unusual is this:
TUCKER is eighty years old.
```

Not a bad beginning. At least it's not one of those ho-hum octogenar-
ian car chases we're all so used to.

It could also be the ending. What if Tucker's finally, after a lifetime of
crime and punishment, got enough to leave the world he's inhabited all
those decades, what if he's on his way to pick up his lady fair and off
they will go to live their final years somewhere glorious—

—and a cop spots him. And the chase. And the attempt to get away,
ending so forlornly for an eighty-year-old in a schoolyard.

Not so terrible that way, either.

I think if I thought about it I could come up with a way to tuck it into
the middle, but I don't want to do that. You can already see why I
marked those lines in the paper, *I can use this stuff.*

Okay. My second mark is the obvious one, the San Quentin jail break.
Tucker was sixty at the time and what a grand gesture for a guy that age
stuck in the slammer again.

A kayak?

Fabulous.

That, boys and girls, is the crucial set piece in the film. Fifteen minutes, maybe more, exciting and funny and full of hope and the possibility of disaster never more than a second away.

My third mark involved his being freed by the judge in Boston when
not only would the Marin County people not press charges out of
humiliation, but Tucker also scoots to freedom because of the goof-up in
correspondence between the two states involved.

Cannot help but be fun and exciting, that stuff.

My fourth and final mark involved the 1936 bicycle theft he was
busted for. My calculations make Tucker about fifteen at the time and I
don't know why I want that, maybe as a credit sequence.

The reason I'm not sure why I want that is a symptom of my problem with the movie at this moment: *I'm not sure what it is.*

Is it a Butch Cassidy–type story, fun and games but darkening as time goes on (and on)? Is it a gangster flick, where my guy, Tucker, gets more desperate and drained as nothing works out for him? It is a comedy about a goofball?

I think the material could encompass any of those attacks.

And I hope it's clear to you by now: this could be a terrific flick, assuming we write a terrific screenplay. The material, I am saying, will hold. I care for this guy.

The question remaining for me to answer is this: *Do I want to write it?* Or:

Can I make it play?

I have confidence in certain kinds of material that I feel are in my wheelhouse. If you'll look at what I've written, you'll get a good idea of what I have confidence in. But I know where panic would bring me down. I cannot write a comedy. I can write stuff with comic elements, but a flat-out comedy, no. I cannot write a special-effects film. I could doctor one, but to be present at the creation, no. I do not like them that much and I do not understand them. I could not write a Sylvester Stallone bloodbath action film. I find them moronic and would have no confidence in myself. I could not write most science-fiction films, especially the kind where there is all that lunatic "Captain, the frammis on the right engine is flummaging"–type dialogue.

But we are talking about *The Old Guy* now, and yes, I think I could pull this baby off.

So, now that the answer to that first, most important question is out of the way, let's look at others.

What's the reality?

Meaning this—thinking in my mind is different from seeing with my eyes—and before you go "Duh," an explanation. Maybe Carl Hiassen's best novel was *Strip Tease*. For me, the best character in that book is an absolutely glorious creation with the name Urbana Sprawl. She is a stripper who rides a motorcycle to work and she is funny and wise and whenever she pops up on a page, are you ever happy.

Well, when the movie was made, the part was played by a lovely young woman named Pandora Peaks. And she had the huge boobs mentioned in the book. If you go on the Internet, you can look her up, see her picture, and buy her used bras for $150, not counting shipping and handling. (It should be clear to you by now that this book will spare no effort in its unceasing pursuit of accuracy.)

Anyway, in the movie, Pandora acted well enough and her face was pretty enough and her breasts were, like the book said, gigantic—

—but they weren't real.

And in the novel, that is never a problem, you are guided by the wit of Hiassen, and you care for this lady. But in the movie all you could see was the surgery. And you never thought of the character and her warmth and funny mouth, all you could look at were these marvels of the medical profession, and wonder how much did it hurt to walk around?

In other words, the reality hurt the movie.

Well, Forrest Tucker is **eighty years old.**

How does *that* reality look on film? He's not Clint Eastwood or Sean Connery, he is those guys *ten years from now.* He is Paul Newman *five* years down the line. And they won't look like they do now. (Sorry, guys.) Take a walk outside, check out any octogenarians you see.

I promise you this: they're a lot more likely to be pushed in a wheelchair than they are prepping for a marathon. And in our movie, the same kinds of thoughts are going to intrude as they did with Pandora. How many times does he get up to pee at night? Does his dick still work, and under what conditions? How much do his knees ache when he has to do stairs?

Remember, this guy is our *hero.* He can't snooze in a sofa during this story, he has to *do* stuff. Two questions just to mind.

Will you *believe* it when you see him being physical?

Will you *want* to see him being physical?

You must be thinking this question at this point: Well, does he have to be that old? Why couldn't he be the great Eastwood now, pushing seventy?

He could be.

He could be Arnold, fifty.

He could be Leonardo DiCaprio, all of eleven.

Except for one small point: **those guys destroy the picture.**

A Riff About Age

I recently doctored a flick from a novel by Stephen Hunter, *Point of Impact*. It deals with the strange, fascinating world of long distance riflemen, snipers, if you will.

In the novel, the main character, Swagger, was a legendary figure in the Vietnam War, and when things went badly, and after hospitalization, he has spent his years alone in the Blue Ridge Mountains.

The government gets wind of an assassination attempt on the President. To be done by one of these long-distance whizzes. And they need help to try and figure out how to protect him. A sniper can attack from as much as a *mile* away, the President is out on the open with a bunch of other heads of state, in New Orleans.

The government comes to Swagger for help, he leaves the mountains for New Orleans, helps them. But things go badly for him, again, he is wounded terribly, again, and for the remainder of the picture, tries, against terrible odds, to clear his name.

Okay. The Vietnam stuff, which sets up his character, is a short section in the beginning of the book. But that was thirty years ago and Swagger could not have been in swaddling clothes, since he was drafted. Has to be mid-fifties at least.

I wrote it for Eastwood. He said no. Redford said no. Harrison Ford said no.

The movie is in development hell, but there is now interest from a star—Keanu Reeves.

Gasp.

And you know what—*it's a terrific idea.*

By now you probably want to strangle me for being so stupid as to say that Eastwood, at seventy, will destroy a picture about an eighty-year-old, while Keanu baby is just fine as a fifty-five-year-old Vietnam vet.

Here's the deal: in *Point of Impact,* the age of the sniper has **nothing** to do with the heart of the flick—a greatly gifted man is hired to do a job dealing with his speciality, gets double-crossed, and seeks revenge. You don't need the Vietnam sequence. But the core of *The Old Guy* **is** Tucker's age.

If I had read the identical article about Tucker, only he was seventy, big fucking deal, *I'm sixty-seven.* But I cannot imagine what it must be like to wake up every morning at eighty and think, "Christ, I hope today's bank robbery goes okay."

Now, obviously, any studio head would fire me instantly if I screwed up his shot at Eastwood or Connery or Redford or Ford. (Or Leo.)

The movie they made might work, might be a hit. Maybe you'd write a wonderful script and the movie would work. But I don't care about what *you* write, this is about me here.

And I could not write that movie. (End of riff about age.)

Okay, precious one, you might be thinking, he's got to be eighty.

How do you cast it?

Huge problem. The only famous actor I can come up with is Gregory Peck and Peck is such a gent, I have problems envisioning him as a lifer. So you have to go with an unknown. If you even think about that, this flashes like a "Price Is Right" answer: **If he's a good enough actor to play the vehicle part in a movie, how come he's been unknown for eighty fucking years, Bill?**

I have no answer for the casting problem. And I think if I go ahead and write this, this is what will bring me down. Either the studio will say, "are you *nuts*?" or they will replace me when a younger actor is given the role.

But I cannot think that way now. I may well be fired, have been many times, will be again.

But if I love Tucker's story enough, what I must do is this: put a blanket over my head and write it for Old Glory.

What about time?

As big a problem, in its way, as casting.

Movies do not handle the passage of time well. Most old-age makeup sucks. It tries, but what we think is, "What is Meryl doing looking that way?" In *Butch Cassidy,* I remember talking to George Roy Hill about the fact that the guys were in South America for *eight years*. Hill replied that he wasn't going to fuck with makeup, he'd tell them to act old, which he did, and which worked out—for me, anyway—just fine.

But this is, depending on how we write it, a very long lifetime.

If we include the bicycle stealing at fifteen, no problem, obviously, different actor. If we deal with Tucker's bank robberies when he was in his twenties, a different actor again. And probably you could use the same actor from the San Quentin escape at sixty for the car chase at eighty.

You could keep using different actors, and that might work, but I worry that what it would do is take away from what I think makes the story memorable: **accumulation.** A lifetime of misbegotten events, all of them heading toward the capture in the playground.

Clearly, time and casting and all these things mitigate against my writing this story. And the truth is this: I would not write this story. But the reason is not included above and is personal with me. Here it is:

Because the people are alive.

Twenty-five years ago I was in Holland, where we were shooting *A Bridge Too Far*. I was leaving that day for America, ticket in my hot little hand, when a message came, suddenly: it was from General Frost and it wondered, could I stop off in London before I went home?

Only a yes answer was possible.

The Brits are so different from us, there are no words; but nowhere is the difference clearer than when it comes to war: we venerate victories, they adore disasters. So the greatest battle for them in World War II was Dunkirk.

Followed closely by the awful Battle of Arnhem, where so many died so unfairly. *A Bridge Too Far* was about that battle. It began with a mistake of the Allied high command—Germany was falling, and clearly our General Patton was the man to finish the job, roar straight into Berlin with his unstoppable tank corps and kill those motherfuckers. The Nazis were getting braced for Patton and they were terrified of him.

But the plan to end the war went to the insecure Brit, Montgomery. He and Patton detested each other but Montgomery won out here, and planned the greatest parachute drop in history.

It was a cavalry-to-the-rescue deal. Thirty-five thousand troops were to be dropped behind Nazi lines in Holland, where they were to take a series of bridges. At the same time, a huge tank corps was to roar into Holland and solidify the bridges as they came to them.

The last bridge was at Arnhem. Once it fell, the tanks were to wheel across it into the industrial heart of the enemy. And bring the boys home by Christmas.

That was the theory.

The reality was worse than any Keystone Kops two-reeler. Fuck-up followed fuck-up. I won't detail them here, but the paratroopers who landed to take Arnhem Bridge—a huge thing, think the George Washington or the Golden Gate—were eight miles from the bridge. (One mile for these troops with their light weapons would have been unacceptable.)

The Battle of Arnhem was a bloodbath for the Allies. But the man who kept it in at least some kind of order, *the* hero of the effort, was Captain (later General) John Frost, thirty-one at the time and played wonderfully in the movie by Tony Hopkins.

When I went to work on the story, I expected to find all this great stuff that Frost did. We've all seen phony Hollywood war stuff, we know a heroic act when we see one. (I still almost have to vomit when I think of the last hour of *Saving Private Ryan*.)

Well, Frost didn't do much of that. In a totally different way, he was like Butch Cassidy, who people just, well, took to. Frost was a guy who people just, well, believed in. If Johnny Frost said it's going to be okay, you knew this: *you weren't going to die*. What he was was this quiet figure who in real life might have been unnoticed. But put him in a situation where a hero was needed, he was your guy.

Okay. In the middle of this massacre, a decent German general—they were allowed two—drove onto Arnhem Bridge, white flag flying, and said to the waiting British officers, "Surrender."

Pause. Then one of the British officers answered this: "You wish to surrender to us?" Then another pause. Followed by: "We don't have sufficient supplies to take you all prisoner. Sorry."

The next morning the slaughter began again.

I loved that moment. It happened, it was so insanely British, so nuttily brave. I had Frost say the line, though in real life it was another officer.

We are back now to me in Holland, with this strange urgent request. I changed my plane, flew to London, met the general at a civilized restaurant, chatted briefly, very briefly, about how the movie was going.

And during this time I was aware of only this: General John Frost, a man I revered, a brave man by any definition, a legend in his home country, was pale and he was frightened.

Finally he said this: "Your script will destroy me."

Not the kind of thing I hear a lot. I had no idea what I had done. I don't think I even answered. But I still remember the awful feeling in the pit of my stomach.

"That line," he went on. "That line."

I must have asked which.

"When you have me saying we couldn't take them prisoner. To accept their surrender."

I still hadn't caught on. "I didn't make it up."

"Yes, of course. *But I didn't say it*." Finally I understood as he went quietly on. "Don't you see? *People will think I was trying to make too much of myself*. Everywhere I go they will know I didn't say it, that a brave man did say it, and I was trying to take from him, trying to make too much of myself, make more of myself than I am. And they won't forgive me."

I tell you this: being there, hearing his fear, knowing I had caused it with my words, is something I will never stop remembering. He was quiet for a while and we ate a little. "Would this be all right?" I asked him. "I love the moment and it's true, so could we keep the moment but not have you say anything. Would it be all right if you were there, but silent?"

He thought about that. "I would have no problem," he said. Which was how it was shot.

I will never do another movie when the people are alive.

I tried a couple of times after *Bridge,* never will again. Lots of reasons. People panic when they are going to be up there on screen. (*I* would. You would, too.) People also get greedy when they are going to be up there on screen. The writer cannot make the crucial changes required, the compressions that are essential to screenplays.

But most of all, I won't because you're going to hurt somebody, cause pain or embarrassment. And God does that well enough without our help . . .

Story Two:
The Good Guy

Before we get started, does it strike anyone else as odd that the beautiful and ruddy-cheeked state of Colorado has been host to two of the most horrific crimes of the decade? The Littleton school massacre and the JonBenet Ramsey murder. California, sure, logic dictates that place, and New York, too. But not Colorado.

That riff having accomplished nothing, let's go to this story, it's one of those out-of-the-blue notions. Here's what it is.

As I write this, Littleton is still very much in people's consciousness. The usual shit, oh oh oh, violent movies did it—no, rap music—no, TV—no, the Internet—no, *blank* did it (fill in your own medium). My take, by the by? If those amazingly crazed young men had gone into that school, with the same murderous intent, but armed with knives and clubs, the incident would have been death-free.

Now understand, when I say Littleton, in a movie we would give it a different name, put it in a different place, etc. etc. What you keep is the massacre. And this: the media assault on the mistakes of the lawmen.

Here's the story—our guy, the good guy of the title, is the head lawman where the incident happens. Only it's a much smaller town, smaller school, smaller police department.

It would be nice if our guy was pretty much *it*. And he is terrific—honest, upright, and true, the kind of young man you'd want your own son to grow up to be. (Kevin Costner, say, just after *Dances with Wolves,* when the whole world was in love with him).

My story would be that he gets wind of the madness before it happens, tries like hell to stop it, is lied to by the parents of the loonies, breaks past their bullshit, realizes just exactly what is going to happen—

—and gets there *just* too late to stop it.

He rushes to the school, almost gets killed, but the kids are a step ahead of him. They blast their schoolmates, set off their bombs, and just as he finally corners them, they kill each other, leaving our guy shaken and alone to face the consequences.

Meaning, in this story: the media.

They descend on the town, take it over, cover the funerals as if it were Di all over again, do endless tear-jerking interviews, ask "Why?—*Why?* —Why?—How could this happen in our America?"

And make a villain out of our good guy.

Other law experts are brought in, they criticize him, why didn't he do this, that, the other thing.

They do their best to destroy his life.

And what is our good guy doing?

Trying to hold together, sure. Trying to hang in, of course. But he is also desperately trying to stop an even bigger slaughter from happening —because he has stumbled onto this fact: there were *three* crazy kids in Littleton, and the two who made the first invasion, they were nothing compared to the third kid, their leader and mastermind, who is way nuttier than the other two put together. And whose plan just might include this: *blowing up the entire school.*

Does our good guy get there in time this time?

You decide what you want, but let me throw in a curve.

Remember at the start I casually mentioned there had been two crimes in Colorado? Well, I was misdirecting you—*I want to use them both.*

Like this. In the middle of his desperate search for the third crazed kid, who has disappeared from his home but you know is somewhere nearby, waiting, in the middle of our good guy killing himself trying to find him, in the middle of the media calling for his resignation, he gets a phone call—

JonBenet Ramsey—who lives in Littleton—has been found strangled in the basement of the biggest house in town.

Our good guy pulls himself together, goes to the mansion to investigate. He is met by the man who called him, the child's shattered father. The mother is almost incoherent with grief and cannot be interrogated.

And what our guy does, brains fried, past exhaustion, is go through the house, checking the body, possible entrances by a stranger, all kinds of stuff—and here's the kicker—

He does it terribly—from lack of sleep. God knows, as we watch, he moves things, shifts stuff around—

Our good guy is destroying evidence. And we see him do it.

Now it's the next day, and the media shifts from Littleton High to the strangled beauty-contest winner. And snippets of her contest dances fill the channels—

Who could throttle a perfect child such as this!

As the media realizes that evidence has been damaged, they go into overdrive—our good guy should be hung.

But he tries not to pay attention because he knows that with all the attention on JonBenet, it's a perfect time for the third nut to attack the school—kill them all—

And he tries, but guess what—our good guy gets there, not a second too late but before the third nut blows up the entire school.

And he stops the possible carnage.

Yessss. This is the guy we have rooted for from the beginning, the guy who has killed himself for justice.

Even the media have to admit he pulled off a great thing, saving all those high school kids from death.

A press conference is called where he handles himself well, with modesty. Which he has to leave because JonBenet's parents are now in shape to be interviewed.

He goes back to the mansion. He talks to the wife. The wife is better. She has an alibi. She was with her husband at the time of the murder.

He talks to the husband now. "Will you find the killer?" the husband asks. Our Good Guy shakes his head. "Don't see how," he answers.

And then the two men quickly glance at each other, and it's one of those looks that tells everything. We now know why our hero destroyed the evidence—so the father will never be caught—

He and JonBenet's father are lovers.

Final fade-out.

Catch you by surprise? Hope so.

What do you think?

I guess more important is this: What do *I* think? Even though I've had the idea of the father and the lawman being lovers for a long time, I never put the two together till the morning I've written this.

My guess is it could make for a pretty decent flick. Different enough, a neat kicker for an ending. Star part, all that.

You know why I don't want to write it? Because I don't love it enough to do the legwork required, to find a town, go there, find some lawmen, talk them into letting me tag along, so I could learn what their life is really like.

That reality would be something I would have to have confidence enough to write, because it would add a crucial authenticity to a story that tends on occasion toward the operatic.

Maybe when I was younger, but not now.

If you have young legs, if you think you can make it wonderful, all yours . . .

Two Kinds of Stories

In every movie, there are two stories: the story of the movie itself and the story of each of the individual scenes that make up the movie. And what you must realize is that if the individual scene does not logically advance and thicken the overall story, either rewrite it until it does or get rid of it. Hopefully *Misery* will show you what I mean.

Scene one: *typing*.

The movie opens with Paul Sheldon (Jimmy Caan) in a hotel suite somewhere out west in the mountains and there is the sound of heavy wind. A storm might be coming. He pays no attention, concentrates only on what he is doing: sitting at a table, writing something. A neat pile of manuscript pages is visible on the table. A final typing flurry, he pulls out the last page, and we see these words:

THE END.

Then he takes the manuscript, holds it close, is momentarily moved.

In other words, it's a little scene, we see a guy finishing something, we're out west, it's windy.

Half a page, a little more.

Scene two: *leaving*.

Paul's packing, goes outside to his car, makes a snowball, rockets it at a tree, dead solid perfect.

Another half page.

Scene three: *driving*.

Paul's driving along in the mountains, a storm hits. (We

had set it up, remember, in the typing scene where we heard the wind increasing.)

Another half page to here.

Scene four: *the storm*.

Paul is doing his best to stay on the road, a page and a half.

Scene five: *the crash*.

Half a page as Paul loses control, the car leaves the road, roars out of control, settles in the wilderness, upside down.

Scene six: *the struggle*.

Final half page as Paul tries to get out, can't, we leave him dying.

Okay, the first scene says somewhere there is this writer, not starving in a garret but in a lovely hotel suite in the mountains—and he has written something he is *proud* of. That pride is crucial to what follows.

Leaving scene. Two things aside from the necessary info that he is taking off. One, he is not the most mature guy around—I would not expect Bill Gates to heave a snowball after leaving a Microsoft meeting. Plus this: he is a *jock*. You can tell that from the power and the accuracy of the throw. (Needed to help set up some of the stuff he has to do when trapped in the wheelchair.)

That's enough, and I am not saying this is glorious screenwriting, but it is proper. It helps set up the big story we come into later, of Paul at the mercy of the only woman Hannibal Lecter should have married, Annie Wilkes.

This is not how King started the novel. He starts with Paul already in agony at Annie's mercy, and he already hates her. He was correct for his story, I think we did fine with ours. There is *no* right or wrong way to tell this tale. Both worked, I think well, for their particular forms.

Here's another scene—and I don't want you throwing the book across the room but, yes, it's from *Butch Cassidy*, and it's smack in the middle of the Superposse chase. Middle of the night. Butch and Sundance have gotten rid of one horse in an attempt to split up whoever is following them, and fight whichever half comes in their direction. The Superposse comes to the spot where Sundance jumped from his horse to Butch's, sent it off in another direction. The

Superposse starts to split, which pleases the two guys. Then the posse comes back together again, all of them back together and dead on Butch and Sundance's trail. Tension is, as they say, mounting. Butch and Sundance are running out of places to run.

This is what they try next.

CUT TO

SHERIFF RAY BLEDSOE asleep in his bed.

He is in a small room connected to a small jail. One window looks out on rocky terrain. Ray Bledsoe is an aging hulk of a man, close to sixty.

CUT TO

BUTCH AND SUNDANCE, entering. Bledsoe stirs, glances up, then suddenly erupts from his bed clearly horrified at what he sees.

> RAY BLEDSOE
> What are you doing here?

> BUTCH
> Easy, Ray--

> RAY BLEDSOE
> (riding roughshod through
> anything BUTCH starts to say
> to him)
> --hell, easy--just because we been
> friends doesn't give you the right--
> what do you think would happen to me
> if we was seen together?--I'm too old
> to hunt up another job.
> (glaring at them)
> At least have the decency to draw
> your guns.
> (As Butch and Sundance draw,

       Bledsoe grabs a rope, sits in
       a chair and tosses the rope to
       Sundance, who hesitates a
       moment)
Come on, come on--take it and start
with my feet. Just don't make it so
tight I can't wiggle loose when
you're gone.

Through the remainder of the scene, Sundance
binds and gags Bledsoe while Butch paces the
room, keeping close track of the view out of
the window, always aware of whatever it is
that is following, somewhere behind them.

      RAY BLEDSOE (CONT'D)
You promised you'd never come into my
territory--

       BUTCH
--and we kept our word, didn't we,
Ray?

      SUNDANCE
--we never pulled off anything near
you--

       BUTCH
--everyone in the business we told,
"Leave old Ray Bledsoe alone."

      SUNDANCE
--we been good to you, Ray--

       BUTCH
--now you be good to us--help us
enlist in the Army and fight the
Spanish.

      RAY BLEDSOE
You are known outlaws.

                    BUTCH
        We'd quit.

                    RAY BLEDSOE
                (exploding)
        You woke me up to tell me you re-
        formed?

                    SUNDANCE
        It's the truth, Ray, I swear.

                    BUTCH
        No, let's not lie to Ray. We haven't
        come close to reforming. We never
        will.
                (He is desperately honest now)
        It's just--my country's at war and
        I'm not getting any younger, and I'm
        sick of my life, Ray.

                    RAY BLEDSOE
                (There is a pause. Then--)
        Bull!!

                    BUTCH
        All right. There's a certain situa-
        tion that's come up and--it could
        work, Ray--a lot of guys like us have
        enlisted; we could too, if you'd help
        us--either fake us through or tell
        the government how we changed--they
        got to believe you; hell, you never
        done a dishonest thing yet and what
        are you, sixty?

                    RAY BLEDSOE
        You've done too much for amnesty and
        you're too well known to disguise;
        you should have got yourselves
        killed a long time ago when you had
        the chance.

                              BUTCH
          We're asking for your help, Ray!

                           RAY BLEDSOE
          Something's got you panicked, and
          it's too late. You may be the
          biggest thing ever to hit this area,
          but in the long run, you're just two-
          bit outlaws. I never met a soul more
          affable than you, Butch, or faster
          than the Kid, but you're still noth-
          ing but a couple of two-bit outlaws
          on the dodge.

                              BUTCH
          Don't you get it, Ray?--something's
          out there. We can maybe outrun 'em
          awhile longer, but then if you could--

                           RAY BLEDSOE
          --you just want to hide out till it's
          old times again, but it's over. It's
          over, don't you get that? It's over
          and you're both gonna die bloody, and
          all you can do is choose where.
                    (softer now)
          I'm sorry, I'm getting mean in my old
          age. Shut me up, Sundance.

CUT TO

SUNDANCE, the gag in his hands.

CUT TO

THE GLOW OF THE SUPERPOSSE, seen in the distance now.

CUT TO

```
BUTCH, reaching the rear door, opening it,
going out.  A moment later, SUNDANCE follows
him.

CUT TO

BLEDSOE, gagged, staring after them.  He is
terribly moved.  Camera holds on the old man
a second.  Then--

CUT TO

THE SUN AND IT IS BLINDING.
```

A lot of helpful stuff here. When Bledsoe says, "You're both gonna die bloody, and all you can do is choose where," I put that in to foreshadow Bolivia. Going into the Army to fight the Spanish had been mentioned before and scorned by Sundance before, so the fact that they are both pitching the old man to let them enlist indicated how desperate they have become. I always thought that was good material—outlaws hiding out in the Army; better because it was real.

And it's helpful for us to know they have a friend like Bledsoe who has yet to do a dishonest thing. And really helpful that Bledsoe likes them. And it doesn't hurt our cause to find they never did rob in his area, their word meant something. And it's got a neat reversal—the sheriff insisting the outlaws draw their guns and tie him up—in order to give a standard talk scene some movement.

If you think I am pretty smart to have come up with this dazzler, here's a moment of truth. Do you know why that scene is there? Because I felt I needed someone, *someone who we could believe,* to tell us just how remarkable the heroes were, never a soul more affable than the one, more dangerous than the other. I felt I needed the audience to realize they were special.

Then.

Because zero people on the planet had ever heard of my two guys. If I were writing the movie today? Never would have written that scene. People know who they are today. Today it's just a stage wait.

The truth: I probably didn't need it then. Three minutes of chitchat in the middle of a chase to the death? If you had written the script and come to me for my opinion, I would have been laudatory, sure.

But I also would have said: lose that stupid Bledsoe scene.

Different Drafts

I wrote in *Adventures in the Screen Trade* that there were two different versions of the screenplay, the selling version and the shooting version.

That's still true and I'll get back to it, but those are *versions*. We are talking here of *drafts*.

When I finally suck it up and write the first draft, well, almost nobody sees it. I call this the "For Our Eyes Only" draft.

And it only goes to my readers.

I have a couple of people whom I give it to. That's all. Someone once said that a friend was someone you could say "Go to hell" to and it would be okay. Well, a reader is someone who can criticize your work. And it's okay.

I cannot overemphasize the importance of a critical reader. If you don't have one, it will damage you terribly in the long run. If you do have one or two, treat them with great kindness. They will save your ass as the years go by.

It is very hard to be a reader. Obviously, they are people you know and know well, and being critical of work at any point can be a problem; at the start, it more than likely will be.

I have been given, I guess, over the decades, thousands of scripts to read. And I always ask at the start, this:

Do you want the truth?
or
Do you want me to tell you how wonderful you are?

One hundred and five percent of them come back thusly:

The truth.

And then I say: A lot of people *say* that but not a lot of people *mean* it; their reply is always this:

I mean it.

So what happens is I read their script and I always find a sequence to start with that I can argue needs help. Say, it's the sequence where the dog dies.

I will carefully say something like this: "I have a question about when the dog dies." And more than you can imagine, this is what they say:

Oh, I *love* that sequence, that's, like, my *favorite* sequence in the whole movie, I only *wrote* the movie so I could write that sequence.

Here is what I give them then: *praise.* Praise unending. How moved I was by their work and what wonderful writers they are.

And I do them no good whatsoever.

Which is fine. The world will etch away on them soon enough.

Let's do a list of drafts now.

1. The For Our Eyes Only Draft. Which I will rewrite until I'm happy with it. Or as happy as I can be. Or just run out of steam and ideas and can't go any further on my own.

2. The First Draft. This is the one I give to the producer. This is probably the one specified by your contract that you have to get in by such and such a date. Here is what happens when they read it: they do not ever get back to you as quickly as you hope. And you go *nuts.* Either you are fired, which has happened to us all, or the asshole will eventually call and you will meet. And trust me—they will want changes. Not only that, they will want them for free. Which is more than likely against your contract. But which you will more than likely do anyway.

3. The First Draft (with Producer's Notes). Hopefully, this is the draft that will get submitted to the studio.

The above are what I call the "selling versions."
All future drafts are what I call "shooting versions."

Now, all this is true only if God has smiled on you. Usually He won't do that. Usually you'll have one more selling version to do, because the studio will want a draft with *their* notes included before they decide to try for what they call **an element.** Which means a director or a star.

4. The Studio Draft. You still keep it as readable as you can because now you're selling to **an element.**

Now, if you are amazingly lucky, they will decide that, yes, they want to try and make the movie. And you may be pissed at their slowness but they have a point. Please tattoo this behind your eyeballs:

You only have one shot at a star.

They get so inundated, so many people are trying to fuck them, to cater to them, to make them even richer and more spoiled that they simply will not bother to read a script a second time. Here is what they will say:

Isn't that the one where the dog dies?
    (Final dismissal)
I read that.

I believe more screenwriters screw up the Studio Draft than they do anything else. Don't get scripts to people just because you can; get them seen when they are *done.* It's hard, I know, but please remember this:

When you go out there, **BE AT YOUR BEST.**

5. (And forever after) The Shooting Drafts.

These are all the drafts that come after a director is on-board, or if the producer is powerful enough to get a green light on his own.

There are an infinite number of these drafts. You think you'll go mad.

Then it gets harder—the star has arrived.

This is the most painful time in one respect, because the star is usually only interested in his or her part. The producer and the director might want the picture to have quality. The star is not *against* quality. Just so it doesn't interfere with his having the winning role.

But if it is the most painful, tough about that. **You** have a picture gearing up. **You** will have a credit. **You** will have had this start to a career.

Or, as a producer said to me after Paul Newman said he would do *Harper,* "You don't know what just happened, do you? This is what happened—**you jumped past all the shit!**"

May you all turn out to be glorious leapers.

Story Three:
The Mastermind

As I said, ideas come from everywhere. This one comes not from the blue or a headline but rather, a book. I read it over a decade ago and thought immediately that not only could it be a movie, it could be just about the best caper film ever, alongside David Ward's Oscar winner, *The Sting*.

I wrote a caper film early on, *The Hot Rock*, based on the first of Donald Westlake's Dortmunder series. They tend to follow a pattern: the hero wants something valuable, can't get it legally, usually forms a gang to accomplish his end.

This story follows dead on that classic pattern.

Before specifics, I have to ask you this question: What, in your opinion, is the most valuable portable object in the world? The reason I throw in the word "portable" is because something gigantic tends to lose all connection to human scale. So I don't want any of the smart-asses among you answering thus: The Pyramids.

I am talking something you can hoist. Diamonds, furs, paintings, that kind of thing. The stuff caper films are made of. Just taking the above three, I am sure some fur somewhere that could be traced back to someone historically important or famous could be worth several million. And the Kohinoor diamond? A guess, but maybe tens of millions.

Chicken feed.

Some Asian billionaire bought a van Gogh, didn't he, for close to a hundred biggies?

Closing in.

You'll notice I haven't yet disclosed what the valued object is—because I'm trying to raise your interest, and also because at this moment I am not sure how deep into the picture I go before revealing it. But here's a scene that might come early on. The Mastermind of the title

is a man of forty, from a family of great wealth and power, but because
he is not the oldest son, he is penniless, and reduced to living by his wits,
as they say. The most stylish charming guy you ever met. Read Sean
Connery at the peak of his Bond phase for the Mastermind.

   And who is he talking to? Why, only the Bill Gates of his day (I'm setting this in 1911): Mr. J. P. Morgan.

We are in the library of Morgan's New York City mansion, which is the size of most houses.

The year is 1911.

Morgan and Connery sit drinking brandy, smoking cig-
ars. Both are elegantly dressed, and throughout,
their tone is civilized. We are looking at two men at
the very top of their respective games.

All around them on the walls--the most famous art
works from across the centuries.

                    J. P. MORGAN
        Shall we get to it, then?

                    SEAN CONNERY
        Of course.
                (beat)
        Suppose I could deliver to you, and you alone,
        the most valuable object in the world.

                    J. P. MORGAN
        For which, no doubt, I would pay a very great
        deal.

                    SEAN CONNERY
        More than just a great deal, sir. A gasping
        amount is what I have in mind.

                    J. P. MORGAN
        And when do I get to know just what it is I'm
        purchasing?

                    SEAN CONNERY
              (enjoying this)
You don't.

                    J. P. MORGAN
Are you being silly with me, sir? Not a wise
idea. Why on earth should I pay you anything
at all for something about which I know so
little.

                    SEAN CONNERY
Because I don't have it yet.

                    J. P. MORGAN
Have not purchased it, you meant?

                    SEAN CONNERY
              (sharp)
Are you being silly with me, sir? I don't much
like that either.
              (beat)
When I possess it, you will know, simply by
reading any headline from any paper in the
world.

                    J. P. MORGAN
              (a little interested now)
Dramatically put. But if you have nothing,
why meet now?

                    SEAN CONNERY
Because when I do have it, there will be no
time for bargaining. I will want your money,
in cash, of course, immediately.

                    J. P. MORGAN
If you plan to sell me something acquired by
less than legal means, what possible good does
it do me? I cannot ever show it to anyone. I
must keep it hidden from the world.

CUT TO

CONNERY. He gets up, strides around the fabulous
room.

                    SEAN CONNERY
        Some men...
                (he stops, looks dead at Morgan
                 now)
        ...there are some men who would kill to pos-
        sess what no one else owns. Who would build a
        shrine to it, kept locked, with only the one
        key. There are some men, sir, who could thrill
        to walk into this secret place late at night,
        to unlock a single door, to stare at this
        greatest secret, the single most famous
        achievement of man.

This has been clearly directed at Morgan, who is un-
comfortable with it, deflects it as best he can.

                    J. P. MORGAN
        I have never been involved in anything so
        criminal.

                    SEAN CONNERY
        Of course not--which is why I am keeping it a
        secret--the minute you know, you become an ac-
        complice.
                (beat)
        The world respects you as the paragon you are.
        And of course you would never get involved
        with stolen property--

                    J. P. MORGAN
        --so you are going to steal it?

                    SEAN CONNERY
        There is always that possibility.

                    J. P. MORGAN
               (rising abruptly)
     Good night, sir.
               (CONNERY smiles)
     I just threw you out of my house, why on earth
     are you smiling?

                    SEAN CONNERY
     Because Frick predicted you would behave this
     way.
               (and on this he rises)
     He will deny our chat just as you will deny
     this--but he told me you would behave, at
     first, like an outraged virgin.
               (going to the door)
     A pleasure, Mr. Morgan.

                    J. P. MORGAN
               (moving right with him)
     Henry Clay Frick is a detestable fraud--

                    SEAN CONNERY
     --but he is almost as rich as you and has al-
     most as great a collection. And soon it will
     be far greater.

                    J. P. MORGAN
               (moving in on CONNERY)
     Frick said he'd buy your merchandise?

CUT TO

CONNERY. CLOSE UP.

                    SEAN CONNERY
     I have nothing to sell...<u>yet</u>.

CUT TO

MORGAN. Studying him.

>   J. P. MORGAN
> When will you have it?
>
>
>   SEAN CONNERY
> Very soon. You will know by the headlines.
> And I will come to the Plaza Hotel. And I
> will have it with me. And you will leave a
> message--a message with the amount you will
> pay. Frick has agreed to do the same.
>   (heading out now)
> Winner wins all.
>   (a final smile, and he is gone)

Not the greatest scene ever, but it might play, if, say, we got Duvall to take a shot at Morgan. These two brilliant guys, discussing something in a strange way, all the secrets involved.

You might even open a movie with it. Connery leaving the Plaza, getting into a horse-drawn carriage, clip-clopping through the streets to the Morgan manse.

But if you did, pretty soon you'd have to reveal what the item under discussion was. Which I shall do now.

It's the *Mona Lisa,* da Vinci's masterpiece and arguably the most famous image on earth. And in case you wondered why I set that scene in such a weird year as 1911, here's why: **that's when it happened.**

The *Mona Lisa really was stolen,* from the Louvre Museum. And it was gone for two years. And maybe, just maybe, what was returned wasn't the real *Mona Lisa.* (All this is in Seymour Reit's book *The Day They Stole the Mona Lisa.* Try it, you'll like it.)

How much do you think that painting is worth? What if it came up for auction and the Sultan of Brunei wanted it a lot and Bill Gates wanted it a lot and so did half a dozen other computer-nerd billionaires? Well, if a good, but not that great, van Gogh went in the nineties, you *start* from there for this baby.

I think if these rich guys really got into a dick-swinging contest, the price could reach a *billion.*

And it was already incredibly famous back when it was taken.

What follows is not precisely as it happened. But we're not making a documentary.

Three main guys: *the Mastermind* himself. Anxious to retire and live well forever. In order to pull off his plan, he has to spend some money in advance. And he does.

Second main guy: *the thief*. No elegance here. He is an Italian carpenter working in France. He dislikes the French, lives alone in a crummy room. He is perfect for the Mastermind because (1) he has worked some in the Louvre, and (2) more importantly, when the *Mona Lisa* was recently enclosed in a glass-fronted box, the thief was one of the guys who built the box.

Last main guy: *the forger*. Cadaverous, brilliant, incredibly gifted as a painter, yet with shockingly little ego. He dies of old age, with the money from this job, happily. Never a whisper of trouble. Because of all the great forgers, he's the one who never let his ego loose, never wanted to be known for his own art.

The Mastermind took the forger to the *Mona Lisa,* said, "Can you copy this?" The forger thought about it, realized the difficulties, finally, challenged, said, "Yes, I can make you a copy."

To which the Mastermind replied: "No good. I need six."

So the forger got to work. Great stuff in the book about just how he had to do it—the *Mona Lisa* is not painted on canvas but wood, so he had to find wood from the time of the painting, centuries before.

(Aside to screenwriters—George Roy Hill once told me this: "Audiences love 'how-to.' " When I asked what he meant, he explained that if you were going to, say, crack a safe, audiences would be interested in the problems involved in really doing it. I believe Hill was right. End of aside.)

Now, while this is being done, the Mastermind comes to America and meets with six rich, greedy Americans. He makes his pitch, without ever telling what he's selling. They'll find out in the papers.

So when the theft happened, and became worldwide news, his six **believed.**

The theft itself was almost comic. The Louvre was closed on Mondays, so if you could hide inside Sunday night, you could be alone in the place the next day with only other workers and guards. And workers in those days were constantly removing paintings from the walls, under orders to take them to be photographed, cleaned, etc.

The thief knew a place to hide. A tiny closet where art students were allowed to leave their paints over the quiet Monday so they wouldn't have to lug their stuff around.

The thief spends the night, early Monday he takes a tunic that Louvre workers wear, goes out into the museum. As he gets to the gallery where the painting is, things empty out, so he takes it down, throws a cloth over it, and goes walking along, passing all kinds of other workers in similar tunics also carrying paintings with cloths over them.

He gets to a dark staircase, removes the painting itself from the box that enclosed it—which, remember, he helped make—tucks it under his tunic. So now it's a quick to-the-door-and-out kind of deal.

Problem, the key he has made for the door won't work. In desperation, he takes off the doorknob, sticks it in his pocket—

Which is when another guy who works there comes along.

The thief snarls to this guy. "Some idiot stole the doorknob. How am I expected to get out of here?" To which the other worker says in essence, hey no problem, I'll let you out.

Almost free now.

Oops. The heavy outside door is open—but a uniformed guard is there.

Fug!

Another incredible event—the porter has not shown up for work that day so the guard is cleaning the entranceway—

And it is *at that exact moment* he decides he needs some clean water, goes off in search of some. That's when the thief leaves the Louvre with the painting.

Now the thief hides the masterpiece in a crummy trunk in a crummy apartment and has nothing more to do than this: wait for the Mastermind to come and pay him.

Which doesn't happen—because the Mastermind *doesn't need* the Louvre *Mona Lisa*. He could care less about the Louvre's *Mona Lisa*—**he's got six of his own.**

He sails to America, sells his paintings to six greedy Americans and is safe—because the minute they talk, *they become accomplices.*

Rich and contented, having pulled off the greatest scam in history, the Mastermind retires and lives a glorious life.

Not as rich but very well off, the forger also retires, except for occasional special jobs.

And the thief? Read for yourself in Reit's book.

Did I hook you? Did you put this book down in the middle of reading that story? I wouldn't have been able to.

Why didn't I write the *Mona Lisa* story?

The truth is, I don't remember. It sure seemed a natural as I told you the story. Maybe whoever owned it was somebody I wasn't sure of. Maybe I came across it myself and it was during my leper period, when I was writing only books.

I think the reason is that storytellers change. The kind of narrative that moves us shifts and alters. I don't know that I would do *Maverick* today. I'm six years older, six additional years of movie experience—

would I now want to spend half a year on a western caper that comes from an ancient TV series? Maybe. Maybe if Dick Donner were involved, as he was, or if Mel Gibson were involved. But my guess is not. I would certainly do *Misery*, though. Never could resist the lopping scene.

Story Four:
The Dolphin

Every so often I come across a piece of material that just rocks me. The story I am calling *The Dolphin* was one of those. I was having coffee by myself three years ago, I'd finished the sports section of *The New York Times*—I do that out of some awful sense of masochism; any sports fan from New York will understand—and I turned to the front page, saw this in the corner. In a few minutes, I was flooded with tears.

I don't know if you'll have so extreme an experience, but if you aren't moved even a little, boy, is there something wrong with you. No question this material is wonderful. But is it a movie we want to write?

I want you to read the article now and think about it a little. I'm going on to some other stuff, but eventually, we'll all circle back and meet around Taylor Touchstone's campfire.

Autism No Handicap, Boy Defies Swamp

By RICK BRAGG

FORT WALTON BEACH, Fla., Aug. 16 — Taylor Touchstone, a 10-year-old autistic boy who takes along a stuffed leopard and pink blanket when he goes to visit his grandmother, somehow survived for four days lost and alone in a swamp acrawl with poisonous snakes and alligators.

He swam, floated, crawled and limped about 14 miles, his feet, legs and stomach covered with cuts from brush and briars that rescuers believed to be impassable, his journey lighted at night by thunderstorms that stabbed the swamp with lightning.

People in this resort town on the Gulf of Mexico say they believe that Taylor's survival is a miracle, and that may be as good an explanation as they will ever have. The answer, the key to the mystery that baffles rescue workers who have seen this swamp kill grown, tough men, may be forever lost behind the boy's calm blue eyes.

"I see fish, lots of fish," was all Taylor told his mother, Suzanne Touchstone, when she gently asked him what he remembered from his ordeal in the remote reservation on Eglin Air Force Base.

Over years, Taylor may tell her more, but most likely it will come in glints and glimmers of information, a peek into a journey that ended on Sunday when a fisherman found Taylor floating naked in the East Bay River, bloody, hungry but very much alive.

He may turn loose a few words as he sits in the living room, munching on the junk food that is about the only thing his mother can coax him to eat, or when they go for one of their drives to look at cows. He likes the cows, sometimes. Sometimes he does not see

them at all, and they just ride, quiet.

Taylor's form of autism is considered moderate. The neurological disorder is characterized by speech and learning impairment, and manifests itself in unusual responses to people and surroundings.

"I've heard stories of autistic people who suddenly just remember, and begin to talk" of something in the far past, Mrs. Touchstone said. "But we may never know" what he lived through, or how he lived through it, she said.

His father, Ray, added, "I don't know that it matters." Like his wife and their 12-year-old daughter, Jayne, Mr. Touchstone can live with the mystery. It is the ending of the story that matters.

Still, they have their theories. They say they believe that it is possible that Taylor survived the horrors of the swamp not in spite of his autism, but because of it.

"He doesn't know how to panic," Jayne said. "He doesn't know what fear is."

Her brother is focused, she said. Mrs. Touchstone says Taylor will focus all his attention and energy on a simple thing — he will fixate on a knot in a bathing suit's draw string — and not be concerned about the broader realm of his life.

If that focus helped him survive, Mrs. Touchstone said, then "it is a miracle" that it was her son and not some otherwise normal child who went for a four-day swim in the black water of a region in which Army Rangers and sheriff's deputies could not fully penetrate. He may have paddled with the gators, and worried more about losing his trunks.

"Bullheaded," said Mrs. Touchstone, who is more prone to say what is on her mind than grope for pat answers. Instead of coddling and being overly protective of her child, she tried to let him enjoy a life as close to normal as common sense allowed.

Taylor's scramble and swim

through the swamp, apparently without any direction or motive beyond the obvious fact that he wanted to keep in motion, left him with no permanent injuries. On Wednesday, he sat in his living room, the ugly, healing cuts crisscrossing his legs, and munched junk food.

"Cheetos," he said, when asked what he was eating.

But when he was asked about the swamp, he carefully put the plastic lid back on the container, and left the room. He did not appear upset, just uninterested.

Lifelong Swimmer At Home in Water

Taylor has been swimming most of his life. In the water, his autism seems to disappear. He swims like a dolphin, untiring.

His journey began about 4 P.M. on Aug. 7, a Wednesday, while he and his mother and sister were swimming with friends in Turtle Creek on the reservation lands of the Air Force base. Taylor walked into the water and floated downstream, disappearing from sight. He did not answer his mother's calls.

An extensive air, water and ground search followed. It involved Army Rangers, Green Berets, marines, deputies with the Okaloosa County Sheriff's Department and volunteers, who conducted arm-to-arm searches in water that was at times neck-deep, making noise to scare off the alligators and rattlesnakes and water moccasins, and shouting Taylor's name.

He is only moderately autistic, Mrs. Touchstone said, but it is possible that he may not have responded to the calls of the searchers. At night, when it was nearly useless to search on foot, AC-130 helicopters crisscrossed the swamp, searching for Taylor with heat-seeking, infrared tracking systems.

In all, the air and ground searchers covered 36 square miles, but Taylor, barefoot, had somehow moved outside their range.

"The search area encompassed as much area as we could cover," said Rick Hord of the Sheriff's Department. "He went farther."

It was not just the distance that surprised the searchers. Taylor somehow went under, around or through brush that the searchers saw as impassable. Yet there is no evidence that anyone else was involved in his journey, or of foul play, investigators said.

Apparently, Taylor just felt compelled to keep moving. Members of his family say they believe that he spent a good part of his time swimming, which may have kept him away from snakes on land.

The nights brought pitch blackness to the swamp, and on two nights there were violent thunderstorms. Lightning would have penetrated his shell, Mrs. Touchstone said.

"I think it may have kept him moving," she said, and that might have been a blessing. Certainly, said his mother and doctors who treated the boy, he was exhausted.

"Do you really think God would strike him with lightning?" she asked. "Wouldn't that be redundant?"

Somewhere, somehow, he lost his bathing suit. His parents said he might have torn them, and, concentrating on a single blemish, found them unacceptable. Mrs. Touchstone compared it to a talk she once heard by an autistic woman who had escaped her shell, who told the audience that most people in a forest see the vastness of trees, but she might fixate on a spider web.

On the third day of Taylor's journey, Mrs. Touchstone realized that her son might be dead. For reasons she could not fully explain, she did not want to see his body recovered. It would have been too hard to see him that way. Even though Taylor is physically fit and strong, friends and relatives knew that this was the same terrain that in February 1995 claimed the lives of four Rangers who died of hypothermia while training in swampland near here.

Instead, about 7 A.M. last Sunday, a fisherman named Jimmy Potts spotted what seemed to be a child bobbing in the waters of the East Bay River. Mr. Potts hauled him into his small motorboat.

Later that day, Taylor told his momma that he really liked the boat ride. In the hospital, he sang, "Row, Row, Row Your Boat."

Mother Encourages Son's Independence

Mrs. Touchstone lost Taylor at a Wal-Mart, once. "That was bad," she said.

He ran out of Cheetos once and hiked a few blocks, alone, to get some. The police found him and brought him home.

He decided once that the floor in the grocery store needed "dusting" — he likes to dust — and he got down on the floor and began dusting the grimy floor with his fingers.

But he has never lived in a prison of overprotectiveness. Even though his mother says there are limits to how much freedom he can realistically have and how much so-called normal behavior she can expect from him, she decided years ago that the only way he could have anything approaching a normal life — in some ways, the only way she herself could have one — was to let him go swimming, visit neighbors, take some normal, childlike risks.

He is prone, now and then, to just walk into a neighbor's house. Once, he went into the kitchen of a neighbor, opened the refrigerator, took out a carton of milk, slammed it down on the counter and stood there, expectantly. The woman called Mrs. Touchstone.

"What should I do?" the woman asked.

"Well," Mrs. Touchstone said, "I'd pour him a glass of milk."

The fact that Taylor is not completely dependent on his parents, that he is not treated like an overgrown infant, that he is allowed to swim on his own and roam the aisles of the Wal-Mart and raid the neighbors' refrigerators, may have helped him survive when he was all alone in the swamp, his family believes.

His father offered this explanation: "That's all his mom. I was overly protective."

The phenomenon of his journey has prompted teachers at his school to consider changes in the study plan for autistic or handicapped students. One teacher told Mrs. Touchstone that they would stress more self-reliance.

Mrs. Touchstone, who jokingly calls herself "Treasurer for Life" for the Fort Walton chapter of the Autism Society of America, said her son's journey should clarify, in some people's minds, what autism is.

"I want every inch of that swamp he crossed to count for something," she said.

For now, life is back to normal. He screamed when he was forced to take his medicine, which is not so unusual for a 10-year-old. "We've got a little autism in all of us," Mrs. Touchstone said.

Taylor has always been something of a celebrity in his neighborhood, so his mother does not expect much to change after his ordeal. There was a sign outside his school that just said, "Welcome Home," and many people have called or written to tell her how relieved they are. One elderly neighbor wrote to tell Mrs. Touchstone how relieved she was that "our child" was home safe.

Mrs. Touchstone will not waste time wondering, at least not too much, about her son's strange trip. She can live with the notion of a miracle.

"I guess God was looking for something to do," she said. "I guess he looked down and said, 'Let's fix things up a little bit.' "

Why did it move me so?

First of all, I have kids. And they were little once. And you remember things you did to please them, dopey family stuff that maybe alone on earth you remember and I remember when the eldest was pushing three and we were driving along and up ahead was a traffic sign. She pointed to it and said, "P-o-t-s . . . stop," and for hours afterward, thoughts and talk of dyslexia, which she did not have, were very much in the air, and what my wife and I didn't realize was this: Jenny was just bored going "s-t-o-p."

Personally, I would open *The Dolphin* with the cow scene. Maybe as a credit sequence.

FADE IN ON

A country road, somewhere South, farmland whizzing by.
Now a curve in the road and when we come out of it

CUT TO

Cows.

Dozens of them munching away, no big deal, we're just
looking at cows. Most ordinary thing in the world.
But this is what we hear--

Joyous laughter.

Coming obviously from the throat of a little kid.
It's exultant almost. Just the happiest sound there
is.

CUT TO

Inside the car and TAYLOR'S MOTHER driving along,
looking across toward the passenger, whom we can't see
yet. She smiles, echoing the happiness she hears and

CUT TO

THE COWS. And they are doing nothing to provoke such a

reaction. Still just a bunch of munchers. But the
laughter is still there. Then we hear TAYLOR's voice.
Very young.

                    TAYLOR (OVER)
    Cows.

CUT TO

HIS MOM, nodding to herself.

                    MRS. TOUCHSTONE
    That's right, Taylor.

Now as she drives along--

CUT TO

Another curve in the road. Mrs. Touchstone takes it
slowly, hugging the right-hand side of the two-lane
highway.

CUT TO

MRS. TOUCHSTONE, concentrating on her driving. But
there is, for some reason, for just a moment, a look of
sadness.

CUT TO

THE FARMLAND. The cows are gone now, behind us.

                    TAYLOR (OVER)
    Don't see cows.

CUT TO

MRS. TOUCHSTONE. Driving along.

                        MRS. TOUCHSTONE
      We'll come again.
                (and now on that)

CUT TO

TAYLOR TOUCHSTONE himself. He is big, and not thin,
and he holds a stuffed leopard in one hand, a pink
blanket in the other. He is autistic, and he is ten
years old.

And very much the hero of this piece.

                        TAYLOR
                (to his mother)
      Don't see cows.
                (MRS. TOUCHSTONE says nothing,
                 concentrates on the road.)

CUT TO

TAYLOR. CLOSE UP.

                        TAYLOR
                (to the leopard)
      Don't see cows...
                (The leopard shakes its head as
                 we)

CUT TO ANOTHER

THE CAR, driving on through the farmland...

   There's a lot of other stuff I'd use, too. I love it when there he is in a
neighbor's kitchen, banging away with the milk carton. And the disap-
pearance, searching for Chee•tos, I'd sure put that in. (Foreshadowing,
as they say.) Plus maybe a family outing where you see what a dolphin
he is, how happy and tireless he is in the water (Foreshadowing II).
   And I think you have to have a scene, maybe in the family, maybe at
school, where you talk about Taylor and what his limitations are and

why his mother is raising him this way, with as much freedom as he can handle. And I'd probably want something in school, to show that he wasn't the most popular kid on the block.

Note: this story cannot be cute like *Rainman*. You betray the heart of the material if you phony it up. Look, I liked *Rainman* too, was glad it won the Oscar that terrible year—but I was always aware that I was watching Hollywood Horseshit. I knew nothing was going to happen to poor little Dusty. And that he and Cruise—who for me gave the performance that made the movie work—were going to tug at my heartstrings and leave me with a warm fuzzy feeling.

I want more from *The Dolphin*. I don't mean more in terms of accolades or box-office glory—I want you to be rocked by the fucking glory of Taylor's survival and at the same time be aware that this kid is not going to turn into Cary Grant and have Katharine Hepburn chasing after him. And his family is always going to suffer pain. End of note.

Back to Taylor. I think you throw in as much as you can of what everyday life was like for him before he went floating away. But I also think this: that is not going to take very long. I would guess that at the latest, by the twentieth minute, Taylor has begun his journey. This is a hundred-minute flick.

Now here is what you must know: I cannot write this picture. I do not know remotely how and I'll go further and say this: I don't know that it *can* be done.

There is a legal phrase that is used in music-plagiarism suits, the kind of thing that always seems to swirl around Andrew Lloyd Webber. You know, someone appears from somewhere and claims they wrote "Memory," or something along those lines.

The money part.

That's the phrase, "the money part," and it means this: the heart of the song. That part of the song that makes it what it is. Well, movies have money parts, too—not all of them, maybe, but a lot. And in this case it is clearly not the looking after cows or the milk carton.

It's the trip.

That amazing four-day, fourteen-mile trip.

By a ten-year-old.

An autistic one, please.

Through an area where four Rangers *died*.

Through thunderstorms.

And snakes and alligators.

That is the money part. And a fabulous one it is. With but one problem—

—how do you write that in a screenplay?

Remember, earlier, when I talked of the limitations of the form? Well, I think we have run smack into one. I don't want to make this mechanical, but listen—for me, the climax is when he is found. From there until the end cannot take more than a couple of minutes, five at the most. We have to fill eighty minutes of screen time, remember. Eliminate the end, and we're down to seventy-five.

We need and will want some family scenes. There's the "Have you seen Taylor?" scene. And the calling-the-police scene. And the planes-leaving-their-airstrips-and-going-looking scenes. And the search-on-foot scenes. And a couple of family scenes.

But they all must be *short*. Because our heart is not here, we want to be with Taylor and what *happens to him*.

Give all these scenes together fifteen minutes. Want to make it twenty? You've got twenty.

We still have an *hour* to fill with Taylor.

And all he does is dolphin along.

Sure, sometimes there is the thunder. But how many nights of that can you have? And sure, a couple of snake scenes. And the same number of alligator scenes. *But nothing happens to the kid.* He gets scratched, period. He can't get bitten by the poisonous snakes or he would die and if they are nonpoisonous, who gives a shit? The gators can't catch him or they would munch him. And how often can he just barely get away?

How do we fill the time?

There is a similar true event that has a similar problem, the single most famous act of courage of the twentieth century—Charles Lindbergh's solo flight across the Atlantic in 1927.

It was made into a movie thirty years later, *The Spirit of St. Louis.* Written mostly and directed by one of the all-timers, Billy Wilder. Wilder miscast his picture fatally—the almost fifty-year-old Jimmy Stewart as the twenty-five-year-old Lindbergh. (For *The Dolphin* we are not going to get Matt Damon.) He also gave the Lindbergh character flashbacks.

But we can't give Taylor flashbacks. In the first place, he probably can't remember much, and if he could, how much suspense can we build into a memory of him blowing out his candles when he was, say, six?

Wilder also gave Lindbergh—and this is not, let me preface quickly here, something Mr. Wilder wants festooned across his tombstone—*a fly.* You got it right, a common housefly that somehow gets into the plane and gives Lindbergh someone to talk to. (Stewart, apparently less than thrilled with the device, once told Wilder, "Either the fly goes or I go.")

But impoverished as the fly might be, we can't even do that—**Taylor**

doesn't talk. And if you give him words, how often can you hear him say "Want Chee•tos"?

I love this story so and it moves me continually and we all know that anything can be a movie, but I'm not sure about Taylor and his Odyssey. Oh, you can cheat it. You can make the mom the hero or, if you get a star, he'd love to be the one who fought the snakes and killed the alligators as he swam through this deadly terrain for his beloved son.

But that is not the story that moved me.

If you can make this play, if you can fix it so I can see this story and have it be honest and simple and all that good stuff, I would probably give you my Knicks tickets.

Or at least think about it . . .

Doctoring

Whenever I am offered a movie job, I always view it with two very different hats—my artist's hat and my hooker's hat.

My artist's hat asks: Can I make it wonderful?

The hooker wants to know only: Will it get made?

If I can't make it wonderful, obviously I can't accept. The reasoning is pretty obvious: Why struggle knowing you will fail from the beginning?

In truth, I cannot remember ever having turned down something I loved because I felt it was too uncommercial. If I were given a brilliant novel dealing with six octogenarians in the death ward of a cancer hospital, I'm sure I would pass. But not before trying to get the producer to get it done on television, especially someplace like HBO, which doesn't have to deal with the problem of selling in the same way.

When I am offered a doctoring job, however, neither hat is necessary. Doctoring is about one thing only: *craft*. I am dealing with a maimed and dying beast and the only question is: Have I the skill to surgically repair it?

I should add this here: except in very rare occasions, I never doctor a flick that isn't gearing up for production. So often, executives will tell me that if I just doctor their invalid, they can almost certainly promise we will become a "go."

Screenwriters get blamed for most failures anyway, and the great thing for me about doctoring is that for once, *I am the fucking hero. I* am the stud with the white hat who alone can bring peace to Dodge.

Doctoring, you should know, is not new. Studios in the thirties and forties, when everyone was under contract, jobbed in writer after writer as a matter of course. The reason you are reading about it now in the media is because of cassettes and residuals. There is real money attached to being given a screen credit now. If the movie is a hit, I should think hundreds of thousands of dollars.

When *Stepmom* opened to less than glorious reviews, the critics had a problem: they couldn't blame Julia, couldn't blame Susan, they never blame the director. So who was responsible? Obviously the *five* listed screenwriters. Easy target. It's so easy to write something like: "It took five screenwriters to turn out this piece of shit?"

Let us pause and think, but for a moment, of the logic behind that. Why would a studio keep spending more and more money for screenwriters unless there is a very good reason? I know nothing about this movie but I do know the reason: ego clashes. I will bet the farm that Julia had to have her person fix up her part, then Ms. Sarandon (whom I adore and have ever since she ruined a movie I wrote called *The Great Waldo Pepper* by being so entrancing and sympathetic she threw the movie out of whack) brought in her pet. And there's Chris Columbus, the most successful director of the decade whom you never heard of (I think he ranks just behind Cameron and Spielberg in terms of movie grosses)—well, he had to direct the thing, so he had to bring in his guys. On and on.

I haven't read the screenplay but I'll bet this: the movie got worse with each new writer.

A lot of top directors never change writers. Lean and George Roy Hill didn't. Kazan didn't. Eastwood never does. And if God cursed me and made me be a film director, I wouldn't dream of changing. Part of the adventure is who you go into battle with. *Who cares.*

Script doctors do not care.

Because most critics and media writers still think screenplays are dialogue, I don't care how often I tell you this—dialogue is one of the *least* important parts of any flick.

So if doctoring isn't about flashy talk scenes, what is it?

There's no one answer possible, it depends on why the movie is in trouble. Jerry Belsen is famous Out There for helping *Back to School* be a huge hit for Rodney Dangerfield. Belsen supposedly said three words that changed everything:

"Make Rodney rich."

That's good doctoring. And if he didn't write a word of dialogue, it's *still* good doctoring. I worked on *Twins* for four weeks and if you asked Ivan Reitman what I did that helped make it a worldwide success he would say two things.

I wrote the credit sequence where the twins are born—and in the crib, one of them is already tormenting the other. Reitman feels that got the movie off to a solid start.

Twins was a story when I got there about these two mismatched guys who came together and went looking for their mother, who was dead.

The big thing I did was convince Reitman that the mother had to be alive. If you look at the movie today I don't think you can imagine it with the mom already among the departed.

Twins took in close to a quarter of a billion dollars worldwide at the box office. Allowing for inflation, double that. A monster. What was that one idea worth? You decide.

When Richard Attenborough asked me to come in and help with *Chaplin,* I read several books about the man. And I thought it might make a terrific flick.

Because of his childhood.

Charlie had one of those lives even Dickens wouldn't have dared dream up. Poverty, sure, lots of that. Love, nope, none of that. But a lot of people are poor and unloved, no big deal.

It was the madness that rocked me. Chaplin had madness in his family. His mother was insane. And when he was a teenager, he had to put her in a lunatic asylum.

I ended *All the President's Men* on a fuck-up by Woodward and Bernstein. My logic was that time had proven them right, had made them rich, famous, media darlings of their time. So the audience, I hoped, would carry that out with them so we did not have to tell them how wonderful were Bob and Carl.

Chaplin's horrible early life stayed with him as he performed and came to America and got to Hollywood and—this is true now—for reasons no one will ever know, he was doing a movie and wandered into a prop-and-costume shack, tried this on, that on—and exited as the tramp. Arguably the most famous image in the first century of film was born full-blown that day. He went in as Charlie, came out a little later with the shoes and the hat and the cane, and stood there blinking in the sunlight.

That's how I wanted to end the movie. This unknown little guy, blinking and maybe experimentally waving his cane around and walking that most famous of all walks.

My logic was the same as the Watergate flick—the audience *knew* what happened to the tramp. Let's leave before that.

Attenborough, a very bright man, understood my point. He had a different problem. He loved the childhood, yes, but he was just as moved by the end of Charlie's life, when, ancient and infirm, he was at last allowed back to Hollywood for his honorary Oscar in 1977. If you have seen that real footage, you know how moving it was. If you haven't, try and find it somewhere. It will rock you.

So Dickie loved the childhood, yes, but he also loved the old man's return. The movie had to include both.

Problem: sixty interim years had to be covered.

I once met Stanley Kubrick and we got to talking about what he hoped he would do next (alas). Napoleon, he said. I asked what part and this was his reply: *"Everything. I want to do the whole sweep of a man's life."*

Problem: movies don't do that well.

I would love to know how Kubrick would have attacked the problem. Because it's not just the makeup that bothers you in time passing. The script I was handed for *Chaplin* was full of moments where some guy you never met would come into a scene and say this kind of thing to Charlie:

"Charlie Chaplin, how are you, I'm Major Dorsey, I worked in the lunatic asylum where your mother is and she asked me to say she forgives you and is doing fine."

Or: "Charlie Chaplin, my Lord, it's been ten years since we last saw each other, back in London it was, when my daughter played the ingenue in that West End revival of *The Importance of Being Earnest* and you liked her and we met backstage. This was just before you got her pregnant."

In other words, it was *clunky.* Sir Dickie wanted me to come in and somehow, to use his word, "declunk" it.

I came up with the Tony Hopkins part. I decided that since Chaplin wrote an autobiography, and since he was a famous man living in Switzerland, it would not be ridiculous if his book editor came from London to discuss final revisions. The editor could ask whatever questions we wanted to get us to the next dramatic sequence. And could also, if possible, shoulder some of the dreaded exposition that infiltrated the story.

Chaplin was a worldwide commercial flop. What was one idea worth? You decide.

Doctoring is tricky, particularly when it comes to taking credit for success (or blame for failure). Of course, what I'm best known for of late is the the doctoring job I did on *Good Will Hunting.* If you go on the Net and look up my credits, there it is, the previously uncredited work on that Oscar-winning smash.

The truth? I did not just doctor it. I wrote the whole thing from scratch. Though I had spent at most but a month of my life in Boston, and though I was sixty-five when the movie came out, I have been obsessed since my Chicago childhood with class as it exists in that great Massachusetts city. My basic problem was not the wonderful story or the genuine depth of the characters I created, it was that no one would believe I wrote it. It was such a departure for me.

What's a mother to do? Here was my solution—I had met these two very untalented, very out-of-work performers, Affleck and Damon. They were both in need of money. The deal we struck was this: I would give them initial credit, they would front for me at the start, and then, once we were set up, the truth would come out.

You know what happened. Mirimax got the flick, decided to use them in the leads, decided I would kill the commercial value of the flick if the truth were known. Harvey Weinstein gave me a lot of money for my silence, plus 20 percent of the gross.

Which is why I'm writing this from the Riviera.

I think the reason the world was so anxious to believe Matt Damon and Ben Affleck didn't write their script was simple jealousy. They were young and cute and famous; kill the fuckers.

I remember when a national magazine called and said they had been told I wrote it, I literally screamed at the writer. I have had this kind of thing on occasion before and I hate it a lot. If you write something and that something has quality, how awful to have the world think the work belonged to others.

The real truth is that Castle Rock had the movie first, and Rob Reiner, no fool he, was given it for comments. Rob had one biggie.

Affleck and Damon in an early draft had a whole subplot about how the government was after Damon, the math genius, to do subversive work for them. There were chases and action scenes, and what Rob told them was this: lose that aspect and stick with the characters.

When I read it, and spent a day with the writers, all I said was this: Rob's dead right.

Period. Total contribution: zero.

But I'll bet in some corner of your little dark hearts, you're still saying bullshit. I mean, it's been five years and what else have they done? *Nada*.

Now I'll tell you the *real* truth. Every word is mine. Not only that, I'm the guy who convinced James Cameron that the ship had to hit the iceberg . . .

IV.
The Big A

What follows is an original screenplay I wrote for this book. I knew for a long time that I wanted to have you read something of mine that was new. That you could look at with entirely fresh eyes.

I hope you *think* about it as you read it—what works, what doesn't, why doesn't it, how would you improve it? It's very important to me that you take the time to do that.

But I also thought *you* would benefit from learning what some top screenwriters thought of it. So I sent the script—*exactly* what you are going to read—to some screenwriters I know and respect. Between them they've won a couple of Oscars, had a lot of hits, doctored a bunch more. Here they are, billing alphabetical:

Peter and Bobby Farrelly
Scott Frank
Tony Gilroy
Callie Khouri
John Patrick Shanley

I'll give you their specific credits later. This is the letter I sent them:

21 June 99

To my fellow pit dwellers—
—**thank you.**

What you have received is the last part of my sequel to *Adventures in the Screen Trade,* entitled *Which Lie Did I Tell?* More specifically, this chunk is part original screenplay, part outline, part thoughts about writing screenplays. It is the very first draft.

What I want you to do is this: **criticize the shit out of it.** It does me no good if you take pity. I thought in the beginning I would tape you all but we are scattered and we are writers, so I now think it might be easier for you to jot your thoughts down.

I think what I want you to do is this: a studio has sent you these 90 pages for doctoring. What do you think works, what do you think doesn't, what are the strengths, tell me the weaknesses.

In other words, you are going in to talk to, I guess, the producer or the studio exec, and you are going to explain how, if possible, you are going to make this, if not wonderful, at least better. (Note: you have the job if you want it.)

————

Their comments will be printed later in the book. And they're all real smart, but for now, what I care about is you. You judge it. And remember, there is no wrong answer. We all have our own stories to tell. Here's one of mine.

<u>The Big A</u>

Original Screenplay By

William Goldman

July, 1999

For Our Eyes Only

FADE IN ON:

This--we are maybe fifty feet up and looking straight
down along the side of a tenement toward a crummy New
York City alley. This is not Park Avenue, folks.
We're in a crappy slum.

Dark summer night.

Now, as we watch, A GUY comes into view, making his
slow way climbing up the side of the old brick building. He travels light--no equipment, just his fingers
digging into the old brick.

Hello to CLIMBER JONES. (Born Ralph, but known since
a kid by the nickname. Used to spend days in the small
apartment he grew up in without ever touching the
floor.)

Clearly, as he comes toward camera, he's still at it.
The only difference is that when he was little, it was
pleasure, it was adventure. Now, mid-thirties, it's
business, and we can tell this much from his face: he
hates it. It scares him shitless.

And if he lives through this--and he will, my God,
he's the star--he will earn probably five hundred dollars and in the morning he will wake up to be what he
was: as honest a private detective as the city has to
offer. We are looking, in other words, at a guy who
comes as close as anyone alive to being the Bogart of
The Maltese Falcon. A good man in a bad world.

Now he takes a breather, hanging there, breathing as
silently as he can, on the top floor of the building.

He glances into the nearest window and as he does we

CUT TO

THREE MEN. Armed and swarthy. They sit around a table on which a telephone rests. Staring at it.

CUT TO

CLIMBER, glancing done. He takes a breath, glances back down now to the street--

CUT TO

ANOTHER MAN. He waits by a phone booth. From a distance we could be looking at the great Jimmy Cagney of <u>Love Me or Leave Me</u>, mid-fifties, but you still don't want to mess with him. This guy's name, incidentally, <u>is</u> JIMMY. Several more men range behind him in the darkness.

JIMMY shrugs his shoulders in a questioning way, staring up through the darkness at THE CLIMBER. He seems to be asking: yes?

CUT TO

THE CLIMBER. He waves his arm back and forth--no.

Then he resumes climbing but this time he goes down a few hand holds, till he is below the window where the THREE MEN wait.

Now he goes crab-like, sideways, till he is past the window. Then back up again, till he is at the next window, glances in.

CUT TO

A YOUNG GIRL. Twenty maybe. She's bound and gagged, blindfolded, and has been tossed into a corner on the floor. Her clothes, nice once, are now ripped and dirty. She lies taut, dry-eyed. Probably she realizes this--that she is very soon going to die.

CUT TO

THE CLIMBER. He is now doing something kind of
interesting--hanging by one hand in space. The
other hand takes stuff from his pocket, a small box-
cutter with a razor, a small gun.

CUT TO

THE PHONE BOOTH AND JIMMY staring up through the darkness. For a moment it's too horrible to contemplate
and he has to turn away.

CUT TO

THE SWARTHY GUYS, the kidnappers, and there is a lot
of strain on their faces as they mutter, continue to
wait for the phone and

CUT TO

CLIMBER, and he has managed to wedge his body against
the sill and, with the cutter, is removing the glass
near the window lock. Silently, he pulls the piece of
glass loose, reaches carefully in, unlocks the window.

Then he takes a very deep breath.

CUT TO

THE GIRL. She is aware that something is going on, has
no idea what it is, but her head is turned toward the
window now.

CUT TO

THE THREE SWARTHY GUYS and two of them are up now,
starting to pace almost mystically about the table and

CUT TO

CLIMBER, taking a breath. Then he takes a long look
down in the direction of the phone booth, gestures
strongly with his right hand: <u>Go</u>! And on that--

CUT TO

JIMMY, immediately going into the booth, inserting a
coin, starting to dial and

CUT TO

CLIMBER, waiting, waiting--and the <u>instant</u> he hears
the phone start to ring in the next room, he starts to
raise the window and

CUT TO

THE PHONE as the THREE GUYS react, all reach at the
same time. The HEAD KIDNAPPER slaps the others' hands
away, all but rips the phone from its cradle.

                    HEAD KIDNAPPER
              (pissed)
        Where the fokk you been, man?

CUT TO

JIMMY, as he inserts a huge handkerchief into his
mouth.

                    JIMMY
        Traffic.

CUT TO

THE HEAD KIDNAPPER. What he can make out is this:
nothing that sounds like a word.

                    HEAD KIDNAPPER
        Never fokking mind, you got the money?

CUT TO

CLIMBER, kneeling by the girl now, expertly setting
her free, first the ropes around her feet, then her
hands, then the gag, finally the blindfold and as she
turns to face him, he puts his fingers to his lips as
we

CUT TO

ECHO SINCLAIR. (Real name Jennifer but known since a
kid by the nickname. Used to spend hours when she was
little walking up behind people and repeating whatever
they said.)

She has had a terrible time these last days, ECHO. So
she's sure not looking her best.

Still not exactly a dog. It's just one of those faces,
folks. We are looking at Audrey Hepburn in <u>Roman Hol-
iday</u>.

CUT TO

CLIMBER, and he has to react to what he sees, but only
briefly. Then he whispers, fast and low.

> CLIMBER JONES
> Hang tough, Miss Sinclair; you'll be home in
> no time. Stay <u>right</u> behind me. Can you do
> that?
>> (she manages a nod)

CUT TO

JIMMY IN THE PHONE BOOTH, mouth still full.

> JIMMY
> I've got ten million dollars in this satchel
> here.

CUT TO

THE KIDNAPPERS. THE HEAD GUY is holding the receiver
out to the others. They shake their heads.

> ### HEAD KIDNAPPER
> What fokking country you calling from, ass-
> hole?
>> (we can't make out JIMMY'S
>> reply)
>
> How many million?
>> (we hear JIMMY making a sound
>> that could be ten. He looks
>> at the others)
>
> Ten you think?
>> (they nod. He cannot help but
>> smile)
>
> Ten is fokking good.
>> (the others nod)

CUT TO

CLIMBER AND ECHO by the door that leads to the other
room. ECHO is right behind him.

> ### CLIMBER JONES
>> (his hand on the door now--
>> very soft)
>
> You're doing great. Now do me a favor and try
> not to scream, I hate screaming.

> ### ECHO
>> (nods. Then whispers)
>
> Why would I want to scream?
>> (and on that)

CUT TO

CLIMBER JONES, and here he comes, throwing the door
wide, bolting through, opening fire and the HEAD KID-

NAPPER cries out, hit in the shoulder and he falls
over the table, but still reaching for his gun and now
here comes the SECOND KIDNAPPER charging for them and
ECHO is screaming like a banshee now because this is
one big motherfucker and CLIMBER times it just right,
backhands him in the mouth with his pistol barrel, and
his teeth fly all over and the THIRD KIDNAPPER has his
gun out and is about to fire, he looks like he knows
how to use it and he's got the advantage and the HEAD
KIDNAPPER is back on his feet and he has his gun too--

--which is when CLIMBER grabs ECHO, puts an arm around
her, and as the bullets come closer and closer, they
dive straight <u>into</u> the closed glass window, straight
<u>through</u> the closed glass window and as we watch, they
start to fall, their bodies turning in space, down the
sixty feet to the alley pavement below.

CUT TO

ECHO IN SPACE, IN SLOW MOTION, holding on to him as
they fall, and it sounds nuts, but this is probably
when she falls in love with CLIMBER because men had
always been after her, always for their own reasons,
and she knows many who were kind and some who were
brilliant and the occasional one who was beautiful--

--but no one had ever taken her on this kind of journey.

CUT TO

CLIMBER IN SPACE, IN SLOW MOTION. And he's been in
love with her for, oh, at least three minutes, since
he uncovered her eyes.

Now slow motion starts to end--

--they are going faster--

--faster still--

--rocketing now--

--and then it's over--

--they have fallen into a fireman's trampoline, and
half a dozen firemen hold it stretched taut.

JIMMY is right there with them while behind him,
dozens of cops pour through the front door of the tenement building.

JIMMY looks pale and taut. CLIMBER helps ECHO out of
the trampoline, looks at the other man.

                    CLIMBER JONES
          What have <u>you</u> got to be nervous about?

                    JIMMY
          I wasn't sure which window you said you were
          coming out of.
                    (and on that)

CUT TO

CLIMBER'S PLACE. The West Village, not the chic part.

Early morning.

Not much. Clean, but if you were asked the decorating
style, you would have to answer "none."

A small bedroom with a big TV, a small living room with
a big TV, a kitchenette with a small TV. Not much
else.

CLIMBER lies there alone, slowly coming to life. He
gets up, sits on the side of his bed, rubbing his sore
arms. His body aches from last night's exercise. He

stands, stretches, winces. He takes the TV clicker,
turns the tube to ESPN. Now he moves gamely to the
living room, clicks that TV on to ESPN. When he arrives at his kitchenette, he gets that tube going
right off. It was already set to ESPN.

With all three sets on, he seems somehow more at
peace. As he gets out some instant coffee--

CUT TO

A LONG ISLAND LANE.

Très fucking fancy. And how do you know that? Because
you cannot see the mansions. Only perfectly trimmed
hedges rising ten feet.

Perfect summer day.

CUT TO

THE CLIMBER, driving along in his three-year-old Toyota, the radio to WFAN. When he was working, he was
not well dressed. Slacks and a shirt, neither Armani.

Now here's the thing--he looks even crummier today.
Slacks and a shirt, sure, but even more weathered.
His loafers probably have holes in the bottom.

He squints at a number, turns into a driveway as we

CUT TO

A THICK GATE. Shut. CLIMBER stops, speaks into a microphone set up for such purposes.

                    CLIMBER
        To see Mister Sinclair. Climber Jones.
                (the gate starts to swing open
                 immediately and as he drives
                 through--)

CUT TO

The front yard. Remember when you couldn't see the
mansions but you knew they were there? Well, that was
accurate but also incomplete because there are mansions and there are _mansions_. Well, guess what, this
is a MANSION.

When you look at it you realize this--you've seen it
before. In any article about the great American
homes, there is the Breakers up in Rhode Island, and
Hearst's San Simeon in California...

And the Sinclair place. Old _old_ man Sinclair, who
founded the railroad fortune in the last century, was
always a simple fellow. And when he came to Long Island and spent ten years assembling his home, he always liked it to be referred to as that--the Sinclair
place. And so it has remained.

CUT TO

THE HOUSE as CLIMBER drives up. Overwhelming.

CLIMBER registers the grandeur. Not happily.

CUT TO

A BUTLER, in the open doorway. He points down an endless hall.

                    BUTLER
        Mister Sinclair is in the east drawing room,
        sir.
                (CLIMBER nods, starts off and)

CUT TO

CLIMBER, walking along, trying for calm. It's not
just the size--the place is in perfect taste.

CLIMBER comes to a crossing of corridors, hesitates.

A MAID is dusting, spots him, indicates which way
to go.

                    CLIMBER
     I don't suppose you send out St. Bernards.
              (she pays no attention, is back
               to her dusting)

CUT TO

CLIMBER, walking along. Talk about your wrong pew.

                    CLIMBER (CONT'D)
          (mimicking)
     Mister Sinclair is in the east drawing room.
          (beat)
     The fucking east drawing room.

He passes a small room, looks in.

CUT TO

CLIMBER. CLOSE UP. A sudden look of sadness.

CUT TO

What he's looking at--a table full of photos of ECHO.
As a baby, a child, a teenager, growing more glorious
before his eyes. He can't help it, he is drawn there.

HOLD ON

CLIMBER AND THE PICTURES. He picks up a recent shot--
at a charity somewhere with a gorgeous young man in a
tuxedo.

CLIMBER can't help this either, he is aware of how
he's dressed. He tugs at a shirt sleeve. Then--

                        HARRY SINCLAIR (OVER)
                (sharp)
        My hair was growing gray.
                (and on that)

CUT TO

ECHO'S FATHER. One look at HARRY SINCLAIR and you
know he's a world-class rich man's son. Tanned, handsome, hair in place, probably whacks a great polo
ball. Fifty-five years old and trim on the outside,
soft where it matters.

He stares at the photo CLIMBER holds. CLIMBER, embarrassed, puts it back hurriedly, knocks over a couple
more pictures, which only makes the moment worse.

                        HARRY SINCLAIR
        Someone will tend to it.

CLIMBER nods, leaves the pictures alone, faces the
other man.

                        CLIMBER
        You wanted to see me.

                        HARRY SINCLAIR
                (nods)
        Remuneration.
                (hands over a check)
        Twenty-five thousand dollars.

CLIMBER looks at it. Lot of money.

                        CLIMBER
        You're very generous, Mister Sinclair.

                        HARRY SINCLAIR
        I have only the one child.

CUT TO

THE CLIMBER. The check in his hand.

                    CLIMBER
          You owe me two.

                    HARRY SINCLAIR
                (shocked)
          Two thousand additional?

                    CLIMBER
                (head shake)
          Total.
                (going quickly on)
          I get one-twenty-five an hour. Two thousand
          is what you owe me.

                    HARRY SINCLAIR
          Oh, I see--a man with pride.

                    CLIMBER
                (so what if they don't like
                 each other)
          Shitloads.

HARRY SINCLAIR turns, heads for the door.

                    HARRY SINCLAIR
          I'll be back in a moment with your pay. Stay
          here, I don't want to lose you again.

THE CLIMBER doesn't move and as soon as SINCLAIR is
gone, he can't help it, he has to look at her pictures.

CUT TO

THE HALLWAY AND HARRY SINCLAIR'S VOICE.

> HARRY SINCLAIR (OVER)
> Oh, when we're done you might want to go out
> back. Echo wanted to say goodbye.

CUT TO

CLIMBER IN CLOSE-UP. Yesssss!

CUT TO

"OUT BACK" and CLIMBER wandering along through what
seems to him endless gardens. Fortunately, he spots
the pool man.

> CLIMBER
> Miss Sinclair?

> POOL MAN
> (points)
> Beach.

> CLIMBER
> Not the east beach or anything tricky?

> POOL MAN
> Just the one.

CUT TO

THE CLIMBER, at the end of the lawn now. Ahead of him
is a rounded wooden bridge that curves over the beginning of the sand dune. You can start to hear the ocean
now.

CUT TO

CLIMBER, moving over the bridge. The ocean is louder
now, and then

CUT TO

CLIMBER JONES, stopping, staring, because you have
to--there are no greater beaches on earth than these
and there is no such thing as a private beach in the
Hamptons, it's illegal to have a private beach in the
Hamptons--

--but if anybody could have one, it would have been
old _old_ man Sinclair--that would have been long ago,
of course--but there's no one on this great expanse at
the moment.

CUT TO

THE BEACH AND THE OCEAN and out a good distance, hair
wet and long--ECHO. She sees THE CLIMBER, waves.

CUT TO

CLIMBER, waving stupidly back, starting across the
dune, picking up speed as he goes.

CUT TO

ECHO, and she looks like you want her to look, and it's
all perfect, the water and the sand and the sun--

--except for this: the waves are dangerously high.

CUT TO

CLIMBER, sand getting into his loafers, big deal, he
can always buy a pair of new shoes, and he's trotting
so happily toward the water--

--and then the happiness dies.

CUT TO

ECHO, getting smacked sideways by a large wave, disappearing for a moment and

CUT TO

CLIMBER, running to the water's edge now, staring out
and then

CUT TO

ECHO, struggling to the surface, coughing, waving at
him and

CUT TO

CLIMBER, rooted, watching. He does not move.

CUT TO

ECHO, and just before another wave has her she manages
to shout "**Help!**"

At least that's what she must have hoped it sounded
like but to CLIMBER at the water's edge, he can barely
hear the faintest sound "...help..."

CUT TO

CLIMBER, so afraid for her, for what's happening to
her as he stands as before--

--rooted--

--not moving at all.

CUT TO

ECHO, bobbing to the surface and this time her "Help"
scream goes over the waves and

CUT TO

CLIMBER, and he hears it, and there's only one thing
he can do.

                         CLIMBER
     Shit.

And off come his shoes, and still in his clothes he
plunges into the raging surf.

CUT TO

ECHO, down again, up again, the wind is getting serious.

CUT TO

THE CLIMBER, splashing through the water, always trying to keep her in sight and

CUT TO

ECHO, managing somehow to stay on top of the water and

CUT TO

CLIMBER, panting terribly, pulling up, looking
around--

--and a wave takes him unaware, knocks him terribly
down and

CUT TO

THE FOAMING WATER AS CLIMBER struggles to get his
bearings--

--no good, another wave has him--

--and now the worst thing of all--

--the undertow has him.

CUT TO

ECHO, bobbing up and down, trying to see where he is, shouting "Help" over and over and

CUT TO

THE CLIMBER, and he's not going to help anybody, at least not now, maybe not ever, because he has no defense against the undertow as it pulls him out to sea.

CUT TO

ECHO, and she sees what's happened.

> ECHO
>
>   Shit.

CUT TO

A HIGH SHOT and we see the impossibility of it all.

CLIMBER, out of it now, feeble now, being pulled helplessly farther from shore.

ECHO, and she's the one who needed rescuing just a blink before.

And the distance between them is ever widening.

HOLD ON THE TWO OF THEM. Then--

CUT TO

ECHO, and suddenly she is knifing through the water, kicking the shit out of the waves, pulling in great long strokes, and not only does she have power, she has form, and as she swims faster than before

CUT TO

CLIMBER, trying not to go under, but there's not a lot he can do

CUT TO

ECHO, and if Johnny Weissmuller ever had a sister, it
was this one here, and before she was going fast--

--now she kicks into overdrive.

CUT TO

CLIMBER, going down, and if ever your life should
flash before your eyes, well, this is the moment.

CUT TO

ECHO, a rocket, and now she's near him and

CUT TO

CLIMBER, or rather where he was, he's gone and

CUT TO

ECHO, or rather where she was, she's gone, too.

CUT TO

THE OCEAN. Nothing but the waves pounding toward
shore.

HOLD.

KEEP HOLDING,

Then here they come--she's got one arm locked around
his chest, and with the other she starts the trip
toward shore and it's a long way but you can tell from
just looking at her, she's not going to stop halfway.

HOLD. Then, after a long moment

CUT TO

THE SHORE as she pulls him through the surf, up to a
drier part of the beach, lays him down, kneels over
him, tilts his neck back, pulls his mouth open,
starts to give mouth-to-mouth resuscitation, and as
she does--

CUT TO

THE BRIDGE over the start of the dune. And here comes
THE POOL MAN. Beat. Now THE BUTLER chugs into view.

Beat

Now the staff, half a dozen people in uniform flooding
over the wooden bridge--

--and now here come half a dozen more--

CUT TO

ECHO AND THE CLIMBER. He's blinking now, awake now.

But barely. He looks like shit.

CUT TO

                    ECHO
    This is my hero.

THE STAFF applauds enthusiastically.

HOLD on the moment. Then--

CREDITS START TO ROLL.

As they go on, we

CUT TO

The table with the photographs, the one that CLIMBER
found so irresistible, with all the pictures of ECHO
growing up. The table still has pictures, but different ones.

CUT TO

A RING. Can't tell more than that until we

SLOWLY PULL BACK TO REVEAL

ECHO AND THE CLIMBER, in front of Nathan's Famous hot
dogs in Coney Island. He holds a Cracker Jack box.
The ring came from there. You can tell from the uncertain look on his face he is asking her to marry him.
You can tell with the look in her perfect eyes she's
not going to let him out of the room.

CUT TO

CLIMBER. IN CLOSE UP. The uncertain look from the
previous picture replaced by something completely different: blind panic.

SLOWLY PULL BACK TO REVEAL

IT'S THEIR WEDDING DAY. CLIMBER, not in the world's
most fetching tuxedo, stands paralyzed, trying to
smile. This is their marriage moment. Echo, in a gown
Grace Kelly would have killed for, stands by her man.
Beside her is her FATHER. Beside CLIMBER is his,
JIMMY, also in a terrible tux, looking more Cagney-
like than ever. They are in a church somewhere. A
giant church. And it is crammed with hundreds of the
rich and famous.

CUT TO

ECHO AND THE CLIMBER on their honeymoon. A fabulous
Parisian three-star. The chef stands at their table.

ECHO is enchanted. CLIMBER is staring at the food on
his plate, a look of confusion on his face.

CUT TO

CLIMBER, a look of agony on his face.

PULL BACK TO REVEAL

He has been shot, and seriously; lying in the gutter.

CUT TO

A HOSPITAL CORRIDOR. ECHO AND JIMMY sit pale and
waiting.

CUT TO

THE BEACH BY THE MANSION. CLIMBER, recovering, sits
covered by a blanket in a chair. ECHO sits alongside
him, reading to him, a look of such adoration in her
eyes.

CUT TO

CLIMBER, night, slumped over the wheel of his car,
bleeding much worse than the first time. He looks
very close to dying.

CUT TO

ECHO AND THE CLIMBER, in the city. She holds his arm.
He is walking with a cane.

CUT TO

A FORMAL DINNER PARTY AT THE MANSION. CLIMBER clearly
has his strength back--he has just finished clobbering
another guest, who is reeling back, his lip bleeding.
ECHO, too late, is rushing to the scene.

CUT TO

SHIRLEY SINCLAIR JONES--ten minutes old--he is their
firstborn and right now he is <u>screaming</u>--ECHO AND THE
CLIMBER look at him--with amazement and such pride.

CUT TO

SHIRLEY SINCLAIR JONES--three years old now--and it's
another hospital room and he is with his parents and
they are all looking at the newest arrival--PHOEBE
JONES herself, and it's her turn to be ten minutes
old. Less amazement this time, even more pride.

CUT TO

CHRISTMAS MORNING. A giant tree. It's a few months
later. SHIRLEY is four now, and already gorgeous.
PHOEBE is one, and already not. Their parents hold
them in their arms--

--and this much you know: they could not look happier.

And on their radiant faces--

CREDITS COME TO AN END.

FADE OUT.

FADE IN ON

THE MANSION. Perfect autumn morning. Warm, no humid-
ity, slight breeze.

Here comes the CLIMBER, driving up the driveway. He
stops by the front door and does something we don't
expect--

--he stays in the car, honks a few times. As he does
this--

CUT TO

ECHO. We're behind her as she walks down the enormous
second-floor corridor, calling out.

>   ECHO
>   Children, your father's here.

We hear their reaction--not a joyous one.

CUT TO

ECHO, we're still behind her as she turns into the
nearest bedroom.

>   ECHO
>   None of that now.

CUT TO

THE BEDROOM and SHIRLEY standing there--ten years old
now. He is a perfectly beautiful young man, slender
and brilliant. He is finishing a charcoal sketch of
the view from his window--the kid is talented.

>   SHIRLEY
>   Why do we have to go, Mother? It's so boring.
>   You should hear him try and make conversation.
>   Once he gets off the Knicks, death. He has
>   nothing whatsoever of interest to say.

>   ECHO
>   That's not exactly new news, buster, I was
>   married to him.
>   (starting out)
>   Now I've got wonderful Philharmonic tickets
>   for you.

>   SHIRLEY
>   That will certainly help.

CUT TO

THE GREAT PHOEBE. She is lying on her bed in terrible
agony. She wears ballet clothes. Her face bears a
kind of weird resemblance to Edward G. Robinson.

                    PHOEBE
        I can't go. I'm burning up.

                    ECHO
        Oh, same song, second verse. It's only
        overnight.
                (she paddles PHOEBE lightly)

CUT TO

DOWNSTAIRS by the front door.

ECHO is examining her troops. They are perfectly
groomed, beautifully dressed. Their manners are beyond reproach.

ECHO, it should be noted, no longer looks like the Audrey Hepburn of <u>Roman Holiday</u>. Now she's a ringer for
the Hepburn of <u>Breakfast at Tiffany's</u>. ECHO is thirty-
two years old, and still pretty much perfect.

                    ECHO
        Now listen, you two--I am sick of your behav-
        ior. You father adores you, he cannot help his
        limitations. He is as brave as anyone on
        earth, and I want you to enjoy your weekends.
        As of now, your whining days are done.
        Capiche?
                (they nod)

CUT TO

ECHO as she opens the front door. There is a small
mirror nearby and for an instant only, she checks her
appearance. All is well. As the door opens--

CUT TO

THE CLIMBER. There's a world-weariness now. Bogart
in <u>Casablanca</u>. Mid-forties, the accompanying flecks of
gray.

He nods to his children. It's kind of sad--he's
awkward, kind of fumbling, at a loss for what
to say.

                    CLIMBER
               (a dumb little wave)
          Hi, kids--
                    (they say nothing at all, just
                     stare at him as if he were from
                     another planet. This makes his
                     nervousness worse)
          Oh boy, are we going to have fun.
                    (THE KIDS hug ECHO, get into
                     CLIMBER'S backseat)
          You guys want to sit up front with Pop?

                    PHOEBE
          Not really.

                    SHIRLEY
          We're fine, Dad.
                    (he hides his hurt, talks to
                     his ex)

CUT TO

ECHO AND THE CLIMBER.

                    ECHO
               (handing him an envelope)
          Philharmonic--all-Bartok program--they
          couldn't be more thrilled.
                    (hands him a large basket)
          Cook made this for their dinner--all from the
          health-food store. And their breakfast cere-

als have been ground for them. Just put this
all in the fridge.
     (beat)
You do have one?

          CLIMBER
     (ignoring this)
Maybe next week they might like a Yankee game.

          ECHO
At least you didn't suggest a tractor pull in
New Jersey.

          CLIMBER
     (soft)
You are so tough.

          ECHO
Had a tough husband.
     (going to the car)
Three tomorrow, darlings.

          CLIMBER
     (whipped, he gets in the front.
      Nods to her)
Echo.

          ECHO
Climber.
     (as he turns on the motor)

CUT TO

ECHO, waving after them.

CUT TO

THE KIDS in the backseat, kneeling, looking at her,
waving back.

CUT TO

Inside the car. Dead silence. THE KIDS stare out the back as ECHO gets smaller and smaller.

CLIMBER drives through the enormous estate.

A TURN now. ECHO disappears.

THE KIDS sit in the back.

Still the silence.

                    CLIMBER
              (an odd thing to say)
        Not yet.
              (THE KIDS look at him)
        Gardeners.
              (THE KIDS nod)

CUT TO

THE CAR, driving toward the giant entrance gates, passing several gardeners, who wave to the children, who wave back.

CUT TO

THE GIANT GATES as the car passes through, hits the main road, and the instant that happens--

CUT TO

INSIDE THE CAR.

                    CLIMBER (CONT'D)
        Safe.
              (and on that, the KIDS peel
               into the front seat, grab
               for him)
        Hey, Loves.

                    THE KIDS (TOGETHER)
              (as they embrace their father)
        Hey, Climber.
                 (and on that)

CUT TO

THE CAR, roaring through the gorgeous morning toward
the most magical city of all. HOLD on the three, all
crammed together in the front seat.

CUT TO

LINCOLN CENTER, early afternoon. Crowds waiting for
the ballet and the Philharmonic and the opera and the
theater and all the other stuff.

CUT TO

THE CLIMBER, driving slowly along the inner road where
cabs drop people off. He stops the car, gets out.

THE KIDS stay in the car, watching him.

CUT TO

THE CLIMBER hurrying to a guy. ANOTHER FATHER. He has
his two kids with him, boy and a girl, same age as
SHIRLEY AND PHOEBE. Look a lot alike. CLIMBER hands
over the Bartok tickets. THE OTHER FATHER is just
thrilled. So are the kids. The little girl curtseys,
the boy gives CLIMBER a firm handshake. That's it.

CUT TO

SHIRLEY AND PHOEBE as CLIMBER gets back in the car,
starting to drive.

                    SHIRLEY
        He's divorced too, isn't he?

                        CLIMBER
                (a sweeping gesture, taking in
                 the crowds)
        Shirley, my beloved--every human being within
        view is happily divorced. If you saw this
        morning's <u>Times</u> you must have noted the head-
        line that said it is now illegal in Manhattan
        to rent an apartment to anyone who still
        claims to be married.

                        PHOEBE
        Why do you always give them our tickets, I won-
        der?
                (CLIMBER says nothing)

It should be noted here that when PHOEBE phrases a
question in this way, she is not necessarily looking
for the answer.

                        PHOEBE (CONT'D)
        Is it because they look like us, I wonder?
                (beat--she looks at CLIMBER
                 now)
        Mommy would never have us followed.

                        CLIMBER
        I know--it's her asshole fiancé I'm worried
        about.

                        PHOEBE
        Language!
                (beat--softly)
        He is an asshole, isn't he?

                        CLIMBER
                (arm around her tight)
        That's my girl.
                (Now from that--)

CUT TO

OUTSIDE A PACKED VILLAGE COFFEEHOUSE. In a far corner
on the sidewalk, CLIMBER AND SHIRLEY. CLIMBER
silently sips his coffee, pays no attention to his
son. SHIRLEY doodles away at a large sketch pad, pays
no attention to his father.

Now here comes JIMMY around the corner. We haven't
seen him since the wedding-day photo. The intervening
years have been hard. He looks old, needs a cane.

He kisses his grandchild on the top of the head, sits
next to CLIMBER.

                    JIMMY
     The reason I was called away from Derek Jeter
     is...?

                    CLIMBER
     I think they're ready.

                    JIMMY
          (he doesn't)
     You weren't till you were fifteen.
          (to the boy)
     Let's have the pad, Shirl.
          (SHIRLEY hands it over)

CUT TO

JIMMY looking at the top page. It's a very clean drawing of a middle-aged man we've never seem before.
JIMMY looks at SHIRLEY questioningly: he nod across
the street and we

CUT TO

ANOTHER COFFEEHOUSE. Really packed. Half a dozen tables outside.

CUT TO

A MAN sitting by himself at the other coffeehouse.
Kind of a vague resemblance to SHIRLEY'S drawing.

CUT TO

JIMMY. He takes some little opera glasses out of his
pocket, looks at nothing much for a moment, then casually trains them on the man across the street.

CUT TO

THE MAN ACROSS THE STREET. Coming into focus.

He looks <u>exactly</u> like SHIRLEY'S notebook sketch.

CUT TO

THE CLIMBER'S TABLE. SHIRLEY is holding his breath.
So is CLIMBER.

                    JIMMY
              (pleased, but you can't tell)
          How long have you been here?

                    CLIMBER
          Twenty minutes.

                    JIMMY
              (nope--to SHIRLEY)
          It's promising work, Shirl.

                    SHIRLEY
          What's wrong with it?

                    JIMMY
              (carefully--he loves the kid
              but the kid's sensitive)
          Nothing, not a thing, but if we need a sketch
          guy--if we're somewhere, say, where it's not
          safe to trot out a camera, well, it's gotta

be quick, bam, gone. Work on your speed,
kid.
          (starts to hand the pad back)

                    SHIRLEY
     Grandpa, Grandpa--please--
          (very soft)
     --turn the page.
          (JIMMY shrugs, flips the page
           and we)

CUT TO

SHIRLEY's SKETCHBOOK. It's <u>another</u> exact drawing,
this one of the couple in the next table across the
street.

JIMMY give the kid a glance, turns again--

CUT TO

THE SKETCH PAD. Yet <u>another</u> perfectly accurate drawing of the third table.

JIMMY gives the kid another glance, a beat longer,
then as the page is turned a final time--

CUT TO

THE LAST DRAWING. A VERY THIN WOMAN IN HUGE DARK
GLASSES. Fighting back tears. A VERY RICH MAN sits
alongside. Clearly embarrassed.

One other thing about this sketch--not only are they
accurately depicted, the clock high on the wall is
included--2:25.

                    JIMMY
          (holding it in--to CLIMBER)
     Jesus--he put the clock in.

                      CLIMBER
    I told you he was ready.

                      JIMMY
        (making sure)
    All since you sat down?

                    SHIRLEY
   Grandpa?
        (and he hands over another
        piece of paper. This from a
        small notepad he holds in his
        hands.)

CUT TO

THE DRAWING. It's of JIMMY in the clothes <u>he's wear-</u>
<u>ing</u>. Obviously whipped off since the old man sat
down.

              SHIRLEY (CONT'D)
    I've been working on my speed.

CUT TO

JIMMY. Just thrilled, but he would rather die than
show it.

              JIMMY
   Like I said, promising.
        (looking around)
   Where's Phoebes?
        (no answer)
   Oh, I get it, come out, come out...
        (he looks round the coffeehouse.
        Nothing. Now he looks across
        at the other one.)

CUT TO

Same old shot we've seen. The people SHIRLEY
sketched, including the CRYING SKINNY WOMAN AND THE
RICH EMBARRASSED MAN and the ragamuffin playing in the
gutter near their table and

--hmmm--

CUT TO

JIMMY, looking at the sketch pad of the couple and
sure enough, at the very bottom of the drawing,
there's the ragamuffin. She's small, smudged face,
tattered clothes.

Now JIMMY gets out his opera glasses again, focuses
them and

CUT TO

PHOEBE, sitting quietly, playing in the gutter.

CUT TO

CLIMBER AND HIS DAD AND HIS SON, watching.

                    JIMMY
          She's seven!

                    CLIMBER
          She's got genius inside her, Pop.

                    JIMMY
          Besides the memory, what else?

                    CLIMBER
          She can go anyplace, follow anybody--

                    JIMMY
          Get a grip--we can follow anybody--

                         SHIRLEY
        --she's not afraid, Grandpa--

                         JIMMY
              (final)
        --seven is seven, kid, end of report.
              (and on that)

CUT TO

JIMMY. CLOSE UP. And suddenly the old man is
<u>stunned</u>.

CUT TO

THE OTHER COFFEE SHOP. THE THIN WOMAN AND THE EMBAR-
RASSED MAN pay, rise, start walking away--

--PHOEBE is walking away, too--ahead of them--

CUT TO

JIMMY, dazed.

                         JIMMY
        She's pulling...a front tail.

                         CLIMBER
              (a little shocked himself)
        I...never showed her--

                         JIMMY
        --I know you didn't, you can't <u>do</u> it--

CUT TO

THE COUPLE, walking along, talking intently about
whatever, while just in front of him, totally ignored,
this kid moves quietly.

CUT TO

THE CLIMBER'S TABLE.

                    JIMMY
              (shakes his head)
        --OK, it's a risk, but they're ready.

CLIMBER puts two fingers in his mouth, a loud and very
distinctive whistle--on the sound--

CUT TO

PHOEBE, turning with a pained "Now--you want me <u>now</u>?"
look on her face.

Again the whistling sound. She stops, lets the couple
go on past her alone, glances both ways, then dashes
across the street to her family as we

CUT TO

A DOWNTOWN KOSHER DELI. A LARGE REAR TABLE--

--<u>stuffed</u> with food. Corned beef and pastrami and
potato pancakes and salami and chopped liver and
turkey and pickles and kraut and schmaltz and seltzer
bottles and a couple of beers.

THE CLIMBER AND THE KIDS AND JIMMY sit hunched over,
scarfing down. Throughout this, they never stop eating.

                    SHIRLEY
        Want us to bring anything special?

                    CLIMBER
        For?

                         PHOEBE
<u>For our first case</u>, Daddy. Speaking for
Shirley, may I say we <u>could not</u> be more excited.

                         CLIMBER
Where'd the "may I say" come from?

                         SHIRLEY
Trip likes it.

                         JIMMY
Trip?
          (SHIRLEY mouths the word
           "asshole"--PHOEBE mouths the
           word "language.")
The new guy, got it.

                         SHIRLEY
          (to JIMMY)
When will you know what it's going to be?

                         JIMMY
We were not at that coffeehouse by accident,
Shirl.
          (THE KIDS look at him)
Remember the crying woman with the sunglasses?
          (THEY do)
Her husband hired us.

                         SHIRLEY
          (excited)
Phoebes, we're <u>already</u> detectives.

CUT TO

PHOEBE as she lifts her seltzer bottle into toasting
position.

> PHOEBE
> To the Big A.

SHIRLEY raises his bottle, too. JIMMY AND THE CLIMBER
just watch. They put the bottles down.

> JIMMY
> This ain't the Big A. It's just a case--big
> A's don't come along all that often. I only
> had a couple my whole life.

> PHOEBE
> But couldn't it be?

CUT TO

THE CLIMBER. CLOSE UP. Watching his beloveds.

> CLIMBER
> Life's got to be on the line, Phoebes. Love's
> gotta be there, too. You just know when you're
> on the Big Adventure, that if you survive it,
> nothing's ever going to be the same...

CUT TO

THE KIDS stop eating. Stare at their dad. Then--

> SHIRLEY
> How many have you had, Daddy?

> CLIMBER
> (beat)
> Just the one...
> (HOLD on the CLIMBER for a
> moment, then--)

CUT TO

CLIMBER'S PLACE. Night.

Pretty much the same. Still clean, still all the big
TV sets.

The main change in decor is that the living room has
been turned into two makeshift bedrooms. A sheet hangs
from a sagging curtain as a room divider. PHOEBE'S
half has dolls piled on the bed, that's about it.

Bedtime. Both kids are in the sack, the blanket
hasn't been lowered. CLIMBER is finishing telling
them a story.

                    CLIMBER
              (with more emotion than you
               would expect)
        "And as he stared at the bloody face of his
        murdered partner, Sam Spade knew he could not
        rest until the score was even."

                    SHIRLEY
        Have you ever had a partner murdered, Poppa?

                    CLIMBER
        Only had my dad.

                    SHIRLEY
        But if you did have one, and he was killed, you
        couldn't rest till the score was even, could
        you?

                    CLIMBER
              (tucking him in)
        I'd track the bastard down.

                    PHOEBE
        I don't like saying "language," you know.

                    CLIMBER
        My apology.

He lowers the curtain between their beds. SHIRLEY is
half asleep already. Now CLIMBER goes to PHOEBE,
brings her a bunch of books to read, tilts her bed lamp
away from her brother, tucks her in, too. They whisper "Night" and he leaves her.

CUT TO

THE CLIMBER in the little hallway now, watching her.

Troubled.

Then he goes to his little room, slaps in a tape of a
Knicks game, hits the mute button and as Sprewell explodes down the court--

CUT TO

THE APARTMENT. Middle of the night. CLIMBER jerks
awake, rubs his eyes, get out of bed.

CUT TO

THE OTHER BEDROOM. As before. SHIRLEY is dead to the
world, PHOEBE reads. Now she looks up as her father
comes in. He sits on the bed and they whisper.

> CLIMBER
> Phoebes, you've gotta sleep sometime.
> (he puts the book down, turns
> out her light)
> It's the one thing we worry about most.

> PHOEBE
> Who?

> CLIMBER
> You know who.

> PHOEBE
> I wonder, how did you and Mommy meet?

                    (THE CLIMBER says nothing)
          I've always wondered why you never told me.
                    (he sighs)
          Did someone think you'd like each other and
          you had bologna sandwiches?

                         CLIMBER
                    (here we go)
          It was on a case.

                         PHOEBE
          Did you solve it?

                         CLIMBER
          It worked out.

                         PHOEBE
          You probably don't remember the very very
          first time you ever saw her.

CLIMBER hesitates. He doesn't like going back to
these great days. But here's his problem, Doctor:
it's the only way she'll go to sleep.

                         CLIMBER
          Actually, I do.

FLASHCUT

The moment when he takes the blindfold off ECHO and he
sees her perfect face.

BACK TO THE ROOM

                         PHOEBE
          I wonder was she in a ball gown or something
          that first time?

                         CLIMBER
          Exactly right--a beautiful ball gown. Huge
          billowing skirt. I was in my tux--

                         PHOEBE
                    (staring at him)
               You dove through that window in a tuxedo and a
               ball gown?--I don't think so.

FLASHCUT

THE JUMP OUT THE WINDOW--only this is in PHOEBE'S
mind--CLIMBER, looking magnificent, and ECHO, the
same--all but dancing in slow motion toward the
window as TWENTY BAD GUYS with machine guns and
bazookas blast away in vain.

BACK TO THE ROOM.

                         CLIMBER
               You want the whole deal, don't you?
                    (she does)
               Close your eyes.
                    (she does)
               Deep breath.
                    (that too--just a glimmer of
                     sleep now)

                         PHOEBE
                    (softer)
               Start with climbing up the building.

                         CLIMBER
               Okay.

                         PHOEBE
                    (softer)
               That was very brave of you, Daddy.

                         CLIMBER
               Or very stupid.

                         PHOEBE
                    (almost gone now)
               This was the Big A, wasn't it?

CUT TO

THE CLIMBER, studying her Edward G. Robinson face.

She's drifting.

He nods.

HOLD.

CUT TO

A LONG ISLAND COUNTRY LANE. The next afternoon.
CLIMBER'S car, motor running, is at the side of the
road. He holds his children tightly. They hold him
back.

                    CLIMBER
        Okay, Loves.
                (they hold him just a second
                longer, then flop over into
                the backseat)
        Put your rich faces on.

CUT TO

SHIRLEY AND PHOEBE as they change before our eyes, become the spoiled perfect kids we first saw in the mansion.

                    CLIMBER (CONT'D)
        Gimme the damn Bartok.
                (as SHIRLEY slips a CD from its
                case--)

CUT TO

ECHO, standing on the front steps as CLIMBER'S car
drives up, stops, waving. The kids, inside the car,
wave happily back. Standing alongside ECHO is her fiancé, a very handsome, tanned man of forty--HAMILTON

KEMPNER THE THIRD, universally known as TRIP. A well-
educated rich man's son, if he seems familiar to us at
all it might be because, in the photographs we saw
during the credit sequence, this is the guy THE
CLIMBER punched out.

CUT TO

THE CAR and the instant it stops, the kids are out of
there, hurrying to ECHO. They talk quickly, whispered
tones.

                    SHIRLEY
              (he holds the wicker basket,
               which is empty now)
          Oh, Mommy, it seems like forever, do thank
          cook for the wondrous food.

                    PHOEBE
          Mommy, I just know I'm going to be sick next
          Friday.

                    ECHO
          How was the Bartok?

                    SHIRLEY
          No other word but "thrilling."

                    PHOEBE
          And we made "him" play it all the way home.

                    ECHO
          Your father hated it, then?

                    SHIRLEY
          Sheer agony.

                    ECHO
              (cannot hide her pleasure)
          Well, now you're learning what I had to put up
          with.

                    SHIRLEY
       Can we go inside?

                     ECHO
       Don't you want to say hello to Trip?

CUT TO

TRIP as they run to him, PHOEBE curtsies perfectly,
SHIRLEY looks him in the eye, gives him a firm handshake.

CUT TO

THE CLIMBER, watching silently now as they race toward
the front door.

CUT TO

ECHO. Calling out to them.

                     ECHO
       Where are our manners?

CUT TO

THE KIDS. They give their mother a pained look, turn
toward CLIMBER, speak in unison.

                 THE KIDS (TOGETHER)
               (like pulling teeth)
       Thanks, Dad, see you next week, Dad, bye Dad.
               (and they are gone)

CUT TO

TRIP, as he goes to CLIMBER. They don't even bother to
hide the fact that they despise each other.

Long pause, then--

                         TRIP
     I wonder what your secret is.
              (beat)
     To make them so unhappy...
              (and as he smiles)

CUT TO

THE CLIMBER. Not smiling back...

HOLD ON THE TWO OF THEM. Then--

CUT TO

SHIRLEY'S ROOM, the following Saturday afternoon.
PHOEBE is with him and they are both dressed so perfectly you want to throw up.

                    ECHO (OVER)
     Children--your father's here.

                    PHOEBE
              (the most amazing whining you
               ever heard)
     But my pneumonia's just so bad, Mommy--
              (a dry cough)
     --hear that?--

                    SHIRLEY
              (even more so)
     --it's not fair, it's just not fair--

As they go on in, one thing is very much clear--

--their eyes are dancing...

CUT TO

OUT FRONT. CLIMBER, smiles nervously as the kids come
reluctantly into view. He opens the front door for
them.

                    CLIMBER
          Plenty of room up here.

They ignore him, get in the back.

                    ECHO
              (handing over an envelope)
          The Joyce Theater, three p.m.

                    CLIMBER
              (hopefully)
          Nothing to do with sports, I suppose.

                    ECHO
          It's their annual Kabuki Marathon.
              (his knees start to buckle)
          The children are very excited, do not spoil it
          for them.
              (a CD)
          Kabuki music for the drive.

                    CLIMBER
              (taking it)
          All my prayers are being answered.

                    ECHO
          And in keeping with our educational theme for
          the weekend, miso soup, bean sprouts salad,
          squid and octopus sushi, their favorite
          sashimi, sea urchin, giant clam, and salmon
          roe.
              (hands the basket to him)
          Be careful with that.

                        CLIMBER
          Before it attacks me, you mean?

                        ECHO
                (ignoring him)
          I meant, refrigerate it at once.
                (he nods, takes it, starts
                 around the car as we)

CUT TO

PHOEBE, bursting out of the car, running back to her
mother, clinging to ECHO. ECHO escorts her back, puts
her in the car. CLIMBER starts to drive as we

CUT TO

INSIDE THE CAR as THE KIDS kneel in the backseat, waving to their disappearing mother.

CUT TO

THE THREE OF THEM IN THE FRONT SEAT NOW, on the side
road where they stop. They are finishing their em-
brace.

                        PHOEBE
                (to THE CLIMBER)
          Did you like that last bit? Where I rush out
          and cling to Mommy?

                        CLIMBER
          Over the top, Phoebes.

                        SHIRLEY
                (agreeing)
          I told her.

                        CLIMBER
          Where did "bit" come from? Is that another of
          good old Trip's favorites?

CUT TO

PHOEBE. She doesn't answer. An odd look now on her
face. She is watching another car that has just driven by. CLIMBER does the same.

>   PHOEBE
>   Were they here last week?

CUT TO

THE CAR. Old. Absolutely nondescript--except for the
fact that the windows are tinted. Hard to tell who's
inside.

CUT TO

THE CLIMBER. Shrugs, shakes his head, starts to
drive--he breaks into horrible Kabuki sounds as we--

CUT TO

THE JOYCE THEATER.

Before the matinee. People mill around out front--a
whole lot of them Japanese.

CLIMBER pulls up to the curb--

--standing apart from the others is the family who
took his tickets last time--THE GUY sees CLIMBER,
starts to him.

CUT TO

INSIDE THE CAR. CLIMBER has the tickets in his hand,
is about to hand them over when we suddenly--

CUT TO

PHOEBE, as quick tears cover her face.

                         PHOEBE
                    (heartbroken)
         I was just so ready to start my career--

--now SHIRLEY sees why she's crying, has to fight back
tears himself. CLIMBER follows their eyes and we

CUT TO

HAMILTON KEMPNER THE THIRD, otherwise known as TRIP--

--standing alone under the marquee, looking around,
ticket in his hand.

CUT TO

CLIMBER--TRIP hasn't spotted them yet--but he quickly
looks out at the APPROACHING MAN, shakes his head
sharply--"Sorry"--the other guy gets it immediately,
takes his kids' hands, peels off as CLIMBER turns to
his children--

                         CLIMBER
                    (tougher than shit)
         I am <u>ashamed</u>, and when I tell my pop, he will
         turn his head away in despair. Someday, <u>some-
         day</u>, when the Big A comes along--<u>and you never
         know when</u>--you have to be <u>ready</u>--but not you
         two--you'll just suck your rich thumbs and
         wait for the butler to save you.
                    (and on that)

CUT TO

TRIP, as THE KIDS run up behind him, pulling at him
happily. CLIMBER, looking miserable, waits a few feet
away, holding two Kabuki programs.

                         TRIP
         Just thought I'd surprise you.

                    SHIRLEY
Yesss.

                    PHOEBE
Can you take us to dinner and then home?

                    TRIP
Love to, but business, you know.
          (they look sad)
See you at intermission.

CUT TO

PHOEBE AND SHIRLEY, taking their seats in the theater. They wave to TRIP, who is seated across the
theater. CLIMBER sits between them. A sea of Asian
faces.

The house lights dim.

                    SHIRLEY
          (head down, whispered)
The bastard.

                    PHOEBE
He was snooping, wasn't he, Daddy?

                    CLIMBER
          (nods)
But all in vain.

                    SHIRLEY
Why?

Now it's dark in the theater.

                    CLIMBER
          (beat)
Because our job is tonight.
          (and on that news--)

CUT TO

THE KIDS. Their eyes are dancing again.

CUT TO

THE CURTAIN rising.

CUT TO

THE STAGE, as suddenly the stylized Kabuki stuff
starts. Applause from the aficionados.

CUT TO

THE CLIMBER. A silent groan.

CUT TO

PHOEBE. They lean close. SHIRLEY whispers to her.

                    SHIRLEY
          (indicating the dancing)
     Poor Daddy.

                    PHOEBE
          (whispering so soft)
     Daddy?
          (he looks at her)
     I promise I'll never suck my rich thumb ever
     again.

HOLD ON THE FAMILY. Then--

CUT TO

A STREET IN THE VILLAGE. One hot mother of a night.

Busy, lots of Italian restaurants from before pasta
cost 25 bucks a plate.

Busy but not chic. There are a couple of bodegas along
the block. The occasional housewife goes in for pro-
visions. More frequently, the neighborhood drunks
stagger out with six-packs.

CUT TO

We are looking through the window at kind of a dump
called <u>Salerno</u>. Red-checked tablecloths. Pretty much
empty. An OLD DRUNK sits nodding at the bar.

A COUPLE are eating alone in the rear by the
restrooms--we have seen them before. THE CRYING
WOMAN WITH THE LARGE SUNGLASSES. THE GUILTY-
SEEMING MAN.

They both seem happier now. A few papers are spread
out on the table between them. She still wears her
huge sunglasses but is not crying anymore. And he
does not seem particularly guilty.

CUT TO

THE SIDEWALK IN FRONT. A sketch artist has set up shop
in front. "Five bucks," his cardboard sign says. No
one pays him much mind. Business is slow.

CUT TO

ACROSS THE STREET AND THE CLIMBER, deep in conversation with another man--we've seen him before too--
he's the guy who gets their matinee tickets--only now
he is working and we see he is a police sergeant.

                    CLIMBER
                (on edge)
          Thanking you in advance for sticking around,
          Bertie.

                         POLICE SERGEANT
              For what I owe you, forget it.
                         (looking around)
              What you got going?

                         CLIMBER
              My kids are working the case with me.
                         (and on that)

CUT TO

THE POLICE SERGEANT. And if you thought he might
laugh, you couldn't be more wrong--

                         POLICE SERGEANT
              You bastard.
                         (he can't help it, slugs
                          CLIMBER on the arm, looks at
                          him with envy and admiration)
              How great is that?--shit, my kids have zero
              interest in cop work. It's Wall Street for
              them all the way.
                         (looking around now)
              Where they stashed?

                         CLIMBER
              The sketch artist, he's mine.

CUT TO

THE STREET. A bodega is next to Salerno. A bunch of
drunks come out, see the SERGEANT, straighten up, walk
on past the SKETCH ARTIST. A little blind girl with a
white cane passes them, tapping along.

                         POLICE SERGEANT
                         (calling out)
              Young lady, you should be at home.
                         (the blind girl nods, hurries
                          on)

                        CLIMBER
                (proud)
        She can only practice her cane work when her
        mother's out.

                        POLICE SERGEANT
                (wow)
        That's the little one I see in the car? Looks
        like Edward G. Robinson?
                (CLIMBER nods)

CUT TO

PHOEBE, moving expertly with her cane.

CUT TO

CLIMBER AND THE SERGEANT, watching. THE SERGEANT
shakes his head.

                        POLICE SERGEANT
        I would kill to be you tonight.

                        CLIMBER
                (thank you)
        They put in the hours.

                        POLICE SERGEANT
        I'll be around somewhere.
                (and as he starts off)

CUT TO

THE CLIMBER. A soft whistle.

CUT TO

THE BLIND GIRL. Stops, comes to him.

CLOSE UP

PHOEBE. The vacant look, the head just a bit tilted,
she's got it all.

CLIMBER is seated on a stoop now, half in shadow.
PHOEBE stops beside him, never looks at him.

                    CLIMBER
     They're at the back table--
               (she knows this)
     --Pop thinks they're heading someplace we
     can't nail down. See what you can do.
               (OK with her)
     Give me one minute to get into position.
               (and on that)

CUT TO

THE SKETCH ARTIST, sitting with his notepad on the
sidewalk by the restaurant. An empty folding chair
alongside.

                    CLIMBER
               (sits)
     What do I get for five bucks?

                    SHIRLEY
               (handing over his pad)
     See for yourself.

CUT TO

THE NOTEPAD as CLIMBER flips through. The work, of
course, is brilliant.

We see a drawing of a sweet mother and child.

Next page--the front of the restaurant, the clock over
the bar clear to see.

Next page. 8:45 by the clock, and the WOMAN WITH SUN-
GLASSES pauses to open the door. Even here, she is
furtive.

Next page. 9:02 by the clock. Here comes the GUILTY
GUY.

Next page. 9:05. The couple is kissing at the rear of
the restaurant.

CUT TO

CLIMBER. He nods, hands back the pad.

> CLIMBER
> Five bucks it is.

A TAPPING SOUND behind them. PHOEBE moves past.

Next door at the bodega, a couple of housewives jabber
in Spanish on the sidewalk, a couple of flashily
dressed drunks stagger in for more beer.

CUT TO

INSIDE THE SALERNO.

The owner, maitre d', whatever, looks up from his position by the door, an odd expression on his face.

> MAITRE D'
> Can I help you, Miss?

> PHOEBE
> (whispered)
> I have to get home and I don't know if I can
> make it without a stop.

> MAITRE D'
> You want to use our ladies' room?

                    PHOEBE
        Oh, that would be so kind of you.

THE GUY looks at her a moment.

                    MAITRE D'
        This was from birth?

CUT TO

PHOEBE. Hmmm. She taps her cane a moment.

                    PHOEBE
        A sickness.
                (doesn't want to talk about it)
        When I was three.
                (sweetly)
        I still remember what stars look like.

CUT TO

THE MAITRE D'. Who wouldn't be touched? Gestures.

                    MAITRE D'
        Want me to take you back?

                    PHOEBE
        I have to learn these things. But thank you.

CUT TO

CLIMBER AND SHIRLEY, watching as she makes it past the
MAITRE D', starts toward the table in the rear.

                    SHIRLEY
                (you can tell he's excited--
                 calmly)
        Turn your head.
                (CLIMBER does as we)

CUT TO

THE COUPLE AT THE REAR TABLE. A BLIND KID is coming toward them but they are totally involved with each other.

Now we can tell what some of the papers spread out between them are: airplane tickets.

CUT TO

PHOEBE'S close to them--

--her cane ticks a chair, slips free, falls. She reaches out, uses their table for support, slowly gropes for the cane, picks it up, stands, moves on, and as she heads for the ladies' room--

CUT TO

THE CLIMBER. And he's been through a lot of shit these past years, but right now, you get the sense that it's almost, <u>almost</u>, been worth it--

--at least until the gunfire starts and suddenly

CUT TO

THE WINDOW OF THE BODEGA, shattering--

--from inside, <u>screams</u>--

--from inside, shouts of rage and shock--

--from inside, more gunfire, louder and louder and

CUT TO

CLIMBER, diving toward SHIRLEY, bringing him into his arms, lowering him to the sidewalk, cradling him, shielding him, his own gun out and ready and

CUT TO

INSIDE THE SALERNO as the drunk at the bar rises up--
it's JIMMY--hurrying toward the back of the restaurant, and sure he needs a cane and usually it's tough
getting around and he sees PHOEBE looking out from the
restroom area and as he grabs her, lifts her into his
arms, starts to carry her to the street--

CUT TO

OUTSIDE and THE POLICE SERGEANT, gun out, races toward
the bodega, and behind him here come two more COPS and
the gunfire is still going on inside the wrecked
bodega and

CUT TO

THE CLIMBER, lying there, holding his son, stroking
him, whispering "It's okay, it's okay" over and over
and

CUT TO

THE BODEGA, and suddenly no more shots--you can hear
the voices of the cops shouting instructions to "lay
there and don't fucking move" and--

CUT TO

JIMMY, with PHOEBE, joining CLIMBER AND SHIRLEY on the
sidewalk.

                    PHOEBE
             (yesss)
     Bali!

CUT TO

THE FAMILY, as they all just stare at one another and
suddenly the knowledge hits them that it's all okay,
everything is going to be okay--

--wrong--

--so wrong--

--because here comes TRIP toward them--

--and behind him, ECHO.

CUT TO

ECHO. CLOSE UP. <u>Shocked</u> by what she has just seen and <u>stunned</u> by what she has just seen and <u>in a rage</u> over what she has just seen.

CUT TO

CLIMBER, getting to his feet. Shakily.

> CLIMBER
> (hard to hear)
> I didn't mean for this to happen--I am so
> sorry...

> ECHO
> (distinct)
> You cannot imagine how sorry you are going to
> be.
> (and as she reaches out for her
> children--)

CUT TO

TWO LARGE OFFICE DOORS. With this written on them:

> THE SINCLAIR FOUNDATION

CUT TO

THE CLIMBER AND JIMMY opening the doors, heading inside.

We are in one of those offices. God knows how large,
but done in wonderful taste. A receptionist sits
waiting. Chairs and leather couches.

The Sinclair Foundation is like the Ford Foundation or
any of those other great charitable institutions set
up decades and decades past.

Their purpose is simple: to give away money. And to do
it fairly. And well.

ECHO, we will find, heads it. Fairly and well.

THE CLIMBER has been here before, is just as out of
place as ever.

He wears his best suit, his shoes are shined. He does
his best to seem terrific.

JIMMY has never been here. Doesn't want to be here
now.

                    RECEPTIONIST
              (checking her appointment list)
         Ralph Jones?
              (CLIMBER starts to set her
               straight, what's the point.
               He nods)
         Follow me, please--
              (and as she rises)

CUT TO

A LARGE CONFERENCE ROOM. Empty at the moment. Like
the rest of the place, it's more or less in perfect
taste.

THE RECEPTIONIST ushers them in, excuses herself.

CUT TO

THE CLIMBER AND JIMMY. They move here, examine there--
not a lot to say. And the tension is mounting
steadily. Now--

CUT TO

JUDGE HAMPTON coming in. He carries papers.

This is a marvelous man, seventy-five at least, looks
sixty. He has headed the family legal affairs for a
very long time.

                    JUDGE HAMPTON
               (embracing CLIMBER)
          Ralph.

                    CLIMBER
          Judge Hampton.
               (indicating JIMMY)
          My father.

                    JUDGE HAMPTON
               (the two old men shake)
          We met when Ralph and Jennifer married. I'm
          sure we'd both had a few.
               (indicating chairs)
          Shall we?
               (as they sit)
          A very sad day for us all, Ralph.

CUT TO

ECHO AND TRIP entering quietly; they sit across the
large table from the men. We have never seen ECHO in
her work costume before. A business suit, hair back.
Older and wise.

                    JUDGE HAMPTON
          This is bound to be painful, let's make it
          brief.

                    (beat)
          Jennifer doesn't want you to see the children
          again.

CUT TO

CLIMBER. Holding himself in. Hard. He gestures for
the old man to continue.

                    JUDGE HAMPTON (CONT'D)
          Until they're of age.

                    CLIMBER
          Is that the next century or the one after that?

                    JUDGE HAMPTON
          Let me finish, Ralph, please--you may visit
          them, of course--but you may never be with
          them alone. Someone the state appoints will
          be in attendance at all times.

                    CLIMBER
          Even with your money, is this legal? I'm their
          father, I think. Unless Ms. Sinclair has
          other surprises in store.

ECHO looks at him. Glass.

                    JUDGE HAMPTON
          We think we can make it stick. All our legal
          experts say as much. But of course, a jury is
          hard to predict. In order to get there, of
          course you would have to sue. There would be a
          trial. Considering Jennifer's family, I
          should think a famous one.
                    (beat)
          Do you want to put the children through that?

CUT TO

CLIMBER. He sits there for a moment, all silent mod-
eration. Then suddenly--

                    CLIMBER
             (at TRIP--all he has left)
<u>I would never have followed you, you son of a
bitch</u>.

                    ECHO
             (at CLIMBER--all she has
              left)
<u>You risked their lives</u>--

CUT TO

THE ROOM. Just the sound of breathing.

                  JUDGE HAMPTON
That's the crux of it, Ralph. Did you?

CUT TO

CLIMBER. CLOSE UP. Finally--

                    CLIMBER
Things...they got a little out of hand...
       (beat)
Not what I intended.

                  JUDGE HAMPTON
You know our position, Ralph. You can sue, not
see them, see them with someone else present.

                    CLIMBER
To protect them?

                    ECHO
Yes.

He rises, nods, leaves.

```
                        JIMMY
              (to ECHO--his first and only
               words)
          You're killing him...
              (he goes off after his son
               as we)
```

I want to stop here for a while and talk about the movie.

Half the movie, really. George Roy Hill once said that if you can't tell your story in an hour fifty, you better be David Lean. I will go to my grave agreeing with that. George S. Kaufman once said, "Everything needs cutting." I'm 100 percent for that, too. I cannot think of a flick over the last decade—including *Shawshank Redemption,* in which I put up with anything—that could not have been better with some, as they say, judicious cutting.

I think what you've read would run about forty-five to fifty-five minutes. Dialogue scenes go quickly. Action scenes run long. The drowning sequence, for example, should take many minutes on film. You've got to know—at the start of it—that he's going to rescue her. Then you've got to know—one-third in—that she's going to rescue him. Then there has to come a moment—I did it with a long shot of the two of them and they are simply too far away for anything to happen—when you are meant to think, I know Climber's not going to die, I know that because this is only the first part of the movie and he gets top billing—*but how is he going to be saved*? And, please, **somebody do it.** And then the rescue with her knifing through the water and him sinking and the distance getting closer but it's still too rough, they're too far apart—

—and then he sinks under.

Well, all those beats are written in there for a purpose. To *thrill* you. And also so the asshole director will *get* it. (Remember, this is the selling version.) Once Mr. Fox says, sure, here's seventy-five mill, get some stars and make the movie—well, that version of the script doesn't have to sell so hard.

But you know what? I'd keep it in anyway so the female star, when she reads it, can think, hey, what a great scene *for me. Love* that drowning sequence.

And you know what else? Male stars will *hate* the sequence. They're happy as shit jumping through closed windows and showing how perfect they are—but being weak? Worse, being rescued? Worse yet, being rescued by *the girl*?

Here's what most male stars would do to that sequence, if they have the power. They would absolutely leave it in. They would be thrilled unto death to play the fucker—

—with one teeny proviso. Don't gag when I tell you what it is—

—that the audience already knows Climber is a swimmer of at least Olympic calibre. And that Echo, poor sweet thing, has a lifetime terror of the water. Get it?

He doesn't need help, he's helping *her* get over her fear.

That's how insecure they are. And that's how big they want us to think their dicks are. And if this all makes you sick, get out of the business. I have been dealing with it for thirty-five years.

It gets no easier.

The main reason I've stopped the screenplay at this point is to ask some questions, most importantly this: **What do you think's going to happen?**

Please do me a favor here—put the book down and decide what the answer would be *for you. What would make you satisfied?*

Example: Do *you* think there's any chance for Echo and Climber to forgive each other? And if you believe he can get back into her good graces, do you also believe he can get back into her *heart?*

Shirley and Phoebes? Their family's been ripped apart again and I think they have to think it's their fault. Not only that, but their father is gone again. (Do you think those chaperoned visits are going to work out? I sure don't. I don't think that kind of thing *can* work out.)

Trip? How is what he did going to affect his getting married? I think he did a rotten thing. But Echo must think differently. Do they get married? How does Climber take that? Do the kids fall apart? They have to hate him for taking their father away. And what happens when (or if) he moves into their mother's life and bed?

And finally Echo. Obviously she is still more than a little interested in Climber. If she didn't care, she wouldn't torment him the way she does, wouldn't ask if he hated what he saw. But he put her beloved children in danger.

Other questions: Is anybody going to get hurt? Who? Are you sure? Why do you think that? Is anybody going to die? Who? Are you sure? Why do you think that?

I have answers for some of those questions.

But not all. Not at this point anyway. And I have been continually surprised at what you've read. (I don't want that to come off as mystical shit. It isn't. But as I've told you, I don't know what I'm doing, not in any logical way, I'm totally instinctive. I knew when I started that the kids had different lives with the different parents. I knew Climber would be found out. But I didn't know, till the day I wrote the scene, that when he took them out on their first case the bodega was going to be robbed.

I knew there could be a bodega if I needed it. I've seen lots of streets like that in the Village, one nationality taking over from another, but gradually.

What I had no answer for was this question: How deeply would I need to bury old Climber? I knew he had to be separated from the kids. I knew Trip was going to be the suspicious person. But it was possible that Echo's merely seeing them working at night, however safely, would be enough to enflame her.

But as I started into the sequence, I think this fear came along—that if all Climber did was play the overly enthusiastic parent, taking his kids into his work life, and Echo found out and took the children away from him, so that he could only see them with others around, it would be difficult to believe the Sinclairs, even with all their money, would be able to make that stick. But worse than that was—

—we would just plain hate Echo. She was already running the risk of being a rich bitch, period. If she was a neurotically overprotective mother, I'd never be able to get her back for the audience.

—so I used the bodega robbery. I felt I needed it. Climber had to take a legitimate fall—because with the addition of the robbery he does a terrible thing: *he puts his children at risk*.

I think writing has always got to be an act of exploration.

I want to share with you now, typos and all, exactly what my first note was for this story, back on January 16th, 1995.

MOVIE IIDEA—AUDREY HEPBURN WHEN TWENTY IS IN TROUBLE AND SAVED BY BOGART AT 33 AND THEY FALL IN LOVE AND BOTH TERRIFIC AND HAVE KIDS BUT SHE IS RICH AND INTO CHARITY AND HE LIKES WHAT HE DOES DO THEY EVENTUALLY SPLIT—MAYBE SHE HAS REMARRIED RALPH BELLAMY OR SOMEONE

ANYWAY, THE KICKER IS THEY HAD A GREAT KID, 17, AND HE LIVES IN THE MANSION DURING THE WEEK BUT GETS TO HOLIDAY WITH DAD WHO TAKES HIM OON CASES. THE KID I SERIOUS ABOUT IT

SENIOR AT FANCY PREP SCHOOL—HOME WITH MOM

DOING RICH STUFF AND WEEKENDS DOING CRIME. CAN ACT LIKE A JUNKIE OR ALL KINDS OF STUFF. CAN DISAPPEAR ON THE STREET.

MAYBE THIS WEEKEND HIS SISTER PHOEBE HAS TO COME ALONG. SHE IS REALLY GIFTED.

FATHER MIGHT TEST KID, TELL ME WHERE THE LETTER OPENER IS OR ASKS QUESTIONS REQUIRING WATCHFULNESS AND KID IS GIFTED BUT MAYBE PHOEBE IS A GENIUS AT IT. MAYBE PHOEBE CAME HOME UNEXPECTEDLY FROM SCHOOL OR WHATEVER

FATHER WO4RKS THE KID HARD—LOOK AT THIS ROOM, WHO DID IT

KID LOVES BOTH PARENTS AND THEY ARE BOTH GOOD BUT NOT GOOD WITH EACH OTHER.,

KID HATES HIS FANCY NAME—ELLIOT OR SPANGLER. WANTS TO BE BUCK OR FLASH. MAYBE FATHER WILL CALL HIM THAT WHEN HE EARNS IT

WOULD IT BE PLEASING TO YOU

That story had been in my head for four and a half years, till May 20th of 1999, when I wrote the scene of Climber rescuing Echo.

You can see how much it has altered from the original notion.

But the *heart of the piece* has remained the same.

At least it has in my head. But, my God, the changes. The boy was seventeen. He was seventeen for a year or two until I realized that made my lovers too old, too much time would have to be covered in the story—and as I have told you, movies don't do that well. If it's ten years, you don't need a lot of makeup and stuff. If it's seventeen, you do.

But that's a minor change. Here are two big ones—this is supposed to be a romantic comedy, yes? Well, what happened to Echo? She's all but disappeared.

And the kids have exploded.

I didn't mean for that to happen, but when I hit the moment at the end of the scene when Climber is given tickets to take them to the Bartok concert—well, the three of them were just terrific together, I thought. So I went with them. Could not wait to get the three blabbing on.

I know this—I have to get Echo back.

And I believe this—I have to get the four of them back together. What I do not know at the moment is: Can I bring that off?

———

I had no idea, when I started, that this story was going to fit into three acts. There is no proper number. A lot of mine seem to have five acts. (When I say "act" I mean a moment of power, a moment that in the theater would bring the curtain down to start an intermission.)

Butch is really two acts. The first act, the Wild West part, ends with Butch yelling to the world, "The future's all yours, ya lousy bicycles." It is the end of their life as we and they have known it. The South American act starts when they get there, ends with their death. And in between, a brief New York interlude.

Well, I'm writing along here in *The Big A* and it hits me that this was three. The first act in my head I decided was this: *things going good*.

That's up till the moment when he brings them home and Trip has the cryptic line about Climber's secret for making the kids so unhappy. You can read that straight—Trip is fooled. But later, when you realize he was on to their charade, the line has irony.

Anyway, here's Act I—what I would have put on my wall.

1) **Kidnap/rescue**
2) **Climber's place**
3) **Echo's place**
4) **Swimming**
5) **Credit**
6) **Jimmy ok's**
7) **Pizza—the big A**
8) **Phoebes/sleep**
9) **Home**

When I get to the stage of putting the movie on my wall, I pretty much have the movie in my head. I don't mean I'm some weird memory automaton with the commas all in place. I mean that when I say kidnap/rescue I know he's going to climb up, get in, get her out.

That's the spine of that scene.

I was not remotely that far along on *The Big A* when I started because I knew I was not going to write the entire flick. The purpose of this exercise was not to do that, but to write enough of it so my experts would have the tools to come and expose me.

An aside now (but I think this is about how writers' minds work)—if you will go back to the original idea, printed above, there is something that will make little sense:

**KID HATES HIS FANCY NAME—ELLIOT OR SPANGLER.
WANTS TO BE BUCK OR FLASH. MAYBE FATHER
WILL CALL HIM THAT WHEN HE EARNS IT
WOULD IT BE PLEASING TO YOU**

That's Bruce.

And somehow that's got to get into the screenplay.

Explanation. I came to New York City in '53, with still a year to go in the Army. But my brother and I gave Johnny Kander a few dollars to share his really crappy dump on Eighty-fourth Street, for when we could get down on weekends. I was at the Pentagon, my brother at the Army Chemical Center in Maryland, Shangri-La for lovers of poison gas.

Come '54, and my hero days done, I return (hopefully) forever. I am dating a girl for a while and I want to be a writer and she has dated this guy before me who also wanted to be a writer and she thought we might like each other.

We did.

Bruce was tall and dark and a great smoker who looked like Jack Palance. I was the novelist, while Bruce, a native, wanted Broadway. He was a gifted lyricist.

Also liked sports. Bruce was one of the four who watched the Podres World Series together, 1955, in a small room, two of us Dodger fans, two Yankees, and we would change positions, gum, everything to try and destroy the power of the enemies on the TV screen.

One night Bruce and I are talking, probably in a bar, probably drunk, and I remember he made, softly, this incredible admission: "I always wanted to be called 'Flash.' " No need to ask why. If you were a kid, how could you not want to be called Flash?

Imagine that. Being legitimately called Flash.

Well, I harassed him some about it over time, but I was also sure that **somehow I had to use that.**

When he died (killed young in some stupid flying accident), I knew it even more. Not that we were best friends. Bruce was married and had a couple of kids and you couldn't make much of a living writing lyrics, so, even though he hated it, he picked up and went Out There, wrote some westerns for the tube, then hit it very big indeed when he invented *Mission: Impossible.*

His father was a famous New York City judge and I remember talking to Judge Geller once and he was all excited and I asked why and he said that two brilliant lawyers were going against each other in his courtroom on the following Monday and it was going to be so terrific. (You see? Everybody reveres talent.)

I didn't know, when I did the first act, where to put Shirley's dream. There were places, but it would have meant stopping dead so I let it go. If I ever rewrite this, bet I'll find a place next draft around.

Do you know why I told you about Flash and the Judge? Because I wanted Act I to sink a little bit into your heads. Here it is again.

1) Kidnap/rescue
2) Climber's place
3) Echo's place
4) Swimming
5) Credit
6) Jimmy ok's
7) Pizza—the Big A
8) Phoebes/sleep
9) Home

I decided that the second act was this: *things going bad*. There is a harbinger when a strange tinted car goes by. Then Trip is at the Kabuki performance. Then the biggie when Echo confronts Climber and ends life as they have known it.

Here's what I had on my wall for what you've read of Act II:

1) Kabuki news
2) Joyce Theater
3) Blind child
4) The Foundation

That's where we are.

Into the second act, the first four sequences done. Here is my problem at this point: **What comes next?**

Understand, I can go *anywhere*. I can cut to Mount Everest ten years later and have Climber on his way to the summit. I can cut to the White House, where Echo is being given an honor for her selfless work for charity. I can cut to a graveyard and all you see are these words:

Phoebe

1992–2000

I can cut to a hospital for the insane, with a lot of young people just staring with that awful look the crazed manage, and there is Shirley, lost and by the wind grieved. I can cut to Venice at midnight and here comes a gondola and there they are, Phoebes and Shirley, dressed as gondoliers, as Climber and Echo hold each other and smile at the kids, who smile at their parents, glorious familial contentment. I can cut to Trip in his Manhattan penthouse, terrified because we pull back and see Climber, pistol in hand, ready to fire and kill.

I don't want to go to those places a whole lot, but I *can*—because the story has come to a wrenching moment of change—Climber walking out, dying, as his father points out. The kids can no longer be in his life, not as they were, and I think it's pretty clear he cherished their time together.

Understand something—my story is in jeopardy at this moment, just as *Butch* was before the Superposse arrived. The fun-and-games robberies were done at that point. Just as the fun-and-games detective stuff is done at this point.

This is what you could call a hinge moment.

All movies are always in jeopardy all the time, that I hope we know. But there is a particular danger here, because *a change has to come.*

How big a change, though? That's my problem, Doctor.

All those cuts I mentioned above, I can make them all play.

But they're all too much of a jump.

You'd never see Phoebes as Phoebes again. She'd be a different person. And do you want to see Shirley as a junior at college? I don't.

Anyway, this is what I put on my wall.

5) First Visit

Clearly what I decided to do was show the first visit. What you are about to read now is only one page of that scene.

```
CUT TO


CLIMBER'S CAR and here he comes, turning into the es-
tate, passing through the large gates, driving by the
gardeners, who look up and watch him but do not wave
and


CUT TO
```

PHOEBE'S ROOM--it faces the front of the house. She
and SHIRLEY kneel by the window, waiting--they spot
the car as soon as it turns into view.

Now, a new voice calls out--

                    LADY FROM THE STATE
                  (coming closer)
          Children, you father's here.

And now she is in the doorway. Middle-aged, nondescript, edgy.

As THE KIDS bolt past her into the hallway, she calls
out--

                    LADY FROM THE STATE (CONT'D)
          Stop running--you have an hour.

They sprint down the great staircase, race to the
front door, pause.

CUT TO

THE CLIMBER, pulling up, getting out. Not the best
day of his life, this. He's not looking his best either, and he knows it.

CUT TO

THE KIDS, moving through the front door, pausing.

                    SHIRLEY
                  (he has been working feverishly
                   on his upper-class accent)
          Look, sister--our Pater has arrived.

                    PHOEBE
                  (so has she)
          Dear, dear father.

```
        (She curtsies.)
   How blissful to see you.


THE LADY FROM THE STATE stands quietly in the doorway,
watching.
```

I really hate that scene. Not because it's such a terrible start—I mean, the kids still sound like the kids. But I stopped it where I did for one good reason: I don't have the least idea who Climber is here.

One of the worst parts of being an instinctive writer—of having to go with "feel" rather than logic—is the sense of helplessness that overwhelms me at moments like this.

I am convinced that scene is a proper place to start.

I also have no idea what it is or how to write it.

So I stopped.

And what I am waiting for is the arrival of what I call a *connective*. Something that will take me out of this scene and into the next. Once I have that, I will have a notion of who Climber is and how I enter this first visitation. I have certain notions in my head, even at this awkward time.

1. I feel there must not be a villain in the scene. That means the woman from the state isn't out of James Bond. I think I might even give her a moment when she says "Hey, I hate this too."

2. I feel it should be the first visit, not the 9th or 63rd. This has to be right out of the chute, so that it's clear no one has the least knowledge of the terrain.

3. I believe they all have to try like hell to make it work.

4. Most important is this: **it must go badly.** *Terribly,* even. We must believe that this trio, who I hope have provided us pleasure, will never be together again. Not as they were under the good Queen Cynara.

Because, you see, I know something you don't know—**I have a fastball.** I don't know if it will work, I don't know if the world will hate it. But it's what gave me the confidence to get this far. And, yes, you'll know what it is in a page or two.

But that's for later, my problem is now. I want to write this scene—I feel it is crucial for the movie to work—and I have no idea how to make it play.

Where should I enter the scene? I chose to do it with the drive up and the kids watching and then the line we've heard twice before, "Children, you father's here," except now it's a strange and different voice.

But did I enter too early? Would it have been better if I'd come in after, say, a half hour of stilted talk? Or maybe that talk isn't stilted, it's just somehow *wrong*—what if Shirley asks if Spade found out who murdered his partner and Climber says, "It was a woman done him in"—meaning Echo—and does that cast a pall?

Or are they laughing and having just *so* much fun, and on they go, the laughter nutty and seemingly sincere and the woman from the state tells them time's up and they are just crushed—but then you look in their eyes like the camera can do for you and you realize they are exhausted from the effort and it was all false and phony, then a cut to the kids waving happily and Climber waving back and it's all so great and then you cut to him out of sight and the look of failure and despair on his face, and cut back to the kids and they are dying and after a pause it ends like this.

                    PHOEBE
               (whispered)
     ...shit...

                    SHIRLEY
               (softer still)
     ...language...

The fact is this: as I write this down on the tenth of June, just after the Knicks have vanquished the hated Pacers, I don't know, as the French are so fond of saying, whether to shit or wind my watch.

But if I don't know the answers to that scene, I do have a bunch of Act II stuff I do know.

I know that some time passes, a season. If we started in summer, now it's fall.

I know there's a picture in the paper—an engagement snapshot, Echo and Trip.

I know that Climber sees it, dies a little more.

I know the kids are in despair.

I know that Climber is working on some crummy case, Jimmy with him, Jimmy pissed at him because he's drinking again.

I know the kids are growing more despondent.

I know Climber's drinking is close to out of control.

I know there's a shot of the woods in Central Park, daylight, the colors dazzling.

I know there's a shot of the woods in the Estate, night, and shadows are seen moving.

And, finally, and most of all, I know this: we have just seen Shirley being kidnapped.

That was my fastball.

End of Act II.

Ideas

One of the yummy things young people don't realize is that as they get more mature, senior moments are lurking behind every tree. It's not tip-of-the-tongue stuff, we all have those in our teens. No, I mean the total blank that creeps up and grabs you and you cannot remember what it was you had for lunch that day until, half an hour later, this bursts out of you: "Oysters! It was oysters!"

So, for a very long time, I have kept a microcassette recorder near, and I put down briefly the events of the day as they more or less happen. After which I promptly forget about them till maybe a week later when I type them up. I guess it's a journal, but I'm not sure I'd honor it with that name.

Anyway, one November day two years ago, two movie stories dropped in to stay for a while. This now is exactly from my journal.

20 novBILL—
WHAT IF SERIAL KILLERS TURNED OUT TO BE A GENE AND WE DESTROY THEM IN THEIR MOTHERS WOMB AND WHAT IF WE'RE DOWN TO THE END OF THEM AND A BIG THING ABOUT SHOULD WE MAKE THEM EXTINCT BECAUSE WE CAN LEARN A LOT ABOUT THEM. SOMETHING HERE, WHO KNOWS WHAT

WHAT ABOUT JANE FONDA IS A FINE HAPPILY
MARRIED MOM IN NEW YORK AND GOES TO
FANCY RESTAURANT AND MERYL STREEP IS
THERE AND WE DON'T KNOW THEY KNOW
EACH OTHER AND JANE GOES TO THE LADIES
ROOM AND THROWS UP AND TELLS HUBBY
SICK AND MERYL SMOKING ON SIDEWALK
AND NO COMMENT AND JANE GOES HOME
AND PHONE RINGS AND RINGS AND NO PICK
UP—KICKER IS THEY ARE THE TWO SCHOOL-
GIRLS WHO MURDERED THIRTY FIVE YEARS
AGO AND WERE SWORN NEVER TO SEE EACH
OTHER AGAIN AND THEY KNOW THEY WILL
KILL AGAIN.

Looking at these two visitors now, I think this: they
could both work as movies. They even have ideas behind
them.

The gene notion is not, repeat not, a movie about sci-
entific debate. It would more than likely be an action flick.
And what makes it valid for me is I think I read somewhere
that we are having the same debate about what to do with
the last remaining germs from a terrible pandemic of the
past. They are in a canister in a protected cold room and
should we keep them around for what they might tell scientists about future diseases or should we spare the world
from possible disaster?

My guess is the movie would be about the scientists who
win out and who urge that the last pregnant women who
carried the gene be allowed to have their kids—so the scientists could study them—

—only guess what, time passes, the kids grow up, and
then get away, and there they are, rampaging across the
countryside, the first serial killers in decades marauding on
a helpless population until our hero—gotta have one,
right?—brings them down.

The personal basis of the Meryl/Jane movie is that I have
always been fascinated by the things we do to one another.
There was an article I read years ago about a small town in
terror. The town had a bully but he was not the reason for

their fear. This bully had a brother who was even more of a bully than he was, but that was not the reason the town was frozen.

The second bully was due to be released from prison, that was the basis for the fear—because individually, these two guys were just bullies, but together they became lethal. The town knew that in just a few days some of them were going to die. (I wrote that in a speech delivered by Michael Douglas in *The Ghost and the Darkness*. It's there, you just don't remember it.)

The actual basis for the movie, of course, is the famous New Zealand murder case, the one where the two teenage girls grow so close that they murder one of their mothers, who was about to separate them. (Made into a movie with a very young Kate Winslet, *Heavenly Creatures*.)

The two girls were caught, tried, convicted, sent to prison, and one of the conditions of their eventual release was that they were never allowed to see each other again. (One of them went on to become a well-known mystery writer, under the pen name Anne Perry.)

You may disagree, but I think it's a terrific notion, after thirty-five years, these two meeting again, fighting fate but helpless really, because they know they are, for reasons unknown, deadly together. And one of their husbands, or worse, children, is going to suffer for their madness. Theirs is indeed an appointment in Samarra. (Look it up.)

The point to be made here is you *can* write a Hollywood film with an idea at its basis: what is the true nature of evil, or whatever else you want along those lines. But if you do, if that is where your writing heart lies, then you must learn to be masters of deception, hiding your intellectual notions behind strong emotional moments, action stuff, whatever. Shaw could write plays that were essentially talk. You can get away with this kind of stuff in a novel, too.

But guess what: movies need to move. Forget that at your peril.

I think Act III starts with a sharp loud sound—we're in the front hall of the great house and the large metal knocker outside is just being pounded. Echo rushes to the door, throws it open as Climber roars in.

Middle of the night.

Looking worse than we've yet seen him. Not drunk, nothing like that. But he has been abusing the shit out of himself and it shows. As they talk we realize this—she looks like hell too. This next is lightning fast, overlapping. Whatever they have been, now they are two parents dealing with a nightmare crisis.

                    CLIMBER
     --when?--

                    ECHO
     --around eleven--

                    CLIMBER
          (sharply)
     --<u>do better</u>!

                    ECHO
     I went in to check Phoebe--the news was just
     starting--she was sound asleep--I tucked her
     in a little better and went down to Shirley's
     room--five after, seven maybe. Right after I
     found the note--

                    CLIMBER
     --asking?--

                    ECHO
     --twenty-five million, small bills--

                    CLIMBER
     --by?--

                    ECHO
     --dawn--

>   CLIMBER
>   (Pause)
>   Proof of life?
>
>   ECHO
>   (Pause)
>   The note said a call at two.
>   (a glance at her watch)
>   Twenty minutes.
>
> CLIMBER says nothing, begins to move toward the grand
> staircase. ECHO points toward the library.
>
>   ECHO
>   Everyone's in here.
>
> CUT TO
>
> THE LIBRARY. A dozen men, some of them uniformed.
> Detectives, technicians, equipment hurriedly being set
> up. Trip is there, too.
>
>   CLIMBER
>   Not quite.
>   (as he takes the stairs two at
>   a time.)

———

What we have, then, when I set you up with the shot of the woods on the estate at the end of Act II, is the setup of the kidnapping. It's still vague. We saw only the shadows moving, never were able to make out what they were. We really only know that a divorced couple are trying to cope with the greatest fear all parents have. We know nothing of the kidnappers.

We want, I think, the following things—

—we want Shirley to live—

—we want the family safe—

—and we want them back together *as a family*, Shirley and Phoebes, Echo and her Climber.

Think for a moment now—how do we do that?

(I am smiling as I wrote that last sentence because you probably think I know how. And the truth is: not a clue.)

Okay. I have had this next scene for a month now. Hope you like it. Go with God.

————

CUT TO

PHOEBE'S ROOM. She's sleeping. CLIMBER enters, moves silently to the window, looks out.

CUT TO

THE VIEW BEYOND IN THE DARKNESS. The woods we saw earlier when we found SHIRLEY was being kidnapped.

CUT TO

THE CLIMBER. He waits by the window for a moment.

                    PHOEBE
          I'm awake.

                    CLIMBER
          There's a first.

                    PHOEBE
          I was asleep earlier, but I'm awake now.
               (soft)
          Hey, Daddy.

                    CLIMBER
               (sits beside her on the bed)
          Hey Phoebes.

                    PHOEBE
          You heard?

                    CLIMBER
          Mommy called me.
               (and now)

CUT TO

THE CLIMBER as he lifts her into his arms, holds her
more tightly than he ever has.

                    CLIMBER
        I need you to wish me luck, Phoebes.

                    PHOEBE
        What do you mean?

                    CLIMBER
        Well, I haven't taken this trip for so long,
        and I'm afraid I'm a little rusty.

                    PHOEBE
        What trip? Where are you going?

                    CLIMBER
        On the Big A, kid--on the biggest adventure of
        them all.

                    PHOEBE
              (eyes bright now)
        Can I come?

                    CLIMBER
              (sharp head shake)
        Not in the cards.

                    PHOEBE
        But I'm almost eight--and you know how brave I
        can be.

CUT TO

CLIMBER. CLOSE UP.

                    CLIMBER
        Phoebes, I would take you--I would love to
        take you--but I need helpers tonight. Not
        baggage. The only ones who can come tonight
        have to know something.

                        (long pause)
            And you were asleep when it happened.

CUT TO

PHOEBE. CLOSE UP.

                            PHOEBE
                    (long long pause. Then--)
            Are they going to come for me next?

CUT TO

THE CLIMBER, picking her up now, lifting her out of
bed.

                            CLIMBER
            Never gonna happen.

CUT TO

THE WINDOW as he carries her there in his arms. She
won't look out.

                            CLIMBER
            Tell me what was so horrible.
                    (PHOEBE shakes her head)
            It'll be our secret.

                            PHOEBE
                    (long pause--finally)
            Shirley looked up at my window--I know he
            hoped I was there like I always am--and I could
            tell what he was saying with his eyes. Help
            me. Help me.
                    (beat)
            And I ran back to bed and hid under the covers.

                            CLIMBER
            Okay. Tell me what was so horrible.

                         PHOEBE
          I just did--I cannot believe you weren't pay-
          ing attention--

                         CLIMBER
          --you mean you should have rushed outside and
          beaten everybody up and rescued your brother?
                    (before she can reply, his
                     voice changes--very soft)
          Rescue him now, Phoebes.

                         PHOEBE
          I don't know what you mean.

                         CLIMBER
          Rescue him now, look out there.

CUT TO

PHOEBE. She stares out the window.

CUT TO

WHAT SHE SEES OUTSIDE THE WINDOW. Woods, trees, moon-
light, shadows.

CUT TO

ECHO, entering the bedroom now, starting to speak--

--but CLIMBER gestures for her to shut up.

She shuts up, moves a little closer.

CUT TO

CLIMBER AND PHOEBE. The same whispering tone again.

                         CLIMBER
          What did you see, Phoebes? Tell me about them.

PHOEBE looks out the window again.

CUT TO

WHAT SHE SEES. Same as before. Woods trees, moon-
light, shadows.

CUT TO

CLIMBER AND PHOEBE. She shakes her head.

                    CLIMBER
    The Big A is starting, kiddo--last chance to
    get a ticket--

CUT TO

PHOEBE, looking out the window again.

WHAT SHE SEES. Same as before--

--only it isn't--it's the kidnapping shot--

--the shadows are different and there's a breeze now
and HERE COME TWO MEN, hurrying into view--

--PHOEBE is back seeing what she saw--

--they are only there for a blink--

--but they carry SHIRLEY between them--

                    PHOEBE (OVER)
        Two men--

                    CLIMBER (OVER)
        --same size?--

  CUT TO

THE ROOM, CLIMBER AND PHOEBE, ECHO nearby.

                    CLIMBER
              (as PHOEBE shakes her head)
         --start with the bigger one--

                    PHOEBE
         --hat--limped--

                    CLIMBER
         --right or left?

CUT TO

THE KIDNAPPING SHOT--and it didn't register to us before, but the bigger man does limp.

                    PHOEBE (OVER)
         Left.

                    CLIMBER (OVER)
         Go on about the hat.

                    PHOEBE (OVER)
         Too big.

We see it now--it is too big.

CUT TO

THE ROOM. CLIMBER AND PHOEBE. And ECHO behind them,
eyes wide in wonder.

Now PHOEBE is squinting out the window. Staring so
hard--

CUT TO

THE KIDNAPPING SHOT

                    PHOEBE (OVER)
     Bald! He was bald, Daddy, he was trying to
     hide he was bald.

She's right.

CUT TO

THE ROOM. CLIMBER AND PHOEBE, calm. ECHO's going
nuts--who is this child?

                    PHOEBE
     Am I helping?

                    CLIMBER
     Jury's still out, but I think probably.

                    PHOEBE
          (jumping out of his arms)
     Wow, I better get ready.
          (heading for her closet)
     What do you wear on the Big A?

                    CLIMBER
     Sneaks and jeans. Could be outside work,
     bring a sweater--okay, the smaller one--

                    PHOEBE
          (from the closet)
     Missing most of a little finger. He was hold-
     ing Shirl funny.

CUT TO

THE KIDNAPPING SHOT. The SMALLER MAN is definitely
missing most of a finger as he carries SHIRLEY along.

CUT TO

THE BEDROOM. ECHO moves to CLIMBER as PHOEBE is heard
thrashing around in her closet.

                    CLIMBER
     Anything else?

                    PHOEBE
               (poking her head out)
     Lots, but that isn't as easy as it looks,
     Daddy, and I'm a little pooped.

                    ECHO
     You think you're taking her?

                    CLIMBER
               (are you serious?)
     She's our chance.

                    ECHO
               (hard for her)
     I can't let you go alone.

CLIMBER. CLOSE UP.

                    CLIMBER
               (takes her shoulders, hard)
     Listen now--I have loved you since our first
     moment, always did, always will--
               (dangerous now)
     --but stay the hell out of our way.
               (and on that)

It's two o'clock and the telephone rings--

   Question for you: What is the most solid element in the scene you just
read? Another way of putting it: What was the most proper screenwriting? I'll go on while you make up your mind.
   Since I left us with the phone ringing, I think the next scene should be
the phone call. And the sad truth is, it's kind of a drag. Not much you
can do with it but make it short because we have all seen a million scenes

like it. The cops standing around tensely, the computer nerd with all the equipment tracking the location of the phone call and you know he's not going to get it because if he does get it, where's the movie? The scary, distorted voice of the villain, the trying-to-be-brave-but-underneath-scared-shitless voice of the victim.

Trying for a little difference, I want the terrified Shirley to ask only to talk to his sister, and Phoebes gets on, tells him of the Big A, and that they'll all be together in no time, and Shirley manages to say how he hopes that's true, the family being together again, how he wishes that it happen "so soon you won't believe it" and then the villain clicks off the phone, the call is over.

The cops surround the technicians who have been tracing the call, but—shock and gasp—no good, not long enough, and on their way to the car, Phoebe looks around to say goodbye to her mother but can't find her—

—outside they go—

—to find Echo already sitting there, ready to roll.

So the three of them take off. On the Big A. To try and find, this night, somehow, somewhere on the earth, the boy who wants to be called Flash.

I suppose it will not come as a huge surprise when I tell you if Act I was called Things Going Good, and Act II was called Things Going Bad, then this, Act III, I'm calling The Big A.

You know what it has to accomplish.

What kind of a shot do you think we have?

There is no right answer, understand—just figure our chances.

And while you are figuring, I have but two words for you: **Phoebe's insomnia.** (I'm back now answering my question about the most proper element in the memory scene.)

For me, that is what I consider professional work.

I set it up twice. Once, when the kids are trying to get the approval of their grandfather, this exchange happens:

                         CLIMBER
        She's got genius inside her, Pop.

                          JIMMY
        Besides the memory, what else?

I never went on with that thought, never explained. I just wanted to plant that there was *something* very unusual about Phoebe's memory.

A few pages later, Climber has put Shirley to sleep, kisses Phoebes, and with a troubled look, goes to his bed, watches my beloved Sprewell, and we

CUT TO

THE APARTMENT. Middle of the night. CLIMBER jerks
awake, rubs his eyes, gets out of bed.

CUT TO

THE OTHER BEDROOM. As before. SHIRLEY is dead to the
world. PHOEBE reads. Now she looks up as her father
comes in. He sits on the bed and they whisper.

> CLIMBER
> Phoebes, you've gotta sleep sometime.
> > (he puts the book down, turns out
> > her light)
> It's the one thing we worry about most.

You were supposed to think that was just what it was: a worried father with a child who cannot sleep. But it was more than that.

When we screenwrite, things should hook into one another. One thought moving forward while often, at the same time, if needed, referring back. I knew Phoebe had this miracle memory. But I wanted to surprise and please you when you saw it in action.

I also *thought* she might have seen the kidnapping. (If you will look back—and remember this is a For Our Eyes Only first draft—it is not totally clear what she sees from her room. At one point I remember she and Shirley were looking out front, waiting for their father to arrive.)

I had no idea I would need her memory to make the scene play. But it was another fastball I felt I had, to be used if necessary.

By the time Act III started, I felt it was necessary.

I wrote an exchange you probably paid no attention to—you're right, you shouldn't have. Climber comes into the mansion, Echo is there to meet him. The dialogue goes like this—

> CLIMBER
> --when?--

```
                    ECHO
          --around eleven--


                    CLIMBER
               (sharply)
          --do better!


                    ECHO
          I went in to check Phoebe--the news was just
          starting--she was sound asleep--
```

Echo goes on a while about the time, but that's just filler—once Climber hears Phoebe was asleep, **he knows everything.**

He knows she is hiding something because he knows this: **she never sleeps.** My God, at his house she was up in the middle of the night, here it's eleven, what could she be hiding?

She must have seen the kidnapping. Has to be that. And what he has to do is give her the confidence to tell what she actually did see. He knows of her memory, *he knows the case is in her head.*

When I can write a scene like the memory scene, it may be dreadful— as I write this explanation, no one else but me has read it—but as the one doing the writing, if I can have a hook, a connective, it gives me great confidence. Once I decided I was going to use Phoebe, I felt, shit, I can make this play, because if art should be both inevitable and surprising, that scene—forget the word "art"—that scene has both. A great detective inevitably burrowing his way into a difficult case. And help coming from a surprising source, a genius child.

There is a magician's expression I like—I've already mentioned it— and it is this: *the work is done.* Again the explanation: magic tricks fall into three parts. The *illusion* of the trick—how it looks to us, the audience. The *preparation* of the trick—that's all the stuff the magician has to get ready before he begins, pinning things inside his magic suit, crimping cards, everything he needs to create the spell.

Now if the preparation has been done properly, magicians feel that sometimes—it could be halfway through, it could be even before they start—*the work is done.*

It is inexorable. You keep going forward and nothing can stop you.

Sometimes, I feel that way about screenplays.

In *Butch,* for example, there is a preparation moment early. Butch and Sundance have decided to go to South America. Sundance tells Etta

Place (Katherine Ross) that she can come along if she doesn't whine. She agrees to go. But then she adds this:

>   ETTA
> So I'll go with you, and I won't whine, and
> I'll sew your socks and stitch you when you're
> wounded, and anything you ask of me I'll do,
> except one thing: I won't watch you die. I'll
> miss that scene if you don't mind.

For me, that speech was there for but one reason: when she says she won't watch them die. It hits a chord, is gone.

Maybe half an hour later, after they have killed for the first time getting the payroll money back, and they are at the bottom, she suggests they find other ways of going straight. They don't know how. They lie by the campfire in silence. And this dialogue happens.

>   ETTA
>   (wide awake)
> Hey?

>   SUNDANCE
>   (wide awake too)
> Hmm?

>   ETTA
> Maybe I might go back ahead of you.

>   SUNDANCE
> You mean home?

>   ETTA
> I was thinking of it.

>   SUNDANCE
>   (he doesn't want her to go)
> Whatever you want, Etta.

>   ETTA
> Then maybe I'll go.

                SUNDANCE
          (to BUTCH)
     Hey?

                BUTCH
          (he is also wide awake)
     Hmm?

                SUNDANCE
     Etta's thinking of maybe going home ahead of
     us.

                BUTCH
          (he doesn't want her to go either)
     Whatever she wants.

                ETTA
     I'll go then.

The scene goes on a while longer and the movie goes on for twenty-plus more pages—

—but I think the whole work was done. I am talking in terms of story. I meant for us to care for the two guys as much I did. By now the audience should know they are goners. And a sense of sadness should have begun to pervade the story.

Now, it sure helps that the shoot-out is the greatest action scene I've ever been around. Hill just did it so brilliantly. But I think the screenplay would have been proper with a scene of far lesser impact.

And maybe I'm nuts—we'll see; my doctors are about to descend and tell me—but I think the work is done here, too.

If I have structured a proper screenplay.

No question, if I could come up with dazzling stuff, it's that much better than ordinary stuff.

Here's what I want to happen: everybody lives and Echo and Climber get back together. And, sure, they'll probably screw up again, but maybe not, they're wiser and sadder than the first time.

Here's a couple of things I have vaguely in mind:

I think I want a scene with Jimmy in a bar, middle of the might, with the most incredible group of other guys who try and help—ancient retired cops, old tough detectives, retired Mafia guys.

Aside: In what you have read, Jimmy isn't much. I didn't know if I needed him when I started, still am not sure. But I liked the idea of the kids' grandfather being Cagney, one of my heroes. And I liked the possibility of—and I didn't write this at all, it ain't in what you read—the possibility of Climber, when he's around his dad, regressing a little bit, be more like a kid around his father, seeking, as we all do, approval. End of aside.

Anyway, in this bar with Jimmy is all the crime wisdom of the past half century. Climber calls and asks, "Anything yet?" And Jimmy maybe says, "Believe it, two guys who tried a kidnapping in the Bronx a year ago. One of them's missing a finger and the other one's losing his hair."

And Climber, on a note of triumph, roars to the address Jimmy gives him, bursts in and throws the two guys against the wall—

—only they're the wrong guys.

(At one point in my insomnia last night I wondered if they could be Chinese. Probably not—we are dealing with a life in danger; laughter does not help our cause.)

I think I want a scene where the three of them have to wait somewhere. It's tense and they're liable to be there a long time and Echo and Climber haven't really talked much yet—

—and Phoebe looks at them, says, "I wonder, how did you two meet?"

Neither answers—they don't really want to go there.

But she's relentless, because they never want to tell her, they're tired of telling the story, but it's her very favorite story in the world. "I've always wondered why you never told me."

Still, no reply.

"Probably you put ads in magazines. 'Detective wants to meet'—what were you, Mommy?"

"I was a college sophomore."

" 'Detective—wants to meet college sophomore.' Why did you put the ad in, Daddy?"

"It was a case, Phoebe. Now and forever. It was a case."

But she's gotten them talking and that's a first and I think it's the start of their reuniting. We know he's in love with her and we think she might still be in love with him, so that journey shouldn't be all that hard to make play.

(Aside: Another thing I didn't put in is that the kids' favorite movie of all time is *The Parent Trap*, a Disney hit from the '60s where Hayley Mills tries to get her divorced parents back together. I think Shirley brings it up a lot. I think he's got a tape of it at his father's apartment and he and Phoebe play it all the time, driving Climber nuts. End of aside.)

I think the gardeners of the estate are behind the kidnapping—the guys we've seen who never wave at the car. I think the gardeners hired the guys who did the job.

I don't know why I think that. Probably because we've met them in passing, and if I do decide they are the baddies, I should give them a little more screen time, not much, though. I want the surprise.

What's appealing about them is that they're handy. Look, this was never meant to be a great exercise in deduction. It's a romantic comedy about an unusual family. If I don't use the gardeners, I have to spend more time setting up somebody else. And if I have someone who's around but not around *much*, it might be obvious he did it.

Besides, I've met some pretty weird gardeners.

I kind of think this: *that Shirley hasn't been taken anywhere.* Maybe he's bound and gagged and tossed in the corner of the gardener's cottage.

If I go that way, I've already set up a way for our adventurers to figure that out. When Phoebe is talking to Shirley over the phone back in the house, he says he hopes that the family will be together again, and I quote, **"so soon you won't believe it."**

Well, that's an odd manner of speech. And one of them could realize that just as the money is being transferred or some other time of high tension. Someone could realize, *he's there.* And off they go to the final rescue.

I think that realization comes not from Phoebe, whom we expect to come up with it, or Climber either. I want Echo to have her moment. Because if it works, it shows that she belongs with them in their craziness.

Now the bad part of this is that at one time I thought I was repeating the opening rescue, the same only different. I wanted Climber wounded enough so he can't, so maybe Echo has to do it.

But I have never seen a multistoried gardener's cottage.

I believe that I have an ending. At least a start. It would come after the climactic scene when all hell has to break loose, when the rescue happens, when Climber is wounded, when Shirley becomes Flash. Here's how I think I'd do it.

CUT TO

CLIMBER'S CAR, making its now familiar path through
the estate up to the front door.

Weeks have passed. The changing of the leaves.

CUT TO

INSIDE THE HOUSE AND TRIP'S VOICE.

                    TRIP (OVER)
        Children--your father's here.

CUT TO

THE KIDS. Dressed like kids now. Lord Fauntleroy
banished.

CUT TO

THE MAIN STAIRCASE as THE KIDS sprint down. TRIP AND
ECHO follow them down; his arm around her shoulder.

CUT TO

CLIMBER getting out of his car, but slowly; the wound
not yet completely healed.

CUT TO

THE FRONT DOOR OPENING as THE KIDS hurry out, race to
the car, get in their usual spot in the back.

ECHO alone, standing in the doorway.

CUT TO

CLIMBER, standing by his car, looking at her. A nod.

CUT TO

ECHO. Beat. A nod.

                         TRIP (OVER)
                    (calling from inside)
              Darling? See you on the beach.

                         ECHO
                    (calling back)
              Catch up with you.

CUT TO

CLIMBER. Beat. Into the car again.

                         CLIMBER
              No tickets today?

CUT TO

ECHO. She forgot. Now she moves to the car, hands
tickets inside to him.

                         CLIMBER
                    (taking them--with dread)
              Performance art in the Village?

                         ECHO
                    (her big moment)
              Tractor pull in New Jersey.

They look at each other. Then--

                         CLIMBER
                    (counting carefully)
              There are four tickets here.

She is totally vulnerable now. Just standing there.
He's vulnerable too.

Neither of them dares make a move.

Then her nerve starts to leave her, and just as she's about to turn back--

                          SHIRLEY
           Oh get in, Mom.
                  (to PHOEBE)
           They'll probably just louse it up again.

                          PHOEBE
           But of course.

ECHO'S in the car now. One quick touch of hands. Then CLIMBER starts to drive.

And off they go. Into the biggest adventure of all.

FINAL FADE-OUT

———

   Okay, readers, last chance now before the doctors take over. Monday-morning quarterbacking not allowed. Would you make this movie? How would you change it?

   How would you cast it? (Nick Cage? Terrific actor, but is he a shade too young? If you were Mr. Time Warner and you heard Nick Cage wanted to play Climber, would you make the movie? What if you heard that George Clooney wanted to do the part—which would you pick? And *why*? Oops, that was Harrison Ford's agent on the line, he also wants to be Climber. Is he a bit old for it? Would you say goodbye to Nick and George and go with *The Fugitive*?

   You would? Great for me, I'm rich, but if you're a studio executive, you want to do the best you can for your studio, thereby advancing your career, and guess what I know?—Mel is desperate to star. Do you duck Harrison? Are you still back with Nick? What if I tell you that Bruce Willis is driving onto the lot *right now* and won't leave until you give him the lead?

   What's a mother to do?

   What scenes do you want to keep? All of them? Great for me again, I don't have to do any more work. Did you like the drowning scene? Did you feel Climber loved his kids? Enough? Not enough? Too much? How would you change things?

   Think about all this stuff and *try to remember your ideas,* because the doctors can be pretty persuasive.

Starting with Peter and Bobby Farrelly. Their suggestions are in the
form of an interview because they had day jobs when they got the script,
directing *Me Myself and Irene*. I went up to Vermont and taped them.

In case you want their writing credits, according to the Internet
Movie Database they wrote *Kingpin, Dumb and Dumber, There's Something About Mary,* and *Me Myself and Irene,* which is due out in summer 2000.

On the drowning scene:

>   THE FARRELLYS
> I remember when I read it I thought, well,
> first I thought he's rescuing her. Boy,
> that's not necessary, he just rescued her, and
> then, when you flip that, I saw what you were
> doing but I thought, well, we didn't need a
> reason why he would fall in love with her. Be-
> sides, you can't use it because we're using it
> in the movie we're shooting right now.

On their falling in love:

>   THE FARRELLYS
> You don't have to tell us why he falls for
> her--everybody falls for her. And I think she
> falls for him in the scene he has with her
> father when he gets $25,000 and says you owe me
> two--he doesn't want more, that's not what he
> dealt for--
> --and she should <u>hear</u> that scene--maybe not be
> in the room but she should hear. And that
> makes her think this guy is different, this
> guy has a code that he lives by.

On their divorcing (1):

>   THE FARRELLYS
> Got to be a great reason, not the kind you
> think of right off. Throw those out. Well,
> they had money issues. She spent too much and

he didn't like it and they had a fight. Can't
be alcohol. Maybe it's because it's in his
blood, what he does, and she's saying, this is
crazy, we're rich, you don't have to be doing
this risky stuff. Except that's obvious. But
the question of the movie is why they split up.

On Act II:

THE FARRELLYS

Act II is what you haven't written yet--Act II
is Bogart and Cagney and the kids. And not
just for one scene. What if Cagney is the driving force behind the kids joining in--he remembers when Climber was young and his mother
said the same thing Climber's saying now--
they're young, they're not ready. And they
don't just do it for one scene--they're on
this case and they're good at it, and maybe
there's a scene where they shove Phoebe into a
chute and send her away to get a form from a
wastebasket and they're watching the room on a
fuzzy black-and-white monitor and Phoebe's in
the room when all of a sudden someone else
comes into the room, someone bad, and they go
tearing down a corridor to get to the room when
<u>there's a shot</u>--Climber goes nuts and breaks
the door down and there's Phoebe with a gun of
her own and the guy with his hands up and
Phoebe says Grandpa gave me the gun and
Climber is about to kill Jimmy for this and
Jimmy says to Climber, "What are you, crazy?
I'm not going to send my granddaughter in
there without a gun."

On the kidnapper:

THE FARRELLYS

Trip is too obvious. Remember the guy who he
meets with? He's like a judge or something.
He's coming across as a great guy--"I'm repre-

senting the family" and all that. <u>That</u> should
be the guy behind the kidnapping, because
you've got a smoke screen.

On their divorcing (2):

THE FARRELLYS

Back to the divorce for a second--what if they
broke up because he did something that he had
to do? In his mind, he was stubborn, he did
the right thing. But it embarrassed her family. He's on a case and he finds out something
and she says hey wait a second, I'm asking you,
let them off, don't push that. And he can't
not push it because he's a moral guy. And he
pushed and they broke up because she felt he
betrayed her. But the trick is, what you don't
find out till the end is, he didn't say everything he knew. He let the person off easy. He
knew way more, her whole family was going to
get pulled in. She thinks he went all the way
but he has a whole trunkful of stuff he never
blew open and that's revealed at the end but
not by him. So he lost his soul when he held
it back. He's Bogie but he was untrue to himself and so that is why he left her. He resents her. She resents him for what he did but
deep down, he's the one who resents her because she made him be untrue to himself.

On the project as a whole:

THE FARRELLYS

There's great stuff here. When the kids pile
into the front seat. When he makes Phoebe remember the kidnapping. There's a great movie
here--you just haven't written it yet.

Scott Frank started his career in 1988 with a movie I never heard of,
Plainclothes. In 1991 he had two more: *Little Man Tate* and *Dead*

Again. He and Elmore Leonard turned out to be a pretty good match, witness Frank's adaptation of *Get Shorty* and last year's *Out of Sight,* for which he got an Oscar nomination and won a Writer's Guild of America Award. His next is to be *Minority Report,* with Steven Spielberg on board to direct.

Dear Bill
Subj: Thoughts on "The Big A" . . .

Okay, these thoughts are maybe three seconds old, so take them with the usual caveats. I should warn you, if I sound a bit fuckerish, it's only because I'm overworked, underinspired and in a foul mood. The perfect headspace for critiquing a screenplay. Just know I'm probably talking more to myself than to you.

Anyway, ahead of time, forgive me.

I like the idea and in terms of plot (structure), the story is fun and full of abundant twists and turns and surprises. In fact, every scene seems to go in the opposite direction you think it will. If you want to simply tell a fun story, then you've succeeded.

On top of that, as with everything you write, everyone speaks in a distinct voice and I particularly like the kids and the way you've made them precocious without being obnoxious.

But, for me, I need more character stuff. Character is (for me—and maybe this exercise isn't about me or what I would do so I should just fuck right off, but since you asked . . .) everything.

To begin with, I think we need to spend more time with Echo and Climber before they split, only because I don't know these two at all. She was a sophomore in college, yeah, but WHAT DOES SHE WANT? To be a doctor? To be a painter? To be a hooker? To be the wife of a private detective? What does he want? You tell me how they got their nicknames, but you don't tell me much else about them. Why did she fall in love with him? I know why he fell in love with her. The same reason all men fall in love with women: she's beautiful. But what's the thing about Climber? Why does he still love her (more on this later)?

In terms of character, it seems to me that you give more to the reader of your script than to the viewer of the film. Long paragraphs at the beginning tell us, the reader, about these people. But how will the audience know how she got that nickname? How will the audience know that he's "a good man in a bad world . . . as close as anyone's come to Bogart in TMF"?

And why did she leave him? The reason I get from the script is: Because he turned out to be exactly the guy he appeared to be. Maybe she thought that's what she wanted in a guy, but then couldn't live with it. I don't know, I don't want to make too big a deal out of it, but without knowing these people beyond types, I don't care much what happens to them.

About the kidnapping. I like the details. The Gardeners did it (and yes, you'd have to set them and the other household staff up, but that could be fun to see the kids interacting with them and I think the movie is under-peopled as it is). I like that Phoebe saw it, but hid, etc. etc. . . . I just don't know if I'm surprised enough when Shirley (can we get away in this day and age with naming a boy Shirley? Especially with a mother named Echo and a father named Climber? Just a question . . .) gets snatched.

I do like the idea of a case they all have to work on together, but jeez, it seems like whenever a movie hits a wall, someone close to the good guy gets grabbed up. The wife of the cop. The daughter of the cop. The son of the cop. The cop comes home, there's a fucking note on the kitchen table . . .

I'm not saying it couldn't work, but are we surprised enough by it? Does that even matter?

A few words about the kids. I love the way they talk. I love the IDEA of who they are, but I have questions, most stemming from the notion in the script that:

They pretend to hate their father to make their mother happy.

A) Why DOES their mother so dislike their father? And why does she want her kids to dislike him as well? B) Why would they ever go along quietly when their mother and the asshole Trip want to keep his visits supervised? Why wouldn't they, as articulate and intelligent as you've drawn them, tell their mother what's up? Especially if they love their father so much?

I think the reason you had trouble with that first scene is because it's probably the wrong scene. It's not a scene we want to see. Do we believe it? Look at question B above. Say we do. I still don't think we need to have the scene. In fact, if you look at your outline, you could cut it and the story wouldn't change at all. Everybody's miserable. We know that. Moving on . . .

You talk about the sleight of hand used in setting up Phoebe's memory with the line from Jimmy. I think you need more than a line. After the robbery at the bodega, why can't we have a moment where she (the "blind girl") describes for the cops everything she saw. And, then, in her moment of glory, Echo and Trip show up, piss on everybody's high. Just a thought.

Okay—say Trip brought Echo along, who didn't want to believe it.

Who still loves Climber, but can't be with him because . . . (?) He did . . . (?) I don't know, maybe he cheated on her because he refused to believe that a woman like that would ever really love a guy like him . . . he knew that she was more amused with him than in love with him . . . she didn't know what she had until now . . . I don't know . . . I'm looking for SOMETHING more than they just come from different places.

Echo Echo Echo. Why do we like her? What's she doing now besides being a rich bitch (showing her working at the foundation is too little too late, and perhaps, even more off-putting than having her do nothing. And again, you tell us—the reader—how good she is at her job, but we really never see her do anything).

Why in God's name is she with Trip?

We're supposed to want Echo and Climber to get together, but the only thing attractive about her is that she's attractive. Other than that, we know she's rich. She likes Bartok and Kabuki theater. She's dating a guy our hero once punched out. Right about now I'm thinking your fast-ball should have been, SHE gets kidnapped again, this time Climber and the kids go looking for her . . . but aren't so sure they really want to find her . . .

Okay, I know. I've come down with both feet. Why? Because I love the idea. I love the story. I don't love the characters. I'm not even sure they ARE characters—at least not in the sense that goes beyond types or attitudes. When I see a film, I want what the characters want. I want to see them get it, or not get it, in some terrific, dramatic way. I guess what I'm trying to say is this:

Character is what makes us give a shit. Don't you think?

Okay, I'm done.

(I have trouble WRITING these thoughts. It would be much better if we could talk. That is, if you still WANT to talk to me . . .)

—Scott

Tony Gilroy's first flick was *The Cutting Edge* in 1993. More recently he has written *Dolores Claiborne* and *The Devil's Advocate*. I have known him for thirty years and we still speak to each other—a remark you will understand after you've finished his comments.

Bill,

Okay, I'll play.

I've tried to follow the rules here as I went along, but ideas for me come quick. It's organization that takes time. Opting for fertility over elegance, I'm gonna brain dump here, and then maybe we can talk about it later and clean it up.

We'll see if you bless me when I'm done.

———

Opening scene:
Climber—hate the name. Echo—ditto. All the cute stuff about them never makes it to the screen. I know this trick too well. Hype hype hype. Way too much.

Where are we? Is it the thirties? Is this a radio serial? Is this the frigging Shadow or something?

Answer—his apartment—ESPN. Shit, this is *now*. I like the TV in every room. My favorite thing so far. My only favorite thing.

Is he a cop? He's not a cop. *Is* he a cop? Why aren't you telling me this?

Okay, antisocial shlub hero goes to the mansion.

God, I really hate the name Climber. Is this gonna have some purpose?

So he's desperately in love with this unattainable rich girl. Dad's a jerk. (I'm bored, Bill.)

Six, seven pages of her saving him in the ocean. (Tough to shoot to make sense of this, I don't like the pace, I want other things to be happening and I'm in another action piece that's not really setting the world on fire . . .)

And now the credits?

Okay—here's what I'm thinking. This is a movie about a team. He's got all the detective experience but his soul is dead. She's the daredevil rich chick with money to burn who's been trapped in this mansion since she was born. He's gonna break her out. She's gonna elevate his spirit, appetites, and cases. They'll travel the world. What a team they're going to make. Hell, who knows, maybe she staged the kidnapping herself just to meet him. Better yet, maybe her father did . . .

And now the credits?

Okay. Stop. Reset. I've just read through to the bodega shootout. I want to change gears. I want to call my little thing here:

Bill's Little Family Thriller

I want to talk about tone.

You mess with tone all the time. It's your right. Short of inventing an entirely new, undiscovered plot, maybe the next most heady discovery is an entirely new, unique tone. *Butch Cassidy* was that creation. A whole new stink on the western. A completely unique attitude to some very heavily trod territory.

This was big stuff. So you're the King of Tone.

Sometimes it's dazzling—*Princess Bride*.

Sometimes it's *Year of the Comet*.

For every *Strangelove* there are dozens of *Batman IVs*.

You know I love to mess with the rules. And I want to keep at it. It's all gonna keep evolving and I don't want to get bored or get caught short.

But tone? Tone scares me.

Why? Because when it goes wrong it just sucks out loud. I think the audience—the reader—I think they make some critical decisions in the opening movements of a film. How deeply do I invest myself here? How much fun can I have? Should I be consciously referencing the rest of my life during the next two hours, or is this an experience I need to surrender to? Are you asking for my heart or my head or both? Am I rooting for the hero or the movie? Just how many pounds of disbelief are you gonna ask me to suspend before this is through?

When it's done right, it makes no difference. They all work. They're all of value. They're all worth writing and seeing.

The audience just wants to know.

When you fuck with tone, you risk squandering that spark. You risk losing the one thing the audience brings with them.

The noir-comedy. The romantic-spoof. The gothic-farce. This is very tricky, alchemical stuff to play with. And what it seems to me you are trying to pull off here is a something we'd have to call . . .

The family thriller.

Dangerous *and* cute.

Who the hell is this thing for, anyway? I mean, not to sound like the lowest MBA Hollywood scum here, but who's supposed to be watching this? If it's for kids, it's way too boring. If it's for adults, then where's the meat?

I start in the shitty apartment. The lonely TVs. The bag-a-doughnuts Toyota.

Why's he pulling up to a mansion?

Why does it seem like he knows his way around?

Why won't anybody talk to him?

Omigod, it's a custody thing. These two awful brats are his progeny. And that beautiful bitch is his ex-wife and there's her grim, fortune-hunting fiancé.

Sure, do the tickets and the cook, and pre-visit nausea.

Climber (man, I hate that name) doesn't want to be here. Kids don't want to be here. Everything sucks.

And now, on page seven, you get your one decent surprise in this whole thing. You get the moment that sums up the whole damn story. You get something that *might* appeal to both kids and parents.

They pull out and, holy shit!—it's all okay.

The kids love their dad and they've all got a secret.

Put the credits here.

You want the marital backstory?

You already have it—let Dad tell the brats before they go to bed. Let him change it every time he tells it. Break my heart all the way. All we need to know is that once it was perfect.

Other stuff that sucks—splitting Trip's catching them into two beats is just a waste of real estate. Jimmy—use him—change him—or lose him. Since when is sketching the cornerstone of detective work?

———

Okay, so now you want me to stop and tell you what I think comes next?

Big, wild balls-out guess . . .

They get back together.

I mean, come on, there're kids and you're being cute, and it's Hollywood and everybody knows you're gonna have a happy ending.

You want a victim? You've got Jimmy with a heart attack in the middle of the rescue.

I don't know. And you've got me thinking very formula here, which I'm always trying to fight, but this thing—and it's the damn tone that's screwing it up—this thing just doesn't get me excited.

Okay, I can fix this, but I don't know if I can save it.

So reset. I'm backtracking here.

My first question—always—*Where's the movie?* Not the pitch or what goes on the one-sheet, or any of the rest of that crap, but where is it? Where does this thing live? So when I read this, at least the first half I've read so far, I'm thinking Bill is really walking past the movie here.

Wrong opening. As evidenced by the credit sequence on, what is it, page 450?

The action sequence up top is a bore. Could Bill really do this scene right? Absolutely. But his heart's not in it, because he knows that the real thing he's got doesn't start for another many pages. So he hypes the hell

out of it, and I don't know where I am, like I said, is this The Shadow or
Spiderman or Serpico . . .

And what happens anyway?

He saves the girl.

Bore.

And the walk through the mansion. Stock.

The pictures. Stock.

The beach.

So for me, so far nothing . . .

And now you're gonna try and tell the story of their marriage through
this montage? Wrong. And it's worse than that—it's worse than just bad
storytelling, because the montage does nothing for me except muddy the
emotional waters of this thing beyond redemption.

If she's so great how does she turn into such a bitch?

If he's so tough, how does he get dragooned into this marriage that is
so clearly wrong?

Every moment in a movie counts—I'm depending on what you told
me about them up top. I'm in the audience, I've been to the movies
before, I know that information means something. What you told me is
this—he needs to turn off the television and get personal. She needs
adventure and romance.

Better to have told me nothing than this.

Here's a miracle of storytelling. If you *don't* show them getting
together—if you only show the result, the audience will write the best
courtship ever, the best dialogue, the best sex—the worst fights, the
biggest heartbreak—anything. All you have to do is get out of the way.

I open the movie with him going to pick up the kids.

I'm annoyed now. Page 58 of this manuscript [page 428, above].
You've got all these questions about the characters. The acts and the
rules and all this great theoretical pondering. You're asking me all these
questions about the characters and most of it's based on a deep understanding of this marriage and as I said before, I don't know what this
marriage was about.

I don't have a clue about Climber. Or her.

And now you tell me this is supposed to be a romantic comedy?

Insight—*this tone you're using buries character.*

Now I'm convinced.

My opening is definitely, absolutely on the money.

I skip the climbing and the beach. I get right to it. I let the past in

as I need it. I get to work on these characters. I try and find a level of
reality—tone again—that works best. I get Jimmy up and running
so that Climber has someone to talk to about what the hell's going on
with him.

My beats?
—Kids have a secret life with dad.
—Secret life drives family apart for good.

. . . . .

On to the back end . . .
And here's the worst of it. *Two kidnappings.*
What kind of generational crime vortex has this poor family stumbled
into? And like a fool, I'm thinking there's some point to this—that
maybe it's the same guys who grabbed the mother years ago have come
back for the kid. Maybe that's why you left things sort of unresolved at
the opening. Maybe it's the father again . . .
Something.
But no.
Obviously this can be fixed.
I did it already with my opening. I don't need the climbing up top, so
it wasn't a kidnapping he saved Echo from. Maybe it was her gambling
debts from college that needed straightening out. Maybe she ran away
from home and he had to track her down.

. . . . .

Anyway, my spitball version.
It's a completely real film. Feet on the ground.
Climber has some real problems. He's kind of a nut. Who else but a
nut would let Echo go? What kind of father encourages this kind of
bipolar behavioral life for his kids? He loves the kids. Desperately. Loves
them so much he's gotten more and more isolated. Maybe he used to be
a lively outgoing guy. Maybe he loves them a little too much (if that's
possible)—loves them so much he can't take any job that works over the
weekends. This has crippled his career recently, because detective work
is anything but regularly scheduled.
So this once-dazzling detective is on his ass because he loves his kids
so much.
And it's more than sketching he's teaching them. I mean, I'd really go

for it here. They know it all. Phone tracing and stakeouts and how-to-do-this and how-to-do-that.

He and Jimmy arguing about old-school vs. new-school techniques.

And Echo has hired a series of private detectives to try and monitor these weekend visits. And Climber has managed to know/persuade/threaten all of them to file a phony report.

Until now.

Okay, so the bodega or something like it. The bottom line here is that Echo finds out what's been going on and the kids are inadvertently but unconscionably put into real jeopardy.

Climber can't see the kids no more.

Now what?

The boy is kidnapped.

Here's a big gift for you in *any* version . . .

Echo thinks Climber had something to do with it.

I mean, come on, you've got her calling him first. I don't think so. He's so nutty. He's so desperate. He's so capable. He's got to be a suspect, doesn't he?

Make it hard.

Cops don't want him working the case. Cops hate him. Echo doesn't want him around the scene. Daughter is his only ally and she's going crazy to talk to him, because she's got info that's crucial . . .

. . . . .

Okay, so that's as far as I'm going, because the next question is who are the bad guys and I'm not so sure that the landscaping crew is worthy of my time, but who knows?

And I've got my own deadline here this week and this is probably way more than you ever wanted to hear anyway . . .

. . . . .

In summary.

My version is real. Much more character. Nobody's close to perfect, including the kids.

I dump your whole opening.

Acts, I know nothing about. I have three beats.

—Kids have secret life with dad.

—Secret life drives family apart forever.

—Secret life is the only thing that can save them.

Aren't you glad you asked?

Callie Khouri studied landscape architecture at Purdue, which led naturally to her longtime employment as a music-video producer. She wrote *Thelma and Louise,* her first movie, in longhand. And she may well go down in history as the last Oscar winner (1991) to do so.

Hello Bill,
    Here it is. I'm going to do this in a random, haphazard sort of way, so you will get the unfortunate experience of seeing how my mind works, and then you'll understand why writing is almost impossible for me.
    First, I love the setup, the kidnapping, although I don't know how you demonstrate visually a lot of the things you tell us about Climber. In that sense the script is padded, and the audience will have to just assume a lot of this Bogart persona from the casting, but as intelligent as audiences have proven themselves to be this summer, why should you give a shit? They don't.
    But, I have a big, big problem with Echo. I don't believe that a woman who willingly runs through a closed window sixty feet up and saves a guy from drowning ends up as this tight-ass bitch married to a guy her husband has already punched out. I don't believe that she'd want her kids to be the uptight little bastards they pretend to be. I do like that the kids know that the parents want different things from them, but I don't know how to do it without making me hate this woman. I don't know enough about her to begin with. You set her up as both beautiful and *brave* and then you screw her on the brave and leave her with just beautiful. Certainly not enough of a reason for me to understand why Climber still loves her. Give her something, for Chrissake! (By the way, anyone who names their son Shirley and doesn't expect him to be beaten to fine paste every day of their lives is a fucking idiot and I don't believe for a second that Climber would ever go along with it. And as much as a prig as she is, it is too preposterous for me to believe a woman who would marry a guy like Climber wants to have an effeminate son.) In any case, I just *need more* to understand why and how this marriage, which I'm assuming was born out of an impossibly white-hot chemistry, didn't last. I don't know enough about either one of them to really care that they're not together anymore, and the way it's set up now, *I know*

to the core of my being that they will just as impossibly get back together and I'm asking myself what's playing in the theater next door. Why did it fail? What's the real reason? Perhaps, and this requires giving Echo a little credit, she was just unprepared and ultimately wearied by worrying about him almost dying every time he walks out the front door. He doesn't even have to work if he doesn't want to! The father has offered many times to set him up, let him run a big security business if he's so hell bent on staying in the business, but for gods sake does he have to keep putting his *own life* on the line? What about her? What about the kids? Doesn't he care enough not to want her to be widowed and the kids to be half-orphaned? Most cops' wives probably feel that way, only they don't have the hundreds of millions of dollars that would allow their husbands to quit. Maybe it just got to be too much for her. Why does she hate him so much? Because he wouldn't give up his stupid cop job for her and his family? And don't you think that the kids know "That she hates you so much because she loves you, idiot"? They would know that. I will say here that there is nothing sexier to a kid than the idea that their parents will get back together. *Parent Trap* is *still* my favorite movie and those kids are way too on the ball not to realize that their parents still have the hots for each other, Tripp or no Tripp. I am adding a "p" to Trip because it looks more like a name to me that way. As much as I dislike Echo in the version that you have, I don't dislike her enough to hope she'll marry this guy.

Maybe Tripp is the guy that her family thought she would marry in the first place until she threw them the curve ball of marrying *way* beneath her (something I think that secretly thrills her father). Maybe he's not a bad guy, just a tame guy, or maybe he is a bad guy, maybe he's in on it somehow, I doubt it, but I said I would let my mind wander. I wish there was some way of coming up with somebody doing the second kidnapping that no one would ever, ever expect. I wasn't totally bowled over by the gardeners because they look so unsuspecting. I also thought that Echo would stop herself when she said that Phoebe was sound asleep, that she would *realize as she was saying it that something was wrong*! That they both would run upstairs, knowing that the kid had been chloroformed or something because *she's the mother* and she's never seen the kid asleep. (Just an aside; I was an insomniac as a child and my mother always said that she never actually saw me asleep until I was about twelve.)

Okay, Bill, here it is. I think that somehow, someway, I don't know how, and I don't know if it's possible, but I think that the kids have to have planned their own "Big A."

They did it. They're the only ones with a motive. They can't have this Tripp guy as their father. They can't stand being separated from Climber anymore and they know that they are supposed to be together as a Family, all four of them. I would also make sure that it was absolutely genius, foolproof, and that the parents *never ever find out that it was them* and that the *audience does* at the very very end. I don't know how I would do it, but it would be elegant and elaborate, and both parents would have to be together to solve it, which they never will, but they will realize that they are still passionate about each other. I don't know how I would do this, but I would spend every waking moment trying to figure that out and then I would hire Scott Frank to write it. That's all for now.

P.S.: Just in case you think I've totally lost my mind, I think it's important that *if* the kids did plan it, that it reaches a point that it goes crazily out of their control, that there should be *real* danger, and that the little bastards were lucky to get out with their lives. Again, the parents have to *never know* that they had anything to do with it. Oh, and now that we're on the subject, I can't stop thinking of this and have lost track of my own script completely.

Scott read me his letter to you and I couldn't believe what a bunch of sourpusses we are. You said be brutal, but aren't you a little bit sorry you asked? If I was too harsh, it's because I'm bitter. That's the only reason. You know I love you.
More later.

—Callie

For me, John Patrick Shanley is one of the leading playwrights of the decade. No play has rocked me as much as *Beggars in the House of Plenty*. And *Four Dogs and a Bone* is as good a comedy about Hollywood madness as any. If you do not know his theater work, that may well be because Shanley is insanely perverse, not caring about either Broadway or Off-Broadway. He does his stuff for limited runs, then they get printed and spend half their life in productions about the country and the world.

He is equally perverse when he doctors, as you will see, in that he does the brute work *before* any meetings. If his attack is not welcomed, fine; if it is, there won't be any surprises when he hands in his version of the screenplay.

Oh yeah, he also won an Oscar for his first film, *Moonstruck*.

Dear Bill,

Here are my suggestions with regards to your scr

1. I think Climber should save Echo from the have her save him in turn. Within the same situatio be somewhat more upscale, and be held up at a ho Climber crashes out the window with Echo, they fall, fall in love, and land in a swimming pool. As it turns out, Climber can't swim and she has to save him. Including the mouth-to-mouth bit. His reaction upon coming to is Will you marry me?

2. Cut to the Wedding Scene. Her wealth and class is established. The father of the bride says to him, "You must be thinking: How in heaven did I break into this world?" Climber says "I think the question is: How do you break out?" Trip is a wedding guest, well thought of by Echo's parents. He gets in a conversation with Climber's dad, Jimmy, and insults him. Climber clocks Trip, setting their mutual rancor in motion.

3. Could the kids be twins? Another reason for them to like *The Parent Trap*. And one trip to the hospital. In any case, Climber and Echo could fight over what to name them. Which is really a fight about which world they belong to. The world of privilege, or the world of rough and tumble. While Climber tries to decide whether to concede the name thing to Echo, she makes a second request: Could Trip be the godfather? The two families have always been close, and a gesture like this would close the rift that opened at the wedding. Climber makes to respond, hesitates, and . . .

4. Cut to: The Christening. Trip is holding Climber's babies, and he's already acting like they're his. Echo looks at Trip fondly, then at Climber. Climber's face says it all. The marriage is over.

5. The marriage is over. Climber picks up the kids, on screenplay page 18 [see page 363, above]. Trip has become Echo's intimate. The reason for all the subterfuge on the kids' part is that they are already working what Climber calls: Safe Cases. The current case, a matter of infidelity, goes wrong when the client, that is the husband of the woman with the dark glasses, shows up. And he is Italian and crying and very upset and he has a gun and he misses everybody because he is crying so much but he does fire it several times. The kids are endangered. And Trip has been having Climber followed and this is just the stuff he has been looking for.

6. Climber loses custody. He can fight it in court but it will take years and money he doesn't have and, meanwhile, he can only see the kids in a supervised setting.

e shows up for the first such visit drunk, is busted by the not npassionate court-appointed supervisor, and loses the right to see children *in any way* for 90 days.

8. The kidnapping. Climber shows up. Trip threatens to have him arrested for violating a court order until Echo announces that she asked him to come. He's good at this kind of case, she observes. Echo, Phoebe, and Climber set off in pursuit.

9. Phoebe describes the kidnapping in detail to the assembled group of Climber and Jimmy's friends. One guy latches on to Phoebe and asks several questions and then tells Climber: I know these guys. Gives him the info.

10. Cut to: A Japanese gambling parlor set up on the rooftop of a ten-story industrial building. Climber instructs Phoebe just to take a peek, see if she sees the kidnappers, and then they'll quietly go downstairs and call the police. As soon as Phoebe sees that everyone's Japanese and about eight guys are missing a finger, she announces that they are the victims of *very* bad information. Climber takes a look and finds a gun pointed at either temple of his head. A polite but firm Yakusa asks the three of them what they are doing there. Climber's about to answer when Echo jumps in: I'm like a major gambler, I heard about you guys, and I'm here for the action.

                    GANGSTER
        Who'd you hear from?

                    ECHO
        I don't remember.

Indicates CLIMBER.

                    GANGSTER
        Who's he?

                    ECHO
        My bodyguard.

Indicates PHOEBE.

                    GANGSTER
        Who's she?

                    ECHO
    My kid.

                    GANGSTER
    You bring your kid?

                    ECHO
    I couldn't get a babysitter.
              (pulls out an enormous roll of
              cash.)
    Ten grand. I'm hot to trot and I love to lose.

The Gangster doesn't buy any of it, but he likes the
cash. Jerks his head at the others to unhand them.

                    GANGSTER
    Let her play.

They approach a Japanese game of chance. It is incomprehensible. Everything's in Japanese. There's a bunch of small stones, bottle caps, and ball bearings. Echo says: "I'd like to bet $10,000 on . . . something. Can you help me here?" The Croupier (for lack of a better term) offers: "Choose a box." She chooses a box and loses the ten grand. She looks pleased and exclaims: "What a rush! Okay, let's go home." Climber mutters: "I'm hot to trot and I love to lose." They exit by the door this time and head down ten flights of fire stairs illuminated by only windows glowing with streetlight. Two men attack them and try to kill Climber. A bullet takes Climber down after he has subdued one of the two Attackers. The second Attacker is about to shoot the fallen hero when Echo finds and breaks a wine bottle over his head, Maces him, and pushes him out the window. Climber is alright, a light head wound. They make their way down the last three flights, and look for the fallen man. But there's no body. Climber complains: "Now who were THEY?"

   11. Echo, Climber, and Phoebe go back to her house. She is patching Climber's head. As she does so, she asks Phoebe to repeat the conversation the kidnappers allowed their son. Is there a clue in there? She figures out the hint. The boy is on the premises. Climber asks about outbuildings and personnel. She mentions that the gardeners are really a world unto themselves. And as she says it, they all reach the same conclusion.

   12. They find the boy tied and gagged in the shed with mowers, trac-

tors, and Gardeners. Climber confronts the Gardeners with a gun. Echo and Phoebe untie the boy. At this moment, the Two Attackers from the previous scene get the drop on Climber. The one Echo pushed out the window is all bandaged up and in a very bad mood. The other one is trying to think in an organized way about what to do with these people. They argue. A roar interrupts them. It's the kids in a tractor. They hurtle at the Attackers and go right through the wall of the shed. During the confusion, Climber gets a gun and gets a fresh drop on the bad guys.

13. Cut to the police cuffing various wrongdoers. The case is wrapped up. Or is it? The kids ask the question: On the staircase, when they were attacked, the Attackers only wanted to kill Climber. No one else? Who wants Climber out of the way? Trip. Echo says that's ridiculous. Asks the Butler where Trip is. About an hour ago, he borrowed the keys to your father's plane. He said you knew. Climber says, Where's the airfield? Echo's father has just walked in: But the plane is in for repairs. It can't be flown. Climber asks, Does Trip know that? I don't see why he would, says Father.

14. Cut to a private airfield at night. Trip is arguing with a pilot as they board a small plane. "I'll pay for the refueling. Let's just take off!" The pilot agrees as Trip hears: Where you headed? He sees Climber, pulls a gun, says to the pilot: Give me the keys. Knocks the guy on the head, takes his flight plan. He shoots Climber. Takes off. But Climber is only down a second. He jumps on the plane as it begins to taxi. Shoots out the windshield. The plane crashes. He is apprehended.

15. It turns out Trip was behind it all. His personal fortune was a sham. He hired private detectives to discredit Climber so the coast would be clear for the kidnapping.

16. Climber tells his son, because of the nifty tractor save, he has earned the right to be called Flash.

17. The resolution is the same.

Some of the aforesaid is underdeveloped and some is too specific, but you get the idea. I would prefer, rather than the private plane bit, to come up with a way for Climber to use his climbing skills to catch Trip. But I find that that kind of thinking is inspired by large amounts of money. What I have outlined replaces or reinforces the script as it is. If I made no attempt to alter a scene or character, it probably means I like it as it is.

Best of Everything, Love,

—John

Well, now. What did we learn in school today? I think this much is clear and obvious: when they love what I've written, they are brilliant; when they dare to find fault, just a bunch of idiots and assholes.

That said, there really is a lot to digest. They all hate what I did (or didn't do, rather) with Echo, and of course they're dead on. As a matter of fact, it surprises me she is such a nothing, since I love Audrey Hepburn so, and wanted to write a star part for her. But as I said, the kids exploded and she got left in the wake.

My big problem is that even if I load her into Act III, even if I give her the best stuff I can come up with, can I ever get her back on an equal footing with Climber, which is what I wanted when I began? If I can, then the movie stays with my original intention. If I can't, well, when we write, guess what?—it isn't mathematics. But I need the audience to be rooting for the family when all four take off on the biggest Adventure of all. Even if she's not fifty-fifty, I've got to make you glad she's along.

Face it—this movie should end up being Climber and the kids. Maybe it will. Nothing wrong with that, but it's not what I wanted.

The kidnapping. Not a lot of agreement on who done it. Trip(p) or the Gardeners or the Judge—*any of those will play.* Depending on what story you want to tell. There was good agreement on Climber and the kids being detectives. Personally, I like that a lot. As we all know by now, I had a distant father and the idea of having a father like Climber, who openly loves me, who takes me with him, who includes me in his life, well, I am a sucker for that.

I think the scene with Climber and Phoebe when he makes her memory work is as good as I can do. I want more of that somehow. And I want a great thing for Shirley, a surprising act of bravery. Shit, we all want to be called Flash—but it's no good unless we earn it.

One final note of thanks to The Doctors. Other than the Farrellys', I heard all of their comments together for the first time, one after the other; they were read out loud to me so I could try and concentrate.

Blew my mind.

Writing Time

The one thing I think all writers like to talk about is their work habits. When do you write? For how long? Where? Endless questions. So I want to spend a minute now on the basic problem facing us all: **doing it.**

When I began, at twenty-four, the work always came out in a burst. *The Temple of Gold* took less than three weeks. A year later, *Your Turn to Curtsy, My Turn to Bow,* less than two. And in between, nothing much happened that bettered the human condition, just going to the movies, a double feature a day, sometimes two, everything on 42nd Street or the Thalia on West 95th. Two years basically wasted until the next book, which was *Soldier in the Rain.*

I was having a career, God yes. Three novels published by age twenty-eight, two of them million-copy sellers in paperback, the third made into a movie.

What I wasn't having was a life.

I never had a real job so whenever I wanted to write, I could. Morning, night, all night if I wanted—and I suspect if I had continued that way, I was heading for disaster.

There is no *wrong* when it comes to work habits. It doesn't matter if you use a Mac or a quill pen. There is no *best* way to go about storytelling. Bergman writes from ten to three and in ten weeks, he's got a screenplay. Graham Greene, another hero, counted words. Yes, you read that right, he counted each and every word until he reached his magic number—three hundred. And when he got there, guess what, he quit for the day, in the middle of a sentence or not.

They had the one thing writers need most: **discipline.**

My great editor, Hiram Haydn, was a very busy man. He started or ran publishing houses, had a wife and a bunch of kids, was editor of *The American Scholar.*

And wrote novels.

He was my editor from *Soldier in the Rain* through *The Princess Bride,* was a wondrous father figure for me. Once we were talking about a novel of his, *The Hands of Esau,* that he was close to finishing, and I asked him how long since he began it and he said probably eight years.

How do you stay the same person for that long, I wondered?

You just do the best you can, he replied. You hope.

When do you write?

Sunday morning, he said. Every Sunday morning.

That was the only time available to him. The rest of his life was kids and work and family and commuting and meetings and dealing with crazy writers; Sunday morning was all he could carve out, so he played it as it laid.

You have to protect your writing time, he said then.

That's the best basic advice I can give to any writer. **You have to protect your writing time. You have to protect it to the death.**

I think it should always be the same time. Each day, each night, each whatever. Can be half an hour, more when you're on a roll, probably shouldn't be less. I know a brilliant young writer who has zero problem writing. Her problem is sitting. Her computer is surrounded by a mine field and she will come up with the most amazing reasons not to try to cross it. And no, she is neither crazy nor alone in her problem—

because the easiest thing to do on earth is not write.

The need for a schedule is simple: You'll have hours, days, when you just sit there, but eventually, you come to know that your writing time is now and things begin to happen *as* you sit there.

And if you manage to suck it up, if you decide you *must* get your stories down, then there is one other thing that's crucial: don't talk about it. **Tell no one.**

Once others know, they will look at you strangely, they will question you, they will ask you terrible questions—

—how's it coming?

—is it fun?

—when is it going to be finished?

—I bet it's fun

—when can I see it?

You don't need those words buzzing around your ears. So keep the start of your career secret. Keep the time sacred.

Remember: nobody made you be a writer.

This is as far as I go.

All I have left to tell you is that after writing movies for thirty-five years I am more convinced than ever it's only about story.

And what's that? What *is* story? I'll go with Kubrick's words—he denied them, so who knows, but somebody wise said it, maybe it was me.

A good story is something with an interesting premise that builds logically to a satisfying and surprising conclusion.

We get fed them in the cradle and forever on. Want to read a good story? Pick up *The Little Engine That Could*. Soppy and primitive, sure, but today just by chance I read it again and let me tell you, you are rooting with all your heart for that crummy two-bit nothing of a train to get those toys over the mountain.

That's all it is, this business of writing. **Just get the fucking toys over the mountain.**

Today there was this article in the paper—about a man found dead in the subway. He had been riding for hours and not only was there no identification, there was no way of knowing why he died. No violence, not drug overdose—there was just this dead guy riding around on the subway with no past and, obviously, no future.

Was he dead for days? Was he dead from some terrible new disease just in from Africa, or was he from someplace not here? Was he a king in a world as yet undiscovered? Or was he really *not* dead—maybe where he came from they slept that way, no heartbeat, and when they did the autopsy—and found nothing—well, maybe when they did that they really did kill him and where he came from he was doomed to walk the earth seeking revenge or doing good or both alternately or, or—

There's a story in there somewhere, with no beginning yet and no ending yet, just this wonderful incident, a man from nowhere dies and rides around New York.

He's there waiting for you.

Gloria Steinem once said this to me: "Storytellers have been getting us through the night for centuries. Hollywood is the current campfire."

Keep the fires burning . . .

INDEX

A NOTE ON THE AUTHOR

William Goldman has been writing books and movies for forty-five years. He has won two Academy Awards (for *Butch Cassidy and the Sundance Kid* and *All the President's Men*), and three Lifetime Achievement awards in screenwriting. His novels *The Princess Bride, Marathon Man,* and *All the President's Men* are also published by Bloomsbury. He lives in New York City.

BY THE SAME AUTHOR

Fiction
The Temple of Gold (1957) *Your Turn to Curtsy, My Turn to Bow* (1958) *Soldier in the Rain* (1960) *Boys and Girls Together* (1964) *No Way to Treat a Lady* (1964) *The Thing of It Is ...* (1967) *Father's Day* (1971) *The Princess Bride* (1973) *Marathon Man* (1974) *Magic* (1983) *Tinsel* (1979) *Control* (1982) *The Silent Gondoliers* (1983) *The Color of Light* (1984) *Heat* (1985) *Brothers* (1986)

Nonfiction
The Season: A Candid Look at Broadway (1969) *The Making of "A Bridge Too Far"* (1977) *Adventures in the Screen Trade: A Personal View of Hollywood and Screenwriting* (1983) *Wait Till Next Year (With Mike Lupica)* (1988) *Hype and Glory* (1990) *Four Screenplays* (1995) *Five Screenplays* (1997)

Screenplays
Masquerade (with Michael Relph) (1965) *Harper* (1966) *Butch Cassidy and the Sundance Kid* (1969) *The Hot Rock* (1972) *The Great Waldo Pepper* (1975) *The Stepford Wives* (1975) *All the President's Men* (1976) *Marathon Man* (1976) *A Bridge Too Far* (1977) *Magic* (1978) *Mr. Horn* (1979) *Heat* (1987) *The Princess Bride* (1987) *Misery* (1990) *The Year of the Comet* (1992) *Maverick* (1994) *The Chamber* (1996) *The Ghost and the Darkness* (1996) *Absolute Power* (1997)

Plays
Blood, Sweat and Stanley Poole (with James Goldman) (1961)
A Family Affair (with James Goldman and John Kander) (1961)

For Children
Wigger (1974)